Publication of *The Complete Works of George Orwell* is a unique
bibliographic event as well as a major step in Orwell
scholarship. Meticulous textual research by
Dr Peter Davison has revealed that all the current editions
of Orwell have been mutilated to a greater or lesser extent.
This authoritative edition incorporates in Volumes 10-20
all Orwell's known essays, poems, plays, letters, journalism,
broadcasts, and diaries, and also letters by his wife, Eileen,
and members of his family. In addition there are very many of
the letters in newspapers and magazines of readers' reactions
to Orwell's articles and reviews. Where the hands of others
have intervened, Orwell's original intentions have been restored.

Keeping Our Little Corner Clean
1942–1943

Eric Arthur Blair – better known as George Orwell – was born on 25 June 1903 in Bengal. He was educated at Eton and then served with the Indian Imperial Police in Burma. He lived in Paris for two years, and then returned to England where he worked as a private tutor, schoolteacher and bookshop assistant. He fought on the Republican side in the Spanish Civil War and was wounded in the throat. During the Second World War he served as Talks Producer for the Indian Service of the BBC and then joined *Tribune* as its literary editor. He died in London in January 1950.

Dr. Peter Davison is Professor of English and Media at De Montfort University, Leicester. He has written and edited fifteen books as well as the Facsimile Edition of the Manuscript of *Nineteen Eighty-Four* and the twenty volumes of Orwell's *Complete Works*. From 1992 to 1994 he was President of the Bibliographical Society, whose journal he edited for twelve years. From 1961 Ian Angus was Deputy Librarian and Keeper of the Orwell Archive at University College, London, and from 1975 Librarian of King's College, London. With Sonia Orwell he co-edited the *Collected Essays, Journalism and Letters of George Orwell* (4 vols., 1986). Since early retirement in 1982 he has divided his time equally between assisting in the editing of this edition and growing olives in Italy.
Sheila Davison was a teacher until she retired, for some time teaching the deaf. She checked and proofread all twenty volumes of the complete edition and assisted with the research and indexing.

Down and Out in Paris and London
Burmese Days
A Clergyman's Daughter
Keep the Aspidistra Flying
The Road to Wigan Pier
Homage to Catalonia
Coming Up for Air
Animal Farm
Nineteen Eighty-Four
A Kind of Compulsion (1903-36)
Facing Unpleasant Facts (1937-39)
A Patriot After All (1940-41)
All Propaganda is Lies (1941-42)
Keeping Our Little Corner Clean (1942-43)
Two Wasted Years (1943)
I Have Tried to Tell the Truth (1943-44)
I Belong to the Left (1945)
Smothered Under Journalism (1946)
It is What I Think (1947-48)
Our Job is to Make Life Worth Living (1949-50)

Also by Peter Davison

Books: *Songs of the British Music Hall: A Critical Study; Popular Appeal in English Drama to 1850; Contemporary Drama and the Popular Dramatic Tradition; Hamlet: Text and Performance; Henry V: Masterguide; Othello: The Critical Debate; Orwell: A Literary Life*

Editions: Anonymous: *The Fair Maid of the Exchange* (with Arthur Brown); Shakespeare: *Richard II;* Shakespeare: *The Merchant of Venice;* Shakespeare: *1 Henry IV;* Shakespeare: *2 Henry IV;* Shakespeare: *The First Quarto of King Richard III;* Marston: *The Dutch Courtesan; Facsimile of the Manuscript of Nineteen Eighty-Four;* Sheridan: *A Casebook; The Book Encompassed: Studies in Twentieth-Century Bibliography*

Series: *Theatrum Redivivum* 17 Volumes (with James Binns); *Literary Taste, Culture, and Mass Communication* 14 Volumes (with Edward Shils and Rolf Meyersohn)

Academic Journals: *ALTA: University of Birmingham Review,* 1966-70; *The Library: Transactions of the Bibliographical Society,* 1971-82

Keeping Our Little Corner Clean

1942-1943

GEORGE ORWELL

Edited by Peter Davison
Assisted by Ian Angus and Sheila Davison

SECKER & WARBURG

———

LONDON

Revised and updated edition published by Secker & Warburg 2001

2 4 6 8 10 9 7 5 3 1

First published in Great Britain in 1998 by
Secker & Warburg
Random House, 20 Vauxhall Bridge Road,
London SW1V 2SA

Random House Australia (Pty) Limited
20 Alfred Street, Milsons Point, Sydney,
New South Wales 2061, Australia

Random House New Zealand Limited
18 Poland Road, Glenfield,
Auckland 10, New Zealand

Random House South Africa (Pty) Limited
Endulini, 5A Jubilee Road, Parktown 2193, South Africa

The Random House Group Limited Reg. No. 954009
www.randomhouse.co.uk

A CIP catalogue record for this book
is available from the British Library

ISBN 0 436 40407 9

Papers used by The Random House Group Limited are natural,
recyclable products made from wood grown in sustainable forests;
the manufacturing processes conform to the environmental
regulations of the country of origin

Typeset in Monophoto Bembo by
Deltatype Limited, Birkenhead, Merseyside
Printed and bound in Great Britain by
Mackays of Chatham PLC

CONTENTS

Titles may be modified and shortened
TBF = BBC Talks Booking Form; dates booked for broadcasts are given in
numerals

Contents

Contents

Contents

Contents

Contents

Contents

INTRODUCTION to VOLUME XIV

1 September 1942 to 28 February 1943: *Keeping Our Little Corner Clean*

Towards the end of Volume XIII Orwell's first attempt at a broadcast form of the literary magazine is reproduced (*1373*). Orwell intended that this 'magazine' should appear each month and so it did until the sixth 'issue', a special Christmas number, broadcast on 29 December 1942. In the context of a broadcasting service designed to be part of Britain's wartime propaganda effort, this is, perhaps, the strangest series of all those Orwell devised and the least overtly propagandist. Orwell himself described the programmes as 'a small and remote outflanking movement in the radio war' in 'Poetry and the Microphone'. Because the programmes were aimed at Indian university students, 'a small and hostile audience, unapproachable by anything that could be described as British propaganda', and there was no hope of more than 'a few thousand listeners', that 'gave us an excuse to be more "highbrow" than is generally possible on the air' (*2629*; XVII, 75). He then describes what can be read in this volume and though he admits the results might seem 'Slightly ridiculous and also rather patronising' it did enable difficult verse to be got across to listeners. He goes on to point to one of the most significant characteristics of these programmes. When practicable he had the poets speak their own poetry: 'I was early struck by the fact that the broadcasting of a poem by the person who wrote it does not merely produce an effect upon the audience, if any, but also on the poet himself' (XVIII, 76). He goes on to wonder 'whether it would not be possible even now to rescue poetry from its special position as the most-hated of the arts' (XVII, 78). Orwell was too dismissive of the wasted years he spent at the BBC (see Introduction to Volume XV). 'Voice', his monthly magazine, did show the way forward. T. S. Eliot reading his 'What the Thunder Said' from *The Waste Land* (in 'Voice,' 5, the script of which is, alas, lost) really would then have been a revelation, as later recordings show. That Orwell was essaying this in 1942 is remarkable, the more so in the context of the purposes of the service for which he was working. It is true that the discussions are stilted, as Orwell realised, but the reason was simple: to pass the double censorship for Security and Policy, everything had to be written out: discussion was shackled even about poetry. But this was an imaginative attempt by Orwell to rid poetry of the air of sounding 'like the Muses in striped trousers' (XVIII, 79). Because of the importance of what was chosen – precisely what – permission has been obtained to print the poems and passages of prose he broadcast. Those who took part included, as well as T. S. Eliot, Herbert Read, Edmund Blunden, and the West Indian poet, Una Marson (all of whom read their own poems), Narayana Menon, Mulk Raj Anand, Tambimuttu, William Empson and, of course, Orwell himself. Although the series ran for only six numbers, he planned to continue the series. Why this was not done is not known.

Orwell continued with the educational series designed for Indian university students and based on the syllabuses of Calcutta and Bombay Universities. Plans were laid in December 1942 for some of these talks to be printed in pamphlet form and two booklets were published by Oxford University Press, but not until 29 October 1946 (see *1301*, XVIII, 454). two of Orwell's talks were included, those on Shaw's *Arms and the Man*, and Jack London. Unfortunately it was so long after the talks had been given that relatively few copies were sold, though they were priced cheaply. On 6 November 1942, Norman Marshall began his series on the fundamentals of drama production, "Let's Act It Ourselves", with Damyanti Sahni (who had worked with the Shakespeare Memorial Theatre) and her husband, Balraj. Once again, Orwell persuaded a distinguished expert to work for him (see Introduction to Volume XIII). Norman Marshall was currently producing *The Petrified Forest* in London with Constance Cummings and Owen Nares and was to become Head of Drama for Associated-Rediffusion Television in 1955. There were not only talks about drama in the educational series and these instructional programmes, but Orwell organised a number of performances of Indian plays such as *Malti and Madhav* and *The Little Clay Cart* (translated from Sanskrit; see *1713*, *1726*, and *1873*).

Other innovations Orwell introduced in the period of this volume were a 'Story by Five Authors' and an essay competition for Indian students. The story was not really a success. Orwell had the idea of starting off a story and having it continued by four others. L. A. G. Strong, Inez Holden, and Martin Armstrong continued what he initiated and then he persuaded E. M. Forster to conclude the experiment. The essay competition (it was at one time thought a play competition might be organised) attracted fewer entries than had been hoped but although there is not a great deal of information as to the degree of its success, Orwell must have thought it worthwhile for soon after he launched a short-story competition when he became literary editor of *Tribune*. One of Orwell's most inventive broadcasts was his imaginary interview with Jonathan Swift, 6 November 1942 (*1637*).

Orwell continued to write newsletters and from 21 November he read them using his pen-name. When this was mooted, Orwell agreed on the grounds that the commentaries had 'always followed what is by implications a "left" line' (*1571*). He continued to read the newsletter to India until 13 March 1943 when that service ceased. However, though it has been suggested that this cessation was to deny Orwell a hand in direct propaganda, he was already, from the day before he first read one of his newsletters to India, reading one to occupied Malaya, No. 8 in that series, and he continued to read these throughout the period of this volume (see *1669*). (Except for a few excerpts, none of these newsletters has been traced.)

Some idea of how hard Orwell worked can be appreciated by glancing at the week beginning 16 November 1942. On that day Gujarati Newsletter 38 was broadcast, for which he had written the English version; he wrote to T. S. Eliot about his reading "What the Thunder Said" in 'Voice,' 5; sent Norman Marshall proposals for "Let's Act it Ourselves" with the Sahnis' questions; and wrote a memorandum on news commentaries for Malaya. The following day he wrote to Desmond Hawkins proposing anniversaries that might be celebrated in December. On the 18th he suggested to E. M. Forster that he discuss Narayana Menon's book on Yeats, asked V. E. Yarsley to speak on plastics for a science programme, and sent a memorandum to Programme Accounts about fees for Dame Myra Hess and Scott Goddard. On the 20th his article, 'Background of French Morocco' was published in *Tribune*; he read to Malaya the first of his news commentaries for that country (which he had written). On the 21st his review of Liddell Hart's *The British Way in Warfare* was published in *The New Statesman and Nation*, and he read a news commentary to India (also which he had written); that day a Bengali newsletter was broadcast for which he had written the English text, and he sent letters to T. S. Eliot, Bahadur Singh, Noel Sircar, Shridhar Telkar, and V. E. Yarsley.

He could certainly be said (as he wrote to George Woodcock on 2 December 1942, *1711*, p. 214) to be keeping his little corner of the BBC fairly clean.

A full General Introduction will be found in the preliminaries to Volume X
Reference should also be made to the Introductions to Volumes XIII and XV

ACKNOWLEDGEMENTS and PROVENANCES

specific to Volume XIV

The editor wishes to express his gratitude to the following institutions and libraries, their trustees, curators, and staffs for their co-operation and valuable help, for making copies of Orwell material available, and for allowing it to be reproduced: BBC Written Archives Centre, Caversham; British Library, Department of Manuscripts (for the Orwell papers, Add. Mss 49384 and 73083); Lilly Library, Indiana University, Bloomington, Indiana; Harry Ransom Humanities Research Center, University of Texas at Austin; and the Library of University College London for material in the Orwell Archive.

Thanks are due to Dan Leab and Desmond Hawkins for having made available a letter by Orwell to Desmond Hawkins. I am also much indebted to George Woodcock for having made copies of his Orwell material available to the Orwell Archive.

I would like to thank the following publications for permission to reproduce material which first appeared in their pages: *The Listener* (by courtesy of the BBC and the Independent Television Association Ltd), *The New Statesman, The Observer, Partisan Review* and *Tribune*.

I am grateful to Laurence Brander, Desmond Hawkins and Alan Hollinghurst (Deputy Editor of *The Times Literary Supplement*) for their help and the valuable information they have supplied.

I would like to thank the following for permission to use material whose copyright they own: 'Story by Five Authors,' Part 4, by Martin Armstrong. Published by permission of the Peters, Fraser and Dunlop Group Ltd; 'Story by Five Authors,' Part 5, by E. M. Forster. Published by permission of the Provost and Scholars of King's College, Cambridge; 'Story by Five Authors,' Part 3, by Inez Holden. Published by permission of Celia Goodman; 'Story by Five Authors,' Part 2, by L. A. G. Strong. Published by permission of the Peters, Fraser and Dunlop Group Ltd; 'September 1, 1939' from *The English Auden: Poems, Essays and Dramatic Writings 1927–1939*, edited by Edward Mendelson, Copyright © 1940 by W. H. Auden. Reprinted by permission of Faber and Faber Ltd and Random House, Inc.; 'Rural Economy' and 'Report on Experience' by Edmund Blunden. Reprinted by permission of the Peters, Fraser and Dunlop Group Ltd; two letters by David Cecil to *The Times Literary Supplement*. Reprinted by permission of Laura Cecil on behalf of the David Cecil Estate; letter by Lord Alfred Douglas to *The Times Literary Supplement*. Reprinted by permission of Sheila Colman for the Lord Alfred Douglas Literary Estate; 'The Love Song of J. Alfred Prufrock' and 'Journey of the Magi' from *Collected Poems 1909–1962* by T. S. Eliot, Faber and Faber Ltd and Harcourt Brace & Company,

PROVENANCES

The major part of the documents and letters reproduced in this volume are in the BBC Written Archives Centre, Caversham and it should be taken that any document or letter that does not have its location indicated on the list below is at Caversham. Only documents and letters in other archives have their locations listed below. However, in cases where there are documents or letters at an item that are in different archives, this is indicated, even though one of the archives is the BBC Archive at Caversham, e.g. 1615 Texas, BBC (the top copy is in the Harry Ransom Humanities Research Center in Texas and the carbon copy is at the BBC Archive at Caversham).

For simplicity's sake, the Orwell papers in the British Library, Department of Manuscripts (Add. Mss 49384 and 73083) are not indicated as such in the location list, but are regarded as being available for consultation in the form of copies in the Orwell Archive.

KEY TO LOCATIONS

BBC	BBC Written Archives Centre, Caversham
Leab	Dan Leab
Lilly	Lilly Library, Indiana University, Bloomington, Indiana
OA	Orwell Archive, University College London Library
Texas	Harry Ransom Humanities Research Center, University of Texas at Austin

1443 Lilly
1447 OA
1463 OA
1477 OA
1486 OA
1501 Lilly
1506 OA
1508 OA
1514 Lilly
1522 OA
1546 OA
1562 OA
1564 OA

1573 OA
1583 OA
1615 Texas, BBC
1636 Texas, BBC
1643 Lilly
1654 Lilly
1658 OA
1664 Leab, BBC
1711 OA
1712 Texas, BBC
1721 Texas, BBC
1796 OA

Editorial Note

THE CONTENTS are, in the main, arranged in chronological order of Orwell's writing. Letters arising from his articles or reviews are usually grouped immediately after that item and Orwell's replies to those letters follow thereon. If there is a long delay between when it is known an article or essay was completed and its publication, it is printed at the date of completion. If items are printed much earlier in the chronological sequence than their date of publication, a cross-reference is given at the date of publication. All entries, whether written by Orwell or anyone else, including lengthy notes and cross-references, are given an item number. Because the printing of the edition has taken place over seven years, some letters came to light after the initial editing and the numbering of items had been completed. These items (or those that had in consequence to be repositioned) are given a letter after the number: e.g., *335A*. Some items included after printing and page-proofing had been completed are given in a final appendix to Volume XX and two (received by the editor in mid January 1997) in the Introduction to Volume XV. Numbers preceding item titles are in roman; when referred to in notes they are italicised.

The provenance of items is given in the preliminaries to each volume. Every item that requires explanation about its source or date, or about textual problems it may pose, is provided with such an explanation. Some articles and broadcasts exist in more than one version. The basis upon which they have been edited is explained and lists of variant readings provided. No Procrustean bed has been devised into which such items must be constrained; individual circumstances have been taken into account and editorial practice explained.

Although this is not what is called a 'diplomatic edition'—that is, one that represents the original precisely even in all its deformities to the point of reproducing a letter set upside down—the fundamental approach in presenting these texts has been to interfere with them as little as possible consistent with the removal of deformities and typographic errors. Orwell took great pains over the writing of his books: the facsimile edition of *Nineteen Eighty-Four*[1] shows that, but in order to meet the demands of broadcasting and publication schedules he often wrote fast and under great pressure. The speed with which he sometimes wrote meant that what he produced was not always what he would have wished to have published had he had time to revise. And, of course, as with any printing, errors can be introduced by those setting the type. It would be easy in places to surmise what Orwell would have done but I have only made changes where there would otherwise have been confusion. Obvious spelling mistakes, which could well be the compositor's or typist's (and the typist might be Orwell), have been corrected silently, but if there is any doubt, a footnote has drawn attention to the problem.

In brief, therefore, I have tried to present what Orwell wrote in his manuscripts and typescripts, not what I thought he should have written; and what he was represented as having written and not what I think should have been typed or printed on his behalf. This is not a 'warts and all' approach because gross errors are amended, significant changes noted, and textual complexities are discussed in preliminary notes. The aim is to bring Orwell, not the editor's version of Orwell, to the fore. Although textual issues are given due weight, an attempt has been made to produce an attractive, readable text.

The setting of this edition has been directly from xeroxes of original letters (if typed), typed copies of manuscript (prepared by one or other of the editors), surviving scripts for broadcasts, and xeroxes of essays, articles, and reviews as originally published (unless a headnote states otherwise). For *The Collected Essays, Journalism and Letters of George Orwell* a 1968 house style was adopted but for this edition, no attempt has been made to impose a late twentieth-century house style on the very different styles used by journals and editors of fifty to eighty years ago. Texts are therefore reproduced in the style given them in the journals from which they are reprinted. To 'correct' might well cause even more confusion as to what was and was not Orwell's: see below regarding paragraphing. Nevertheless, although it is not possible *to know*, one may sometimes hazard a guess at what underlies a printed text. Thus, I believe that most often when 'address' and 'aggression' are printed, Orwell typed or wrote 'adress' (especially until about the outbreak of World War II) and 'agression.' Although American spellings (such as 'Labor') have been retained in articles published in the United States, on very rare occasions, if I could be certain that a form of a word had been printed that Orwell would not have used—such as the American 'accommodations'—I have changed it to the form he would have used: 'accommodation'. Some variations, especially of proper names, have been accepted even if they look incongruous; so, 'Chiang Kai-Shek' as part of a book title but 'Chiang Kai-shek' throughout the text that follows.

Hyphenation presents tricky problems, especially when the first part of a word appears at the end of a line. Examples can be found in the originals of, for example, 'the middle-class,' 'the middle class', and 'the middleclass.' What should one do when a line ends with 'middle-'? Is it 'fore-deck' or 'foredeck'? If 'fore-' appears at the end of a line of the copy being reproduced, should the word be hyphenated or not? *OED* 1991 still hyphenates; Chambers in 1972 spelt it as one word. Where it would help (and it does not include every problem word), the ninth edition of F. Howard Collins, *Authors' & Printers' Dictionary*, Oxford University Press, 1946 (an edition appropriate to the mature Orwell) has been drawn upon. But Collins does not include fore-deck/foredeck. On a number of occasions Orwell's letters, or the text itself, is either obscure or wrong. In order to avoid the irritating repetition of *sic*, a small degree sign has been placed above the line at the doubtful point (°). It is hoped that this will be clear but inconspicuous. It is not usually repeated to mark a repetition of that characteristic in the same item. Orwell was sparing in his use of the question-mark in his letters; his practice has in the main been followed.

Paragraphing presents intractable problems. Orwell tended to write in long paragraphs. Indeed, it is possible to show from the use of many short paragraphs that News Review scripts so written are not by Orwell. The key example is News Review, 30, 11 July 1942 (*1267*), for which there is also external evidence that this is not by Orwell. This has twenty-one paragraphs as compared to eight in the script for the following week. It so happens that we know that Orwell was not at the BBC for two weeks before the 11 July nor on that day: he was on holiday, fishing at Callow End, Worcestershire (and on that day caught a single dace). But though paragraph length is helpful in such instances in identifying Orwell's work, that is not always so. It is of no use when considering his articles published in Paris in 1928–29 nor those he wrote for the *Manchester Evening News*. These tend to have extremely short paragraphs—sometimes paragraphs of only a line or two, splitting the sense illogically. A good example is the series of reviews published on 2 November 1944 (*2572*) where a two-line paragraph about Trollope's *The Small House at Allington* should clearly be part of the preceding four-line paragraph, both relating the books discussed to Barchester; see also *2463*, *n. 2* and *2608*, *n. 4*. There is no question but that this is the work of sub-editors. It would often be possible to make a reasonable stab at paragraphing more intelligently, but, as with verbal clarification, the result might be the more confusing as to what really was Orwell's work and what this editor's. It has been thought better to leave the house-styles as they are, even if it is plain that it is not Orwell's style, rather than pass off changes as if the edited concoction represented Orwell's work.

Usually it is fairly certain that titles of essays are Orwell's but it is not always possible to know whether titles of articles are his. Reviews were also frequently given titles. Orwell's own typescript for his review of Harold Laski's *Faith, Reason and Civilisation* (*2309*), which survived because rejected by the *Manchester Evening News*, has neither heading (other than the name of the author and title of the book being reviewed), nor sub-headings. That would seem to be his style. In nearly every case titles of reviews and groups of letters, and cross-heads inserted by sub-editors, have been cut out. Occasionally such a title is kept if it is an aid to clarity but it is never placed within quotation marks. Other than for his BBC broadcasts (where Orwell's authorship is clear unless stated otherwise), titles are placed within single quotation marks if it is fairly certain that they are Orwell's.

Telegrams and cables are printed in small capitals. Quite often articles and reviews have passages in capitals. These look unsightly and, in the main, they have been reduced to small capitals. The exceptions are where the typography makes a point, as in the sound of an explosion: BOOM! Orwell sometimes abbreviated words. He always wrote an ampersand for 'and' and there are various abbreviated forms for such words as 'about'. It is not always plain just what letters make up abbreviations (and this sometimes applies to his signatures) and these have regularly been spelt out with the exception of the ampersand for 'and'. This serves as a reminder that the original is handwritten. Orwell often shortened some words and abbreviations in his own way, e.g., Gov.t, Sup.ts (Superintendents), NB. and N.W (each with a single stop), and ie.; these forms have been retained. In order that the diaries should readily be apparent for what they are, they have been set in sloped roman (rather than italic, long passages of which can be tiring to the eye), with roman for textual variations. Square and half square brackets are used to differentiate sources for the diaries (see, for example, the headnote to War-Time Diary II, *1025*) and for what was written and actually broadcast (see, for example, Orwell's adaptation of Ignazio Silone's *The Fox, 2270*). Particular usages are explained in headnotes to broadcasts etc., and before the first entries of diaries and notebooks.

Orwell usually dated his letters but there are exceptions and sometimes he (and Eileen) give only the day of the week. Where a date has to be guessed it is placed within square brackets and a justification for the dating is given. If Orwell simply signs a letter, the name he used is given without comment. If he signs over a typed version of his name, or initials a copy of a letter, what he signed or initialled is given over the typed version. There has been some slight regularisation of his initialling of letters. If he omitted the final stop after 'E. A. B', no stop is added (and, as here, editorial punctuation *follows* the final quotation mark instead of being inside it). Sometimes Orwell placed the stops midway up the letters: 'E·A·B'; this has been regularised to 'E. A. B'.

Wherever changes are made in a text that can be deemed to be even slightly significant the alteration is either placed within square brackets (for example, an obviously missing word) or the alteration is footnoted. Attention should be drawn to one particular category of change. Orwell had a remarkably good memory. He quoted not only poetry but prose from memory. Mulk Raj Anand has said that, at the BBC, Orwell could, and would, quote lengthy passages from the Book of Common Prayer.[2] As so often with people with this gift, the quotation is not always exact. If what Orwell argues depends precisely upon what he is quoting, the quotation is not corrected if it is inaccurate but a footnote gives the correct reading. If his argument does not depend upon the words actually quoted, the quotation is corrected and a footnote records that.

So far as possible, I have endeavoured to footnote everything that might puzzle a reader at the risk of annoying some readers by seeming to annotate too readily and too frequently what is known to them. I have, therefore, tried to identify all references to people, events, books, and institutions. However, I have not been so presumptuous as to attempt to rewrite the history of this century and, in the main, have relied upon a small number of easily accessible histories. Thus, for the Spanish Civil War I have referred in the main to *The Spanish Civil War* by Hugh Thomas; and for the Second World War, to Winston Churchill's and Liddell Hart's histories. The former has useful and conveniently available documents, and the latter was by a historian with whom Orwell corresponded. They were both his contemporaries and he reviewed the work of both men. These have been checked for factual information from more recent sources, one by Continental historians deliberately chosen as an aid to objectivity in an edition that will have world-wide circulation. It is assumed that readers with a particular interest in World War II will draw on their own knowledge and sources and the annotation is relatively light in providing such background information. Similarly, biographical details are, paradoxically, relatively modest for people as well known as T. S. Eliot and E. M. Forster, but far fuller for those who are significant to Orwell but less well known and about whom information is harder to track down, for example, George(s) Kopp, Joseph Czapski, and Victor Serge. It is tricky judging how often biographical and explicatory information should be reproduced. I have assumed most people will not want more than one volume at a time before them and so have repeated myself (often in shortened form with cross-references to fuller notes) more, perhaps, than is strictly necessary. Whilst I would claim that I have made every attempt not to mislead, it is important that historical and biographical information be checked if a detail is significant to a scholar's argument. History, as Orwell was quick to show, is not a matter of simple, indisputable fact. In annotating I have tried not to be contentious nor to direct the reader unfairly, but annotation cannot be wholly impartial.[3]

Each opening is dated. These dates, though drawn from the printed matter, are not necessarily those of the text reproduced on the page on which a date appears. The dates, known or calculated of letters, articles, broadcasts, diaries, etc., will correspond with the running-head date, but, for example, when correspondence (which may have run on for several weeks) springs from an article and follows directly on that article, the date of the article is continued *within square brackets*. Sometimes an item is printed out of chronological order (the reason for which is always given) and the running-head date will again be set within square brackets. Wherever practicable, the running-head date is that of the first item of the opening; if an opening has no date, the last date of a preceding opening is carried forward. Articles published in journals dated by month are considered for the purpose to be published on the first of the month. Inevitably some dates are more specific than is wholly justified, e.g., that for 'British Cookery' (*2954*). However, it is hoped that if readers always treat dates within square brackets with circumspection, the dates will give a clear indication of 'where they are' in Orwell's life.

Great efforts have been made to ensure the accuracy of these volumes. The three editors and Roberta Leighton (in New York) have read and re-read them a total of six times but it is obvious that errors will, as it used to be put so charmingly in the sixteenth century, have 'escaped in the printing.' I offer one plea for understanding. Much of the copy-preparation and proof-reading has been of type set during and after the war when newsprint was in short supply and mere literary articles would be set in microscopic-sized type. Many of the BBC scripts were blown up from microfilm and extremely difficult to puzzle out. When one proof-reads against xeroxes of dim printing on creased paper, the possibilities for error are increased and the eyes so run with tears that vision is impaired. We hope we have corrected most errors, but we know we shall not have caught them all.

P.D.

A slightly fuller version of this note is printed in the preliminaries to Volume X.

1. *George Orwell, Nineteen Eighty-Four: The Facsimile of the Extant Manuscript*, edited by Peter Davison, London, New York, and Weston, Mass., 1984.
2. Information from W. J. West, 22 July 1994.
3. The problems of presenting acceptable history even for the professional historian are well outlined by Norman Davies in *Europe: A History*, Oxford University Press, Oxford and New York, 1996, 2–7. I am obviously attempting nothing so grand, yet even 'simple' historical explication is not always quite so simple.

REFERENCES

References to Orwell's books are to the editions in Vols I to IX of the *Complete Works* (edited P. Davison, published by Secker & Warburg, 1986–87). The pagination is almost always identical with that in the Penguin Twentieth-Century Classics edition, 1989–90. The volumes are numbered in chronological order and references are by volume number (in roman), page, and, if necessary (after a diagonal) line, so: II.37/5 means line five of page 37 of *Burmese Days*. Secker editions have Textual Notes and apparatus. Penguin editions have A Note on the Text; these are not identical with the Secker Textual Notes and Penguin editions do not list variants. There is a 32-page introduction to the Secker *Down and Out in Paris and London*. Items in Volumes X to XX are numbered individually; they (and their notes) are referred to by italicised numerals, e.g. *2736* and *2736 n. 3*.

REFERENCE WORKS: These are the principal reference works frequently consulted:

The Oxford English Dictionary, second edition (Compact Version, Oxford 1991): (*OED*).
The Dictionary of National Biography (Oxford 1885–1900, with supplements and *The Twentieth-Century*, 1901–   ): (*DNB*).
Dictionary of American Biography (New York, 1946, with supplements).
Dictionnaire biographique du mouvement ouvrier français, publié sous la direction de Jean Maitron, 4ᵉ ptie 1914–1939: De la Première à la Seconde Guerre mondiale (t. 16–43, Paris, Les Éditions Ouvrières, 1981–93).
Who's Who; Who Was Who; Who's Who in the Theatre; Who Was Who in Literature 1906–1934 (2 vols., Detroit, 1979); *Who Was Who Among English and European Authors 1931–1949* (3 vols., Detroit 1978); *Contemporary Authors* and its *Cumulative Index* (Detroit, 1993); *Who's Who In Filmland*, edited and compiled by Langford Reed and Hetty Spiers (1928); Roy Busby, *British Music Hall: An Illustrated Who's Who from 1850 to the Present Day* (London and New Hampshire, USA, 1976).
The Feminist Companion to Literature in English, edited by Virginia Blain, Patricia Clements, and Isobel Grundy, Batsford 1990.
The New Cambridge Bibliography of English Literature, edited by George Watson and Ian Willison, 4 vols., Cambridge, 1974–79.
Martin Seymour-Smith, *Guide to Modern World Literature*, 3rd revised edition, Macmillan 1985.
The War Papers, co-ordinating editor, Richard Widdows, 75 Parts, Marshall Cavendish, 1976–78.

The following are referred to by abbreviations:

CEJL: *The Collected Essays, Journalism and Letters of George Orwell*, ed. Sonia Orwell and Ian Angus, 4 volumes, Secker & Warburg 1968; Penguin Books, 1970; references are by volume and page number of the more conveniently available Penguin edition.

Crick: Bernard Crick, *George Orwell: A Life*, 1980; 3rd edition, Penguin Books, Harmondsworth, 1992 edition. References are to the 1992 edition.

Eric & Us: Jacintha Buddicom, *Eric and Us: A Remembrance of George Orwell*, Leslie Frewin, 1974.

Lewis: Peter Lewis, *George Orwell: The Road to 1984*, Heinemann, 1981.

Liddell Hart: B. H. Liddell Hart, *History of the Second World War*, Cassell, 1970; 8th Printing, Pan, 1983.

Orwell Remembered: Audrey Coppard and Bernard Crick, eds., *Orwell Remembered*, Ariel Books, BBC, 1984.

Remembering Orwell: Stephen Wadhams, *Remembering Orwell*, Penguin Books Canada, Markham, Ontario; Penguin Books, Harmondsworth, 1984.

Shelden: Michael Shelden, *Orwell: The Authorised Biography*, Heinemann, London; Harper Collins, New York; 1991. The American pagination differs from that of the English edition; both are given in references, the English first.

Stansky and Abrahams I: Peter Stansky and William Abrahams, *The Unknown Orwell*, Constable 1972; edition referred to here, Granada, St Albans, 1981.

Stansky and Abrahams II: Peter Stansky and William Abrahams, *The Transformation*, Constable 1979; edition referred to here, Granada, St Albans, 1981.

Thomas: Hugh Thomas, *The Spanish Civil War*, 3rd edition; Hamish Hamilton and Penguin Books, Harmondsworth, 1977.

Thompson: John Thompson, *Orwell's London*, Fourth Estate 1984.

West: *Broadcasts*: W. J. West, *Orwell: The War Broadcasts*, Duckworth/BBC 1985.

West: *Commentaries*: W. J. West, *Orwell: The War Commentaries*, Duckworth/BBC, 1985.

Willison: I. R. Willison, 'George Orwell: Some Materials for a Bibliography,' Librarianship Diploma Thesis, University College London, 1953. A copy is held by the Orwell Archive, UCL.

2194 Days of War: *2194 Days of War*, compiled by Cesare Salmaggi and Alfredo Pallavisini, translated by Hugh Young, Arnoldo Mondadori, Milan 1977; rev. edn Galley Press, Leicester 1988.

A Bibliography of works, books, memoirs and essays found helpful in preparing Volumes X to XX of *The Complete Works of George Orwell* will be found in the preliminaries to Volume X.

CHRONOLOGY

THE BBC YEARS

In the main, Orwell's publications, except books, are not listed

25 June 1903 Eric Arthur Blair born in Motihari, Bengal, India.

---

18 Aug 1941–24 Nov 1943 Talks Assistant, later Talks Producer, in the Indian section of the BBC's Eastern Service.

21 November 1941 First of over 200 newsletters written by Orwell for broadcast to India, Malaysia, and Indonesia, in English; and translated for broadcast in Gujarati, Marathi, Bengali, and Tamil.

8 March 1942 First contribution to *The Observer*.

15 May 1942 *Victory or Vested Interest?* published by George Routledge & Sons, containing Orwell's lecture, 'Culture and Democracy'.

Summer 1942 Moves to Maida Vale, London.

11 August 1942 'Voice 1,' first of six literary 'magazines' devised by Orwell for broadcast to India.

19 March 1943 His mother, Ida Blair, dies.

24 August 1943 'I am definitely leaving it [the BBC] probably in about three months' (letter to Rayner Heppenstall).

18 Nov 1943 *Talking to India* published by Allen & Unwin, edited and with an Introduction by Orwell.

23 Nov 1943 Leaves BBC and joins *Tribune* as Literary Editor. Leaves Home Guard on medical grounds.

Nov 1943–Feb 1944 Writes *Animal Farm*.

---

21 January 1950 Orwell dies of pulmonary tuberculosis, aged 46.

THE COMPLETE WORKS OF
GEORGE ORWELL · FOURTEEN

KEEPING OUR
LITTLE CORNER CLEAN

1435. BBC Talks Booking Form, 1.9.42

K. K. Ardaschir: 'The Moslem Minorities of Europe'; 13-minute talk; recorded 2.9.42; broadcast date not fixed; fee £8.8s. Signed: Z. A. Bokhari. Remarks: 'Please may Mr. Ardaschir's contract be sent by hand to Room 310, 200. O. S. marked c/o Mr. Blair, as he is going away shortly.'

1436. BBC Talks Booking Form, 1.9.42

Cedric Dover: 'Anniversaries of the Month,' 2; broadcast 8.9.42; fee £4.4s. Signed: Z. A. Bokhari. Remarks: 'Mr. Dover will be taking one of four parts in this feature.'

1437. BBC Talks Booking Form, 1.9.42

Lilla Erulkar: 'Anniversaries of the Month,' 2, monthly programme; broadcast 8.9.42; fee £4.4s. Signed: Z. A. Bokhari. Remarks: 'Miss Erulkar is taking one of four parts in this feature.'

1438. BBC Talks Booking Form, 1.9.42

Sidney Horniblow: 'In Black and White,' 1–6; 'writing of 13 minute feature to fill 15 minute period, and also taking part as the Voice of the Daily Express'; broadcast 4, 11, 18, 25.9.42 and 2 and 9.10.42; fee £10.10s each date, to cover preparation of script and participation in programme. On 12 September, a fee of £12.12s was arranged and noted on the form. Remarks: 'The three other voices taking part in this feature are booked through Mr. Attwood.'

1439. BBC Talks Booking Form, 1.9.42

Noel Sircar: 'Anniversaries of the Month,' 2, monthly programme; broadcast 8.9.42; fee £4.4s. Signed: Z. A. Bokhari.

1440. To George K. C. Yeh
2 September 1942   PP/EB

Dear Dr. Yeh,
I daresay you will remember me from [th]at evening when we had dinner together with [Bi]ll Empson.[1] I am wondering whether you could find time to do a talk for us in English on the Indian Service. We are having a series of three talks on Modern Japan, called Japan's Threat to Asia; the first talk will deal with Japan during the Meiji era, the second with Japan between the Sino-Japanese war of 1894 and 1931, and the third will deal with the period from the Manchurian incident onwards. I am sure you are the most suitable person to do this if you can spare the time. The date of the talk would be September 29th, but we should want the script a week beforehand. These talks take $13\frac{1}{4}$° minutes, which means about 1500 words. Could you be kind enough to let me know as soon as possible whether you feel inclined to undertake this?[2]

Yours sincerely,
George Orwell
Talks Producer
Indian Section

1. William Empson, poet and critic; (see *845, n. 3*), had taught in Japan and China before the war.
2. Dr. Yeh, who was Director of the Ministry of Propaganda at the Chinese Embassy in London, wrote to Orwell on 3 September to say that he could not give a talk on 29 September; he would be out of London then and for all the preceding week. Just over twelve months later, on 20 September 1943, Dr. Yeh recorded a talk in English, 'The World I Hope For,' which had previously been translated and broadcast in the Hindustani Service; see *2275*.

1441. BBC Talks Booking Form, 2.9.42

M. R. Kothari: Marathi Newsletter, 27; written by E. Blair, translated and read by M. R. Kothari; broadcast 3.9.42; fee £5.5s. Signed: Z. A. Bokhari. Remarks: 'Please note last week's Newsletter should read No. 26—not 27. A mistake in the numbering occurred from the 16th July 1942—which should read No. 20.'

1442. Marathi Newsletter, 27
3 September 1942

The English original was written by Orwell. No script has been traced. The programme was broadcast at 1345 instead of 1430 (see *1431*), and the sequence of programmes was correctly renumbered (see *1441*). PasB gives timing as $12\frac{1}{2}$ minutes.

1443. To Leonard Moore

4 September 1942   Typewritten

10a Mortimer Crescent   London   NW6

Dear Mr Moore,

Many thanks for the cheque for £10–17–1, and the accounts. I return the latter.

I am unfortunately far too busy to write anything except casual journalism. Besides being in the BBC I am in the Home Guard, and between the two I don't have many evenings to myself. However, during 1940–1941 I kept a diary, and when I had been keeping it some time it struck me that it might be publishable some time, though I felt it would be more likely to be of interest after a lapse of 5 or 10 years. But events have moved so fast that it might as well be 10 years since 1940 now, and I am not sure the thing is not worth trying on a few publishers. A friend who had also kept a diary had some idea of making a book out of the two, but this idea fell through.[1] At present my diary is being typed,[2] but when that is done, in about 10 days, we might see what we can do with it. Gollancz did hear about° and said he would like to see it, but I am not certain whether people are not rather fed up with war diaries. I should think the best place for publishing a thing of this kind would be America, if one could connect with an American publisher and then the° get the MS through the censorship. My books have never sold well in the USA, but I think I may have built myself up a small public there via the London Letters I have done from time to time during the last 18 months in the "Partisan Review". The editor told me some New York publisher said he thought the London Letters might be worth reprinting in pamphlet form, and if so the diary might have a chance. It is about 25,000 or 30,000 words, an awkward length, and I shouldn't expect such a book to have more than a small sale, but I should think some publisher might think it worth risking a few pounds on.

I hope business is good. Everyone seems to be reading, when they can get hold of books.

Yours sincerely
Eric Blair

1. The friend was Inez Holden (see *1326, n. 1*). On 21 May 1967 she wrote to Ian Angus: 'I see a comment in a contemporary diary of mine in which I note that George Orwell said to Eileen Orwell, "You see there will be these facts on what newspapers are publishing, how much space for advertising, how much for the Derby etc and then Inez will come in with her feminine impressionist writing from her diary."' She said the project for a joint publication did not come off because she wanted to alter anything Orwell said with which she disagreed or believed to be inaccurate. Her diary was published alone as *It Was Different at the Time* (1943). See Orwell's letter to Leonard Moore, 13 November 1942, *1654*.
2. The typewriter used is that on which Orwell typed letters from home. If the typing was being done for him, it was being done either by Eileen or by Nancy Parratt, if she came to the flat to type for him. Yet the typing looks suspiciously like Orwell's.

1444. To Edmund Blunden

[4 September 1942?]

CAN YOU COME TO 200 OXFORD STREET ELEVEN THIRTY ON TUESDAY[1] TO REHEARSE WITH OTHER SPEAKERS

ORWELL BROADCASTS

1. Presumably 8 September 1942, the day of the broadcast.

1445. News Review, 38

5 September 1942

'News Review' is handwritten at the head of this script. It is a very clean typescript; the only changes are one line x-ed through by the typist and the change recorded at *n. 3*. It is marked, in Orwell's hand, 'As broadcast   13' 18"   E.A.B,' and carries no censorship stamps, though 'Censored by Z A Bokhari' is written at the top of the first page by Bokhari. The script was read by Bahadur Singh.

September 3rd was the third anniversary of the outbreak of war. Before giving our usual resume° of the week's news, it may be worth while to look back over the past three years and thus see the present phase of the struggle in its true perspective.

If one looks thus at the whole picture and not merely at one corner of it, the fact which stands out is that after three years of desperate war, Britain is far stronger than she was when the war started. Whereas in the autumn of 1939 the entire British Commonwealth was barely able to mobilise a million trained men, and had only a very small air force and depleted navy, to-day there are several million trained men in Britain alone, putting aside the great armies in the Middle East, in India, and in other places. The R.A.F. has grown till it is more than the equal of the German Air Force, and the Navy, in spite of heavy losses in the unending and difficult work of convoying war materials to Britain, is much more powerful than at the outbreak of war.

When the German commanders survey the situation the fact[1] that their main enemy, Britain, is merely stronger and not weaker after all their attacks—must be the first to strike them. And behind this is the other immense fact that America now stands behind Britain and is re-arming upon an enormous scale and at lightning speed in places where neither the German army nor the German air force can affect the process. The other fact which the German commanders have to take into consideration is the continued resistance of Soviet Russia, the complete failure of the Red Army to disintegrate as it was supposed to do in the Autumn of 1941, and the frightful drain on German manpower which the Russian campaign represents, especially with another winter in the snow looming two or three months ahead.

Looking back we see that there have been really three turning points in the war and at each of them a Fascist victory receded further into the distance. The first was the Battle of Britain, in the late summer of 1940. The Germans, confident of a quick victory, hurled their air force against Britain and not only suffered heavy losses to no purpose, but were brought to realise that they could not win the war quickly, but had got in front of them a long and exhausting struggle in which almost inevitably the rest of the world would end by turning against them. The next turning point was in the winter of 1941, when the German advance on Russia petered out and the Russians drove the Germans back from Rostov. The German attack on Russia had been a direct result of the successful British resistance and the British sea blockade. Unable to break out and establish communications with Asia and America, the Germans had planned to conquer Russia at one blow, after which they would have at their disposal an enormous area which could be plundered of almost all the raw materials they needed, while at the same time they would no longer have the Red Army as a perpetual menace to their rear, so that they could devote their whole forces to a renewed attack on Britain. This also failed, and the Germans, in spite of great gains of territory, found themselves in for an exhausting struggle in which they were fighting against tremendous manpower and impossible climatic conditions, while their air force was so heavily engaged that they could not prevent the R.A.F. from pounding the cities of Western Germany. The third turning point was when Germany succeeded in pushing Japan into the war. The Japanese were mainly concerned with the conquest of East Asia, but the plan from the German point of view was to divert the attention of the Americans and prevent them from sending further aid to Britain. Once again the great gamble failed, for though the Japanese won easy victories at the beginning, they too soon found themselves in for a protracted struggle against a superior enemy, and the Americans, while fighting the Japanese in the Pacific, were not diverted for a moment from sending men and supplies to Europe. In spite of successes which look brilliant on a short term view, each of the three great gambles of the Fascist powers has failed, and they are able to see gradually forming against them a vast coalition of nearly four fifths of humanity with overwhelming resources and unalterable determination to make an end of Fascist aggression once and for all. In 1940, Britain was alone, poorly armed and not by any means certain of being joined by further Allies. In 1942, Britain has beside her the Red Army, the enormous American war industries and the four hundred million human beings of China. However long the struggle may yet be, its end cannot be in much doubt. That is the picture of the war which we see if we look at it in its broad lines and do not allow yesterday's newspaper to occupy the whole of our attention.

We have occupied most of our time in giving this general review of the war, and we shall therefore give only a short summary of this week's events.

In Egypt, the fresh German attack which we foretold in last week's newsletter has begun. It is however too early to give any worthwhile news of it. We will merely utter a warning that the conditions in Egypt are not easy for the Allies, and the fact that the Germans attacked first suggests that they have been successful in replacing the losses of the battles in June and July. The

British, however, have also been reinforced and American troops and aeroplanes are now beginning to take their place on this front.[2] After making a fairly strong attack with their armoured forces, the Germans are now retreating again, but it is not clear as yet whether this is because they found the British defences too strong for them or whether it is some kind of feint or manoeuvre. The allied air forces have been very active in the Mediterranean and have sunk several Axis ships this week. We shall be able to report more fully on the Egyptian situation next week.

The fighting in the Solomon Islands has been a brilliant success for the Allies. The Americans are now more or less in control of six islands and what was particularly important, on the island of Guadalcanal they captured a large air base which the Japanese had almost completed. About five days back, probably in hopes of driving the American fleet away from the Solomons, the Japanese made a fresh landing at Ellne Bay at the south eastern tip of New Guinea. The force which they landed there has been almost completely destroyed by the Australian forces, and its remnants are now in process of being mopped up. From the northern side of New Guinea, the Japanese have made a fresh attack in the direction of Port Moresby, but with indecisive results. They also appear to have made a fresh landing on one of the Solomon Islands. We may expect them to make very violent efforts to dislodge the Americans from the Solomons, for so long as the Americans remain in possession of these islands the Japanese position in New Guinea is threatened and their chance of attempting the invasion of Australia is almost negligible. Probably, therefore, there will be further sea and air battles to report. Although it is several thousand miles distant, India should watch these struggles in the South Pacific with interest, for on their outcome partly depends the possibility of the Japanese attacking India. They probably will not do so unless they can gain naval and air superiority round the shores[3] of the Bay of Bengal, and consequently each aeroplane carrier destroyed by the Americans makes India a fraction safer.

The position in Russia is still very grave, but has not altered materially since last week. The Germans are still hurling all their forces against Stalingrad and in the last day or two have gained a certain amount of ground south west of the city. At this moment the most violent fighting is raging almost within gunshot of Stalingrad and the Germans are throwing all the tanks and aeroplanes which they possess into the attack. But up-to-date the news is that the Russian defences are holding firm. Further south, the Germans have also gained some ground in the drive towards the Grosny oilfields. On the other two fronts, the Moscow front and the Leningrad front, the Russians themselves are still on the offensive.

There have been more heavy air raids on Western Germany, and for the first time in this war Gdynia on the Baltic Sea has been bombed. The fact that a town so far away can be bombed from Britain at this time of year, when the nights are still fairly short, shows the great increase in the striking power of the RAF. The Russian air force has recently bombed Berlin. The various proclamations on the subject of air raids which have been issued by the German press and radio show[4] how seriously the German people, especially in the big industrial towns, is being shaken by ceaseless bombing.

1. the fact] *preceded in typescript by* 'this fact'
2. Slightly more than a line follows, but has been x-ed through in the typing. It cannot be fully made out from the microfilm but refers to Egypt and possibly anticipates the last sentence of this paragraph.
3. A word (seaside?) has been obliterated and 'shores' written above it.
4. Typescript has 'shows'.

1446. Bengali Newsletter, 8

5 September 1942

The English original was written by Orwell. No script has been traced. PasB gives timing as 13 minutes. The transmission time for this Newsletter was changed from 1345 GMT to 1430 from this date.

1447. Unpublished Review of *Retreat in the East* by O. D. Gallagher

The Observer, [6 September 1942?]

This review was rejected by the editor of *The Observer*, Ivor Brown (see *1480*, *n. 2*). The date it was intended to print the review is not known, but *Retreat in the East* was published in September 1942, and reviews usually appeared in Sunday newspapers about the time of publication. Orwell refers to the rejection in a letter to Connolly dated 'Saturday,' placed here at 12 September; see *1480*. On 23 October 1942, Ivor Brown sent Orwell an apology and explanation. He said he had held the review 'because I felt that it would play straight into the hands of those Americans who are looking out for implements with which to make trouble. The publication of the now well-known article in "Life" about Britain and its Empire had made it particularly important that we should not play into the hands of a few ill-disposed Americans in London.' He was sorry that Orwell had found it necessary 'because of a mistake on our part' to return a book on Shaw unreviewed (see letter to Connolly) and he hoped 'we shall have your co-operation' in future. The text is reproduced from a printer's galley; no typescript has been traced.

Though telling us too much about Mr. Gallagher and his fellow-correspondents and too little about the various oriental peoples among whom they made their hurried journeys, this book contains interesting material. As War Correspondent of the "Daily Express" Mr. Gallagher was on board the Repulse when she was sunk, and saw the Malaya and Burma campaigns at close quarters. It is a depressing story that he has to tell, though not a surprising one, and of course the villains of it are the Burra Sahibs and Tuans Besar,[1] the big business men and high officials under whose sloth and greed the Far Eastern provinces of the Empire had gradually rotted. Here is a picture of some of them in the Singapore club:—

There lay the Tuans Besar, in two long rows of chairs. Attached to the arms of each chair were two leg-rests, which were swung out so that the sitter could lie flat out with his legs held up at a comfortable angle for him. The Tuans Besar were nearly all dressed in light-weight, light-coloured suits (not white, mark you, as only Eurasians wore white in Singapore; certainly not the exclusive, well-dressed Tuans Besar). Dark-red mouths opened and closed as they blew out great gusts of curry-laden breath. The bloated bellies heaved. . . .

While the Singapore business men, whose income tax had a ceiling of eight per cent., carried on with their normal round of golf, gin, and dancing, the fever-stricken troops in the jungle lived on bread and jam and chlorinated water. In Burma it was much the same story—an ill-armed, hopelessly outnumbered army with a frivolous incompetent civilian community behind it: the only redeeming features were the courage of the troops, the brilliant feats of the R.A.F. and the American Volunteer Group, and here and there the devotion and initiative of some minor official, who might be either an Englishman, an Indian, or a Eurasian.

A number of people, which Mr. Gallagher estimates at 300,000—even the Governor put it at 200,000—fled from Rangoon as a result of two air-raids which would have been petty ones by our standards. After that the defence of Burma became even more hopeless than before, because of the lack of labour. It was impossible to get ships unloaded, and thousands of tons of American armaments, originally destined for China, had to be destroyed before the Japanese arrived. Mr. Gallagher makes two charges which the ordinary reader has no way of verifying, but which ought to be investigated. One is that fresh troops were landed at Singapore long after its position had become obviously hopeless,[2] in spite of the protests of General Wavell, who wanted them diverted to Burma. The other is that Chiang Kai-shek's offer to send troops into Burma was only accepted grudgingly, and too late. It is also clear from his account that there was a good deal of favouritism in the matter of evacuation. Europeans, at any rate women, could generally get transport, but Indians had to fend for themselves. An interesting passage in the book describes a column of 4,000 Indian refugees on the 1,200-mile march back to India, with not a weapon between them and with Burmese bandits robbing them every night and murdering the stragglers.

Mr. Gallagher also spent some days with the Chinese army in Burma, and went as a passenger on a bombing raid on Bangkok. It is unfortunate that he says little about the political attitude of the ordinary Burmese population, an important question of which conflicting accounts have been given. Otherwise his book is a valuable piece of reporting, likely to ruffle some dovecots which have needed ruffling these twenty years past.

1. These were terms of respect for important Europeans in Burma and Malaya respectively. Orwell makes much use of 'burra sahib' in *Burmese Days*. *Malay Made Easy*, by A. W. Hamilton (Sydney, 1942), defines *Tuan besar* as 'The (European) manager.'
2. This was correct. Troops were landed and within a few hours were Japanese prisoners, many, of course, to die, and all to suffer, in the hands of their captors.

1448. Gujarati Newsletter, 28

7 September 1942

The English original was written by Orwell. No script has been traced.

On 7 September 1942, Bokhari sent a memorandum to the Eastern Service Director, L. F. Rushbrook Williams, following a meeting with Rowan Davies, Empson, Tonkin, Bonwit, and Miss Sam about the use of the 1130–1145 GMT time slot. So far as Orwell's work was concerned, this confirmed the use of this time for Gujarati Newsletters on Mondays, Marathi Newsletters on Thursdays, and Bengali Newsletters on Saturdays. Trade-offs between the Indian and Chinese Sections regarding other times were reported.

1449. BBC Talks Booking Form, 7.9.42

Mulk Raj Anand: 'Voice,' 2, monthly programme; 'half hour programme of poems etc. with discussions lasting about 7 mins. Mr. Anand helped to put the programme together & will take part in the discussions—speaking for about 2 [minutes]'; broadcast 8.9.42; fee: £5.5 'to cover part in discussions & assistance in compilation of prog.' Signed: Z. A. Bokhari.

1450. BBC Talks Booking Form, 7.9.42

Edmund Blunden: 'Voice,' 2; 'reading two poems by himself—for about 4 minutes—copyright being covered by Miss Alexander'; broadcast 8.9.42; fee £3.3s (inclusive). Signed: Z. A. Bokhari.

1451. BBC Talks Booking Form, 7.9.42

Cedric Dover: 'Books That Changed the World,' 1. The Descent of Man; 2. Uncle Tom's Cabin; broadcast 1 and 8.10.42; fee £9.9s each. Signed: Z. A. Bokhari.

1452. BBC Talks Booking Form, 7.9.42

Princess Indira of Kapurthala: 'The Debate Continues'; broadcast 5, 12, 19, and 26.10.42; fee £9.9s each talk. Signed: Z. A. Bokhari.

1453. BBC Talks Booking Form, 7.9.42

Ethel Mannin: 'I'd like It Explained'; 13-minute discussion on female emancipation with Mrs. Fordham (see separate contract)[1] in which Ethel Mannin will speak for about 6½ minutes; broadcast 25.9.42; 'a special fee of £10.10s has been arranged for Ethel Mannin.' Signed: Z. A. Bokhari.

1. Not traced.

1454. BBC Talks Booking Form, 7.9.42

Narayana Menon: 'Books That Changed the World,' 1, Gulliver's Travels; broadcast 17.9.42; fee £9.9s. Signed: Z. A. Bokhari.

1455. BBC Talks Booking Form, 7.9.42

Herbert Read: 'Voice,' 2, monthly programme; 'reading poem by W. H. Auden (September 1941),[1] for about 3 minutes, and taking part in discussions (total length of discussions 7[2] minutes)'; broadcast 8.9.42; fee: £4.4, 'to cover reading of poem lasting 3 minutes & part in discussion.' Signed: Z. A. Bokhari.

1. The title should be 'September 1, 1939'
2. '4' was originally typed but '7' written over it, probably by Bokhari.

1456. BBC Talks Booking Form, 7.9.42

K. S. Shelvankar: 'Books That Changed the World,' The Social Contract; broadcast 24.9.42; fee £9.9s. Signed: Z. A. Bokhari.

1457. BBC Talks Booking Form, 7.9.42

Bahadur Singh: News Review;[1] broadcast 3 and 31.10.42; fee £3.3s + 13s 2d fare. Signed: Z. A. Bokhari.

1. These bookings were for reading the Weekly News Commentary in English prepared by Orwell.

1458. BBC Talks Booking Forms, 7.9.42

Noel Sircar: News Review;[1] broadcast 10.10.42 and 7.11.42; fee £3.3s each reading. Signed: Z. A. Bokhari.
Noel Sircar: Film Commentary; monthly 13-minute talk on films to be released in India shortly; broadcast 22.9.42 and 20.10.42; fee £3.3s each talk, increased to £9.9s each on 22 September. Signed: Z. A. Bokhari.

1. These bookings were for reading the Weekly News Commentary in English prepared by Orwell.

1459. BBC Talks Booking Form, 7.9.42

Shridhar Telkar: Weekly News Review[1]; reading only; broadcast 26.9.42 and 24.10.42; fee £3.3s each. Signed: Z. A. Bokhari.

1. These bookings were for reading the Weekly News Commentary in English prepared by Orwell.

1460. BBC Talks Booking Form, 7.9.42

Shridhar Telkar: 'Topic of the Week;' broadcast 7, 14, 21, and 28.10.42; fee £9.9s each talk. Signed: Z. A. Bokhari.

1461. BBC Talks Booking Form, 7.9.42

G. Woodcock: 'Voice,' 2, monthly programme; 'Mr. Woodcock will be in the studio for rehearsal & transmission and will possibly make one or two remarks in the discussion, but is coming primarily out of interest in the programme. I do not think he should receive a fee'; broadcast 8.9.42; fee £1.1 queried; form bears stamp 'Acceptance received and cheque posted or handed,' but this is crossed out and written over is 'No reply   no fee paid.'[1] Signed: Z. A. Bokhari.

1. See Woodcock's letter to Orwell, 2 December 1942, *1711*.

1462. To Noel Sircar

[7–21 September 1942?]

The carbon copy of this telegram from Orwell is filed between 7 and 21 September 1942; it probably refers to that period. The relevant Fridays were the 11th and 18th.

CAN YOU TAKE PART IN FEATURE PROGRAMME FRIDAY NEXT 9.30 TILL TWELVE NOON

1463. War-time Diary

7.9.42: *There is evidently trouble in Syria. Handout this morning to the effect that—most unfortunately and much against H.M. Government's will—General de Gaulle is insisting that Syria is still under a French mandate and it is impossible yet to make a treaty, as in the case of Irak. General de Gaulle's attitude is considered most deplorable,*[1] *but as he is, after all, the accredited leader of the Free French and the whole legal position is very obscure (the matter should be decided upon by the League of Nations which unfortunately no longer exists) H.M. Government is unable, etc. etc. In other words the Syrians will get no treaty, the blame for this is placed on our puppet de Gaulle, and if possible we shall swipe Syria for ourselves. When I heard this hollow rubbish trotted out by Rushbrooke-Williams[2] this morning and we all had to listen and keep straight faces, there came into my head, I don't quite know why, the lines from Hardy's Dynasts about the crowning of Napoleon in Rome[3]:*

> Do not the prelate's accents falter thin,
> His lips with inheld laughter grow deformed,
> In blessing one whose aim is but to win
> The golden seat that other bums have warmed?

The Daily Worker reappeared today—very mild, but they are urging (a) a second front, (b) all help to Russia in the way of arms etc., and (c) a demagogic programme of higher wages all round which would be utterly incompatible with (a) and (b).

1. *deplorable*] unfortunate *in manuscript*
2. Rushbrooke-Williams] 'R-W' *in typescript. The Eastern Service Director spelt his name* 'Rushbrook Williams.'
3. In *The Dynasts*, Napoleon places the crown on his own head in Milan Cathedral, not in Rome (Complete Edition, 1910, 35; Part I, Act I, Scene 6). On p.34, that edition has 'While' for 'In,' 'seats' for 'seat,' and 'b—s' for 'bums,' Orwell discussed *The Dynasts* in *Tribune*, 18 September 1942; see *1497*.

1464. 'Voice,' 2: A Magazine Programme

8 September 1942

The text below is that used for the broadcast, which was passed for Policy and for Security by Bokhari. The typescript was amended in Orwell's hand, and the typing also looks like Orwell's. Although there is an unamended typed note, 'Not checked with broadcast,' there is also, in Orwell's hand, a note, 'As broadcast 25' 21".' No name is given on the typescript or in PasB for the speaker of the extract from *Revolt in the Desert*; the insertion of Orwell's name here is an editorial guess. In addition to misreadings, Auden's 'September 1, 1939' is called 'September 1941,' line 19 of which begins with 'O' in the typescript. The textual notes following the script record differences between the original typescript and what was broadcast, that is, Orwell's manuscript changes and textual errors. In the margin opposite Orwell's introductory announcement is a list of the participants' names, in capital letters, probably in Orwell's hand: ORWELL G., EMPSON WM., ANAND MULK RAJ, READ HERBERT, BLUNDEN EDMUND, GODFREY KENTON.

ORWELL: This is the second number of VOICE. Here we all are in the editorial office as usual, putting the magazine together. "VOICE" is always chiefly concerned with poetry, especially modern poetry, and this time we are having a number specially devoted to war poetry. The trouble is that—according to some people at any rate—there isn't any war poetry this time. There was even an article about it in "The Times" Literary Supplement a little while back, headed: "Where are the War Poets?" Is that true, Empson, in your opinion? Are there no war poets this time?

EMPSON: Of course it isn't true. There's a whole string of war poets—Henry Treece, J. F. Hendry, F. S. Scarfe, Keidrich Rhys, G. S. Fraser,[1] Roy Fuller, Alan Rook,[2] and I don't know how many more. A quite sizeable anthology of war poetry has just come out—edited by an Indian, by the way, J. M. Tambimuttu. I suppose what The Times Literary Supplement meant was that there are no Rupert Brookes this time. But neither there were last time after 1915.

ORWELL: Of course one might claim that any poem written in wartime is a war poem. But even if one doesn't ignore the war there is a difference between accepting war and rejecting it. I should say the poems being written now are mostly anti-war, are they not?

ANAND: There is very little that is jingoistic being written, and certainly we don't want anything jingoistic in "VOICE". But I can think of poems written recently which do accept the war, though not quite in the same way as Rupert Brooke.

ORWELL: For example?

ANAND: Well, for example, Auden's poem, "September 1941".

ORWELL: Oh, yes, that's a very good one. I was forgetting that. That'll do to start the magazine with. Here it is, then. "SEPTEMBER, 1941" by W. H. Auden. This is Herbert Read reading it:[3]

READ:

SEPTEMBER 1941 [= SEPTEMBER 1, 1939][3]
by W. H. Auden

I sit in one of the dives
On Fifty-Second Street
Uncertain and afraid
As the clever hopes expire
Of a low dishonest decade:
Waves of anger and fear
Circulate over the bright
And darkened lands of the earth,
Obsessing our private lives;
The unmentionable odour of death
Offends the September night.

Accurate scholarship can
Unearth the whole offence
From Luther until now
That make a[4] culture mad,
Find what occurred at Linz
What huge imago made
A psychopathic god;
I and the public know

What all schoolchildren learn,
Those to whom evil is done
Do evil in return.

Exiled Thucydides knew
All that a speech can say
About Democracy,
And what dictators do,
The elderly rubbish they talk
To an apathetic grave;
Analysed all in his book,
The enlightenment driven away,
The habit-forming pain,
Mismanagement and grief:
We must suffer them all again.

Into this neutral air
Where blind skyscrapers use
Their full height to proclaim
The strength of Collective Man,
Each language pours its vain
Competitive excuse:
But who can live for long
In an Euphoric dream;
Out of the mirror they stare,
Imperialism's face
And the international wrong.

Faces along the bar
Cling to their average day:
The lights must never go out,
The music must always play,
All the conventions conspire
To make this fort assume
The furniture of home;
Lest we should see where we are,
Lost in a haunted wood,
Children afraid of the night
Who have never been happy or good.

The windiest militant trash
Important Persons shout
Is not so crude as our wish:
What mad Nijinsky wrote
About Diaghilev
Is true of the normal heart;
For the error bred in the bone
Of each woman and each man
Craves what it cannot have,
Not universal love
But to be loved alone.

From the conservative dark
Into the ethical life

The dense commuters come,
Repeating their morning vow;
'I *will* be true to the wife,
I'll concentrate more on my work,'
And helpless governors wake
To resume their compulsory game:
Who can release them now,
Who can reach the deaf,
Who can speak for the dumb?

All I have is a voice
To undo the folded lie,
The romantic lie in the brain
Of the sensual man-in-the-street
And the lie of Authority
Whose buildings grope the sky:
There is no such thing as the State
And no one exists alone:
Hunger allows no choice
To the citizen or the police;
We must love one another or die.

Defenceless under the night
Our world in stupor lies;
Yet, dotted everywhere,
Ironic points of light
Flash out wherever the Just
Exchange their messages;
May I, composed like them
Of Eros and of dust,
Beleaguered by the same,
Negation and despair,
Show an affirming flame.

WOODCOCK: It sounds rather disillusioned. I should describe it as the poem of someone who had had his most intense war experience before the major war started & had grown rather sceptical of the whole value of war as a political instrument.

ANAND: But Auden is still a political poet. That poem has what you could describe as a direct political purpose.[5]

EMPSON: I think the younger poets who are writing now are really unpolitical. They merely[6] feel that the only way to deal with the war is to start from[7] their personal situation in it. I've got a poem here which illustrates what I mean. It's called "A Letter to Anne Ridler", by G. S. Fraser, who's fighting in Egypt, I believe.

ORWELL: Would you like to read it? That'll do for the second poem in the magazine.

EMPSON: All right. But it's too long. I'll start about the middle & go straight through to the end.[8]

ORWELL: All right, go ahead. "A Letter to Anne Ridler", by G. S. Fraser.

EMPSON: Last part of LETTER TO ANNE RIDLER
                              by G. S. Fraser

Loving the charity of women's love,
Too much a household pet, I see in you
The gentle nurture that now curbs my grief
As I grow tall, beyond that budding grove
Of all the beautiful beyond belief
Within whose shade my windflower passions blew,

Private to me, their shy and secret sun,
Who now with other private suns compete
And seek in man's inverted mode such love
As nerves the will to enter and complete
Its terrible initiation of
Man to these virtues that from pain are won.

And the sick novice whimpers for his home
Who shall be hurt and horribly alone
Before the historic vigil lets him sleep.
Yet for such hurt, such pity might atone
And such an Ithaca for those who roam
Far, that they may at last return and weep.

Why do the towers of Troy for ever burn?
Perhaps that old Jew told us, or perhaps
Since women suffer much in bearing us
We also must show courage in our turn,
Among these forks and dreaded thunder-claps,
Against an endless dialectic tearing us . . .

Or freedom, say, from family love and strife
And all the female mystery of a room
That half supports and half imprisons us
May tear a man from mother, sister, wife,
And every soft reminder of the womb.
Dead Freud in Lost Vienna argued thus.

I hardly know! But Fritz, who's now interned,
(Sober and well-informed like all his race)
Told me this war might last, say, seven years;
But right would be triumphant then, the tide be turned,
Unless indeed (the night fell on his face)
Our hopes are just illusions like our fears.

Perhaps in London, say, in seven years,
We'll meet, and we will talk of poetry,
And of the piety of homely things,
A common past, the flowering library
In which the awkward spirit perseveres
Until a world of letters shines and sings . . .

Unless the vigilant years have numbed my face,
The long humiliation soured my heart,
The madman's silence boxed my veering mood:
Let time forgive me, if I fall apart,

> And fall, as many souls have fallen from grace,
> Through just and necessary servitude.
>
> Or if we never meet, remember me
> As one voice speaking calmly in the north
> Among the muslin veils of northern light;
> I bore the seed of poetry from my birth
> To flower in rocky ground, sporadically,
> Untill° I sleep in the unlaurelled night,

ANAND: We ought to have something about the last war as well, oughtn't we?

X: And isn't it time we had a piece[9] of prose? We can't fill a whole number of a magazine up with verse.

WOODCOCK:[10] I think on the whole the best stuff written about the last war was in prose. But it was very passive, at least the later and better stuff was. The great feature of the last war was its appalling slaughter, and, so far as the people mixed up in it could see, its meaninglessness. This time it isn't quite the same.[11] It's difficult to think of any book about the last war which is still worth reading and which expresses any positive attitude.

ANAND:[12] What about T. E. Lawrence's "Revolt in the Desert"?

EMPSON: Ah, that was a different war. Lawrence was engaged in a minor campaign,[13] and it was fought for limited[14] objects which the people fighting in it could understand. Besides, it was in the open, not in trenches.[15] It wasn't machine warfare, and the individual counted for something.

ANAND: There is a very good description of Lawrence and his Arabs blowing up a Turkish troop train. Look, here it is. Lawrence and his party are lying beside the railway track, waiting to press the electric button which explodes the mine they have buried between the sleepers, and the train is approaching round the bend.

EXTRACT FROM REVOLT IN THE DESERT—Read by [Orwell?]

At that moment the engines, looking very big, rocked with screaming whistles into view around the bend. Behind them followed ten box-wagons, crowded with rifle-muzzles at the windows and doors; and in little sandbag nests on the roofs Turks precariously held on, to shoot at us. I had not thought of two engines, and on the moment decided to fire the charge under the second, so that however little the mine's effect, the uninjured engine should not be able to uncouple and drag the carriages away.

Accordingly, when the front 'driver' of the second engine was on the bridge, I raised my hand to Salem. There followed a terrific roar, and the line vanished from sight behind a spouting column of black dust and smoke a hundred feet high and wide. Out of the darkness came shattering crashes and long, loud metallic clangings of ripped steel, with many lumps of iron and plate; while one entire wheel of a locomotive whirled up suddenly black out of the cloud against the sky, and sailed musically over our heads to fall slowly and heavily into the desert behind. Except for the flight of these, there succeeded a deathly silence, with no cry of men or rifle-shot, as the now-grey mist of the explosion drifted from the line towards us, and over our ridge until it was lost in the hills.

In the lull, I ran southward to join the sergeants. Salem picked up his rifle and charged out into the murk. Before I had climbed to the guns the hollow was alive with shots, and with the brown figures of the Beduin leaping forward to grips with the enemy. I looked round to see what was happening so quickly, and saw the train stationary and dismembered along the track, with its wagon sides jumping under the bullets which riddled them, while Turks were falling out from the far doors to gain the shelter of the railway embankment.

As I watched, our machine-guns chattered out over my head, and the long rows of Turks on the carriage roofs rolled over, and were swept off the top like bales of cotton before the furious shower of bullets which stormed along the roofs and splashed clouds of yellow chips from the planking. The dominant position of the guns had been an advantage to us so far.

When I reached Stokes and Lewis the engagement had taken another turn. The remaining Turks had got behind the bank, here about eleven feet high, and from cover of the wheels were firing point-blank at the Beduin twenty yards away across the sand-filled dip. The enemy in the crescent of the curving line were secure from the machine-guns; but Stokes slipped in his first shell, and after a few seconds there came a crash as it burst beyond the train in the desert.

He touched the elevating screw, and his second shot fell just by the trucks in the deep hollow below the bridge where the Turks were taking refuge. It made a shambles of the place. The survivors of the group broke out in a panic across the desert, throwing away their rifles and equipment as they ran. This was the opportunity of the Lewis gunners. The sergeant grimly traversed with drum after drum, till the open sand was littered with bodies. Mushagraf, the Sherari boy behind the second gun, saw the battle over, threw aside his weapon with a yell, and dashed down at speed with his rifle to join the others who were beginning, like wild beasts, to tear open the carriages and fall to plunder. It had taken nearly ten minutes.

I ran down to the ruins to see what the mine had done. The bridge was gone; and into its gap was fallen the front wagon which had been filled with sick. The smash had killed all but three or four and had rolled dead and dying into a bleeding heap against the splintered end. One of those yet alive deliriously cried out the word typhus. So I wedged shut the door, and left them there, alone.

EMPSON: That describes[16] something which happened according to plan. I think it would be difficult to find its equivalent in war poetry.[17] The characteristic poems of the last war were satire, and political pamphleteering at that.[18] Sassoon's poems, for instance, were effective at the time but they don't wear well.[19]

ANAND: But there[20] was also Wilfred Owen. You remember the poem about "What passing bells for these who die like cattle"?

ORWELL: It's a pity he isn't here to read it. He was killed. But we've got Edmund Blunden here today. He edited Owen's poems, by the way.[21] How about getting him to read one or two of his poems?

ANAND: Ah yes. That will give just the right contrast between the last war and this one.

ORWELL: There is a very good one called "Rural Economy". I suppose Mr. Blunden wrote it about 1917—didn't you?

BLUNDEN: – – – –°

ORWELL: Anyway, here it is. "Rural Economy"—and this is Edmund Blunden reading it.

BLUNDEN:

RURAL ECONOMY 1917
– by –
Edmund Blunden

There was winter in those woods,
And still it was July:
There were Thule solitudes
With thousands huddling nigh;
There the fox had left his den,
The scraped holes hid not stoats but men.

To these woods the rumour teemed
    Of peace five miles away;
In sight, hills hovered, houses gleamed
    Where last perhaps we lay
Till the cockerels bawled bright morning and
The hours of life slipped the slack hand.

In sight, life's farms sent forth their gear;
    Here rakes and ploughs lay still;
Yet, save some curious clods, all here
    Was raked and ploughed with a will.
The sower was the ploughman too,
And iron seeds broadcast he threw.

What husbandry could outdo this?
    With flesh and blood he fed
The planted iron that nought amiss
    Grew thick and swift and red,
And in a night thought ne'er so cold
Those acres bristled a hundredfold.

Why, even the woods as well as field
    This ruseful farmer knew
Could be reduced to plough and tilled,
    And if he planned, he'd do:
The field and wood, all bone-fed loam,
Shot up a roaring harvest-home.

ORWELL: That is a poem that goes into a certain amount of detail. Here's another that gives a more general statement. It's called Report on Experience.

REPORT ON EXPERIENCE
by Edmund Blunden

I have been young, and now am not too old;
And I have seen the righteous forsaken,
His health, his honour and his quality taken.
    This is not what we were formerly told.

> I have seen a green country., useful to the race,
> Knocked silly with guns and mines, its villages vanished,
> Even the last rat and last kestrel banished—
>   God bless us all, this was peculiar grace.
>
> I knew Seraphina; Nature gave her hue,
> Glance, sympathy, note, like one from Eden.
> I saw her smile warp, heard her lyric deaden;
>   She turned to harlotry; —this I took to be new.
>
> Say what you will, our God sees how they run.
> These disillusions are His curious proving
> That He loves humanity and will go on loving;
>   Over there are faith, life, virtue in the sun.

ORWELL: I don't know if anybody has noticed one thing. We haven't yet had a poem *in favour* of war.

SOMEONE: Is anyone in favour of war?

ANAND: Not as an end in itself. But there is such a thing as recognising that war may be necessary, just as a surgical operation may be necessary. Even an operation which may leave you mutilated for life.

EMPSON: Although there aren't any heroics in this war, I maintain that the attitude implied in the poem of Fraser's which I read is actually more heroic than the Rupert Brooke attitude.[22] I think the key phrase is "this just and necessary servitude". It *is* just and necessary, and it *is* servitude. You see he's willing to do more than get himself killed. He's willing to cripple his own personality for the sake of a cause he believes in.

ORWELL: But there can be an actual enthusiasm for war when it's for some cause such as national liberation. I mean one can feel that war is not merely a disagreeable necessity, but that it is spiritually better than peace—the kind of peace you have in Vichy France, for instance.

ANAND: What about an example?[23]

ORWELL: How about[24] "The Isles of Greece"?

ANAND: Of course! That comes very near home nowadays.

ORWELL: Here it is, then. "The Isles of Greece", by Lord Byron.

KENTON:

THE ISLES OF GREECE
read by Godfrey Kenton[25]

> The isles of Greece! the isles of Greece
>   Where burning Sappho loved and sung,
> Where grew the arts of war and peace,
>   Where Delos rose, and Phoebus sprung!
> Eternal summer gilds them yet,
> But all, except their sun, is set.
>
> The mountains look on Marathon —
>   And Marathon looks on the sea;
> And musing there an hour alone,

I dream'd that Greece might still be free;
For standing on the Persians' grave,
I could not deem myself a slave.

A king sate on the rocky brow
   Which looks o'er sea-born Salamis;
And ships, by thousands, lay below,
   And men in nations; —all were his!
He counted them at break of day —
And when the sun set, where were they?

And where are they? and where art thou,
   My country? On thy voiceless shore
The heroic lay is tuneless now —
   The heroic bosom beats no more!
And must thy lyre, so long divine,
Degenerate into hands like mine?

'Tis something in the dearth of fame,
   Though link'd among a fetter'd race,
To feel at least a patriot's shame,
   Even as I sing, suffuse my face;
For what is left the poet here?
For Greeks a blush — for Greece a tear.

Must *we* but weep o'er days more blest?
   Must *we* but blush? — Our fathers bled.
Earth! render back from out thy breast
   A remnant of our Spartan dead!
Of the three hundred grant but three,
To make a new Thermopylae!

What, silent still? and silent all?
   Ah! no; — the voices of the dead
Sound like a distant torrent's fall,
   And answer, 'Let one living head,
But one, arise, — we come, we come!'
'Tis but the living who are dumb.

In vain — in vain: strike other chords;
   Fill high the cup with Samian wine!
Leave battles to the Turkish hordes,
   And shed the blood of Scio's vine!
Hark! rising to the ignoble call —
How answers each bold Bacchanal!

Fill high the bowl with Samian wine!
   We will not think of themes like these!
It made Anacreon's song divine:
   He served — but served Polycrates —
A tyrant; but our masters then
Were still, at least, our countrymen.

Fill high the bowl with Samian wine!
   On Suli's rock, and Parga's shore,
Exists the remnant of a line

Such as the Doric mothers bore;
And there, perhaps some seed is sown,
The Heracleidan blood might own.

Trust not for freedom to the Franks —
    They have a king who buys and sells;
In native swords and native ranks
    The only hope of courage dwells:
But Turkish force and Latin fraud
Would break your shield, however broad.

Fill high the bowl with Samian wine!
    Our virgins dance beneath the shade —
I see their glorious black eyes shine;
    But gazing on each glowing maid,
My own the burning tear-drop laves,
To think such breasts must suckle slaves.

Place me on Sunium's marbled steep,
    Where nothing, save the waves and I,
May hear our mutual murmurs sweep;
    There, swan-like, let me sing and die:
A land of slaves shall ne'er be mine —
Dash down yon cup of Samian wine!

The first reading is that of the text as amended by Orwell (and as printed here); the second reading is that of the unamended typescript.
1. Fraser] Frazer *and throughout except in Empson's reading of the poem*
2. Roy Fuller, Alan Rook] William Rogers
3. This is Herbert Read reading it:] *added to typescript; throughout, the typescript gives* September 1, 1939 *as* September 1941
4. make a] *interlinear insertion;* make *should be* has driven
5. WOODCOCK: It sounds rather disillusioned . . . as a direct political purpose] *two speeches replace:* ANAND: There is a change of mood there. He has grown a good deal less confident. It seems a long time since the Spanish Civil War. But after all it is still a political poem. It has a political purpose.
6. are really unpolitical. They merely] *interlinear insertion*
7. start from] write about
8. But it's too long. I'll start about . . . to the end] It'll have to be cut, though, it's too long. I'll read the later part of it. *The typescript (and broadcast) had these errors:* 16 heart *for* hurt; 22 much *for* must; *and* 34 triumph *for* be triumphant.
9. piece] bit
10. WOODCOCK] EMPSON; *correction handwritten in upper and lower case*
11. the same. It's difficult] the same. Hardly anyone on either side feels that it makes no difference who wins. It's difficult
12. ANAND:] X.
13. that was a different war. Lawrence was engaged in a minor campaign,] that's different. That was about a minor campaign.
14. limited] *interlinear insertion*
15. in the open, not in trenches] in the desert
16. That describes] Yes, that is something rather unusual in war literature. It describes
17. war poetry] verse
18. political pamphleteering at that] not very effective even at that
19. Sassoon's poems . . . don't wear well] Sassoon's poems, for instance, were too angry to make good satire
20. But there] There

21. He edited Owen's poems, by the way.] *interlinear insertion*
22. is actually more heroic than the Rupert Brooke attitude] is nobler than the Rupert Brooke stuff
23. What about an example?] Can you think of a good example?
24. How about] What about
25. Stanzas 2, 10, and 12 of the original have been omitted.

1465. To Martin Armstrong

9 September 1942   PP/EB

Dear Mr. Armstrong,[1]
I believe Gerald Bullett asked you [whet]her you would like to take part in a broadcast called Story by Five Authors, and that you said you would. Could you just let me know for certain whether this is so, and if so, I will let you have all the necessary further particulars.

Yours sincerely,
George Orwell
Talks Producer
Indian Section

1. Martin Donisthorpe Armstrong (1882–1974) was associate literary editor of *The Spectator*, 1922–24, and author of many books of poems, short stories, and longer fiction. He had recently published *Victorian Peep-Show* (1938), *Simplicity Jones* (1940), and *The Butterfly* (1941). He replied to Orwell's letter on 11 September expressing his willingness to participate.

1466. To Inez Holden

9 September 1942   PP/EB/NP

Dear Inez,
We did arrange, didn't we, for you to take part in a broadcast called Story by Five Authors? You might just let me know whether this is O.K., and I will let you have further particulars. Your broadcast will be on October 23rd.

Yours,
George Orwell
Talks Producer
Indian Section

1467. To J. F. Horrabin

9 September 1942   PP/EB

Dear Horrabin,
Thanks so much for your letter. I am glad to hear you are having a nice rest, but I see Dot and Carry[1] are appearing as usual. Yes, we will keep your talk

on Land Reclamation at the original date—October 16th. I am sending herewith a list of the questions I would like you to touch upon. I have not cast this in dialogue form because I don't know enough about this subject to know what aspects you would want to concentrate most on. I have merely written down a number of questions starting various hares which you could follow up or not as you wish. These talks are 13½ minutes, and allowing for the interviewer's questions I don't think your part should be more than 14 to 15 hundred words. If you like to write the whole thing out into the form of a dialogue, putting in the questions to be asked of you, you can do so, or if you prefer you can simply produce a statement in answer to some of the questions I have written down and I will work it up into dialogue form. I would like to have the script not later than October 9th.

Yours,
Eric Blair
Talks Producer
Indian Section

1. One of Horrabin's strip cartoons featured two office girls, Dot and Carrie.

On the verso of Horrabin's letter to Orwell of 7 September are the following questions in Orwell's handwriting. In this transcription, false starts have been ignored, contractions except '&' expanded, and slight styling changes made. For 'colonised' in the second line Orwell originally wrote 'utilised'; in 2b, 'Are the polar regions' was originally written as 'How far the polar regions.' The original is illustrated as plate 15 in West: *Broadcasts*.

"The Deserts & the Poles".

Q.1. Is the earth already populated up to capacity? Are there areas which are now empty but could be colonised?

Q.2. What about areas now seemingly uninhabitable.

    a. *Deserts.* Where are the principle° desert areas & could anything be done to reclaim them? Is it known what produces deserts? Does desert reclamation have any adverse effects elsewhere?

    b. *Polar regions.* Are these inhabitable to any extent? Have any of the artic° or antarctic areas a summer during which cultivation could be practiced?° Is anything being done in this line now? Are the polar regions fully explored? What about the northern polar area as a means of communication between the new & old worlds? Is anything being done in this line? How is arctic transport affected by aviation and meteorology?

1468. To L. A. G. Strong

9 September 1942   PP/EB

Dear Mr. Strong,[1]

I wonder if you would care to take part in a broadcast of an experimental and slightly unusual type which we are projecting in October. This is called Story by Five Authors and the idea is to have a serial story in five parts each written by a different author, who can carry on the story just as he chooses from the last instalment. The instalment we want you to do is the second. I am doing the first, the third will be done probably by Inez Holden, the fourth by Martin Armstrong, and we hope the concluding one by E. M. Forster. I cannot yet give further details because the first instalment which I am doing is only in process of being written. This idea may be a failure but on the other hand it might be rather interesting. Could you let me know whether you will at any rate provisionally accept this, and in that case I can let you have the first instalment from which yours would follow at about the end of this month. Each instalment should take 13½ minutes which means about 1500 words. The date of yours would be October 16th. If you are not able to come on that day we can always record it.

Your sincerely,
George Orwell
Talks Producer
Indian Section

1. Leonard Alfred George Strong (1896–1958) wrote poems, short stories, novels, plays, and books for children. His best novels were probably *Dewar Rides* (1929), *The Garden* (1931), and *Sea Wall* (1933). He edited *The Best Poems of 1923[–25]*, the Gollancz Books for Schools, 1935, Methuen's One-Act Plays, 1939–49, and the Nelson Novels, 1934–35. A series of his broadcasts for schools, *English for Pleasure*, was published in 1941, and with C. Day Lewis he edited *A New Anthology of Modern Verse, 1920–40* (1941).

1469. Extract from Minutes of Eastern Service Meeting

9 September 1942

Programmes for weeks 37 and 38 tabled. Mr. Blair noted that Dr. Joad[1] is available as an occasional contributor of English talks.

1. C. E. M. Joad (1891–1953), philosopher and author, was a colourful radio personality who achieved widespread popularity from his participation in the BBC's 'Brains Trust' programme, 1941–47. He was a conscientious objector in World War I and an advocate of pacifism thereafter. He was Head of the Department of Philosophy and Psychology at Birkbeck College, University of London from 1930–53. He was a lucid writer and able to convey his subject to a lay public. Though an agnostic for much of his life, he discussed his new-found religious belief in *Recovery of Belief*, 1952.

1470. BBC Talks Booking Form, 9.9.42

M. R. Kothari: Marathi Newsletter, 28; written by E. Blair, translated and read by M. R. Kothari; broadcast 10.9.42; fee £5.5s. Signed: Z. A. Bokhari.

1471. BBC Talks Booking Form, 9.9.42

Ellen Wilkinson: 'Women Generally Speaking,' The House of Commons; broadcast 14[1].10.42; fee £5.5s; 'balance of fee to Min of H.S.'[2] Signed: Z. A. Bokhari.

1. Altered in ink from '7.'
2. Ellen Wilkinson (see *422, n. 3*) had been Labour M.P. for Jarrow, and a leader of the Jarrow Protest March of unemployed from her constituency to London in 1936. At this time she was Joint Parliamentary Secretary to the Minister of Home Security, Herbert Morrison, with special responsibility for air-raid shelters. In the first post-war Labour government, she was Minister of Education.

1472. Marathi Newsletter, 28

10 September 1942

The English original was written by Orwell. No script has been traced. PasB gives timing as 11′ 40″.

1473. To Mulk Raj Anand

10 September 1942   PP/EB/NP

Dear Mulk,
Would you like to do War and Peace in our series Books that Changed the World?
Please let me know about this. The broadcast will be on October 15th, at 12.15, and the talk should be 13½ minutes in length. We should want to have the script by October 7th at the latest. It would be a very great help if you could let me have a typed copy of the script.

Yours,
Eric Blair
Talks Producer
Indian Section

1474. To E. C. Bowyer

10 September 1942   PP/EB/NP

Dear Mr Bowyer,
I wonder if you could help me by suggesting a speaker for a talk in one of our series—or indeed you might undertake the talk yourself if you felt competent.
This is another talk in that series "I'd Like it Explained", in which you took part. This one is to be on Transport, and I rather want the emphasis to be on

air transport. Could you suggest anyone capable of dealing with this if you don't care to do it yourself [?][1]

Your sincerely,
George Orwell
Indian Section
Talks Producer

1. Bowyer replied on 11 September to say that he would be happy to speak on air transport but was at a loss as to whom to suggest to discuss surface transport. Were he to be the sole speaker he feared the talk might be open to the objection that it was biased towards air transport. His letter is annotated by Orwell: 'Letter 15.9.42.' This would seem to refer to Orwell's letter dated 16 September; see *1491*.

1475. To R. R. Desai

10 September 1942   PP/EB/NP

Dear Desai,
I wonder if you would like to take part in another series of broadcasts called "Books that Changed the World". This is a series of talks on books which have actually had a direct influence on the big public during the past 200 years. [It] starts off with Gulliver's Travels and ends up with Mein Kampf. I would like you very much to do the talk on the latter, if you would. The date would be October 29th. Please let me know whether you feel inclined to undertake this and I will tell you all about it next time I see you.

Yours,
Eric Blair
Talks Producer
Indian Section

1476. BBC Talks Booking Form, 10.9.42

Narayana Menon: 5-minute talk on the anti-Fascist Youth Rally; broadcast 9.9.42; fee £4.4s. Signed: Z. A. Bokhari.

1477. War-time Diary

10.9.42:   *Lecturing last night at Morley College, Lambeth. Small hall, about 100 people, working-class intelligentsia (same sort of audience as Left Book Club branch[1]). During the questions afterwards, no less than 6 people asked "Does not the lecturer think[2] it was a great mistake to lift the ban from the Daily Worker"—reasons given, that the D. W's loyalty is not reliable and it is a waste of paper.* ⌈*Only one woman stood up for the D W, evidently a Communist at whom one or two of the others expressed impatience ("Oh,* she's always saying that"!)[1] *This after a year during which there has been a ceaseless clamour[3] for the lifting of the ban. One is constantly being thrown out in one's calculations[4] because one listens to the articulate minority and forgets the other 99 per cent. Cf. Munich, when the mass of the people were almost certainly behind Chamberlain's policy, though to read the New Statesman etc. you wouldn't have thought so.*

1. The Left Book Club, founded by Victor Gollancz in 1936, still published a book a month on anti-Fascist or Socialist topics. Local group meetings had been revived in the middle of 1942, and some fifty branches were formed.
2. *think*] think that
3. *clamour*] clamour from Left organisations
4. *calculations*] judgements

1478. News Review, 39

12 September 1942

The heading 'News Review' is handwritten at the top of the first page. Either this typescript or that for the following week was the last to be censored by Bokhari before he left for Liverpool, to sail for India. The script for 19 September is without censorship stamps; that for 26 September was censored by Anthony Weymouth. The script is as broadcast but it is not possible to tell with certainty whether the writing is Orwell's. A curious aspect of this typescript is that although it comes to an end near the top of the fourth typed page (making it very short), a fifth, but unnumbered, page with four more short paragraphs of news follows. The microfilm is not clear, and the page photographed looks to be a rather poor carbon copy. It doesn't seem to be quite the same typewriter face as the main body of the text. Possibly these paragraphs were not written by Orwell. The script was read by Noel Sircar.

Last week we reported that fighting had broken out again in Egypt, and added that we hoped to be able to give fresh news[1] of it this week. This particular phase of the Egyptian campaign is already over, and has resulted in a severe setback for the Germans. They made what was evidently a large scale effort to break through the Allied defensive positions and were repulsed with very heavy losses, especially of tanks and other vehicles. The actual number of tanks lost by the Germans has not yet been officially reported, but Mr. Wendell Willkie,[2] the American envoy to the Turkish government, who passed through Egypt on his way to Ankara, stated that the Germans had lost 100 tanks, which represents 40 per cent of their full strength in Egypt. Mr Churchill also in his recent speech—to which we refer later—has stated that the result of this battle has been to make Egypt safe for some months to come.

It should be remembered, that the Egyptian campaign has not finished, the German forces are not destroyed. The losses they have suffered, however, are undoubtedly serious for them, especially their losses in tanks, because of late they have been finding the sea passage from Italy to Africa very costly. During the past week our submarines alone have sunk or damaged 12 Axis supply vessels, and this is in addition to the damage done by allied aeroplanes. Now that Malta has been reinforced and has fighter planes to guard its aerodromes, it can again be the base from which British bombers attack Axis shipping and ports in Italy and Sicily. On the whole, therefore, we may say that the situation in Egypt has improved very greatly—more greatly indeed than we thought it safe to prophesy a week ago.

Heavy fighting is still going on in central New Guinea, where the Japanese are trying to advance directly over the mountain range which runs along the centre of the island, and reach Port Moresby. They have made a definite advance within the past few days, and are now only about 45 miles from their objective. Port Moresby cannot be considered safe as long as there are Japanese anywhere in New Guinea. The Japanese have failed to dislodge the Americans from the islands they have seized in the Solomon Archipelago in spite of the fresh landing attempt which they made three days ago.

During the past few weeks, the Chinese have regained a good deal of territory in the Eastern provinces, and have so far frustrated the efforts which the Japanese are making to complete their railway communications north and south. The other objective which they have in this area is to prevent the Chinese getting or keeping possession of any base from which Japan itself could be bombed. At present several towns in Chekiang province which are potential air bases for use against Japan are in Chinese hands. The Japanese efforts to capture them have failed. However, even if the Chinese hold on [and] these areas can be consolidated, that does not mean that the bombing of Japan can begin immediately, because the building up of an air base with all its numerous staff of mechanics, its buildings, work shops and supplies of oil, munitions and spare parts for repairs is a long business. Moreover the transport difficulties are very great since the Burma Road, originally the chief route for war materials entering China, is in Japanese hands. Air transport, however, is being improved and new routes into China from India are being opened up. When these are fully established the advantage of possessing bases within bombing distance of Japan can be exploited.

Following on his return from Moscow, Mr. Churchill has made a general statement on the war to the House of Commons. This authoritative statement clears up several points about which information was previously lacking. Perhaps the most important reference Mr. Churchill made in his speech was to the Dieppe raid, which he described as being a reconnaissance in force, necessary in order to obtain information for larger operations later. Mr Churchill naturally made no mention of dates or places, but left it quite clear that an invasion of Europe is contemplated and will be undertaken at the appropriate moment. He explained that in his talks with Premier Stalin he had reached complete agreement and had both convinced himself of the readiness of the Russian people to go on fighting in no matter what circumstances and of our own readiness to make whatever sacrifices may be necessary to take the pressure off our allies. Mr. Churchill added that the Russians felt that they had had to make an unduly great part of the common effort—a feeling which, considering the history of the past year, was not unjustifiable. All they needed from ourselves, however, was an assurance that we would make a diversion when opportunity served, and this assurance they now have. Mr. Churchill also made a statement on the Egyptian campaign and gave an assurance about the defence of Egypt which we have mentioned already. He explained that he had separated the command of the Tenth Army in Persia from that of the Eighth Army in Egypt in order to prevent the Commander in Egypt from being overburdened with what might prove to be a double campaign. For Mr. Churchill also mentioned the possibility of the British army in Persia being used in direct aid to the Russian armies in the Caucasus area. Mr. Churchill also spoke of the recent naval battle in the Mediterranean as a result of which the British convoy reached Malta with much-needed supplies. The arrival of this convoy, he said, had made Malta's position secure for many months and though the Naval losses were heavy—an old aircraft carrier, two cruisers, one of which was a new one, and a destroyer—this price was not unduly high since the effect was to keep Malta in being as an air and submarine base. The Axis losses [in the battle] in aeroplanes and U-boats destroyed and warships damaged were in any case heavy.

Mr. Churchill was also able to disclose that the sea war on which both the food and the armaments of Britain finally depend had taken a decided turn for the better during the past three months. The rate at which Americans are building ships is now decidedly higher than the rate at which Axis submarines are sinking them, and the submarines themselves are being harassed so successfully that there is hardly a day on which the news of a submarine being either sunk or damaged does not come in. Our bombing raids on Western Germany, on the ports in which the submarines are built, also have an indirect beneficial effect on the sea war.

There has been no very great change on the Russian fronts during the past week. The Germans are still making an all-out effort to capture Stalingrad and in places are probably fighting in the suburbs of the city. The Germans have a great preponderance of aeroplanes on this front, especially dive-bombers. Stalingrad's position, though not hopeless, must be regarded as very precarious. Novorossisk on the Black Sea is in German hands, though fighting is still going on in that area. Although Novorossisk is important as a naval base, its loss does not mean that the Soviet Black Sea fleet is out of action, since it possesses another base farther south.

Laval, the French Quisling, has now instituted a persecution of Jews in Unoccupied France in almost the same style as is being carried out in Germany. Thousands of French Jews are being deported to Eastern Europe while their children are confined in concentration camps. This has called forth protests from the Vatican and the Catholic Church generally, and French priests are already being persecuted for giving shelter to Jewish children.

The Daily Worker, the British Communist newspaper, the ban on which has been lifted, re-appeared on September 7th. It is giving full support to the war effort of the United Nations.

The British are taking over fresh areas in the island of Madagascar. They have already seized three more harbours on the west coast, and an important aerodrome from which the planes of the RAF can patrol the whole island. This move has been made necessary by the fact that Japanese submarines were being supplied at various points on the coast of Madagascar, with the connivance of the Vichy French authorities whom the British had formerly allowed to remain in control. By taking over the whole of the island, or all of it that matters, the British will be able to make the passage through the Indian Ocean considerably safer for Allied ships.

1. Words in the first two lines are obscured by the censorship stamp for Policy, but there is no doubt that 'fresh news' is correct.
2. Wendell L. Willkie (1892–1944), industrialist and lawyer, was the Republican candidate for the U.S. presidency against Franklin Roosevelt in 1940. He did much to liberalise his party. In September and October 1940 he visited Egypt, the Middle East, Russia, and China, recorded in his *One World* (1943).

1479. Bengali Newsletter, 9

12 September 1942

The English original was written by Orwell. No script has been traced. PasB gives timing as 12′ 15″.

1480. To Cyril Connolly

Saturday, [12 September 1942?]   Typewritten on BBC letterhead

10a Mortimer Crescent   London   NW6

Dear Cyril,

I am sending back the Shaw book. I don't write for papers which do not allow at least a minimum of honesty. There is no point in reviewing a book unless one can say what is in it.[1] The author of "Retreat in the East" got in some good cracks at the civilian community in Malaya etc. and I merely quoted a typical one. I had no idea that silly owl Brown[2] had anything to do with the literary page of the Observer. He would never stand for what I should say about Shaw, whom I believe he worships.

I am sorry I'm afraid I can't dine with you on Tuesday, though thank you all the same. I may be on night duty here.[3]

Yours
[Not initialled]
Eric Blair

1. See headnote to review of *Retreat in the East, 1447.*
2. Ivor (John Carnegie) Brown (1891–1974), author, critic, and editor, had been drama critic and leader writer for the *Manchester Guardian,* 1919–35, and was drama critic for *The Observer,* 1929–54, and its editor, 1942–48. He wrote novels, several books of essays, several collections of short essay, on words, and studies of Shakespeare, Dickens, Dr. Johnson, Jane Austen, and J. B. Priestley. His *Shaw in His Time* was published in 1965.
3. Either on Home Guard or firewatching duty.

1481. Review of *A Modern de Quincey* by Captain H. R. Robinson

The Observer, 13 September 1942

Unjustified in other ways, the title of this book does have the excuse that its author, like de Quincey, is very much interested in his own reactions as an opium-smoker. An officer of the Indian Army, seconded to the Burma Military Police, he was axed in 1923 and settled down for a couple of years in Mandalay, where he devoted himself almost exclusively to smoking opium, though he did have a brief interlude as a Buddhist monk and made unsuccessful efforts to float a gold mine and run a car-hiring business. After a short visit to England, during which he tried quite vainly to cure himself of the opium habit, he returned to Mandalay, and on being arrested for debt attempted suicide—a ghastly failure, for instead of blowing out his brains as he had intended he merely blew out both eyeballs, blinding himself for life.

This bald outline of the facts does not do injustice to Captain Robinson's book, which, in spite of the long passages devoted to the delights of opium, leaves a great deal unexplained. Those who knew the author in Mandalay in 1923[1] were completely unable to understand why a young, healthy and apparently happy man should give himself up to such a debilitating and—in a European—unusual vice, and on this point the book throws no further light. Captain Robinson merely explains that one night in Mandalay he happened to see some Chinese smoking their opium, decided to try what it was like, and thereafter became a habitual opium-smoker. Some other reason for wanting to escape from real life there must have been. It is never mentioned, but the clue is possibly to be found in the earlier part of the book, which describes Captain Robinson's adventures as a frontier magistrate among the little-known tribes in the north east corner of Burma.

What are the pleasures of opium? Like other pleasures, they are, unfortunately, indescribable. It is easier to describe the miseries which the smoker suffers when deprived of his drug; he is seized with feverish restlessness, then with violent fits of yawning, and finally howls like a dog, a noise so distressing that when an opium-smoker is imprisoned in an Indian jail he is usually, quite illegally, given diminishing doses to keep him quiet. Like many other smokers, Captain Robinson felt himself, while under the influence of the drug, to be possessed of almost divine wisdom. He was aware that he not only knew the secret of the Universe, but had reduced this secret to a single sentence, which he was unfortunately never able to recall when he woke up. One night, so as to make sure of remembering it, he took a pad and pencil when he lay down to smoke. The sentence in which all wisdom was contained turned out to be: "the banana is great, but the skin is greater."

This book is a small but not valueless contribution to the literature of opium. It is amateurishly written, but its facts are truthful. The description of the attempted suicide is worth the rest of the book put together. It is profoundly interesting to know what the mind can still contain in the face of apparently certain death—interesting to know, for instance, that a man can be ready to blow his brains out but anxious to avoid a disfiguring wound. Those who knew Captain Robinson in the old days will be glad to receive this evidence of his continued existence, and to see the photograph of him at the beginning of the book, completely cured of the opium habit and apparently well-adjusted and happy, in spite of his blindness.

1. Orwell was in Mandalay from 27 November 1922 to 9 November 1923 and then from 17 December 1923 to 25 January 1924. Presumably he knew Robinson—he refers again to 'Those who knew Captain Robinson' in the final sentence.

1482. Gujarati Newsletter, 29

14 September 1942

The English original was written by Orwell. No script has been traced.

1483. [A. P. Blair, 'My Debt to India, V']

14 September 1942

PasB states that this was 'translated and read by A. M. Ashraf.' It almost certainly was not by Orwell. A. P. Blair (and Charles Blair, see *1485*) have not been positively identified, but the latter may be John Pilcher; see *882, n. 1*. He worked at the Ministry of Information at the time and had connexions with India.

1484. To J. A. Lauwerys

15 September 1942   PP/EB/NP

Dear Mr. Lauwerys,
I am writing to ask whether you can advise me about some speakers in a new scientific series we are going to broadcast to India. I want to have a series on what one might call popular science, dealing with new inventions and processes which alter the way of life of ordinary people. I would like to have the first talk, which is on October 20th, on de-hydrated food, which is obviously a very important development and makes, for example, the maintenance of big armies in foreign countries a great deal easier than it would be otherwise. I want to have the second talk, four weeks later, on micro-films, which again may, I think, have very important effects. Unfortunately I don't know who are the experts or competent speakers on these subjects.

I also want to have a talk of a slightly different style on ersatz and raw materials, on October 9th. The only person I know who has expert knowledge of this is the German writer, Oswald Deutsch whose English is not good enough for India. I should be very much obliged if you could let me have as soon as possibly° your advice about speakers for these three talks.

Yours sincerely,
George Orwell
Talks Producer
Indian Section

1485. [Charles Blair, Japan's Threat to Asia, 1: 'Japan in the Second Half of the Nineteenth Century']

15 September 1942

The typescript (surviving on microfilm T42, BBC Archives) has a handwritten note, 'As broadcast 13′ E.A.B'. On page 6 is the only other insertion—'their'—and that could be in Orwell's hand. However, the speaker, Charles Blair, had no connexion with Orwell, and has not been identified with certainty. He may be the 'Blair' (without initials) who represented the Ministry of Information at an Eastern Service Committee meeting of 19 November 1941, which was also attended by Orwell (as 'E. A. Blair'). 'Blair' was possibly a nom de plume for John Pilcher (see *882, n.1*), a diplomat who served in Japan, 1936–39, 1967–72 and spoke Japanese. He was at the Ministry of Information 1941–48.

1486. War-time Diary

<u>15.9.42</u>: *Ghastly feeling of impotence over the India business, Churchill's speeches, the evident intention of the blimps to have one more try at being what they consider tough, and the impudent way in which the newspapers can misrepresent the whole issue, well knowing that the public will never know enough or take enough interest to verify the facts. This last is the worst symptom of all—though actually our own apathy about India is not worse than the non-interest of Indian intellectuals in the struggle against Fascism in Europe.*

1487. Indian Section Organization

Z. A. Bokhari, Indian Programme Organiser, had asked permission to return to India, partly on compassionate grounds, partly to enable him to bring his children to England, and partly to assess the reception of the Indian Section's broadcasts in India and to collect materials. He put forward proposals on 27 May 1942, and on 2 June and 11 September 1942. His departure and the date of his return were both much delayed. He left from Liverpool by sea on 29 September 1942, arriving in India on 11 November; he travelled back to England by air and sea, arriving on either 13 or 14 May 1943, the journey taking nearly a month. From 16 September 1942, Mary Blackburn acted on his behalf in the booking of talks; letters survive showing how the others took over his duties. Those aspects of Bokhari's three memoranda dealing with the organisation of the work of the section in London are reproduced; these included Orwell's responsibilities and proposals for who should read Orwell's Newsletters (not, in the event, carried out). Less important details have been omitted, noted by [. . .]. Two talks booking forms for 16 September 1942 pinpoint the changeover of authority. One, for Kothari, is signed by Bokhari; the other, for Ardaschir, is signed by Miss Blackburn.

1488. Z. A. Bokhari (IPO) to Eastern Service Director
27 May 1942

INDIAN SECTION — ORGANISATION

I put forward the following suggestions for your consideration:—

1. During my absence the routine administration of the Indian Section— i.e. Mr. Sahni's office, Mr. Blair's office and my office—should be entrusted to Miss Blackburn, who should co-ordinate the activities of the Indian Section and work as a link between E.S.D. and the Indian Section. Miss Blackburn will therefore be responsible for seeing that the various instructions of E.S.D. regarding Contracts, duration of programmes, etc., etc., are carried out. She will be responsible for getting the various papers, including Booking Slips for Contracts, signed by E.S.D. She will also see that the payment to various artists remains confidential, as it has been hitherto.

   I suggest that during my absence Miss Blackburn should get something over and above her present pay.

2. E.S.D., Prof. Firth, Lady Grigg, Eric Blair and Mr. Sahni should meet at least once a week to discuss the programmes of the next week, and the programmes for the fourth week. The following points will have to be gone into:—

   (i) The Schedule of programmes
   (ii) The dates on which scripts should be in
   (iii) Allocation of duties for Rehearsals and Transmissions.
   (iv) Listeners' letters and their answers
   (v) Talkers' letters and their answers
   (vi) The Rota for week-ends
   (vii) Report on the talkers of the last week and the desirability of engaging them in future
   (viii) Technical defects or difficulties of the last week and their remedy.

3. Mr. Sahni should be made responsible for Hindustani programmes and Mr. Blair for the English programmes. These programmes will have to be censored for Policy by E.S.D. and for security by a Security Censor.

4. *Newsletters.* Prof. Firth[1] is being requested to suggest Switch-censors for Bengali, Marathi and Gujerati Newsletters.

5–9. [. . .]

1. See *846, n. 13.*

1489. Z. A. Bokhari (IPO) to Eastern Service Director
2 June 1942

INDIAN SECTION — ORGANISATION

Further to my note of the 27th May, I am grateful to you for agreeing to the following:—

1. Miss Blackburn's appointment as a liaison between you and the Indian Section and her appointment as
2. secretary to the informal Committee, comprising yourself, Prof. Firth, Lady Grigg, Eric Blair and Mr. Sahni.
3. that Mr. Sahni should be made responsible for Hindustani programmes and that Mr. Blair for the English. That these programmes will be censored for Policy by you and for Security by a Security Censor.[1]
4. *Newsletters.* I suggest the following Switch Censors:
(a) *Bengali* Dr. Sudhin N. Ghose
Mr. Das Gupta
Mr. Das Gupta is working for the Ministry[2] as a Translator and sub-editor of the Bengali 'Haftawar Akhbar'.
(b) *Marathi* S. M. Telkar
(c) *Gujerati* Mrs. Mohan. She is a Gujerat who is the wife of the Secretary to the Nepal Legation — OR —
Irshad Syed
If you approve of these names, will you be good enough to get them through the 'College'[3] urgently[?]
The Students' Messages are received in various languages. The Students send their messages in the vernaculars, together with faithful translations of their messages in English. The above Switch Censors will compare the original message with this translation, and the Security Censor will pass the messages.
5. *Weekly News in English.* I suggest the following people as suitable readers in my absence:[4]
> (i) Princess Indira
> (ii) Noel Sircar
> (iii) C. D. S. Lakshmanan
> (iv) Cowasjee Jehangir
> (v) A. Subramanium

6–11. [. . .][5]

1. In a memorandum of 4 June to the Assistant Controller, Overseas Service, Rushbrook Williams (ESD) said 'Censorship for policy and security for the English scripts will be shared between Mr. Weymouth, Mr. Thavenot, and myself.'
2. Possibly the Ministry of Information. His address was given as '3 Grenville Street   Russell Square.' Russell Square lies at the rear of Senate House, University of London, where that ministry was situated but Grenville Street is actually off Brunswick Square, some 300 yards to the east.
3. For being put through the College. see *845.*
4. In the event, Shridhar Telkar, Noel Sircar, Bahadur Singh, and Princess Indira were given this task. However, Princess Indira did not read the first Newsletter scheduled for her (22 August 1942); her place was taken by Homi Bode.

5. The other omissions refer to purchasing books and records, offering contracts, engaging a five-piece Indian band, asking Indian staff based in London if they wish to return to India (though none are named), arranging for his reports to be transmitted through Laurence Brander, the Indian Intelligence Officer, and arrangements for bringing back his family, including his three children (two over twelve and one under twelve), and the need for a new passport. He wrote, 'It sounds very dreadful, but instead of my wife, I intend to bring a servant with me.'

1490. Z. A. Bokhari (IPO) to Eastern Service Director

11 September 1942

When I am mentaled° in lights velocity, perhaps the following details and suggestions will be of some use to you.

GENERAL:

1. *English Scripts*

   These, I suggest, should be censored for *Policy* by you, and for *Security* by any Security censor available.

2. *Newsletters*

   These are written in English and translated into various languages by our Announcer-Translators. Censorship arrangements as for above.

3. *Messages*

   Students send their messages (with their translations into English) to us in advance. Any Security censor can censor them. Policy censorship does not apply to this programme.

   Soldiers can't and don't write their messages. The Producer is responsible for rehearsing and switch-censoring them.

4. *Hindustani Programmes* — They are:—

   (a) Features

   (b) Talks

   (c) Entertainment

   (d) Messages from India

   I very strongly recommend that you should give five minutes a day to Bakaya or Sahni, who will give you the gist of programmes for your approval, and guidance in regard to Security. Generally speaking, our programmes don't touch the Security borders.

   In several cases the Features are received in English and then translated into the language. In such cases, the English version will be submitted to you.

   A. L. Bakaya should be made responsible for "vetting" the messages received from India. His judgment can be relied upon.

In continuation of I.P.O's memo of 11–9–42.

DETAILS:—

		GMT
SUNDAY:	Middle East Entertainment	0415 — 0445
	Prog. for Forces in Gt. Britain	0925 — 1000
	"Any Questions?" (filling T.E.E. & half-hour English period).	1115 — 1200
	Hindustani Talk	1415 — 1430
	Hindustani Children's Prog. (Ashraf)	1430 — 1445
MONDAY:	Middle East Entertainment	0415 — 0445
	The Debate Continues	1115 — 1130
	Radio Theatre	1130 — 1200
	Gujerati Newsletter	1345 — 1400
	'Indira Sabha'	1415 — 1430
TUESDAY:	Middle East Entertainment	0415 — 0445
	English half-hour period	1115 — 1145
	Through Eastern Eyes	1145 — 1200
	Hindustani Feature	1415 — 1430
WEDNESDAY:	Middle East Entertainment	0415 — 0445
	Through Eastern Eyes	1115 — 1130
	15 mins: Music (E.M.S.)	1130 — 1145
	Women Generally Speaking (arranged by Lady Grigg)	1145 — 1200
	'Hello Punjab'	1345 — 1400
	Greetings — Indian Students' Messages (recorded)	1420 — 1430
THURSDAY:	Middle East Entertainment	0415 — 0445
	Through Eastern Eyes	1115 — 1130
	English — feature	1130 — 1200
	Marathi Newsletter	1345 — 1400
	Hindustani Talk (approx:) (starting sometime in October)	1415 — 1430
FRIDAY:	Middle East Entertainment	0415 — 0445
	English half-hour period	1115 — 1145
	Through Eastern Eyes	1145 — 1200
	'Hello Punjab'	1345 — 1400
	Hindustani Feature	1415 — 1430
SATURDAY:	Middle East Entertainment	0415 — 0445
	Through Eastern Eyes (News Review)	1115 — 1130
	English half-hour period — music presented by Princess Indira	1130 — 1200
	Hindustani Entertainment	1345 — 1440
	Greetings — Indian Students' Messages (recorded)	1420 — 1430
	Bengali Newsletter	1430 — 1445

1491. To E. C. Bowyer

16 September 1942   PP/EB/NP

Dear Mr. Bowyer,

Many thanks for your letter. I think perhaps that in a talk of this length it would be better not to complicate it by a controversy between the different kinds of transport and I suggest that we stick simply to air transport, which is obviously more novel. If you would do this for us I should be very glad. As it is only one person, we will do it in the form of an interview in which you are asked a few leading questions and reply to them. This talk is to take place on October 23rd, which means we should like to have the script not later than October 16th. Within the next day or so I will send you a list of the questions we would like you to answer.

Your sincerely,
George Orwell
Talks Producer
Indian Section

1492. To Ethel Mannin

16 September 1942   PP/EB/NP

Dear Ethel Mannin,

I am sorry we did not acknowledge your script. I have now received Mrs. Fordham's draft and am working the two [manuscripts] into a dialogue. I shall not make you say anything that you did not say, or imply, in your draft but I will try and let you have a copy of the complete dialogue a day or two before the broadcast in case you want to make any last-minute alterations. Can you come to 200, Oxford Street not later than 11.45 a.m. on September 25th—the day of the broadcast—so that we can have time for rehearsal. [?]

Yours sincerely,
George Orwell
Talks Producer
Indian Section

1493. BBC Talks Booking Form, 16.9.42

K. K. Ardaschir: 'Rebirth of Egyptian Nation'; 13-minute talk; broadcast 18.9.42; fee £9.9s. Signed: M Blackburn[1] for I.P.O. Remarks: 'Will you kindly send the contract to my office—310, 200, O.S.—Mr. Ardaschir will not receive it in time otherwise.'

1. On 16 September 1942, Bokhari signed his last talks booking form (*1494*) before leaving for India. Mary Blackburn took over this duty; see *1487*.

1494. BBC Talks Booking Form, 16.9.42

M. R. Kothari: Marathi Newsletter, 29; written by E. Blair, translated and read by M. R. Kothari; broadcast 17.9.42; fee: £5.5s. Signed: Z. A. Bokhari.

1495. Marathi Newsletter, 29
17 September 1942

The English original was written by Orwell. No script has been traced. PasB gives timing as 10′ 43″.

1496. To Francis Yeats-Brown
17 September 1942   PP/EB

Dear Major Yeats Brown,[o1]
This is just to remind you about your broadcast in the Eastern Service on September 25th, at 12.15, in the English Language. I understand from Sir Malcolm Darling that he will be passing on a copy of your script to us within the next few days.

I should be glad if you could arrange to come to my office at 11.30 on the morning of the 25th, in order to give time for a short rehearsal of your talk. My office is at 200, Oxford Street, on the corner of Great Portland Street.

Yours sincerely,
Eric Blair
Talks Producer
Indian Section

1. Francis Yeats-Brown (1886–1944; DFC), professional soldier, airman, author, left the army in 1926 and was assistant editor of *The Spectator*, 1926–28. His books include *Bengal Lancer* (1930), (filmed as *The Lives of a Bengal Lancer*, 1935, with Gary Cooper); *Dogs of War!* (1934); *Yoga Explained* (1937), and *Indian Pageant* (1942). In *European Jungle* (1939) he wrote that it was his 'honest conviction that there is more real Christianity in Germany to-day [under Hitler] than ever there was under the Weimar Republic' (quoted by Malcolm Muggeridge in *The Thirties*, 1940, 237; see Orwell's review, 25 April 1940, 615; and referred to in 'Notes on the Way,' *Time and Tide*, 6 April 1940, 604). On 25 October 1942, Yeats-Brown wrote to Sir Malcolm Darling offering talks on India. He was advised on 3 November 1942 by Hilton Brown, who had organised talks on India for the Home Division, that 'any talk of a general nature on Indian affairs should come just now from an Indian rather than from a European.'

1497. 'Thomas Hardy Looks at War'
Tribune, 18 September 1942

Thomas Hardy's great poetic drama, *The Dynasts*, is of formidable size, and is generally bound in the sort of depressing gritty cover that one associates with school text books,[1] with the result that it has become one of those books which people can't read and therefore feel obliged to praise. It is nevertheless well worth reading, if only because the war it deals with has a ghostly similarity with this one.

The Dynasts is a sort of versified chronicle of the Napoleonic war, which in atmosphere and even in strategy was much liker to the present war than was the war of 1914–18. It is true that the events are happening in a different order, but even so their similarity is startling. The Russo-German pact is Tilsit, the Battle of France is Jena, the Battle of Britain is Trafalgar, the German invasion of Russia is the Moscow campaign, and so on. (Dunkirk is probably not Corunna, but the disastrous campaign in the Low Countries in 1792.) Moreover, the ideological mix-up, the quisling motif, the treacherous nobles and the patriotic common people, the endless line-ups and double-crossings, even such details as the invasion scare and the hasty formation of a Home Guard in Britain, are all paralleled.

However, the main interest of The Dynasts is not in its appositeness to our own times, nor in its historical side at all, for Hardy does not show much grasp of what we should now regard as the underlying issues of the Napoleonic war. The book's theme is sufficiently indicated in its title; Hardy sees the war as simply a clash of power-hungry monarchs, with the common people being slaughtered without any benefit, or even any possibility of benefit, to themselves. Of course, the idea of huge and meaningless suffering appeals deeply to him, and in the form chosen for The Dynasts his strange mystical pessimism gets a freer rein than it could get in a novel, where a certain amount of probability is needed.

Hardy set free his genius by writing a drama which was definitely not meant to be acted, and quite unknowingly—for The Dynasts was written round about 1900—produced something that would do as it stands for the script of a talkie. Though it is mostly in blank-verse dialogue, it contains a great deal of visual description, and its effect is really got by the constant switching of perspective from one end of Europe to the other, and from the earth to the middle air in a way that could only be reproduced on the screen. Apart from the human characters, certain beings described as spirits are introduced as a sort of chorus to comment on what is happening. But even the spirits, though they can foresee the future, are unable either to alter or to understand it. According to Hardy's vision of life, all events are predetermined, human beings are automata, but they are automata with the illusion of free will and the power of suffering. Everything happens at the behest of something called the Immanent Will—it tells one a great deal about Thomas Hardy that he believes in God and his God is always referred to as It—whose purposes we do not understand and never can understand. At certain key points in The Dynasts the Will manifests itself and the landscape turns into a sort of enormous brain in which the struggling human beings are seen to be entirely helpless cells or fibres. For example, at the most desperate moment of the battle of Waterloo:

"SPIRIT OF THE YEARS
Know'st not at this stale time
That shaken and unshaken are alike
But demonstrations from the Back of Things?
Must I again reveal It as It hauls
The halyards of the world?

"A transparency as in earlier scenes again pervades the spectacle. . . .[2] The web connecting all the apparently separate shapes includes Wellington in its tissue with the rest, and shows him, like them, as acting while discovering his intention to act. By the lurid light the faces of every row, square, group and column of men, French and English, wear the expression of people in a dream."[3]

That is effective enough even as it stands. In its context, as a climax to the long and hopeless struggle of Napoleon, it is profoundly moving, and leaves one with the feeling that *The Dynasts* is one of the very few genuine tragedies that have been written in our time.

One might wonder how any truly tragic effect can be produced by Hardy's morbid and almost superstitious view of life. One might also ask how it is that *The Dynasts* gives an impression of grandeur while Hardy's vision of history is, in fact, extremely limited. He shows hardly any awareness that the Napoleonic war was partly a war of ideas—no hint that the fate of both the French Revolution and the Industrial Revolution were involved—and he deals chiefly with the picturesque high-lights of the war, even at moments showing signs of jingo patriotism. All centres round the personality of Napoleon, whom Hardy represents as a mere vulgar adventurer, which he was.

Why, then, is Napoleon's story moving? Because personal ambition is tragic against a background of fatalism, and the more megalomaniac it is, the more tragic it becomes. If one believes that the future is predetermined, no figure is so pitiful as the "great" man, the man who a little more than others has the illusion of controlling his destiny.

In places the verse of *The Dynasts* is remarkable. In the huge formless drama (nineteen acts!) Hardy's clumsy genius had elbow-room, and there are wonderful passages here and there. For example:

Ay; where is Nelson? Faith, by this late time
He may be sodden; churned in Biscay swirls;
Or blown to polar bears by boreal gales;
Or sleeping amorously in some calm cave
On the Canaries' or Atlantis' shore
Upon the bosom of his Dido dear,
For all that we know![4]

This passage is of great technical interest because of its onomatopœic effects. Whereas the third line, for instance, gives an impression of icy cold by means of its long vowel sounds, the easy rhythm of the next three lines seems to call up a vision of a cosy lamp-lit room, with Lady Hamilton waiting beside the fireplace, Nelson's slippers keeping warm in the fender and a dish of crumpets on the hob.

But the main apppeal of *The Dynasts* is not in the verse, but in the grandiose and rather evil vision of armies marching and counter-marching through the mists, and men dying by hundreds of thousands in the Russian snows, and all for absolutely nothing. Hardy's pessimism was absurd as well as demoralising, but he could make poetry out of it because he believed in it; thus showing, like Poe, Baudelaire and various others, that even a half-lunatic view of life will do as a basis for literature provided it is sincerely held.

1. Orwell probably refers to the green of the Complete Edition, published in 1910. The first part of the play had appeared in 1903; seven years later it was published in full, comprising the nineteen acts to which Orwell refers. Judging by his reference to *The Dynasts* in his War-time Diary, *1463, 7.9.42*, Orwell may have written this essay shortly before its publication. It marks his return to *Tribune*; his last contribution had been on 20 December 1940.
2. The ellipsis marks the omission of the original's 'and the ubiquitous urging of the Immanent Will becomes visualized' (Part III, VII. vii; 1910 edition 505).
3. The double quotation marks are an editorial addition to indicate the extent of the quotation from *The Dynasts*.
4. From the Earl of Malmesbury's last speech (Part I, IV. vi; 1910 edition 80).

1498. News Review, 40

19 September 1942

The title 'News Review' is handwritten at the head of the first page. Although the typescript for this broadcast is marked 'as broadcast,' it bears no censorship stamps. The last sentence of the first paragraph has been x-ed out in the course of typing. There are some handwritten amendments in a very small hand (but possibly Orwell's), difficult to read on the microfilm. The script was read by Homi Bode.

British sea, air and land forces have carried out a daring raid at Tobruk more than a hundred miles behind the enemy's lines in Egypt. Although the full results have not yet been disclosed, it is known that the British raiding party lost two destroyers, and probably some prisoners and that they did very heavy damage.[1] Tobruk is now the principal port used by the Germans to bring war materials from Greece or even from Italy, and the object of the raid was to supplement the damage already done by the bombing planes of the R.A.F. [It is outside the range of any but heavy bombers, and the object of a Commando Raid on such a place would be to carry out more accurate destruction than could be achieved from the air.]

We may be sure that there will be further large-scale operations in Egypt and the advantage will lie with whichever side can get ready to strike first. This is largely a matter of bringing war materials over sea. Raids of this type if successfully carried out might upset the German plans almost as effectively as sinking their ships in transit.

The fighting in New Guinea appears to be stationary for the time being and we may hope that the Japanese advance towards Port Moresby has been stopped, though they are certain to make fresh attacks in this direction. During the past week there has been very heavy fighting on the island of Guadalcanal where the Japanese have succeeded in landing fresh troops. The Americans hold the main port of the island and the airfield, and the Japanese efforts to dislodge them have failed. Reports coming from China, however, suggest that a large Japanese fleet is approaching the Solomon Islands and we must expect them to make the most desperate efforts to recapture these islands, which so long as they are in American hands, endanger their whole position in the South Pacific. The Americans express themselves confident of being able to hold on and to use the Solomon Islands as a base for further advances.

The Germans are still concentrating every man, tank and aeroplane they can muster upon the attack on Stalingrad. Since last week they have advanced in certain sectors and in places they have even penetrated into the town where street fighting is said to be going on. Both sides have been reinforced within the past few days. On this front, the Germans have a considerable preponderance of aeroplanes, especially dive bombers, which they are using in immense numbers. The Russians are resisting with the utmost courage and obstinacy but the situation of Stalingrad must be regarded as extremely grave and it is becoming harder and harder to reinforce it. We do not care to prophesy one way or the other as to whether Stalingrad will hold out. If it does not, the Germans probably cannot be prevented from reaching the Caspian Sea, and the Volga ceases to be of any use as a means of communication. If the Germans reached Astrakhan, the Caspian Sea itself would cease to be at any rate a safe route for the transport of oil and other supplies, as almost its whole area could be ranged by German aeroplanes. On the other hand it is already the middle of September and there is no sign as yet that the Germans are within sight of getting across the Caucasus mountains and reaching the Baku oilfields, which are their real objective. Novorossisk on the Black Sea has fallen into German hands and they may possibly attempt to by pass the mountains by moving down the coast of the Black Sea. On the other Russian fronts the Germans are either making no progress or the Russians themselves are taking the offensive. They have just launched another offensive in the Voronezh area. It is significant that the Germans are already making preparations for a winter campaign, are building fortified positions well behind their lines in Russia and are scouring the whole of Europe for furs and other warm clothes. They probably expect, therefore, to have to keep a large army on the Russian fronts, including the northern fronts, throughout the winter, in which case they will inevitably lose great numbers of men from the cold, though their preparations to meet it may be better this winter than last. The importance of the battle now being fought round Stalingrad lies in the fact that if the Germans do not take Stalingrad, they cannot avoid forcing millions of their soldiers to spend the winter in the Russian snow. If they do take Stalingrad, they hope that the northern Russian armies may be unable to get their supplies of oil in which case the Germans could hold these fronts with comparatively few men who could be relieved at short intervals. We do not yet know whether this is the case, because naturally we do not know what stocks of oil and other war materials the Russians have stored at Moscow, Leningrad and other places in the north. The preparations which the Germans are making for a winter war suggest that they have reason to think that the Russians will be by no means incapable of making another offensive this winter.

The operations in Madagascar are proceeding smoothly and the seaports which were the principal objective are already in British hands. The British forces are still 50 or a 100 miles from the capital Antananarivo[, but are likely to reach it within the next few days]. Two days ago [a report was put out that] the French Government of the island [had] asked for an armistice. [This has since been denied and it is probable that] The Vichy Government *however* has put heavy pressure on the French authorities to put up a pretence of resistance *and the Armistice Terms have been refused*. In fact, however, resistance has been negligible and it is quite clear that the Vichy regime has not much support from the French population and little or none from the indigenous population. The shouts of anger which have gone forth from the German radio over the British occupation of Madagascar demonstrate that the Germans rightly regard this island as being of great strategic importance. Points on its coast line were in fact being used for refuelling Axis submarines, and the elimination of this danger will appreciably ease the Allied shipping situation.[2] The local officials are carrying on their work under the British military authorities and there is not likely to be any interruption to the food supplies or the life of the island generally.

It is reported that Axis agents have made an unsuccessful attempt to assassinate the President of Nicaragua. Brazil, the latest ally of the United Nations, is increasing its armed forces. From Argentina comes the news of big popular demonstrations of solidarity with Brazil, making it clear that the common people of the country are much more friendly to the Allied cause than the government of the moment.

The British bombing raids on Western Germany continue, and are now too frequent to be enumerated individually. The R.A.F. are now dropping bombs which weigh no less than 8 thousand pounds or 3½ tons. These bombs do not penetrate into the ground but burst on the surface, devastating the houses for hundreds of yards round. Aerial photographs of Karlsruhe, Düsseldorf and other places show whole areas of hundreds of acres where there is scarcely a house with its roof intact. Neutral travellers arriving from Germany have reported that morale in Western Germany is suffering considerably under the continuous raids to which the German air force seems able to make no reply.

Four days ago, September 15th, was celebrated throughout this country and the world as the second anniversary of the Battle of Britain. Between August and October 1940, after the fall of France, the Germans made an all-out effort to conquer Britain by air and loudly boasted that they would be able to do so within a few weeks. They started off in August and September with daylight raids aimed at destroying the Royal Air Force, and when this had evidently failed, switched over to night raids directed chiefly at the working class areas in the East End of London, aiming at terrorising the civilian population. The whole manoeuvre however was a failure and in about two months of air warfare the Germans lost between two and three thousand planes, with some thousands of irreplaceable airmen. September 15th is celebrated as the anniversary because on that day the Royal Air Force shot down no less than 185 German planes,[3] and it was about that date that the failure of the Germans to overwhelm the British defences by daylight bombing became apparent. Now that we can look back and see the events in better perspective it is becoming clear that the Battle of Britain ranks in importance with Trafalgar, Salamis, the defeat of the Spanish Armada and other battles of the past in which the invading forces of a seemingly invincible monarch or dictator have been beaten back and which have formed a turning point in history.

1. This was an attempt to destroy Axis port installations at Tobruk, and at Benghazi, some three hundred miles west. Air and sea attacks were launched on Tobruk and a motorised column attacked Benghazi. Both attempts failed, and British losses were heavy (see *2194 Days of War*, 286). On 14 September, the Germans sank the anti-aircraft cruiser *Coventry* and the destroyers *Zulu* and *Sikh*. For fuller details, see *1515, n. 2*.

2. Fear that Madagascar would be used as a base for Japanese naval attacks, with the support of the local Vichy authorities, lay behind the takeover. Churchill, quoting many messages passed at the time, outlines clearly the Allies' anxiety (*The Second World War*, IV, 197–212; U.S.: *The Hinge of Fate*, 222–37). General Smuts, Prime Minister of South Africa, telegraphed Churchill as early as 12 February 1942 that he looked upon 'Madagascar as the key to the safety of the Indian Ocean, and it may play the same important part in endangering our security there that Indo-China has played in Vichy and Japanese hands. All our communications with our various war fronts and the Empire in the East may be involved' (198; U.S.: 223). Churchill also quotes a report of 12 March 1942 from the German Naval Commander-in-Chief to Hitler that the Japanese intended to establish bases on Madagascar (200; U.S.: 225). There was a belief, later proved false, that the battleship *Ramillies* and a tanker were struck by torpedoes on 30 May from Japanese submarines operating out of Madagascar (210; U.S.: 236).

3. Post-war records showed that only about one-third of this number of German planes (56) had been shot down (and rather more had been shot down on 15 August); 23 British planes were lost. However, this did mark the turning point in the Battle of Britain. It is still commemorated on the Sunday nearest to 15 September.

1499. Bengali Newsletter, 10

19 September 1942

The English original was written by Orwell. No script has been traced. PasB gives timing as 13′ 05″.

1500. BBC Talks Booking Form, 19.9.42

Princess Indira of Kapurthala: 'Great Cellists'; 'three 30 minute programmes, comprising 5 to 7 mins of spe[e]ch. Rest gramophone records of Cellists. Each script compiled with the assistance of EMS'[1]; broadcast 12, 19, and 26.9.42; fee £6.6s each programme. Signed: M Blackburn for I.P.O.

1. Probably European Music Supervisor, though the official abbreviation was 'Eur.M.S.' Only Eleen Sam, a talks producer in the Eastern Service, had two of these three initials; there was no one on the staff at this time with all three initials. For anyone outside the BBC, a fee would have been payable.

1501. To Leonard Moore

20 September 1942   Handwritten

10a Mortimer Crescent   London   NW. 6

Dear Mr Moore,
Herewith the diary I spoke to you of.[1] I think it is worth printing. I suppose you know my permanent address is as above. I think your office are still sending me things at 111 Langford Court occasionally.

Yours sincerely
Eric Blair

1. See *1443*.

1502. Gujarati Newsletter, 30

21 September 1942

The English original was written by Orwell. No script has been traced. PasB gives timing as 11' 05".

1503. To J. G. Crowther

21 September 1942   PP/EB/NP

Dear Mr. Crowther,
I am writing to ask whether you can ad[vi]se me about someone to do a talk in the Indian service. We have a series called "I'd Like it Explained", in which experts on various subjects of current importance answer questions put to them by an Indian interviewer. We want to have a talk on Ersatz and Raw Materials, and have had some difficulty in finding a speaker. The only expert I know on this subject is Oswald Deutsch whose English is not good enough for the Indian service. Ritchie Calder told me you would probably be able to suggest someone. I wonder if you would be kind enough to let me know about this. The matter is rather urgent, as the date of the talk is October 9th.

Yours sincerely,
Eric Blair
Talks Producer
Indian Section

1504. To J. C. Drummond

21 September 1942   PP/EB/NP

Dear Professor Drummond,[1]

I am writing to ask if you would care [to] do a talk in the Indian service of the BBC. Ritchie Calder suggested to me that you might either be willing to undertake this particular talk or to give me the name of somebody else who would. We have a series called "Science & The People" dealing with new discoveries and processes which affect the lives of ordinary people, and we are anxious to have a talk on dehydrated food, particularly with reference to the possibilities it offers of saving shipping and feeding armies in remote places. These talks are of 13½ minutes duration which generally speaking means about 1500 words, and the date of the talk is October 20th. Could you be kind enough to let me know whether you would like to undertake it, and if so I will let you have further details.

Yours truly,
Eric Blair
Talks Producer
Indian Section

1. Jack Cecil Drummond (1891–1952; Kt., 1944), a nutritional biochemist, was described by the American Public Health Association's Lasker Awards Committee as one of 'the four great leaders' in public health administration. In 1940 he became scientific adviser to the Minister of Food, Lord Woolton. Drummond set minimum food requirements for children and manual workers during World War II and introduced National Milk Cocoa and the supply of orange juice for young people. He replied to Orwell that, though he would be delighted to talk on dehydrated food, there were others better equipped to do so. He suggested Dr. Franklin Kidd (see *1512, n. 1*) or one of his senior staff at the Low Temperature Research Station, Cambridge. On 4 August 1952, Drummond, his wife, and ten-year-old daughter were murdered when camping in France.

1505. BBC Talks Booking Form, 21.9.42

K. K. Ardaschir: 'The Highway of the World'; 13½-minute talk; recorded 22.9.42; broadcast not fixed; fee £9.9. Signed: M Blackburn for I.P.O. Remarks: 'Will you please send Mr. Ardaschir's contract to Mr. Blair, 310, 200 O.S. tomorrow morning?'

1506. War-time Diary

21.9.42: *Yesterday met Liddell Hart for the first time. Very defeatist and even, in my judgement, somewhat inclined to be pro-German subjectively.* ⌈In a great stew about the barbarism of bombing Lübeck. Considered that during the wars of recent centuries the British have the worst record of all for atrocities and destructiveness.⌉ *Although, of course, strongly opposed to the Second Front, also anxious for us to call off the bombing. There is no point in doing it, as it can achieve nothing and does not weaken Germany. On the other hand we ought not to have started the bombing in the first place (he stuck to it that it was we who started it), as it merely brought heavier reprisals on ourselves.*

Osbert Sitwell[1] *was also there.* [He was at one time connected with Mosley's movement, but probably somewhat less inclined to go pro-German than L-H.] *Both of them professed to be disgusted by our seizure of the Vichy colonies. Sitwell said that our motto was "When things look bad, retake Madagascar". He said that in Cornwall in case of invasion the Home Guard have orders to shoot all artists. I said that in Cornwall this might be all for the best. Sitwell: "Some instinct would lead them to the good ones".*

1. Sir Osbert Sitwell (1892–1969) was educated at Eton and served in the Grenadier Guards, 1912–19. In 1916 his poetry, with his sister Edith's, was published as *Twentieth-Century Harlequinade*. He also wrote short stories (*Triple Fugue*, 1924; *Open the Door*, 1941), a number of novels, including *Before the Bombardment* (1926), *The Man Who Lost Himself* (1929), *Those Were the Days* (1938), *A Place of One's Own* (1941), many essays and some critical studies (particularly on Dickens). He selected and arranged the text of William Walton's *Belshazzar's Feast* (1931). In a review in 1948, Orwell described his *Left Hand, Right Hand!*, *The Scarlet Tree*, and *Great Morning!* (1944–47) as 'among the best autobiographies of our time'; see *3418*.

1507. To Ritchie Calder

22 September 1942 PP/EB/NP

Dear Calder,[1]

With reference to that talk I phoned you about, the date is November 17th, which means I would like to have the script by November 10th. These talks are 13½ minutes in length, which means about 1600 words. I would like something rather like the New Statesman article you did,[2] but one has to be careful not to be too technical and to establish in the first few minutes just what microfilms are, as it is certain that some of your listeners will have never heard of them. I should like the important part that these things are likely to play in preventing libraries from being destroyed by bombs or by the police of totalitarian regimes to be emphasised.

Yours,
George Orwell
Talks Producer
Indian Section

1. Peter Ritchie Calder (1906–1982; Baron Ritchie-Calder, 1962) was a scientific author, journalist, and broadcaster, who began his working life as a police court reporter in Dundee. He worked for a number of newspapers in Scotland and London, including the *Daily Herald*, 1930–41, *News Chronicle*, 1945–56, and *New Statesman*, 1945–58. From 1941 to 1945 he worked at the Foreign Office. He held many important posts after the war and received the Victor Gollancz Award for service to humanity in 1969. His many publications included *Birth of the Future* (1934), *Conquest of Suffering* (1935), *Lesson of London* (in Orwell and Fyvel's Searchlight Series, 1941), *Start Planning Britain Now* (1941), *Men Against Ignorance*)for UNESCO, 1953), and *World of Opportunity* (for the United Nations, 1963).
2. 'Science on the Screen,' 22 August 1942.

1508. War-time Diary

<u>22.9.42:</u> *Most of the ammunition for our Sten guns is Italian, or rather made in Germany for Italy. I fancy this must be the first weapon the British army has had whose bore was measured in millimetres instead of inches. They were going to make a new cheap automatic weapon,[1] and having the vast stocks of ammunition captured in Abyssinia handy,[2] manufactured the guns to fit the cartridges instead of the other way about. The advantage is that the ammunition of almost any continental submachine gun will fit it. It will be interesting to see whether the Germans or Japanese come out with a .303 weapon to fit captured British ammunition.*

1. See *1363, n. 6* on the Sten gun. Orwell took one to pieces on 6 August 1942 (see *1363*) and fired one on 9 August 1942 (see *1367*).
2. For an earlier reference to the possible use of captured enemy ammunition, see War-time Diary, *780, 24.3.41.*

1509. To E. C. Bowyer

23 September 1942   PP/EB/NP

Dear Mr. Bowyer,

Thank you very much for letting me know that you are willing to do the broadcast on Air Transport. I am sending a skeleton of the discussion. I have put in questions which I think cover the subject but you can, of course, vary them in any way you wish. These talks take 13½ minutes which usually means about 1500 words so that allowing for the interviewer's questions your part should be about 1400 words. How you allot this between the different questions rests entirely with you. The talk is on October 23rd, at 12.45 p.m. BST, and I would like to have the script by October 16th. Should you be unable to broadcast it on the actual day we could always record it beforehand. If you are able to come on the day, we should like you to come to 200, Oxford Street at 12 o'clock, in order to have time to rehearse the interview before the actual broadcast.

Yours sincerely,
George Orwell
Talks Producer
Indian Section

Skeleton of the discussion sent to Bowyer.

AIR TRANSPORT

Interviewer: I have been reading recently about Mr. Henry Keyser's[1] proposal to build numbers of large freight-carrying aeroplanes to replace cargo ships. I suppose this is something quite new and has only been suggested because of the German submarine menace. Have aeroplanes been used for carrying cargoes before?

E.C.B.	(explains shortly about anything in this line that was being done before the war.)
Interviewer:	But is it really possible to carry large cargoes by air? What is the capacity of a freight-carrying plane?
E.C.B.	(answers this, explaining not only what an aeroplane can carry but how many trips it can make compared with a ship.)
Interviewer:	How does air transport compare with sea transport in the matter of cost?
E.C.B.	(answers)
Interviewer:	Can all kinds of goods and materials be carried in this way? Are there not some things which it would always be uneconomic to transport by air?
E.C.B.	(answers)
Interviewer:	How about the war? In your opinion, has air transport come to stay or is it a wartime measure?
E.C.B.	(answers and sums up the discussion).

1. Henry John Kaiser (1882–1967), a leading U.S. industrialist, had been involved in the construction of the San Francisco Bay Bridge and Boulder, Grand Coulee and other dams. During the war he built and ran seven shipyards in the United States to mass-produce ships to make good those lost to German U-boat attacks. He built 1,490 'Liberty Ships,' at great speed. He also built fifty 18,000-ton aircraft, or 'fleet,' carriers. After the war he was chairman of Kaiser-Frazer (automobiles) and Kaiser Community Homes.

1510. To C. H. Desch

23 September 1942   PP/EB/NP

Dear Dr. Desch,[1]

Following on our telephone conversation I send herewith a skeleton of the discussion. [Of] course you could vary the questions if you wanted to and you might think it better not to answer one or two of them, particularly perhaps the last question but one. We do not want to tell lies in these broadcasts, but on the other hand we have to avoid anything that is bad from a propaganda point of view. These talks take 13½ minutes, which usually means about 1500 words so I think your part, allowing for the interviewer's questions, would be about 1400. How much space you allot to each question rests with you. I would like to have the script by October 2nd. Should you be unable to do the broadcast on the 9th we can record it beforehand. The time of the actual broadcast is 12.45 p.m., so that if you came to my office at 200, Oxford Street at about 12 o'clock, it would give us ample time to rehearse before the broadcast. 200 Oxford Street is on the corner of Great Portland Street, near Oxford Circus.

Yours sincerely,
Eric Blair
Talks Producer
Indian Section

Skeleton of the discussion sent to Desch.

QUESTIONS FOR "ERSATZ & RAW MATERIALS"

Interviewer: What is meant by the term ersatz?

C.H.D.   (Short explanation of this).

Int: I suppose the use of substitutes is a quite recent development, is it not?

C.H.D.   (Mentions progress made in the science of substitutes by Germany (also Britain and U.S.A?) in the last war).

Int: Can substitutes be found for all materials?

C.H.D.   (Gives exposition of what can and what cannot be done in the way of substitutes).

Int: But evidently an ersatz product must always use up corresponding quantities of some other raw material. And what about labour? Does it pay to use ersatz products? Would anyone do it if not compelled to do so? Is autarchy or economic nationalism likely to persist after the war?

C.H.D.   (Answers this question)

Int: Can you give me your opinion as to how the war issue is likely to be affected by the use of ersatz materials?[2]

C.H.D.   (Answers this question).

Int: What about India? Is there any raw material which India lacks and which could be made good locally by means of substitutes?

C.H.D.   (Answers).

1. Dr. Cecil Henry Desch (1874–1958) was Professor of Metallurgy, University of Sheffield, 1920–31; Superintendent, Metallurgy Department, National Physical Laboratory, 1932–39; President of the Institute of Metals, 1938–40; and President of the Iron and Steel Institute, 1946–48.
2. This question was written in by Orwell to replace what had been typed: 'How does it affect the war issue? Is it possible for the Germans over a long period to make good the materials they have not got? And how do Britain and the U.S.A. stand?'

1511. Marathi Newsletter, 30

24 September 1942

From this point onwards there was a change in the arrangements for preparing and broadcasting the Marathi Newsletter. It is unclear whether or not Orwell was involved. Since there is doubt, he has not been credited with writing this or further Marathi Newsletters. His involvement in earlier Newsletters is known because talks booking forms up to that for 29 exist for the translator and reader, M. R. Kothari: those state that Orwell (Eric Blair) prepared the English version.

On 22 September, Bokhari wrote to Kothari to tell him: "We shall not be asking the Contracts Department of the B.B.C. to get in touch with you for the broadcast on Thursday next, as Miss Chitale will be back and in order to bring variety into our Newsletters, we shall be asking her to broadcast the Newsletter on the 24th September. This does not, of course, mean that we shall not be grateful for your help and co-operation in the future."

Two days' notice was rather abrupt. What is more strange is the reason given. The PasB for 24 September states that K. G. Jathar was the announcer/translator; Miss Chitale is not mentioned. This probably means that Jathar read the script, too, and he is specified as doing so from 1 October. It may be that Miss Chitale prepared the English version, but Bokhari's letter was probably somewhat misleading. Jathar was apparently a staff employee, so there was no need to prepare forms, and hence no evidence of whether Orwell was involved or not.

In the circumstances, Marathi Newsletters are not from here on recorded, although Orwell may still have been involved in their preparation.

1512. To F. Kidd

24 September 1942   PP/EB/NP

Dear Dr. Kidd,[1]

I am writing to ask if you would care to do a talk in the Indian Service of the BBC. Professor Drummond suggested to me that you might be willing to undertake this particular talk. We have a series called "Science & The People" dealing with new discoveries and processes which affect the lives of ordinary people, and we are anxious to have a talk on dehydrated food, particularly with reference to the possibilities it offers of saving shipping and feeding armies in remote places. These talks are of 13½ minutes duration which generally speaking means about 1500 words, and the date of the talk is October 20th. Could you be kind enough to let me know whether you would like to undertake it, and if so I will let you have further details. If you were unable to come to London on that particular day, we could always record the talk beforehand.

Yours sincerely,
Eric Blair
Talks Producer
Indian Section

1. Franklin Kidd (1890–1974; CBE, 1950) was Superintendent of the Low Temperature Research Station, Cambridge, 1936–47. From 1947 to 1957 he was Director of Food Investigation for the Department of Scientific and Industrial Research. In addition to scientific papers, he published *Almond in Peterhouse and Other Poems* (1950).

1513. BBC Talks Booking Form, 25.9.42

S. K. Das Gupta: Bengali Newsletters; written by E. Blair, translated and read by S. K. Das Gupta; broadcast 10, 17, 24, and 31.10.42; fee £5.5s; 'extension of present Contract, which expires after 3rd Oct.' Signed: M Blackburn for I.P.O.

1514. To Leonard Moore

Friday, [25 September 1942[1]] Handwritten postcard

10a Mortimer Crescent NW. 6

[No salutation]
Yes, try Gollancz first. If he doesn't want it,[2] I should try some other publisher than Warburg, who to my knowledge hasn't paper to risk on anything but certainties at present.

Eric Blair

1. The card is postmarked 25 September and that was a Friday. It is stamped as received in Moore's office on 28 September 1942.
2. The War-time Diary; see *1443, n. 1.*

1515. News Review, 41

26 September 1942

'News Review' is written at the head of the first page. This text is reproduced from a completely clean typescript. It carries the two censorship stamps, signed, it would appear, by Anthony Weymouth. Orwell has written at the top of the first sheet, 'As broadcast 11 mins E.A.B'. The script was read by Shridhar Telkar.

The situation at Stalingrad is better than we felt ready to predict a week ago. During this week, the Germans have been making desperate efforts to fight their way into the heart of the city and literally every yard of ground has had to be bought with many lives. The Germans, however, have made very little progress and during the past few days the Russians have won back some of the ground which they lost earlier. The Stalingrad battle has no doubt already been a severe drain on German manpower as in this type of fighting it is impossible to gain any objective without heavy loss of life and the advantage is usually with the defenders. The situation is still extremely grave, but even if the Germans were to gain full possession of Stalingrad tomorrow, it would still have held them up for about six weeks longer than they expected.
    The announcements of the German wireless have now ceased not only promising an early end to the war but even promising the early capture of Stalingrad. On the contrary, all the emphasis in the Axis broadcasts is on the

extreme difficulty of the present battle and on the necessity of the German people preparing themselves for a long war. During the past few days one or two of the German broadcasters have begun to suggest that, after all, Stalingrad is not very important, and that its capture is a direct contradiction of what the Germans themselves were saying a few days earlier, and suggests that they are now beginning to be doubtful whether Stalingrad will, in fact, even[1] fall into their hands. We may be certain that they will make further desperate efforts to take it, for if this part of their campaign should fail[2] they will have to retreat to a shorter line for the winter. This would mean relinquishing some of the territory they have won during the summer, and it would then be difficult to prevent the German people from asking why so much blood had been shed in vain. There are some significant signs of restlessness among the minor partners in the Axis. Rumania, Bulgaria and Hungary are hardly likely to get any solid gains from the war in the event of an Axis victory, and the common people in these countries, at any rate Bulgaria and Rumania, are strongly pro-Russian in sentiment. They are doubtless beginning to realise that the Germans are simply using them as cannon fodder and that the prospects which their leaders thought a little while back they had before them of seizing large territories without having to fight for them were illusory. Budapest the capital of Hungary was recently bombed by the Red air force. No doubt this will be repeated and the fact that war is a serious business and not simply a matter of easy looting of defenceless peoples will be brought home more and more to the petty dictators who follow in Hitler's train.

Simultaneously with the attack on Tobruk which took place more than a week ago it is now learned that British land forces made a most daring raid 500 miles or more in the rear of the Axis armies. Reports of this were only released 3 days ago. It now appears that the British land forces raided Benghazi,[3] the main Axis port in Libya, and destroyed 30 aircraft on the ground, made a similar attack on the port of Barce while another force seized the desert oasis of Jalo, held it for two days and destroyed the ammunition dumps and other war materials before returning to their base. It is too early to say whether these raids are the prelude to further large scale operations in Egypt. But their effect must be to force the Germans to use more troops in guarding their lines of communication and thus weaken their main striking force. Reports which have come in suggest that the German commander in Egypt has already begun to regroup his forces.[4]

In the Solomon Islands the Japanese efforts to re-capture the port and airfield on the island of Guadalcanal have failed. There have been several reports of powerful Japanese forces approaching the islands, and during the past week there have been 2 engagements between Japanese ships and American bombing planes. For the moment it appears that the Japanese naval force has been obliged to retreat. There are indications, however, that the Japanese are going to make another strong effort to re-capture the Solomons, and from what they have lost already we must assume that they regard these islands as so important as to be worth very heavy losses. Probably, therefore, there will be more fighting to report from this area during the next week. In the island of New Guinea the Japanese advance towards Port Moresby has been brought to a halt. The Japanese forces which landed at Milne Bay, at the eastern end of the island, have now been completely annihilated.

During the past few weeks several distinguished politicians have succeeded in escaping from France and reaching Britain. This is very important for two reasons. In the first place, it indicates the almost complete lack of popular support for the puppet regime of Vichy, and secondly, through these fresh arrivals we can get first-hand and up to date information about internal conditions in both Occupied and Unoccupied France. There can be no doubt even on the evidence of the Germans themselves that resentment against the German occupation is growing stronger and stronger. For example, only the other day the Germans announced that they had just executed no less than a hundred and sixty[5] people in the single town of Paris. This tale of reprisals and executions is repeated over and over all through Occupied Europe, not to mention those areas like Jugo-Slavia where a state amounting to civil war exists. What we learn, however, from the new arrivals from France, is of the formation of a new political alliance between all patriotic sections in the Occupied countries. Political parties which previously regarded one another as deadly enemies are now completely united in their opposition to the invader. The most distinguished political figure to reach England in recent weeks was M. Andre Philip, the French Socialist. He has been followed by several other socialists, but more recently by M. Charles Vallin,[6] who was previously one of the leading figures of the Croix de Feu—a French Fascist organisation. This Fascist party of course favoured collaboration with the German invader. It now appears, however, that the cruelty and exactions of German rule have become so unbearable that even some of the French Fascists are beginning to revolt and to throw in their lot with the parties of the Left. M. Vallin has come to England to help organise common resistance. All this resistance in the occupied countries, of course, has to go on in secret, but the Germans have been quite unable to prevent it or even to prevent the appearance of secretly printed newspapers, of which great numbers, some of them with circulations of many thousands, are appearing in France and throughout Western Europe.

It was announced during this week that another big convoy of allied ships carrying war materials has arrived safely in northern Russian ports. Some ships were lost on the way but the great majority got through and only one of the naval vessels escorting the convoy, a destroyer, was lost. The Germans lost at least 10 aeroplanes besides several submarines.[7] This route by which war materials are carried to the northern Russian armies is the most dangerous of all because the convoys have to skirt the Norwegian coasts where they can be attacked and observed all the way by land based aircraft. Nevertheless a steady supply of materials has continued to reach our Russian allies by this route and the successful defence of Leningrad can no doubt be partly attributed to these supplies.

British troops have occupied Antananarivo the capital of Madagascar. They were cheered by all sections of the population when they entered the town, and the administration is functioning smoothly. The Vichy governor has fled and declares his intention of keeping up resistance, but it is evident that such opposition as was put up by the French garrison of the island is at an end.

1. The final letter is unclear and 'ever' may be intended.
2. The typescript has 'fall that.'
3. For the seaborne assault of this twin-pronged raid, see *1498* and *1498, n. 1.*
4. The raid on Barce, east of Benghazi, was carried out by the Long Range Desert Group, which did much damage to planes at its airfield. Orwell makes the operation sound successful, but its failure was stated in the official publication for general readers, *The Eighth Army: September 1941 to January 1943* (The Army at War series, Ministry of Information, 1944). That describes as 'pin-pricks' 'experimental raids carried out by sea-borne landing parties assisted by raiding parties operating overland on the night of 13th–14th September.' It then bluntly states, 'They were not a success.' In the main attack on Tobruk, by sea and land, the army lost 38 officers and 419 men. The overland force striking at Benghazi was caught by bombers and withdrew to the oasis at Jalo. The Barce force, after its attack, joined them at Jalo, where they hung on for five days before retreating to Kufra in the face of strong enemy reinforcements (*The Eighth Army*, 70).
5. The number 160 is probably a transcription error for the real figure, 116. Following the executions, 5,000 Partisans were reported jailed for not remaining indoors for thirty-six hours. The executions were for repeated attacks on German soldiers. The Inter-Allied Information Committee gave the number of people executed by the Germans in occupied countries to this date as 207,373 (*Daily Herald*, 22 September 1942). The Military Governor of France, General Karl Heinrich von Stülpnagel, who authorised the executions, later participated in the plot to assassinate Hitler, and was executed by slow strangulation.
6. Charles Vallin (1903–) had escaped from France with Pierre Brossolette, a Socialist and onetime editor of *Le Populaire*. Vallin had represented the Seine district of Paris in the Chamber of Deputies, 1938–42, and was Vice-President of the Fascist Croix de Feu. Before he left France to serve under de Gaulle, he wrote to Marshal Pétain condemning Franco-German collaboration.
7. This was Convoy PQ 18; it arrived in Archangel on 19 September with the loss of thirteen of the forty ships convoyed. The British destroyer lost was *Somali*. The Germans lost three U-boats and forty-one aircraft.

1516. Bengali Newsletter, 11

26 September 1942

The English original was written by Orwell. No script has been traced. PasB gives timing as 11′ 4″.

1517. BBC Talks Booking Form, 26.9.42

Lady Grigg: 'Women Generally Speaking'; broadcast 3, 10, 17, 24, and 31.10.42; fee £8.8s each broadcast. Signed: M Blackburn for I.P.O.

1518. Gujarati Newsletter, 31

28 September 1942

The English original was written by Orwell. No script has been traced. PasB gives timing as 9′ 40″.

1519. To C. H. Desch

28 September 1942   PP/EB/NP

Dear Dr. Desch,

Many thanks for your letter of 26th September. I have altered the last question but one to "Can you give me your opinion as to how the issue of the war is likely to be affected by the use of ersatz materials?" I suppose this is vague enough to be innocuous. As to the last questions, there is no objection to your saying you have no special knowledge of Indian conditions, but will answer to the best of your capacity. The object of this talk is to put ersatz on the map for Indian listeners rather than to talk about specifically Indian problems, but we like to tie these programmes on to India where possible.

Yours sincerely,
Eric Blair
Talks Producer
Indian Section

1520. To F. Kidd

28 September 1942   PP/EB/NP

Dear Dr. Kidd,

Many thanks for your letter of 26th September and the manuscript which I am returning. I am afraid I may have conveyed a slightly wrong impression in my earlier letter. We do not want you to give a detailed account of the processes of dehydration, nor even any large amount of statistics and especially not anything which may convey information to the enemy. All we wanted was a general educative talk putting this subject on the map for India. In these talks, we are trying to keep our Indian listeners au fait with current scientific developments, especially with new processes and inventions which directly affect the lives of ordinary people. Scientific food storage is obviously one such and it has not hitherto entered very much into the Indian consciousness. We do not either particularly wish you to deal with Indian conditions, except to the extent that we like to tie all these talks on to India in some degree. I think if you would undertake it, you could be quite able to give the sort of talk we want on food storage and dehydration without being over-technical or conveying any information to the enemy. Could you be kind enough to let me know as soon as possible whether you are still willing to consider it.

Yours sincerely,
Eric Blair
Talks Producer
Indian Section

1521. To Herbert Read

28 September 1942   PP/EB

Dear Read,
We are having another number of Voice on Tuesday, October 6th, and would like you to take part, if you will. We want to use a piece of about two pages out of "The Innocent Eye" and of course it would be nice if you could read it yourself. Also a poem by D. H. Lawrence. This is a number devoted to childhood, and the poem we want you to read is The Piano, which you doubtless know. As before it means giving up most of the morning, but I believe you are in town on Tuesdays normally. Could you let me know as soon as possible whether this will be all right.

Yours,
George Orwell
Talks Producer
Indian Section

1522. War-time Diary

28.9.42: *Open-air church parade in Regents Park yesterday. How touching the scene ought to be—the battalion in hollow square, band of the Coldstream Guards, the men standing bareheaded (beautiful autumn day, faint mist and not a leaf stirring, dogs gambolling round) and singing the hymns as best they could. But unfortunately there was a sermon with the jingoistic muck which is usual on these occasions and which makes me go pro-German for as long as I listen to it. Also a special prayer "for the people of Stalingrad"—the Judas kiss.* [A detail that gets me down on these occasions is the clergyman's white surplice, which looks all wrong against a background of military uniforms. Struck by the professionalism of the band, especially the bandmaster (an officer in the black peaked cap of the Guards). As each prayer drew to its close, a stirring in the band, the trombones come out of their leather suitcases, the bandmaster's baton comes up, and they are ready to snap into the Amen just as the priest reaches "through Jesus Christ our Lord".[1]

1523. To K. K. Ardaschir

29 September 1942   PP/EB/NP

Dear Ardaschir,

I am returning the enclosed script, because I am afraid we cannot use it. Much as it interested me, it is politically quite impossible[1] from our point of view. I don't mean that there is not a great deal to be said for the views that you express, but we cannot of course broadcast anything that is not in line with our general policy.

Yours sincerely,
Eric Blair
Talks Producer
Indian Section

1. Ardaschir had sent Orwell this talk on 24 September. He told Orwell that, since his talks were heard by Indian students, 'here is something to soothe their Leftist souls.'

1524. BBC Talks Booking Form, 29.9.42

Clemence Dane: 'Women Generally Speaking,' More Books (The Wife of Bath); recorded 2.10.42; broadcast date not fixed; fee £15.15s. Signed: M Blackburn.

1525. Extract from Minutes of Eastern Service Meeting

30 September 1942

a) Mr Blair to furnish Sir Malcolm [Darling] with copy of [news] bulletin in advance and advise E.S.D. of 29 September discrepancy.
b) On the general question of advance publicity in India, agreed to form a sub-committee comprising Mr. Beachcroft, Mr. Brander, Sir Malcolm Darling or his representative, Mr. E. A. Blair or his representative, Mr. Davenport. Mr. Beachcroft to convene meeting to consider and report on what is required from producer departments for publicity purposes. Meantime (a) Mr. Blair to advise Miss Blackburn that the Hindustani programme must be planned definitely earlier in advance, (b) Mr. Beachcroft to be informed of items as soon as they are arranged.
c) COMPETITIONS
Suggestions to institute (a) play competitions and (b) monthly essay competitions for critical essays on English and Hindustani programmes to be considered prior to drawing up concrete proposals at next meeting.

1526. 'T. S. Eliot'

Poetry (London), October–November 1942

This review article discusses Eliot's *Burnt Norton*, *East Coker*, and *The Dry Salvages*, each of which was published separately.

There is very little in Eliot's later work that makes any deep impression on me. That is a confession of something lacking in myself, but it is not, as it may appear at first sight, a reason for simply shutting up and saying no more, since the change in my own reaction probably points to some external change which is worth investigating.

I know a respectable quantity of Eliot's earlier work by heart. I did not sit down and learn it, it simply stuck in my mind as any passage of verse is liable to do when it has really rung the bell. Sometimes after only one reading it is possible to remember the whole of a poem of, say, twenty or thirty lines, the act of memory being partly an act of reconstruction. But as for these three latest poems, I suppose I have read each of them two or three times since they were published, and how much do I verbally remember? 'Time and the bell have buried the day,' 'At the still point of the turning world,' 'The vast waters of the petrel and the porpoise,' and bits of the passage beginning 'O dark dark dark. They all go into the dark.' (I don't count 'In my end is my beginning,' which is a quotation). That is about all that sticks in my head of its own accord. Now one cannot take this as proving that *Burnt Norton* and the rest are worse than the more memorable early poems, and one might even take it as proving the contrary, since it is arguable that that which lodges itself most easily in the mind is the obvious and even the vulgar. But it is clear that something has departed, some kind of current has been switched off, the later verse does not *contain* the earlier, even if it is claimed as an improvement upon it. I think one is justified in explaining this by a deterioration in Mr. Eliot's subject-matter. Before going any further, here are a couple of extracts, just near enough to one another in meaning to be comparable. The first is the concluding passage of *The Dry Salvages:*

> And right action is freedom
> From past and future also.
> For most of us, this is the aim
> Never here to be realised;
> Who are only undefeated
> Because we have gone on trying;
> We, content at the last
> If our temporal reversion nourish
> (Not too far from the yew-tree)
> The life of significant soil.

Here is an extract from a much earlier poem:

> Daffodil bulbs instead of balls
> Stared from the sockets of the eyes!

He knew that thought clings round dead limbs
Tightening its lusts and luxuries.
. . .

He knew the anguish of the marrow
The ague of the skeleton;
No contact possible to flesh
Allayed the fever of the bone.[1]

The two passages will bear comparison since they both deal with the same subject, namely death. The first of them follows upon a longer passage in which it is explained, first of all, that scientific research is all nonsense, a childish superstition on the same level as fortune-telling, and then that the only people ever likely to reach an understanding of the universe are saints, the rest of us being reduced to 'hints and guesses.' The keynote of the closing passage is, 'resignation.' There is a 'meaning' in life and also in death; unfortunately we don't know what it is, but the fact that it exists should be a comfort to us as we push up the crocuses, or whatever it is that grows under the yew trees in country churchyards. But now look at the other two stanzas I have quoted. Though fathered on to somebody else, they probably express what Mr. Eliot himself felt about death at that time, at least in certain moods. They are not voicing resignation. On the contrary, they are voicing the pagan attitude towards death, the belief in the next world as a shadowy place full of thin, squeaking ghosts, envious of the living, the belief that however bad life may be, death is worse. This conception of death seems to have been general in antiquity, and in a sense it is general now. 'The anguish of the marrow, the ague of the skeleton,' Horace's famous ode *Eheu fugaces*, and Bloom's unuttered thoughts during Paddy Dignam's funeral, are all very much of a muchness. So long as man regards himself as an individual, his attitude towards death must be one of simple resentment. And however unsatisfactory this may be, if it is intensely felt it is more likely to produce good literature than a religious faith which is not really *felt* at all, but merely accepted against the emotional grain. So far as they can be compared, the two passages I have quoted seem to me to bear this out. I do not think it is questionable that the second of them is superior as verse, and also more intense in feeling, in spite of a tinge of burlesque.

What are these three poems, *Burnt Norton* and the rest, 'about'? It is not so easy to say what they are about, but what they appear on the surface to be about is certain localities in England and America with which Mr. Eliot has ancestral connections. Mixed up with this is a rather gloomy musing upon the nature and purpose of life, with the rather indefinite conclusion I have mentioned above. Life has a 'meaning,' but it is not a meaning one feels inclined to grow lyrical about; there is faith, but not much hope, and certainly no enthusiasm. Now the subject-matter of Mr. Eliot's early poems was very different from this. They were not hopeful, but neither were they depressed or depressing. If one wants to deal in antitheses, one might say that the later poems express a melancholy faith and the earlier ones a glowing despair. They were based on the dilemma of modern man, who despairs of life and does not want to be dead, and on top of this they expressed the horror of an

over-civilised intellectual confronted with the ugliness and spiritual empti-
ness of the machine age. Instead of 'not too far from the yew-tree' the keynote
was 'weeping, weeping multitudes', or perhaps 'the broken fingernails of
dirty hands.' Naturally these poems were denounced as 'decadent' when they
first appeared, the attacks only being called off when it was perceived that
Eliot's political and social tendencies were reactionary. There was, however,
a sense in which the charge of 'decadence' could be justified. Clearly these
poems were an end-product, the last gasp of a cultural tradition, poems
which spoke only for the cultivated third-generation rentier, for people able
to feel and criticise but no longer able to act. E. M. Forster praised *Prufrock* on
its first appearance because 'it sang of people who were ineffectual and weak'
and because it was 'innocent of public spirit' (this was during the other war,
when public spirit was a good deal more rampant than it is now). The
qualities by which any society which is to last longer than a generation
actually has to be sustained—industry, courage, patriotism, frugality,
philoprogenitiveness—obviously could not find any place in Eliot's early
poems. There was only room for rentier values, the values of people too
civilised to work, fight or even reproduce themselves. But that was the price
that had to be paid, at any rate at that time, for writing a poem worth reading.
The mood of lassitude, irony, disbelief, disgust, and not the sort of beefy
enthusiasm demanded by the Squires[2] and Herberts,[3] was what sensitive
people actually felt. It is fashionable to say that in verse only the words count
and the 'meaning' is irrelevant, but in fact every poem contains a prose-
meaning, and when the poem is any good it is a meaning which the poet
urgently wishes to express. All art is to some extent propaganda. *Prufrock* is
an expression of futility, but it is also a poem of wonderful vitality and
power, culminating in a sort of rocket-burst in the closing stanzas:

> I have seen them riding seaward on the waves
> Combing the white hair of the waves blown back
> When the wind blows the water white and black.
>
> We have lingered in the chambers of the sea
> By sea-girls wreathed with seaweed red and brown
> Till human voices wake us, and we drown.[4]

There is nothing like that in the later poems, although the rentier despair on
which these lines are founded has been consciously dropped.

But the trouble is that conscious futility is something only for the young.
One cannot go on 'despairing of life' into a ripe old age. One cannot go on
and on being 'decadent,' since decadence means falling and one can only be
said to be falling if one is going to reach the bottom reasonably soon. Sooner
or later one is obliged to adopt a positive attitude towards life and society. It
would be putting it too crudely to say that every poet in our time must either
die young, enter the Catholic Church, or join the Communist Party, but in
fact the escape from the consciousness of futility is along those general lines.
There are other deaths besides physical deaths, and there are other sects and
creeds besides the Catholic Church and the Communist Party, but it remains

true that after a certain age one must either stop writing or dedicate oneself to some purpose not wholly aesthetic. Such a dedication necessarily means a break with the past:

> . . . every attempt
> Is a wholly new start, and a different kind of failure
> Because one has only learnt to get the better of words
> For the thing one no longer has to say, or the way in which
> One is no longer disposed to say it. And so each venture
> Is a new beginning, a raid on the inarticulate
> With shabby equipment always deteriorating
> In the general mess of imprecision of feeling,
> Undisciplined squads of emotion.

Eliot's escape from individualism was into the Church, the Anglican Church as it happened. One ought not to assume that the gloomy Pétainism to which he now appears to have given himself over was the unavoidable result of his conversion. The Anglo-Catholic movement does not impose any political 'line' on its followers, and a reactionary or austro-fascist° tendency had always been apparent in his work, especially his prose writings. In theory it is still possible to be an orthodox religious believer without being intellectually crippled in the process; but it is far from easy, and in practice books by orthodox believers usually show the same cramped, blinkered outlook as books by orthodox Stalinists or others who are mentally unfree. The reason is that the Christian churches still demand assent to doctrines which no one seriously believes in. The most obvious case is the immortality of the soul. The various 'proofs' of personal immortality which can be advanced by Christian apologists are psychologically of no importance; what matters, psychologically, is that hardly anyone nowadays *feels* himself to be immortal. The next world may be in some sense 'believed in' but it has not anywhere near the same actuality in people's minds as it had a few centuries ago. Compare for instance the gloomy mumblings of these three poems with *Jerusalem my happy home*; the comparison is not altogether pointless. In the second case you have a man to whom the next world is as real as this one. It is true that his vision of it is incredibly vulgar—a choir practice in a jeweller's shop—but he believes in what he is saying and his belief gives vitality to his words. In the other case you have a man who does not really *feel* his faith, but merely assents to it for complex reasons. It does not in itself give him any fresh literary impulse. At a certain stage he feels the need for a 'purpose,' and he wants a 'purpose' which is reactionary and not progressive; the immediately available refuge is the Church, which demands intellectual absurdities of its members; so his work becomes a continuous nibbling round those absurdities, an attempt to make them acceptable to himself. The Church has not now any living imagery, any new vocabulary to offer:

> The rest
> Is prayer, observance, discipline, thought and action.

Perhaps what we need is prayer, observance, etc., but you do not make a line of poetry by stringing those words together. Mr. Eliot speaks also of

> the intolerable wrestle
> With words and meanings. The poetry does not matter.

I do not know, but I should imagine that the struggle with meanings would have loomed smaller, and the poetry would have seemed to matter more, if he could have found his way to some creed which did not start off by forcing one to believe the incredible.

There is no saying whether Mr. Eliot's development could have been much other than it has been. All writers who are any good develop throughout life, and the general direction of their development is determined. It is absurd to attack Eliot, as some left-wing critics have done, for being a 'reactionary' and to imagine that he might have used his gifts in the cause of democracy and Socialism. Obviously a scepticism about democracy and a disbelief in 'progress' are an integral part of him; without them he could not have written a line of his works. But it is arguable that he would have done better to go much further in the direction implied in his famous 'Anglo-Catholic and Royalist' declaration. He could not have developed into a Socialist, but he might have developed into the last apologist of aristocracy.

Neither feudalism nor indeed Fascism is[5] necessarily deadly to poets, though both are to prose-writers. The thing that is really deadly to both is Conservatism of the half-hearted modern kind.

It is at least imaginable that if Eliot had followed wholeheartedly the anti-democratic, anti-perfectionist strain in himself he might have struck a new vein comparable to his earlier one. But the negative, Pétainism, which turns its eyes to the past, accepts defeat, writes off earthly happiness as impossible, mumbles about prayer and repentance and thinks it a spiritual advance to see life as 'a pattern of living worms in the guts of the women of Canterbury'— that, surely, is the least hopeful road a poet could take.[6]

1. The quotation from 'The Dry Salvages,' *Poetry (London)* omitted the comma after 'us' in line 3. In the second and fourth stanzas from 'Whispers of Immortality' (written about 1918), 'his eyes' was printed for 'the eyes;' 'how thought' for 'that thought;' a semi-colon appeared for a full-stop after 'luxuries,' and a colon for a semi-colon after 'skeleton.'
2. Sir J. C. Squire (see *142, n. 3*) was, according to Martin Seymour-Smith, 'critically obtuse, being all for "straightforwardness" and over-prejudiced against poetry he could not understand. . . . In his parodies (*Collected Parodies*, 1921), however, he was often brilliantly funny. . . . He was a kind and generous man, and a better poet than many who now enjoy temporary reputations and have not heard of him' (*Guide to Modern World Literature*, 3rd ed., 1985, 232–33). His *Collected Poems* (1959) has a preface by John Betjeman.
3. Alan Patrick Herbert (1890–1971; Kt., 1945; CH, 1970), humorist, novelist, dramatist, and author of much light poetry. From 1935 until university constituencies were abolished in 1950, he represented Oxford University as an Independent M.P. Though he wrote frequently for *Punch*, he had a serious side; his play *Holy Deadlock* (1934) dramatised anomalies in the divorce laws, and as an M.P. he introduced the Matrimonial Causes Bill (enacted in 1937), which made significant changes to the divorce laws. He served in the Royal Naval Division, 1914–17.
4. *Poetry (London)* did not hyphenate 'sea-girls'; it added a comma after 'brown'.
5. The original text has 'is not'.

6. Orwell's article was followed by 'Another Reading' by Kathleen Raine (1908–), poet and critic; 'My point of view,' she wrote, 'at once differs from that of Mr. Orwell, and expresses the point of view of many of my generation.' She admired Orwell's article 'in certain limited respects.' He had avoided 'the more obvious pitfalls, in applying political, rational, non-poetic standards, to poetry. Mr. Orwell does not fall into the error that Communists usually make in such cases, of failing to see that a problem exists that is not stated in terms of dialectical materialism.' However, she argued that he had fallen into the error of which he accused Eliot, 'that of pursuing a line of thought that has become a dead end; of accepting certain statements about the universe as final that are, like all knowledge, provisional.' She concluded: 'The Christian believes that the best is accessible to the worst, and the highest to the humblest human soul. Mr. Eliot's consistent adherence to the highest values of Christianity, and the inheritance of civilisation, shows a deeper respect for the ordinary man than any facile simplification of Mr. Orwell, the B.B.C., or the Mass Observers offer to a public that they at heart despise.' The January 1943 issue of *Poetry (London)* printed two letters taking up the Orwell-Raine debate. Herman Peschmann argued that criticism demanded facts and opinions 'and the opinions must be built on facts or the criticism is invalidated.' He complained that Orwell 'sins so badly against these basic principles' that these must first be rectified 'before any adequate reassessment of the three Eliot poems can be attempted.' He argued that the way context conditioned meaning must be taken into account not 'what the critic thought [the poet] wrote or meant' and that the critic's inferences must not be advanced as factual statements. Irene Browne thought Orwell 'a dangerous man to admire,' which she did, with reservations: 'His literary function is the valuable one of provocation.' She felt that he displayed more honesty than sense in criticising Eliot's poetry; 'he was falling into the ranks of Eliot enthusiasts.' She had hard words for Raine's 'rush to defend Mr. Eliot': 'I turned with a sigh from the lucidity of Mr. Orwell to Miss Raine's obscurity of thought.' Orwell's review was reprinted in *Little Reviews Anthology*, edited by Denys Val Baker, 1943.

1527. To Mulk Raj Anand
1 October 1942 PP/EB/NP

Dear Mulk,
You know you are scheduled to do another series of interviews rather like [the] ones you did before, starting on 6th [Nov]ember. I think I talked this over [wit]h you. This series is called "A Day in [My] Life" and you are down to interview various types of ordinary people who are playing a part in the war effort. The first three are—a munitions worker, a soldier, and a merchant seaman. I have no doubt that you have the necessary contacts. As far as possible, however, we would like to know well in advance who is actually taking part, so that we can do some advance publicity about them. We want the speakers in these talks to give a picture of their day to day life and explain just what they are doing to help the war effort. Do you think you could see me about this within the next few days?

Yours,
George Orwell
Talks Producer
Indian Section

1528. To E. M. Forster

1 October 1942   PP/EB/NP

Dear Forster,

I believe your contract for "Some Books" expires on October 14th. We of course want you to continue, and I hope you will want to do so as well. It is just necessary to have this in writing, but if you confirm this verbally when you come next Wednesday that will be all right.

> Yours,
> George Orwell
> Talks Producer
> Indian Section

1529. To Princess Indira of Kapurthala

1 October 1942   PP/EB/NP

Dear Princess Indira,

We are just working out our schedule of talks until the end of the year, and we hope very much that you will go on with your talks in the series "The Debate Continues" each week. I understand from Mr. Lockspeiser that he is anxious for you to go on with the music programme on Saturdays as well.[1] I hope you will agree to continue with both these programmes.

> Yours sincerely,
> Eric Blair
> Talks Producer
> Indian Section

1. Orwell refers to the series 'Great Cellists' in September 1942; see *1500*.

1530. To K. S. Shelvankar

1 October 1942   PP/EB/NP

Dear Shelvankar,[1]

I made efforts to get you on the phone but did not succeed; but I understand that you are in London. If you can manage to come in and see me some time within the next few days I would like very much to consult you about a series of talks we are starting on November 5th. We are going to have a history of Fascism in seven parts, starting with Mussolini's so-called "March on Rome" and ending up with the invasion of the U.S.S.R. I would naturally like you to do one or more talks yourself, but I would also like your advice as to who should do the others, as you know better than I which Indians are acquainted with recent European political history. You might perhaps ring up and let me know if and when you can come in.

Yours sincerely,
Eric Blair
Talks Producer
Indian Section

1. K. S. Shelvankar (see *1050, n. 1*), author of a Penguin Special, *The Problem of India* (1940). There is a certain irony in Orwell asking him to broadcast, for he had warned E. M. Forster not to discuss this book because it had been banned in India; see *1103*.

1531. To Shridhar Telkar

1 October 1942   PP/EB/NP

Dear Telkar,

This is to confirm that we would like you to continue with your weekly talks on Wednesdays, from 4th November to 16th December, under the title "Behind the Headlines". Will you let me know about this?

Yours sincerely,
Eric Blair
Talks Producer
Indian Section

1532. BBC Talks Booking Form, 1.10.42

Mulk Raj Anand: 'Books That Changed the World,' 5, War and Peace; broadcast 15.10.42; fee £9.9s. Signed: M Blackburn for I.P.O.

1533. BBC Talks Booking Form, 1.10.42

E. C. Bowyer: 'I'd Like It Explained,' 13, Air Transport; broadcast 23.10.42; fee £9.9s. Signed: M Blackburn for I.P.O.

1534. BBC Talks Booking Form, 1.10.42

Dr. C. H. Desch: 'I'd Like It Explained,' 11, Ersatz and Raw Materials; broadcast 9.10.42; fee £9.9s. Signed: M Blackburn for I.P.O.

1535. BBC Talks Booking Form, 1.10.42

J. F. Horrabin: 'I'd Like It Explained', 12, Land Reclamation; broadcast 16.10.42; fee £9.9s. Signed: M Blackburn for I.P.O.

1536. BBC Talks Booking Form, 1.10.42

Dr Shelvankar: 'Books That Changed the World,' 6, Das Kapital; broadcast 22.10.42; fee £9.9s. Signed: M Blackburn for I.P.O.

1537. BBC Talks Booking Form, 1.10.42

Miss Zahra Taki: 'I'd Like It Explained,' 10, Interviewing Leonora Lockhart on the subject of Basic English; 13½-minute talk involving speaking for about 2 minutes; broadcast 2.10.42; fee suggested as 1 or 2 gns but £1.1 paid. Signed: M Blackburn for I.P.O.

1538. Weekly News Review, 42

3 October 1942

There are no changes to the typescript of this commentary. The script bears both censorship stamps; although it is difficult to be sure from the microfilm, the initials of the censor seem like those of Thavenot, one of the three censors proposed by Rushbrook Williams on 4 June 1942; see *1489, n. 1.* At the top of the first page of the script, Orwell has written 'As b'cast   11' 38"   E.A.B.' The figure '38' is very faint, so not reliable. The script was read by Bahadur Singh.

The battle for Stalingrad continues. Since last week the Germans have made a little progress in their direct attacks on the city and savage house to house fighting is still going on. Meanwhile the Russians have launched a counter-attack to the north west of Stalingrad which has made progress and must have the effect of drawing off some of the German reserves.

It is still uncertain whether or not Stalingrad can hold out. In a recent speech the notorious Ribbentrop, one-time ambassador to Britain and signatory of the Russo-German pact, was allowed to state that Stalingrad would soon be in German hands. Hitler made the same boast in his speech which was broadcast on September 10th. Elsewhere, however, there has been a marked note of pessimism in German pronouncements and a constant emphasis on the need for the German people to prepare themselves for a hard winter and for an indefinite continuation of the war.

In this connection the report recently given to *The Times* by a neutral who had just left Germany and has also been in the Occupied parts of Russia, is of great interest. The picture as he paints it is something like this. The Germans have now occupied enormous areas which contain almost all that they need in the way of food and raw materials but are barely able to exploit them because they have been unable to obtain the co-operation of the conquered peoples. This neutral visitor describes seeing farms in Ukrainia being worked by German gang labour including boys as young as 14. The intention the Germans previously had of setting up puppet regimes in the occupied parts of Russia appears to have been abandoned. It would be impossible for them to set up any Quisling administration that could gain the obedience of the population and they are consequently obliged to rely on direct military rule. As to Germany's internal condition, this visitor considered that the morale of the German army is still good and that the people are still ready for great sacrifices but that there has been a great falling-off in confidence. The failure of the Russian campaign to bring about any decisive results has disappointed all expectations and so also has the failure of the German Army in Africa, to over-run Egypt and capture the Suez Canal. Meanwhile the R.A.F. raids make life in Western Germany less and less bearable, and it is generally recognised that these are only a foretaste of what is coming when the British and American air forces have reached their full expansion. Corroborating what this neutral observer says, we may notice that German home propaganda during recent months has concentrated more and more on terrifying the German population with stories of what will happen to them should they be defeated. The old fables about an international Jewish conspiracy are brought forth again and the Germans are told that should the war go against them, they have nothing to hope for except slavery. This of course is a lie, but it is exceedingly significant that the German Government should consider it a lie worth telling. For two years ago, or even a year ago, the possibility of defeat was not even envisaged. The tune played on the radio was not 'What will happen to us if we lose', but 'What we shall do after we have won'.

In general the present situation has considerable parallels with the situation in 1918. At that time the Germans had over-run most of the territories they have over-run now, and though it is true that they had not got possession of France or Norway, and had not got Italy on their side, on the other hand they could draw on the vast resources of the Turkish Empire with territories stretching right down to the borders of Egypt. But then as now it was impossible for them to make the conquered territories into a paying concern, and for precisely the same reasons, that the behaviour of the invaders roused such hatred that it was impossible to make the conquered populations work. In the Ukraine the peasants either left the land uncultivated or hid their grain, and the attempt to set up a Quisling[2] was a miserable failure. The reactions of the population at home were also very similar. They had had many victories and yet never seemed any nearer to final victory. And meanwhile the lists of casualties mounted into millions and the food situation got steadily worse. As all the world knows, the German armies suddenly collapsed in the late summer of 1918 only a few months after winning what had appeared to be their greatest victory. We do not predict that a similar collapse will take place before the Germans have received a decisive defeat on land, but we do point out how the general situation has deteriorated from the German point of view and how ominous it must seem to ordinary thinking Germans to see the repetition of events very similar to those which last time led to disaster.

From other fronts than the Russian one there is not a great deal to report. The most important news this week is that the Australian forces in New Guinea have launched a small-scale offensive and made some progress. They have already pushed the Japanese off the central ridge of the mountains that run from end to end of the island, and the latest news was[1] that the advance was continuing. The success of the Australian attack appears to have been largely due to superiority in the air. It should be remembered, however, that the whole of this operation is on a small scale, and it is too early to say whether it will have any decisive results. The Japanese claim to have occupied some more small islands lying between New Guinea and the Australian mainland. This claim has not yet been confirmed from Allied sources and should be treated with suspicion. As long as Port Moresby remains in Allied hands the Japanese are not likely to make any serious attempt on the mainland of Australia and they probably would not make a landing on islands which are in an isolated position and liable to heavy bombing from the air.

During the past 48 hours the British have launched a successful attack in Egypt, straightening out a small salient and driving the enemy back several miles. At this moment fighting is probably still going on. This appears to be *only* a local action and too much should not be expected of it. We may be able to give a fuller report next week.

The position of the Germans in Egypt has probably been much weakened by the successful attacks made on their supply routes by Allied aircraft and submarines. It was recently revealed that during the past four or five months the amount of Axis shipping sunk in the Mediterranean by R.A.F. planes alone was more than sixty thousand (60,000) tons. This is in addition to the sinkings by Allied submarines which during the past week have sunk five Axis supply ships in this area. The effect of these Allied successes is to prevent the Germans from effectively using the port of Tobruk and make them bring their supplies by the comparatively short sea journey from Sicily to Benghazi, which imposes much delay and compels the Germans to feed their armies by a thin supply line running along the coast, where it is subject to constant bombing.

Hitler's latest speech was broadcast on September 30th. Although it mostly consisted of wild boasting and threats, it made a surprising contrast with the speeches of a year ago. Gone were the promises of an early victory, and gone also the claims, made more than a year ago, to have annihilated the Russian armies. Instead all the emphasis was on Germany's ability to withstand a long war. Here for example are some of Hitler's earlier broadcast statements: On the 3rd September 1941: 'Russia is already broken and will never rise again.' On the 3rd October 1941: 'The Russians have lost at least 8 to 10 million men. No army can recover from such losses.' He also boasted at the same time of the imminent fall of Moscow. That was a year ago. And now, on 30th September, the final boast upon which Hitler ended his speech was: 'Germany will never capitulate.' It seems strange to look back and remember how short a while ago the Germans were declaring, not that they would never capitulate, but that they would make everyone else capitulate. Hitler also uttered threats against saboteurs, a tacit admission that the German home front is no longer entirely reliable.

Monsieur Herriot,[3] one-time President of the French Republic, has been arrested by the Vichy authorities because of his courageous stand against the policy of 'collaboration' with the German invader. The arrest of so popular and deeply-respected [a] man is simply one more confession of the political failure of the Vichy regime, and the contempt and hatred in which all decent Frenchmen hold the small clique of so-called collaborators.

1. Typed as 'was'—'is' would make better sense.
2. Presumably 'a Quisling government' was intended.
3. Edouard Herriot (1872–1957), politician and literary scholar, led the Radical Party from 1919 until his death. He held a number of cabinet posts and was Premier in 1924 and 1932. From June 1936 until the fall of France he was President of the Chamber of Deputies (not of the French Republic, as Orwell states). Although he did not join the Free French forces in exile, he strenuously criticised the Vichy regime and was imprisoned by the Germans from 1942 until the end of the war. Elected president of the National Assembly, he held that position until his retirement in 1954. Among his many books are *Philon le Juif* (1898), a study of the Jewish school of Alexandria; *Madame Récamier et ses amis* (1904), *La Vie de Beethoven* (1929), *La Russie nouvelle* (1922), *Impressions d'Amérique* (1923), and *Les Etats unis d'Europe* (1930), many of which were translated into English.

1539. Bengali Newsletter, 12

3 October 1942

The English original was written by Orwell. No script has been traced. PasB gives timing as 12' 20".

1540. Gujarati Newsletter, 32

5 October 1942

The English original was written by Orwell. No script has been traced. PasB gives timing as approximately 11 minutes.

1541. To Franklin[1] Kidd

5 October 1942   Handwritten draft and typewritten versions
PP/EB/NP

Dear Dr. Kidd,
Many thanks for your letter of 3rd October. It will be all right if we get the manuscript by[2] October 12th, and we can record it between then and the

20th, which is the date of the broadcast. Could you let us know as soon as possible[3] what day would suit you for the recording (it will be done at 200, Oxford Street or at Broadcasting House)[4] and we will fix it up.

Yours sincerely,
Eric Blair
Talks Producer
Indian Section

1. Orwell spelt 'Franklin' as 'Franklyn.'
2. by] in *in draft*
3. as soon as possible] *omitted in draft*
4. it will be done at 200, Oxford Street or at Broadcasting House] it will be done here or at Broadcasting House *in draft*

1542. BBC Talks Booking Form, 5.10.42

Martin Armstrong: 'Story by Five Authors,' 4; '4th instalment of 13 minutes' duration of serial story in five parts, each part by a different author'; broadcast 30.10.42; fee £5.5s + 10s 5d fare. Signed: M Blackburn for I.P.O.

Similar forms were issued for Inez Holden and L. A. G. Strong on the same day, but with a fee of only £4.4s each (with no expenses). The one for Strong was marked 'for reading only.' Strong contributed the second instalment, broadcast on 16 October; Holden gave the third on 23 October 1942. In addition to the fee for reading, the Copyright Department paid a fee. A letter of 15 October 1942 to Martin Armstrong from B. H. Alexander survives, which fills in the details:

I understand you are contributing the 4th instalment of a serial story for our Indian programme entitled "Story by 5 Authors", and that each instalment lasts for approximately 15 minutes. The 4th instalment is being broadcast on the 30th October.

As you know the normal fee for two readings of your stories, plus publication in "The Listener" is 25 guineas. On this occasion, however, as the serial is for broadcasting in the Overseas Service in which repeats are not normally given, we only wish to take the right to give one reading. I am wondering, therefore, if you could accept a fee of 15 guineas to cover, as usual, transmission once throughout our system, together with publication in "The Listener" and our overseas journal "London Calling". I very much hope this will be satisfactory.

If it should be desired to give a second reading at any future date, could you agree to a fee of 10 guineas to bring the total fee up to the usual level of 25 guineas for two readings.

Armstrong accepted this on 17 October.

1543. BBC Talks Booking Form, 5.10.42

Sir Aziz-ul-Huque: 'Indians in Great Britain'; broadcast 10.11.42 and 8.12.42; fee £9.9s each talk. Signed: M Blackburn for I.P.O.

1544. BBC Talks Booking Form, 5.10.42

R. Desai: 'Books That Changed the World,' 7, Mein Kampf; broadcast 29.10.42; fee £9.9s.[1] Signed: M Blackburn for I.P.O.

1. Though Desai was still travelling from Aberystwyth, there is no reference to paying his expenses. The broadcast was scheduled for a Thursday; he regularly travelled to London overnight on Sunday to read the Gujarati Newsletter on the following afternoon. The script for this talk has survived.

1545. BBC Talks Booking Form, 5.10.42

Dr R. U. Hingorani: three 13-minute talks: 1: China and the Chinese, 2: Japanese Impressions, 3: Turkey;[1] recorded 5.10.42; broadcast dates not arranged; fee £9.9s each talk. Signed: M Blackburn for I.P.O. Remarks (in Mary Blackburn's hand): 'he is a busy man therefore the Recording of these 3 Talks have° been arranged for one session.'

1. On 27 August 1942, Bokhari had sent Mrs. Talbot Rice, Turkish Specialist at the Ministry of Information, the script of the talk on Turkey and asked her to approve it.

1546. War-time Diary

<u>5.10.42</u>: *New viceroy of India to be appointed shortly. No clue as to who he will be. Some say General Auchinleck—who, it is said, gets on well with leftwing Indians.*

Long talk with Brander, who is back after his 6 months tour in India.[1] His conclusions so depressing that I can hardly[2] bring myself to write them down. Briefly—affairs are much worse in India than anyone here is allowed to realise, the situation is in fact retrievable but won't be retrieved because the government is determined to make no real concessions, hell will break loose when and if there is a Japanese invasion, and our broadcasts are utterly useless because nobody listens to them. Brander did say, however, that the Indians listen to BBC[3] news, because they regard it as more truthful than that given out by Tokio or Berlin. He considers that we should broadcast news and music and nothing else. This is what I have been saying for some time past.

1. Laurence Brander, author and lecturer in English literature in India for twelve years before the war, was employed by the BBC as Intelligence Officer, Eastern Service, 1941–44. In 1954 his study *George Orwell* was published. Pages 8–9 give a succinct insight to Orwell at the BBC:

Everyone liked and respected him and he was the inspiration of that rudimentary Third Programme which was sent out to the Indian student. He soon sensed that the audience for the programme was not so large as was thought by the senior officials and, before I went to India early in 1942 to find out, he gave a great deal of time to discussing the problems with me. I found that our programmes were at a time of day when nobody was listening and that they could hardly be heard because the signal was so weak. Very few students had access to wireless sets. . . .

I was always grateful to Orwell while we worked together in the B.B.C. He laughed very readily at the nonsense that went on, and made it tolerable. This did not interfere with his sense of responsibility, for he knew how important radio propaganda could be, if intelligently organized, and he worked very hard on his own talks, which were always good and usually brilliant. His voice was a great handicap. Thin and flat, it did not go over well on short-wave broadcasting.

Brander goes on to refer to the proposal to put into print the good talks that were not being heard, and it was he who suggested that Blair broadcast under the name Orwell; see *1557* and *1571*. After the war, he was Director of Publications for the British Council.

2. *can hardly*] cannot
3. *to BBC*] to the BBC

1547. 'Voice,' 3: A Magazine Programme

6 October 1942

The text below is from the typescript as amended by Orwell, which was used for the broadcast. The typescript was marked 'Not checked with broadcast,' but Orwell has written 'As b'cast   E.A.B.   21½ mins' at the top of the first page. This is not quite correct; Stevie Smith (see *1582, n. 1*), whose name appears in the 'as broadcast text,' did not participate. Herbert Read read her poem ('quite nicely,' as Orwell wrote to her; see *1582*). Most of the script looks as if it was typed by Orwell, but two passages are typed in a different style on slips pasted over the reworked typescript, evidently to make these passages easier to read in transmission. Textual changes are here recorded in the notes at the end. The participants' names were written in a list in the margin at the top of the first page of the script: 'Orwell, Anand, Read H., Stephen Spender, W. Empson.'

ANNOUNCER: This is London Calling. This is the third number of *Voice*, our monthly radio magazine, and here is George Orwell introducing it:

ORWELL: Good evening, everybody. Much the same people are sitting round the table as last time, but we have 2 new contributors this month. One is Stephen Spender, whose poems are known to you, no doubt, & the other is Stevie Smith, author of "A Good Time was Had by All" & other books.[1]

We have found that this magazine goes better when all the contributions in it revolve round some central theme. Last month you may remember that we had a number devoted to war poetry, and war literature generally. This month we have decided to have a number devoted to childhood—not, of course, literature written *for* children but *about* childhood. The trouble is that the volume of child literature is so enormous that one hardly knows where to start. Once again I

77

think we shall have to narrow the field by only discussing childhood in two or three of its aspects. What is the outstanding characteristic of childhood, I wonder?

ANAND: Innocence, I suppose.[2]

SMITH:[3]   We might start with something by Wordsworth, I suppose it's old-fashioned to say so, but I'm very fond of "Intimations of Immortality in Early Childhood."[4]

ORWELL: That's too long.[5] What about starting with Blake's poem "Holy Thursday"? That gives you the feeling of the innocence of children— not, perhaps, what they really possess, but what an adult sees in them when he looks at them from the outside. Here it is, "Holy Thursday". This is Herbert Read reading it.

READ: 'Twas on a Holy Thursday, their innocent faces clean,
The children walking two and two, in red and blue and green,
Grey-headed beadles walk'd before, with wands as white as snow,
Till into the high dome of Paul's they like Thames' waters flow.

O what a multitude they seem'd, these flowers of London town!
Seated in companies they sit with radiance all their own.
The hum of multitudes was there, but multitudes of lambs,
Thousands of little boys and girls raising their innocent hands.

Now like a mighty wind they raise to Heaven the voice of song,
Or like harmonious thunderings the seats of Heaven among.
Beneath them sit the aged men, wise guardians of the poor;
Then cherish pity, lest you drive an angel from your door.

ORWELL: It's very nice, but[6] Blake is looking at the child from the outside. He is seeing the child as a picture, representing innocence. There are many of his poems that succeed in doing that, but I don't remember one that tells you what the child itself actually feels.

ANAND:[7]   Has any writer succeeded in doing that?

READ: Yes, I think Blake himself does, because his own mind is childlike.[8]

SPENDER: There's also cruelty in children. Nobody perhaps succeeds in[9] conveying the actual feelings of the child, but there is a vast literature dealing with the adult's memories of childhood, and doing it accurately enough to raise the same feelings in a reader. Any programme dealing with childhood which left out the nostalgic element would be incomplete, I think.

SPENDER:[10]   The trouble is there's so much to choose from. In a way all books of childhood reminiscence are alike. The incidents may be different but the essential atmosphere is the same.

ORWELL: It is the atmosphere of childhood. We must have at least one extract of that type. Read, will you read us a bit out of your autobiography,[11] "The Innocent Eye".

READ: All right.[12]

ANAND: Might we have one of Tagore's poems on childhood first?[13] For instance the one called "First Jasmines".

ORWELL: And there is a poem of D. H. Lawrence which I have in mind—

"The Piano" it's called. As those are both short poems, I suggest we do it like this. We'll read them straight through without any comment in between, and then the extract from Read's book to follow. Well, here they are. First of all Rabindranath Tagore's poem "First Jasmines", read by Mulk Raj Anand, then D. H. Lawrence's "The Piano", read by William Empson, and then an extract from "The Innocent Eye", read by Herbert Read himself. Here they are, then:

ANAND: Ah, these jasmines, these white jasmines!
I seem to remember the first day when I filled my hands with these jasmines, these white jasmines.
I have loved the sunlight, the sky and the green earth;
I have heard the liquid murmur of the river through the darkness of midnight;
Autumn sunsets have come to me at the bend of a road in the lonely waste, like a bride raising her veil to accept her lover.
Yet my memory is still sweet with the first white jasmines that I held in my hand when I was a child.

Many a glad day has come in my life, and I have laughed with merrymakers on festival nights.
On grey mornings of rain I have crooned many an idle song.
I have worn round my neck the evening wreath of *Bakulas* woven by the hand of love.
Yet my heart is sweet with the memory of the first fresh jasmines that filled my hands when I was a child.

EMPSON: Softly, in the dusk, a woman is singing to me;
Taking me back down the vista of years, till I see
A child sitting under the piano, in the boom of the tingling strings
And pressing the small, poised feet of a mother who smiles as she sings.

In spite of myself, the insidious mastery of song
Betrays me back, till the heart of me weeps to belong
To the old Sunday evenings at home, with winter outside
And hymns in the cosy parlour, the tinkling piano our guide.

So now it is vain for the singer to burst into clamour
With the great black piano appassionato. The glamour
Of childish days is upon me, my manhood is cast
Down in the flood of remembrance, I weep like a child for the past.

READ: On the south side of the Green were two familiar shrines, each with its sacred fire. The first was the saddle-room, with its pungent clean smell of saddle-soap. It was a small white-washed room, hung with bright bits and stirrups and long loops of leather reins; the saddles were in a loft above, reached by a ladder and trap-door. In the middle was a small cylindrical stove, kept burning through the Winter, and making a warm friendly shelter where we could play undisturbed. Our chief joy was to make lead shot, or bullets as we called them; and for this purpose there existed a long-handled crucible and a mould. At what now seems to me an incredibly early age we melted down the strips of lead we found in the window-sill, and poured the sullen liquid into the small aperture of the mould, which was in the form of a pair of pincers—closed whilst the pouring was in progress. When opened, the gleaming silver bullets, about the size of a pea, fell out of the matrix and rolled away to cool on the stone floor. We used the bullets in our catapults, but the joy was in the making of them, and in the sight of their shining beauty.

The blacksmith's shop was a still more magical shrine. The blacksmith came for a day periodically, to shoe or reshoe the horses, to repair waggons and make simple implements. In his dusky cave the bellows roared, the fire was blown to a white intensity, and then suddenly the bellows-shaft was released and the soft glowing iron drawn from the heart of the fire. Then clang, clang, clang on the anvil, the heavenly shower of ruby and golden sparks, and our precipitate flight to a place of safety. All around us, in dark cobwebbed corners, were heaps of old iron, discarded horse-shoes, hoops and pipes. Under the window was a tank of water for slaking and tempering the hot iron, and this water possessed the miraculous property of curing warts.

In these two shrines I first experienced the joy of making things. Everywhere around me the earth was stirring with growth and the beasts were propagating their kind. But these wonders passed unobserved by my childish mind, unrecorded in memory. They depended on forces beyond our control, beyond my conception. But fire was real, and so was the skill with which we shaped hard metals to our design and desire.

ORWELL: So far we've taken rather a romantic view of childhood.[14] We've dealt with the innocence of childhood and the nostalgic feelings of the grown-up who looks back and remembers the time when he was a child. But childhood also has its pathetic side, & also its nightmare side.[15] A child lives a lot of its time in a very terrifying world. And even seen from the outside a child is a very pathetic thing.

EMPSON: Once again there's an enormous literature in the pathos and helplessness of children. But if you want something that gives that effect in a few lines, there is a poem by W. H. Davies called "The Two Children".

ORWELL: I think that would go rather well with a short poem by Stevie Smith. Read, perhaps you would read that.

READ: And what about something from Dickens, for instance "David Copperfield". Dickens knew that children in spite of all their innocence can suffer torments even when they are not physically maltreated.[16]

ORWELL:[17] Well, I suggest doing it the same way as we did before. First of all Stevie Smith's poem, read by Herbert Read.[18] Then W. H. Davies's poem "The Two Children", read by Wm. Empson.[19] And then an extract from "David Copperfield" which I'll read myself.[20] Here they are:

READ:[21]

It was a cynical babe
Lay in its mother's arms
Born two months too soon

After many alarms
Why is its mother sad
Weeping without a friend
Where is its father—say?
He tarries in Ostend.
It was a cynical babe. Reader, before you condemn, pause,
It was a cynical babe; not without cause.

DAVIES:[22] 'Ah, little boy! I see
 You have a wooden spade.
Into this sand you dig
 So deep—for what?' I said.
'There's more rich gold', said he,
 'Down under where I stand,
Than twenty elephants
 Could move across the land'.

'Ah, little girl with wool!—
 What are you making now?'
'Some stockings for a bird,
 To keep his legs from snow.'
And there those children are,
 So happy, small, and proud:
The boy that digs his grave,
 The girl that knits her shroud.

ORWELL: Shall I ever forget those lessons? They were presided over nominally by my mother, but really by Mr. Murdstone and his sister, who were always present, and found them a favourable occasion for giving my mother lessons in that miscalled firmness, which was the bane of both our lives.

Let me remember how it used to be, and bring one morning back again.

I come into the second-best parlour after breakfast, with my books, and an exercise book, and a slate. My mother is ready for me at her writing-desk, but not half so ready as Mr. Murdstone in his easy chair by the window (though he pretends to be reading a book), or as Miss Murdstone, sitting near my mother stringing steel beads. The very sight of these two has such an influence over me, that I begin to feel the words I have been at infinite pains to get into my head, all sliding away, and going I don't know where.[23]

I hand the first book to my mother. Perhaps it is a grammar, perhaps a history or geography. I take a last drowning look at the page as I give it into her hand, and start off aloud at a racing pace while I have got it fresh. I trip over a word. Mr. Murdstone looks up. I trip over another word. Miss Murdstone looks up. I redden, tumble over half-a-dozen words, and stop. I think my mother would show me the book if she dared, but she does not dare, and she says softly:

"Oh, Davy, Davy!"

"Now Clara", says Mr. Murdstone, "be firm with the boy. Don't say 'Oh, Davy, Davy!' that's childish. He knows his lesson or he does not know it."

"He does *not* know it", Miss Murdstone interposes awfully.

"I am really afraid he does not", says my mother.

"Then, you see, Clara", returns Miss Murdstone, "you should just give him the book back and make him know it."

"Yes, certainly," says my mother; "that is what I intend to do, my dear Jane. Now, Davy, try once more, and don't be stupid."

I obey the first clause of the injunction by trying once more, but am not so successful with the second, for I am very stupid. I tumble down before I get to the old place, at a point where I was all right before, and stop to think. But I can't think about the lesson. I think of the number of yards of net in Miss Murdstone's cap, or of the price of Mr. Murdstone's dressing-gown, or any such ridiculous problem that I have no business with, and don't want to have anything at all to do with. Mr. Murdstone makes a movement of impatience which I have been expecting for a long time. Miss Murdstone does the same. My mother glances submissively at them, shuts the book, and lays it by as an arrear to be worked out when my other tasks are done.

There is a pile of these arrears very soon, and it swells like a rolling snowball. The bigger it gets, the more stupid *I* get. The case is so hopeless, and I feel that I am wallowing in such a bog of nonsense, that I give up all idea of getting out, and abandon myself to my fate.

Even when the lessons are done, the worst is yet to happen, in the shape of an appalling sum. This is invented for me, and delivered orally by Mr. Murdstone, and begins "If I go into a cheesemonger's shop, and buy five thousand double-Gloucester cheeses at fourpence-halfpenny each, present payment" — at which I see Miss Murdstone secretly overjoyed. I pore over these cheeses without any result or enlightenment until dinner-time, when I have a slice of bread to help me out with the cheeses, and am considered in disgrace for the rest of the evening.

It seems to me, at this distance of time, as if my unfortunate studies generally took this course. I could have done very well if I had been without the Murdstones; but the influence of the Murdstones upon me was like the fascination of two snakes on a wretched young bird.[24] . . . As to any recreation with other children of my age, I had very little of that; for the gloomy theology of the Murdstones made all children out to be a swarm of little vipers (though there *was* a child once set in the midst of the Disciples),[25] and held that they contaminated one another.

The natural result of this treatment, continued, I suppose, for some six months or more, was to make me sullen, dull, and dogged. I was not made the less so by my sense of being daily more and more shut out and alienated from my mother.[26] I believe I should have been almost stupefied but for one circumstance.

It was this. My father had left a small collection of books in a little room upstairs, to which I had access (for it adjoined my own) and which nobody else in our house ever troubled. From that blessed little room, Roderick Random, Peregrine Pickle, Humphrey Clinker, Tom Jones, the Vicar of Wakefield, Don Quixote, Gil Blas, and Robinson Crusoe, came out, a glorious host, to keep me company. They kept alive my fancy, and my hope of something beyond that place and time, — they, and the Arabian Nights, and the Tales of the Genii, — and did me no harm; for whatever harm was in some of them was not there for me; *I* knew nothing of it. It is astonishing to me now, how I found time, in the midst of my porings and blunderings over heavier themes, to read those books as I did. It is curious to me how I could ever have consoled myself under my small troubles (which were great troubles to me), by impersonating my favourite characters in them — as I did — and by putting Mr. and Miss Murdstone into all the bad ones — which I did too.[27] I have been Tom Jones (a child's Tom Jones, a harmless creature) for a week together. I have sustained my own idea of Roderick Random for a month at a stretch, I verily believe. I had a greedy relish for a few volumes of Voyages and Travels — I forget what, now — that were on those shelves: and for days and days I can remember to have gone about my region of our house, armed with the centre-piece out of an old set of boot-trees — the perfect realisation of Captain Somebody, of the Royal British Navy, in danger of being beset by savages, and resolved to sell his life at a great price. The Captain never lost dignity, from having his ears boxed with the Latin Grammar. I did; but the Captain was a Captain and a hero, in despite of all the grammars of all the languages in the world, dead or alive.[28]

EMPSON: The extract from "David Copperfield" is very good, but it is about a very peculiar way of treating children, not about normal child life. Conditions have changed now.

ORWELL: Yes, I suppose so. The essential thing in that passage is education as an instrument of torture. It probably isn't quite the same nowadays.

ANAND: I doubt that very much, children still run away from school, don't they?

ORWELL: At any rate there isn't the Victorian theory that you have to "break the child's spirit", as they used to call it.

READ: No, but there are more subtle ways of ill-treating children. In Victorian times, they at least had the advantage of being neglected.

ANAND: And there are still slums and malnutrition, not to mention bombs. Perhaps one can only say that the child's outlook is somewhat more hopeful nowadays.[28]

ORWELL: I think that gives us the note to end on. I should like to end with Stephen Spender's poem "An Elementary School Class in a Slum". It tells the truth about actual conditions, and yet it's hopeful. Here it is. "An Elementary School Class in a Slum", read by Stephen Spender himself:

SPENDER: Far far from gusty waves, these children's faces.
Like rootless weeds the torn hair round their paleness.
The tall girl with her weighed-down head. The paper-
seeming boy with rat's eyes. The stunted unlucky heir
Of twisted bones, reciting a father's gnarled disease,
His lesson from his desk. At back of the dim class,
One unnoted, sweet and young: his eyes live in a dream
Of squirrels' game, in tree room, other than this.

On sour cream walls, donations. Shakespeare's head
Cloudless at dawn, civilised dome riding all cities.
Belled, flowery, Tyrolese valley. Open-handed map
Awarding the world its world. And yet, for these
Children, these windows, not this world, are world,
Where all their future's painted with a fog,
A narrow street sealed in with a lead sky,
Far far from rivers, capes, and stars of words.

Surely Shakespeare is wicked, the map a bad example
With ships and sun and love tempting them to steal —
For lives that slyly turn in their cramped holes
From fog to endless night? On their slag heap, these children
Wear skins peeped through by bones and spectacles of steel
With mended glass, like bottle bits on stones.
All of their time and space are foggy slum
So blot their maps with slums as big as doom.

Unless, governor, teacher, inspector, visitor,
This map becomes their window and these windows
That open on their lives like crouching tombs
Break, O break open, till they break the town
And show the children to the fields and all their world
Azure on their sands, to let their tongues
Run naked into books, the white and green leaves open
The history theirs whose language is the sun.

CLOSING ANNOUNCEMENT: That is the end of the third number of "Voice", our monthly radio magazine. Those taking part were Herbert Read, William Empson, George Orwell,[29] Mulk Raj Anand and Stephen Spender. The next number of "Voice" will be broadcast on November 3rd.

The first reading is that of the text as amended by Orwell, and as printed here, though not quite as broadcast; the second reading is that of the unamended typescript.
1. Good evening . . . & other books] *manuscript addition in Orwell's hand*
2. Innocence, I suppose.] I should say, innocence
3. Smith did not participate in transmission; see headnote.
4. I suppose . . . Early Childhood"] or Blake, perhaps
5. That's too long.] *interlinear insertion*
6. ORWELL: It's very nice, but] X.   As you said. *Colons have been added where speakers' names have been written in.*
7. ANAND:] Y.
8. READ: Yes, I think . . . childlike.] *manuscript addition;* childlike] childhood
9. SPENDER: There's also cruelty . . . succeeds in] EMPSON: Not perhaps in
10. SPENDER:] Z.
11. Read, will you read . . . autobiography,] As Herbert Read is with us, I suggest having a passage out of his autobiography,
12. READ: All right.] *manuscript addition*
13. Might we have one of Tagore's poems on childhood first?] There are also Tagore's poems on childhood. *Question-mark added here.*
14. ORWELL: So far we've taken rather a romantic view of childhood.] X: So far we have only dealt with the favourable aspects of childhood.
15. side, & also its nightmare side.] side.
16. EMPSON: Once again . . . physically maltreated.] *three speeches typed on a slip pasted over the original, amended, text*
17. ORWELL:] EMPSON:
18. Herbert Read] herself
19. Wm. Empson] Herbert Read
20. which I'll read myself] read by George Orwell
21. READ:] SMITH:
22. DAVIES:] READ:
23. know where.] know where. I wonder where they do go, by the by? *Last sentence crossed out*
24. There is a pile of these arrears . . . a wretched young bird.] *crossed out*

25. (though there *was* a child once set in the midst of the Disciples)] *crossed out*
26. I was not made the less . . . from my mother.] *crossed out*
27. It is astonishing to me . . . which I did too.] *crossed out*
28. languages in the world, dead or alive . . . somewhat more hopeful nowadays.] *six speeches and last seven words of reading from Dickens typed on a slip pasted over the original, amended, text. The original typing was heavily amended; retyping was probably to facilitate reading during the broadcast.*
29. William Empson, George Orwell] William Empson, Stevie Smith, George Orwell

1548. BBC Talks Booking Form, 6.10.42

Herbert Read: 'Voice,' 3; 'reading extract from own book (covered with Miss Alexander[1]) — about 3 minutes, & taking part in discussions — total length about 5 minutes'; broadcast 6.10.42; fee £4.4s 'to cover reading & part in discussion.' Signed: M Blackburn for I.P.O.

1. So that a performing fee might be paid for copyright material.

1549. BBC Talks Booking Form, 6.10.42

Stephen Spender: 'Voice,' 3; 'reading his own poem (An Elementary School Class) — about 2½ minutes. And taking part in discussions — total length about 5 minutes'; broadcast 6.10.42; fee £4.4s 'to cover reading of poem and participation in discussion.' Signed: M Blackburn for I.P.O.

1550. To Mulk Raj Anand

7 October 1942   PP/EB

Dear Mulk,
I am sending back your script on War And Peace because I wish you would re-write the later part, roughly speaking from page 4 onwards in order to deal more with the sociological aspect of War and Peace. I think it is quite true that Tolstoy marked the beginning of a new attitude towards the novel, but that in itself is not big enough to justify the title "Books That Changed the World". What I wanted was a talk on War And Peace as exemplifying the new attitude towards war. If not the first, it is certainly one of the first books that tried to describe war realistically and many modern currents of thought, probably including pacifism, derive from it to some extent. I do not of course want pacifist propaganda, but I think we might make valuable use of a comparison between Tolstoy's description of the battle of Oesterlitz[1] and for instance Tennyson's Charge of the Light Brigade.

Gollancz has expressed interest in your idea for a book about India.[2] He says it would have to be done quickly, which however would be quite easy by the method we were projecting of doing it. He wants you, or failing you, me to go and see him today week, October 14th, at 11 a.m. at his office. Do you think you could see me between now and then so that we can draw up a synopsis of the book?

Yours sincerely,
George Orwell

1. Austerlitz, where Napoleon gained a brilliant victory over the Austrians and Russians in 1805. Tolstoy's account is given in Book 3, chapters 14–19.
2. In a letter to Orwell of 11 October 1942 (which discussed factual aspects of the broadcast), Anand added a postscript to say that he would telephone on Monday (presumably the next day) to discuss the book. He said that the only real basis for a symposium was a constructive plan for the defence of India. That might bring together different points of view and 'reveal the idiocy of reaction more strongly.' In a letter of 19 November, Anand tells Orwell he will see him the next day. There is nothing else on file about this book.

1551. To Mulk Raj Anand

7 October 1942   PP/EB/NP

Dear Mulk,

We are starting shortly a series of talks giving the History of Fascism in seven parts. I am wondering whether you would like to take part, and to deal with the talk covering the Spanish Civil War. Please let me know whether you would like to undertake this, and I will let you have more detailed particulars. I should like an answer fairly soon, as the first talk is to be on November 5th.

The date of your talk—the fifth in the series—would be December 3rd, which means that we should want the script not later than November 26th.

Yours,
Eric Blair[1]
Talks Producer
Indian Section

1. This and the previous letter to Anand dated 7 October (see *1550*) are signed differently: one has Eric Blair; the other George Orwell. It may well *not* reflect alleged confusion on Orwell's part. It is noticeable that this letter is set to a narrower measure (just over four inches) than other letters written on this day, which were four and a half inches. Two typists may have been involved. This letter carries Nancy Parratt's initials; the others leave no space for typists' initials. The initials on the letter to L. A. G. Strong (*1552*), despatched by a secretary, could be Miss Parratt's, but that does not mean she typed the letter. Further evidence for different typists lies in Anand's name, at the foot of each letter (not reproduced here): Miss Parratt has 'Mulk Raj Anand,' the usual form; the other letter has 'M. R. Anand.'

1552. To L. A. G. Strong

7 October 1942   PP/EB

Dear Mr. Strong,

I am sending herewith the first instalment of our serial. Your instalment goes on the air on Friday week, October 16th, at 12.15 by the clock, from 200,

Oxford Street. If possible, I would like to have your script by the end of this week, or at any rate not later than Tuesday, the 13th. There is not likely to be any difficulty over the censorship, but your instalment must go on as soon as possible to the next contributor, so as to leave at any rate five or six days for her to write her contribution. I hope you do not find this opening chapter too hard to follow on from. I have left plenty of possibilities. I don't want to lay down conditions, but as the thing has to run for five instalments, I think we ought to say at any rate that neither of the two principal characters who have been introduced ought to die off [in] the second instalment. You can follow [up] the story in any way you choose, and I hope you will be able to leave a fairly good jumping off place for your successor.

Yours sincerely,
George Orwell
Talks Producer
Indian Section
Dictated by Mr. Orwell and
despatched in his absence by:[1]

1. The initials are probably 'NP'—for Nancy Parratt, Orwell's secretary.

1553. To Gladys Calthrop
8 October 1942   PP/EB

Dear Mrs. Calthrop,[1]
I am wondering whether you would like to take part in a series of talks designed to give Indian listeners some hints about amateur dramatic societies. We think that there is probably a growing interest in the theatre in India, together with a good deal of ignorance about technique. We have, therefore, roughly sketched out a series of six talks which would be given principally by some expert such as yourself, and partly by Indians who could supply the background stuff, as they would know what the standard community in an ordinary Indian town would be able to provide in the way of money, personnel and so forth. If you are interested in this, I wonder if you could come and see us so that we could talk it over and get the talks mapped out in greater detail. Perhaps you could let me know, giving one or two alternative dates, what days in the near future would be convenient to you. Of course, I don't want to take up more time than you can afford and I should therefore w[arn] you that this may mean six 13-minute talks on six consecutive Fridays, with a certain amount of discussion beforehand in each case.

Your sincerely,
Eric Blair
Talks Producer
Indian Section

1. Gladys E. Calthrop, artist and stage designer. Her first designs were for *The Vortex* by Noel Coward (1924), and she designed many of Coward's successes thereafter. In 1941 she designed his *Blithe Spirit*, and in 1943 *Present Laughter* and *This Happy Breed*.

1554. To R. R. Desai

8 October 1942   PP/EB/NP

Dear Mr. Desai,
We are starting shortly a series of talks giving the History of Fascism in seven parts. I am wondering whether you would like to take part, and to deal with the first talk, covering the March on Rome. Please let me know whether you would like to undertake this, and I will let you have more detailed particulars. I should like an answer fairly soon, as your talk is to be on November 5th. This means that we should want the script not later than October 29th. We can discuss this further when you come to the office on Monday next.

Yours sincerely,
Eric Blair
Talks Producer
Indian Section

1555. To Cedric Dover

8 October 1942   PP/EB/NP

Dear Dover,
We are starting shortly a series of talks giving the History of Fascism in seven parts. I am wondering whether you would like to take part, and to deal with the talk covering The June Purge.[1] Please let me know whether you would like to undertake this, and I will let you have more detailed particulars. I should like an answer fairly soon, as the first talk is to be on November 5th.

The date of your talk—the third in the series—would be 19th November, which means that we should want the script not later than November 12th.

Yours sincerely,
Eric Blair
Talks Producer
Indian Section

1. The internal blood-letting among Hitler's followers on 29 and 30 June 1934, when perhaps four-hundred people were murdered who were deemed to oppose Hitler, and especially Goering and Himmler. The most notable victim was Ernst Röhm.

1556. To K. S. Shelvankar

8 October 1942   PP/EB/NP

Dear Shelvankar,
This is just to confirm that you are doing the two talks in the History of Fascism [series] about the rise of the Nazi [p]arty and the Invasion of the U.S.S.R.

These are on the 12th November and the 17th December respectively, which means that we should like to have the scripts in the office *at least* a week before the date of the talk.

Yours sincerely,
Eric Blair
Talks Producer
Indian Section

1557. Laurence Brander, Intelligence Officer, India, to L. F. Rushbrook Williams, Eastern Service Director

8 October 1942, with copy to Orwell

Saturday Weekly News Letter

In conversation with Mr. Eric Blair this morning, I discovered that he writes our Saturday Weekly News Letter which is read by some Indian. The audience in India supposes that the reader is the composer, and the present audience is small. As you know, the universal demand amongst our Indian audience is for well-known Englishmen. If, therefore, it could be arranged that this News Letter be no longer anonymous, but the known work of "George Orwell" and read by him[1] instead of largely being ignored as at present, it would be looked forward to with the very greatest interest, as few names stand so high with our Indian audience at present as that of George Orwell.

1. 'and read by him' was a manuscript addition by Brander.

1558. Story by Five Authors

Through Eastern Eyes, 9 October 1942

On 9 September 1942, Orwell wrote to L. A. G. Strong, Inez Holden, and Martin Armstrong asking each to contribute one part of a five-part story to be broadcast to India; see *1468, 1466, 1465*. He proposed to write this first instalment. On 24 October, he wrote to E. M. Forster asking him to write the concluding instalment; see *1610*. The four later instalments are placed here according to the dates they were broadcast: 16, 23, and 30 October and 6 November 1942; see *1574, 1606, 1623, 1638*. Orwell's instalment is taken from his original script, which looks to be typed on Nancy Parratt's machine. The script is marked 'As Broadcast.' One verbal change is noted; mistypings have been corrected silently. The other scripts are printed from BBC fair copies.

Part 1 by George Orwell

It was a night in London in the late autumn of 1940. A bomb came whistling down, piercing the racket of the guns, and a man, a small shadowy figure, darted like a lizard into an already ruined house and flung himself down behind a pile of debris. He was none too soon, for the next instant the bomb exploded with a noise like the Day of Judgment less than a hundred yards away. He was quite unhurt, however, and it was only a few seconds before his ear drums began to work again and he realised that the objects which had spattered him all over were merely chips of brick and mortar.

Gilbert Moss, for that was his name, sat up and brushed some of the dust and plaster off his raincoat, after which he began mechanically feeling in his pockets for a cigarette. He noticed without surprise or even much interest that a dead man was lying face upwards a yard or two away from him. It did not seem to matter, either, that almost within touching distance some fallen beams or floor joists were burning fitfully. The whole house would be on fire before long, but in the mean time it gave a certain amount of protection.

Outside the barking of the guns rose and fell, sometimes bursting forth into an ear-splitting volley as a near-by battery came into action. This was the third time tonight that Gilbert had had to fling himself down to dodge a bomb, and on the second occasion he had had a small adventure, or what would have seemed an adventure in normal times. Caught by the blitz a long way from his own quarter of the town, he had struggled homewards through such a nightmare of gunfire, bomb flashes, falling shrapnel, burning houses and racing clanging fire engines as made him wonder whether the whole of humanity had not gone mad together. Under the rosy sky one had the impression that all London was burning. He had been passing down a side street he did not know when he heard a cry and saw a woman gesticulating to him from beside a demolished house. He hurried across to her. She was wearing blue overalls—curiously enough that was all he ever noticed about her—and a little boy of four or five, with a terrified face, was clutching at her leg. The woman cried out to him that there was a man under the wreckage and no rescue squad was near. With her help he had dug into the dusty pile of rubble, pushing and pulling at lumps of brick and mortar, splinters of glass, panels of smashed doors and fragments of furniture, and sure enough, within five minutes they had uncovered the body of a man, whitened to the eyes with plaster but conscious and almost unhurt. Gilbert never discovered whether the man was the woman's husband or father, or merely a stranger. They had just helped him out on to the pavement when there was the whistle of another bomb. Immediately one thought had filled Gilbert's mind to the exclusion of all others—the child. He had swiftly grabbed the little boy, laid him flat on the pavement and covered him with his own body against the moment when the bomb should burst. However, it was a delayed-action bomb and no roar followed the whistle. As he got up the woman had suddenly flung her arms round his neck and given him a kiss that tasted of plaster. And then he had gone on, promising to inform the next warden he met about the injured man. But as it happened he had not met any warden, and there the incident ended.

That was half an hour ago and Gilbert had already almost forgotten it. On a night like this nothing seemed remarkable. Since entering his new refuge he had hardly given a second glance to the dead man lying beside him. The pile of smouldering beams sent out little spurts of flame which illumined Gilbert and the wreckage of various pieces of furniture. He was a thin smallish man in his middle thirties, with greying hair and a worn, sharp-feature°, discoloured face. It had a sour expression which at most times was accentuated by a cigarette dangling from the lower lip. With his shabby raincoat and black felt hat he might have been an unsuccessful actor or journalist, a publisher's tout, a political agent or possibly some kind of hanger-on of a lawyer's office. He could find no matches in his pockets and was considering lighting his cigarette from one of the burning beams when an A.R.P. warden in overalls and gumboots threaded his way through from the back of the ruined house, flashing his torch from side to side.

"You O.K., chum?"

"I'm O.K.", said Gilbert.

The warden waited for the echo of a gun to die away before speaking again. He flashed his torch briefly onto the prostrate man but seemed too preoccupied to examine him.

"This poor devil's[1] done for", he said. "We got a packet tonight, all right. I better report him. They'll pick him up in the morning, I s'pose."

"No use wasting an ambulance", agreed Gilbert.

The A.R.P. man had just disappeared when the burning beams burst into bright flame and the room was almost as bright as day. Gilbert glanced again at the dead man lying at his side, and as he did so his heart gave a violent, painful leap. It was the figure of a rather handsome man of his own age, the face calm and undamaged, the eyes closed. In the better light, however, Gilbert had noticed two things. In the first place it was not a stranger but a man he knew very well—or had once known very well, rather. In the second place the man was not dead, nor anywhere near it. He was merely unconscious, perhaps stunned by a falling beam.

A change had come over Gilbert's face the instant that the shock of recognition passed. It became very intent, with the ghost of a smile. The expression he wore was not a wicked expression, exactly—rather the expression of a man faced with an overwhelming temptation, an opportunity too good to be missed.

Suddenly he sprang to his feet and began looking for something which he knew he would have no difficulty in finding. In a moment he had got it. It was a heavy billet of wood, part of a broken floor joist, four feet long and tapering at one end to form a natural handle. He tested its weight and then, carefully measuring his distance from the unconscious man on the floor, gripped it with both hands and swung it aloft. Outside the guns were roaring again. Gilbert did not immediately deliver his blow. The man's head was not quite in the right position, and with the toe of his boot Gilbert pushed a few flakes of plaster under the head, raising it slightly. Then he took a fresh grip on his billet of wood and swung it aloft again. It was a heavy, formidable club. He had only to bring it down once and the skull would break like an egg.

At this moment he felt no fear, any more than he felt compunction. Curiously enough the racket of the guns upheld him. He was utterly alone in the burning town. He did not even need to reflect that on a night like this any death whatever would be attributed to the German bombs. He knew instinctively that in the middle of this night-mare° you could do what you liked and nobody would have time to notice. Nevertheless the moment in which he had paused had temporarily saved the unconscious man's life. Gilbert lowered his club and leaned on it, as on a walking stick. He wanted, not exactly to think things over, but to recapture a certain memory, a certain feeling. It is not much use killing your enemy unless in the moment of striking him you remember just what he has done to you. It was not that he had faltered in his intention of killing this man. There was no question that he was going to kill him. But before doing so he wanted, in a sense, to remember *why* he was doing so. There was plenty of time, and complete safety. In the morning his enemy's body would only be one air-raid casualty among hundreds of others.

He leaned his club against a pile of wreckage and again took his unlighted cigarette from his pocket. He still could not find any matches. A thought striking him, he knelt down and felt in the unconscious man's pockets till he came on a slim gold cigarette-lighter. He lit his cigarette and put the lighter back, rather reluctantly. The initials on it were C.J.K.C., he noted. He had known this man as Charles Coburn, the Honourable Charles Coburn. Doubtless he was a lord by this time, though Gilbert could not remember the name of the title he was heir to. It was curious, but the excellent cloth of the man's waistcoat, and the expensive feel of the slender gold lighter, partly brought back the memory that he was looking for. They both felt like money. Gilbert had known Charles Coburn as a very rich young man, horribly elegant and superior, and rather cultured as they used to call it in the nineteen-twenties. With not many exceptions Gilbert hated all rich people—though that in itself was not a motive for killing anybody, of course.

He sat down again and drew the cigarette smoke deep into his lungs. The chorus of the guns stopped for nearly two minutes, then opened up again. It was so hard to remember—not the *fact*, of course, but the social atmosphere in which such things could happen. He remembered in great detail the outrageous, mean injury which this man had done him; what he did not remember so well were his own feelings at the time, the weakness and snobbishness which had made it possible for such a petty, humiliating disaster to happen to him. To remember that he had to remember the England of the nineteen-twenties, the old, snobbish, money-ruled England which was fast disappearing before the bombers and the income-tax came to finish it off. For a moment it eluded him, then suddenly it came back to him in a vision of a Mayfair street one summer morning—the flowers in the window boxes, a water cart laying the dust, a footman in a striped waistcoat opening the door. He could not remember when he had seen that particular street, or whether he had ever seen it. Perhaps it was only a symbolic street. But there it was, in the smell of pink geraniums and newly-drenched dust—fashionable London with its clubs and its gunsmiths and its footmen in striped waistcoats, the London of before the deluge, when money ruled the world and creatures like Charles Coburn were all-powerful because of their money.

Gilbert sprang to his feet again. He had no more doubts now. He did not merely know in an intellectual sense that he hated the man lying at his feet, he knew just why and how he hated him. Nor did it seem to him a barbarous thing to kill your enemy when you have him at your mercy; on the contrary, it seemed to him natural. As though encouraging him, the guns rose once again to an unbroken, rolling roar, like thunder. With an expression on his face much more purposeful than before he once more measured his distance, gripped his club firmly in both hands and swung it above his head, ready for a blow that would settle his enemy once and for all.

Continued by L. A. G. Strong; see *1574.*

1. devil's] 'bastard's' *in typescript, crossed through, and* 'fellow's' *substituted in Orwell's hand; that also is crossed through, and Orwell settled on* 'devil's'

1559. News Review, 43
10 October 1942

There are no censorship stamps on the original of this commentary, nor any indication that this text is as broadcast. The alterations, however, are all in Orwell's handwriting. The script was read by Noel Sircar.

Stalingrad is holding firm, and there is even some reason to think that the Germans may have abandoned the hope of taking it. Both Hitler and Ribbentrop, in their recent speeches, spoke of Stalingrad as though it were about to fall, but more recently the German High Command have issued a statement to the effect that they were going to abandon direct assaults on the town and attempt to reduce it by artillery bombardment. This may mean that they believe that they can blast the remaining defenders out of Stalingrad by using the heavy artillery with which they reduced *Sebastopol*,[1] but it may on the other hand mean that they have given up hope of crossing the Volga at this point and are doing their best to save face with the German home public.

The battle for *Stalingrad*[2] has now been going on for nearly two months, and must certainly have cost the Germans some tens of thousands of men, without any corresponding gain. This is now the beginning of October, and we may say that in spite of the large territories which the Germans have over-run, and even if Stalingrad should fall, the German campaign this year has not quite attained its object, missing it by a narrow margin, as did the campaign of 1941. We may be certain that the German objective this year was to reach the Caspian Sea and to cross the Caucasus Mountains, after which Germany's oil problem would have been a comparatively simple matter. We are safe now in saying that it is too late for the Germans to complete this programme, and in addition the prolonged defence of Stalingrad has given time for the northern Russian armies to be reinforced and to receive fresh supplies. Even if the Germans should capture Stalingrad, cross the Volga River and thus, in effect, cut the Russian front into two halves, this probably will not reduce the fighting power of the Russian armies as it would have done a couple of months ago. We may conclude that the German dream of driving the Russians back behind the Ural Mountains and reducing them to mere guerilla activity will have to be abandoned [at any rate for this year].

We mentioned last week the speech made by Hitler in which a decidedly different tone was apparent *from that of his*[3] triumphant speeches of a year or two earlier. This has been followed by a rather similar speech by Goering, and from this and other indications we can probably infer the new plan of campaign which has been forced on the Germans by their failure to conquer either Britain or Russia.

Both Goering and Hitler dropped the claims made earlier to have destroyed the Soviet armies once and for all. They merely claimed to have driven the Russians far enough back to prevent an invasion of Europe, and at the same time dwelt upon the wealth of the territories they had conquered. Both declared that Germany is ready for a long war and Goering in his speech made it abundantly clear that Germany's new plan is to plunder Europe in order to keep the German war machine going. He said that the British blockade did not affect Germany since the whole of Europe is at Germany's disposal, and added bluntly that whoever went hungry in Europe, it would not be the Germans. We can see, therefore, that the specious talk of a year ago about the New Order, and about Europe, freed from British and American influence, raising its standard of living under German guidance, has been dropped. Instead, the Germans come forward quite undisguisedly as a nation of slave-masters who are going to keep the other European races in subjection and plunder them of their food and other goods in order to sustain the attacks of the United Nations. This is an important development because it means that the Germans are more or less throwing away their opportunities of winning the real allegiance of the countries they have overrun. Quite possibly these speeches are the prelude to some kind of peace offer in which the Germans would claim that they have no wish for further expansion, that the war has consequently lost any meaning. Similar speeches made recently in Tokyo suggest that the Japanese may be contemplating a similar strategy. The United Nations, however, are not likely to be deceived, and the chance of any premature peace which would allow the Fascist Powers to renew their aggressions after a year or two can be written off.

In New Guinea, the Australian advance is continuing and little opposition is being encountered, though the advance is necessarily slow because of the difficult nature of the country. The Allies still have air superiority in this area. The Japanese retreat from the position which they had reached quite near to Port Moresby is capable of several interpretations, and we do not care to comment on it at this stage. There is still serious fighting on the island of Guadalcanal, where the Japanese have several times landed fresh troops under cover of darkness and are attempting to win back the port and airfields captured by the Americans. Further north, at another island in the Solomons group, American planes have made another successful raid and damaged several Japanese warships.

The Americans have occupied fresh islands in the Aleutian Archipelago and are establishing airfields there. As a result, the Japanese-held island of

Kiska is already being bombed by land-based American planes. So far as can be discovered by air reconnaissance, the Japanese have now abandoned the other islands they had occupied in the Aleutian Archipelago and are only holding on to the island of Kiska.

British bombing raids on Germany continue. Now that the nights are longer the bombers can go further east, and several parts of the Baltic Sea have been bombed during the past week or two. More and more American planes are now taking part in the R.A.F. raids. Yesterday, the biggest daylight raid of the war was carried out over northern France.[4] About 600 Allied planes took part and only four failed to return. This may be compared with the biggest daylight raid carried out by the Germans, on September 15th, 1940, when 500 or 600 German planes came over Britain and 185 were shot down.[5]

There have also been successful raids on German bases in occupied Norway. In these raids a new British light bomber, the Mosquito, has played a conspicuous part. The full details of the Mosquito have not yet been released for publication, but it is evident that it is a very light and very fast bombing plane, especially suited to daylight raids. We shall probably be able to give further particulars about it later.

The British and United States Governments have just announced that they are relinquishing all extraterritorial rights in China. This applies to Free China immediately, and will apply to the whole of China after the war. For about a century past various European nations have had concessions in Shanghai, *Tientsin*[6] and other Chinese cities, *and*[7] they were not subject to Chinese law, and [they have] also had the power to station their own troops in China and to enjoy various other privileges. This is now coming to an end as the result of an agreement between the British, American and Chinese Governments. This step not only demonstrates the mutual trust and friendship between China and the rest of the United Nations, but marks the final emergence of China as a modern nation on an equality with the western powers. It is a fitting tribute for today's anniversary of the Chinese revolution.

Yesterday it was announced that Abyssinia is entering into full alliance with the United Nations. Abyssinia was the first country to be overwhelmed by Fascist aggression, and also the first to be liberated. The Abyssinians are now ready to place their military and economic resources at the disposal of those who helped to set them free. In these two events we see how the world-wide struggle of the free peoples against aggression is growing steadily stronger.

1. *Sebastopol*] Odessa
2. *Stalingrad*] it, however
3. *from that of his*] than in Hitler's
4. Daylight bombing was undertaken by the U.S. Air Force and night bombing by the RAF. This item may refer to a force of one hundred U.S. bombers that attacked industrial plants at Lille on 9 October. According to *2194 Days of War*, of the German planes that attempted to intercept this force, a hundred were destroyed or damaged (292). Although northern France was being raided during the day, daylight bombing of Germany was making slow progress. Churchill records that in discussions with General Ira C. Eaker, commander of U.S. Eighth

Air Force Bomber Command, in January 1943, Eaker put the case for a daylight programme with forceful 'earnestness.' Churchill complained that despite there being 20,000 men and 500 planes in East Anglia 'not a single bomb had been dropped on Germany.' However, as Churchill writes, the American plan 'soon began to pay dividends' (*The Second World War*, IV, 608–09; U.S.: *The Hinge of Fate*, 678–80).

5. This figure was later revised to 56; the RAF lost 23 planes (*2194 Days of War*, 74).
6. *Tientsin*] Pekin
7. *and*] within which

1560. Bengali Newsletter, 13

10 October 1942

The English original was written by Orwell. No script has been traced. PasB suggests timing of 11′ 45″.

1561. To E. M. Forster

10 October 1942   PP/EB/NP

Dear Forster,

Many thanks for your script—I thoroughly enjoyed reading it. It has now been typed, and I enclose a copy, together with a copy of last month's talk.

The dates that have been fixed in our new schedule for your next talks are November 11th and December 9th—we haven't yet planned any further ahead, but your talks will follow on, every fourth Wednesday, as usual. If these dates don't happen to suit you, we can always record the talks beforehand, at any time you happen to be in London, although of course it's much nicer to have it direct.

You can certainly have your full time at the mike, there is no question of Lady Grigg's programme encroaching on your time, unless, of course, you under-run, and then Lady Grigg follows straight on in the usual way.

Yours,
George Orwell
Talks Producer
Indian Section

1562. War-time Diary

10.10.42:   *Today in honour of the anniversary of the Chinese Revolution the Chinese flag was hoisted over Broadcasting House. Unfortunately it was upside down.*

[According to D. A., Cripps is going to resign shortly—pretext, that the War Cabinet is a sham, Churchill being in reality the sole power in it.]

11.10.42:   *The authorities in Canada have now chained up a number of*

German prisoners equal to the number of British prisoners chained up in Germany. What the devil are we coming to?[1]

1. The Germans chained some 2,500 Allied prisoners (mainly Canadian) taken at Dieppe because they claimed that British Commandos had chained their German prisoners. The British War Office denied this. Canada then manacled 1,376 German prisoners. On 15 October, the Swiss Red Cross offered to mediate. See Orwell's (unpublished) letter to *The Times*, 12 October 1942, *1564*. On 18 October, Hitler ordered German troops to shoot all captured Allied Commandos 'to the last man.'

1563. Gujarati Newsletter, 33

12 October 1942

The English original was written by Orwell. No script has been traced. PasB gives timing as 10′ 11″.

1564. To the Editor of *The Times*

12 October 1942   Typewritten; carbon copy[1]   Unpublished

10A, Mortimer Crescent, N.W.6.

Sir,

May I be allowed to offer one or two reflections on the British Government's decision to retaliate against German prisoners, which seems so far to have aroused extraordinarily little protest?

By chaining up German prisoners in response to similar action by the Germans, we descend, at any rate in the eyes of the ordinary observer, to the level of our enemies. It is unquestionable when one thinks of the history of the past ten years, that there *is* a deep moral difference between democracy and Fascism, but if we go on the principle of an eye for an eye and a tooth for a tooth we simply cause that difference to be forgotten. Moreover, in the matter of ruthlessless we are unlikely to compete successfully with our enemies. As the Italian radio has just proclaimed, the Fascist principle is two eyes for an eye and a whole set of teeth for one tooth. At some point or another public opinion in England will flinch from the implications of this statement, and it is not very difficult to foresee what will happen. As a result of our action the Germans will chain up more British prisoners, we shall have to follow suit by chaining up more Axis prisoners, and so it will continue till logically all the prisoners on either side will be in chains. In practice, of course, we shall become disgusted with the process first, and we shall announce that the chaining up will now cease, leaving, almost certainly, more British than Axis prisoners in fetters. We shall thus have acted both barbarously and weakly, damaging our own good name without succeeding in terrorising the enemy.

It seems to me that the civilised answer to the German action would be something like this: "You proclaim that you are putting thousands of British prisoners in chains because some half-dozen Germans or thereabouts were temporarily tied up during the Dieppe raid. This is disgusting hypocrisy, in the first place because of your own record during the past ten years, in the second place because troops who have taken prisoners have got to secure them somehow untill° they can get them to a place of safety, and to tie men's hands in such circumstances is totally different from chaining up a helpless prisoner who is already in an internment camp. At this moment, we cannot stop you mal-treating our prisoners, though we shall probably remember it at the peace settlement, but don't fear that we shall retaliate in kind. You are Nazis, we are civilised men. This latest act of yours simply demonstrates the difference."

At this moment this may not seem a very satisfying reply, but I suggest that to anyone who looks back in three months' time, it will seem better than what we are doing at present and it is the duty of those who can keep their heads to protest before the inherently silly process of retaliation against the helpless is carried any further.

Yours truly,
George Orwell

1. The style of the date, '12th October 1942,' (Orwell would have typed 12.10.42), the address (with punctuation), and his name (in block capitals) suggests that a BBC secretary typed this letter, though it is not on BBC letterhead. It was among Orwell's papers at his death. For the chaining of prisoners, see *1562, n. 1.*

1565. To F. Kidd

12 or 13 October 1942

CAN YOU RECORD THURSDAY THREE FIFTEEN TO FOUR FIFTEEN AT TWO HUNDRED OXFORD STREET LONDON

BLAIR BROADCASTS

Dr. Kidd replied by pre-paid telegram on 13 October to say that Thursday would be convenient.

1566. To K. K. Ardaschir

13 October 1942   PP/EB/NP

Dear Ardaschir,
Your talk on the status of women in Europe has been passed for censorship with some minor cuts and I should like you to broadcast it on Tuesday October 20th, at 12.45. That means I should like you to be here by 12 o'clock on that day. I will send you a copy of the script with the cuts as soon as it has been typed and you might bring that copy along with you. Please let me know whether this will be O.K.

The other one, on President Inonu,[1] will be on November 11th. It will have to be definitely a five minute talk which may mean cutting it down a bit, but we can do that on the day.

Yours sincerely,
Eric Blair
Talks Producer
Indian Section

1. Ismet Inönü (1884–1973), Prime Minister of Turkey, 1923–24, 1925–37, and 1961–65; President, 1938–50.

1567. To R. R. Desai

13 October 1942   PP/EB

Dear Desai,
With reference to my letter of 8th October. I wonder whether you would be able to do the third talk in the series instead of the first? I think it may be better if Cedric Dover does the one on Italian Fascism, while you do the one we are calling "The June Purge". I make the change because I know from your open letter to a Nazi that you can deal with German Fascism, and I now find that Dover has made a sort of study of Italian Fascism. No doubt the title "The June Purge" is self-explanatory to some extent but I had perhaps better give you some further particulars. The second talk which Shelvankar is doing, is on the Rise of the Nazi Party and I want you in the third talk to show how the Nazis threw away their quasi-socialistic program, and came to terms with big business and the army, at any rate for the time being, by wiping out the Left Wing of the Party. I hope I shall be able to show you a copy of Shelvankar's script about ten days before yours is due to go on the air. I am sorry to have had to make this change and hope it has not put you out. Please let me know as soon as possible whether you can manage this. The date of the talk will now be 19th November, so we shall need the script by the 10th.[1]

Yours sincerely,
Eric Blair

1. This was Orwell's last letter to Aberystwyth; Desai returned to Cambridge where he had been evacuated. This facilitated attempts to arrange for him to listen to Gujarati broadcasts by All-India Radio, monitored by the BBC at Stratton Street, London. Between 13 and 22 October, Miss Blackburn made arrangements with Major Ferguson of the Monitoring Unit for Desai to listen-in. The first appointment was for Sunday, 25 October, and Desai was allowed his fare and a night's subsistence.

1568. BBC Talks Booking Form, 13.10.42

K. K. Ardaschir: two talks: 1. 13-minute talk on Women of the West; 2. 5-minute talk on President Inonu°; broadcast. 1. 20.10.42; 2. 11.11.42; fee 1. £9.9;

2. £4.4. Signed: M Blackburn for I.P.O. Remarks: 1. replaces cancelled talk, Film Commentary; 2. goes into period 'Topic of the Week' with Telkar. 'N.B. Mr. Ardaschir has moved.'

1569. BBC Talks Booking Form, 13.10.42

Dr Franklin Kidd: 'Science and the People,' 1; fortnightly series; 13½-minute talk on dehydration; recorded 15.10.42; broadcast 20.10.42; fee £9.9s + 12s 0d fares from Cambridge. Signed: M Blackburn for I.P.O.

1570. Extract from Minutes of Eastern Service Meeting

14 October 1942

COMPETITIONS

Sub-committee, comprising Mr. E. A. Blair (convener), Mr. Firth, Mr. Davenport and Mr. Ashraf, to meet in Room 314, Oxford Street, at 4 p.m. on 21st October, to explore possibilities of drama and poetry competitions. Mr. Brander to cable Ahmed Ali for feeling in India towards such competitions.

1571. To Eastern Service Director

15 October 1942   CONFIDENTIAL; Typewritten; original   EB/NP

Weekly News Commentary

With reference to the suggestion that I should write and broadcast the weekly news review in English over my own name, i.e. George Orwell. The four speakers who are at present doing this in rotation have contracts up to November 7th, after which I will gladly take this on. But there are one or two points which it would be better to define clearly beforehand.

If I broadcast as George Orwell I am as it were selling my literary reputation, which so far as India is concerned probably arises chiefly from books of anti-imperialist tendency, some of which have been banned in India. If I gave broadcasts which appeared to endorse unreservedly the policy of the British government I should quite soon be written off as "one more renegade" and should probably miss my potential public, at any rate among the student population. I am not thinking about my personal reputation, but clearly we should defeat our own object in these broadcasts if I could not preserve my position as an independent and more or less "agin° the government" commentator. I would therefore like to be sure in advance that I can have reasonable freedom of speech. I think this weekly commentary is only likely to be of value if I can make it from an anti-fascist rather than imperialist standpoint and avoid mention of subjects on which I could not conscientiously agree with current Government policy.

I do not think this is likely to cause trouble, as the chief difficulty is over Indian internal politics, which we rarely mention in our weekly news commentaries. These commentaries have always followed what is by implication a "left" line, and in fact have contained very little that I would not sign with my own name. But I can imagine situations arising in which I should have to say that I could not in honesty do the commentary for that week, and I should like the position to be defined in advance.

[Signed] Eric Blair
(Eric Blair)

Orwell's memorandum was sent by Rushbrook Williams, the Eastern Service Director, to R. A. Rendall, Assistant Controller, Overseas Service, with this handwritten note:

Confidential

Subject: "George Orwell" to broadcast?

Mr Brander [see *1546, n. 1*] has suggested that as Blair does in effect write the News Commentary for India (weekly) he should deliver it himself and thus enable us to 'cash in' on the popularity of "George Orwell" in India. I mentioned this to Mr Blair, and the result is this characteristically honest and straightforward note.

On the points that Mr Blair raises, I see no difficulty in practice. He and I can, by discussion, always arrange a *modus vivendi*. In fact, I feel strongly inclined to try the experiment.

Is there any difficulty about a Corporation employee broadcasting under a pen-name? [If the matter has to be referred to the Establishment side, may I suggest that Blair's memo. should *not* be forwarded? It was written for my own eye (and I know he would like you to see it also): but to people who do not know him as you and I do, it might be misleading!]¹

LFRW
15/10

This note was annotated and initialled in a hand that has not been identified. The initials cannot be made out; the annotation is in pencil and has partially faded. The second and third points are fairly clear but the word after 'safeguard' and the penultimate word of the first point are uncertain. The first initial seems to be 'G'; the third note suggests that the annotator was a senior member of the BBC's staff. 'G. of I.' = Government of India.

1. G. of I. safeguard. everything subversive about banned books waive ban. G [?]
2. No difficulty about pen name.
3. Not as BBC staff

On 23 October, Rendall wrote to Rushbrook Williams following his discussion with the Controller of the Overseas Service, J. B. Clark:

I have discussed this matter with C(O.S). There is no difficulty about a member of the Corporation staff broadcasting under a pen name, but he should not be announced or billed as a member of the Corporation staff, and the normal conditions about staff contributions to programmes should apply.

C(O.S.) suggests, however, that in this instance it would be advisable to make sure—presumably through the India Office—that the Government of India are not going to raise objections to broadcasts by a man whose books they have banned. The propaganda advantages of Orwell's name are obvious and I should hope[2] they would be appreciated.

This was annotated by Rushbrook Williams on 29 October and sent back to Rendall for the Controller, J. B. Clark:

I have consulted Mr Joyce[3] and his colleagues, and they feel that it would be useful to take advantage of "Orwell's" name.

In view of the fact that several people whose books have fallen under the displeasure of the G. of I. do in effect speak for us, and that their contributions are appreciated, Mr Joyce feels it would be a mistake to refer the matter specifically to the G. of I. If *asked*, the G. of I might feel called upon to adopt a critical attitude. If the question [is] not raised, Mr Joyce thinks they are very unlikely to object!

Clark replied on the verso to Rendall on 2 November:

In view of ESD's [Rushbrook Williams's] note, I fully agree—at least as an experiment (as R. W. suggests in his minute of 15/X). I would like to know of any signs of reaction—official or personal.[4]

Rendall then passed this note to Rushbrook Williams, and Orwell read his first Newsletter on 21 November 1942 (there being no broadcast on 14 November; see *1671*).

1. The square brackets are in the original.
2. hope] think; *handwritten amendment of typed note by Rendall*
3. Alec Houghton Joyce (see *426, n. 1*) was at this time Information Officer, India Office. Orwell had written to him on 12 February 1938 regarding the proposal that he work for the Indian weekly paper the *Pioneer; see 426.*
4. No reaction is reported on the files traced.

1572. To Sidney Horniblow
      15 October 1942   PP/EB/ED[1]

Dear Mr. Horniblow,
I want to thank you for all your help and cooperation over the series "In Black and White", for which we were most grateful.

At present there is no possibility of continuing the series, as we are booked up for some months, but I will certainly bear you in mind and get in touch with you again when I see an opportunity of producing another similar programme.[2]

Yours sincerely,
(Eric Blair)
Talks Assistant

1. The style of typing of this letter is quite different from that of Orwell's regular secretaries and the typewriter fount is much smaller. 'ED' has not been identified with certainty, but there was a Miss E. Dunstan, secretary to the Director of Overseas Presentation (T. W. Chalmers) in the Staff List dated 21.8.43.
2. Orwell appears to have had nothing to do with arrangements for 'In Black and White.' Much correspondence passed between Bokhari (and Miss Blackburn after he left for India), Miss Alexander of the Copyright Department, and Miss Boughen of Talks Booking regarding the fee to be paid. It had been assumed that the programme was all original material, so a fee of £12.12s would be appropriate. But Bokhari explained on 9 September 1942 that it was a compilation programme, intended to give 'a fair and accurate impression of the leading newspapers.' The fee was reduced to £10.10s for the last two programmes. In Bokhari's absence, it was left to Orwell to end Horniblow's engagement.

1573. War-time Diary

15.10.42: *A little bit of India transplanted to England. For some weeks our Marathi newsletters were translated and broadcast by a little man named Kothari, completely spherical but quite intelligent and, so far as I could judge, genuinely anti-Fascist. Suddenly one of the mysterious bodies which[1] control recruitment for the BBC (in this case I think MI 5)[2] got onto the fact that Kothari was or had been a Communist, active in the students' movement, and had been in jail, so the order came to get rid of him. A youth named Jatha, working at India House and politically OK, was engaged in his place. Translators in this language are not easy to find and Indians who speak it as their native tongue seem to tend to forget it while in England. After a few weeks my assistant, Miss Chitale, came to me with great secrecy and[3] confided that the newsletters were still in fact being written by Kothari. Jatha, though still able to read the language, was no longer equal to writing it and Kothari was ghosting for him. No doubt the fee was being split between them. We can't find another competent translator, so Kothari is to continue and we officially know nothing about it. Wherever Indians are to be found, this kind of thing will be happening.*

1. *which*] who
2. This is presumably a reference to the mysterious 'College' to which Orwell refers from time to time; see *845*.
3. The manuscript of 'Volume III' of the Diary ends at this point, followed by '(continued in Vol. IV).' The conclusion of this entry and the entries for 7 October and 15 November 1942 are reproduced from the typescript only. The reference to a fourth volume in the manuscript implies that what has just been completed is a third volume. The manuscript opens without a volume heading at 14.3.4 (see *1025*); the typescript has as its heading, 'WAR DIARY (continued).' There is no indication in either manuscript or typescript that the Diary from 14.2.42 to 15.10.42 is made up of more than a single volume. It looks as if Orwell thought he

was here completing a third, not a second, volume. No 'fourth' volume has been traced. The volume that continued the manuscript may have completed only the entry at 15.10.42 (as found in the typescript), and those of 17.10.42; see (*1583*) and 15.11.42 (*1658*).

1574. Story by Five Authors

Through Eastern Eyes, 16 October 1942

Part 2 by L. A. G. Strong

Gilbert Moss swung his club, and coldly eyed his enemy's head. Though with so heavy a weapon it did not matter where he struck—the sheer weight of the wood must smash in the skull—yet he chose a place with his eyes. He would strike exactly: the deliberate blow of an artist, certain of his aim, exacting vengeance: not a blind, clumsy, resentful smash.

His grip on the club was not right. He shifted his hands, until the balance was good and the great sullen mass of wood swung smoothly. Now! Now, Charles Coburn! now you're going to get it. The only pity is, you'll never know who gave it to you. You'll never know it was Gilbert Moss—Mister Moss, as you were so careful to call him in public, in case any of your friends might for an instant suppose you knew him socially. The remembrance of the humiliations which had been put upon him rose in a red mist. He uttered a strangled cry of rage and pain, and swung the club up wildly, but his hands were shaking so much that it fell with a thud on one of the broken pieces of wood by the unconscious man's head, causing the head to jerk idiotically upwards and fall again. Gilbert could not tell whether it was his own eyes or a trick of the light from the burning beams, but for a moment he thought the eyelids flickered and the colour of the face changed. Steady, you idiot! Steady! You're imagining things.

Gilbert was sweating now, sweating and shaking all over. What a fool he had been to delay. A couple of minutes ago, his resolve was firm, he was cold and impersonal, an executor of absolute justice. Now he had let himself be worked up into a state. He'd always despised Hamlet for missing that chance of killing his uncle, by stopping to philosophise. Hamlet had been weak, and was only finding excuses for his weakness. Here was he now, Gilbert Moss, with his training as a scientist—yes: that had been another of Coburn's sneers, blast him, inferring by his tone that a laboratory assistant was not a scientist but just a menial, a bottle-washer; getting all that into the word scientist: how *did* they get those implications, those overtones of patronage, damn them, *damn* them!—here was he, Gilbert Moss, hesitating, dithering, telling himself that a vengeance was no vengeance if the victim never knew who struck him: that for all Coburn would know he might have been killed by the bomb that blew him where he lay.

A burning beam twenty feet away fell with a crash, making Gilbert jump. The flames flared up, lighting the unconscious face on the ground, and sent strange shadows chasing across it. In the new light, it seemed to wear a smile of disdain. "Excellent", the Honourable Charles Coburn seemed to be saying, "excellent. Hit a man when he can't defend himself. Splendid, Moss, splendid". Not Mister Moss when they were alone—oh, dear no. Moss—as if he were a footman.

"Well", Gilbert said, between his teeth. "You've put it across me for the last time. Smile away. We'll see how you'll smile after this".

Savagely he swung the club. So heavy was it, it swung too far, and all but jerked him off his feet. Panting, steadying himself, he made to raise it again, and stopped—just in time. In front of him, clear in the dancing light, a man stood, staring at him.

Gilbert let the end of the club fall, and stood, leaning on it, staring back. The man said nothing. He continued to look at Gilbert. His face was blank, but beneath its blankness Gilbert could see, even in this light, something calculating, nervous, alert: the face of one loitering with intent when a policeman suddenly walks round the corner. The hardships of the last few years had taught Gilbert a thing or two about the niceties of facial expression.

The man's eyes left Gilbert, almost casually, and looked past him. Then they came back again. He passed his tongue across his lower lip, and spoke.

"Ullo, mate".

Gilbert cleared his throat. His voice, when it came, sounded to him stilted and pedantic.

"Hullo".

The man moved a step nearer. He was looking around quickly now, but without moving his head.

"Wotcher doin'? Tryin' to bust somethink open?"

Gilbert thought in a flash—he hasn't seen. Coburn might be hidden from where he was standing. Then he realised that he wasn't answering the man's question, and that it was unpleasantly apt. His answer came before he had time to consider it.

"Well—yes, in a way".

As he spoke, he looked on the ground, to see if there were any object he might conceivably have been trying to batter open.

"Can I give you a 'and?"

He had come closer. Shabby, clean-shaven, long upper lip, a muffler round his neck—still he wasn't looking at Gilbert. His little eyes were taking stock of everything round about—quick, accomplished eyes, the eyes of a pickpocket or a tout, the predatory, hunted eyes of a man who lived by his wits, and didn't live well.

"I don't think so, thanks".

"Please yourself. Sure? Two's better than one—sometimes".

He was eyeing the club now—a slanting glance from under his eyelids. He edged closer. Before Gilbert could stop himself, he heard his voice cry out in nervous exasperation.

"Leave me alone. What are you doing here?"

The outcry produced no visible effect. The stranger, still glancing about him, came closer still.

"All right, mate. No offence. No bones broke. Come to that, wotcher doin' 'ere yourself?"

There was no threat in the words, and he did not look at Gilbert as he said them.

"I? I just . . . found myself here".

"Just dropped in, like, for a social call. To see an old pal, per'aps. 'E don't seem to know yer very well—does 'e?"

Gilbert drew himself up. "As a matter of fact", he said, "he does. Too well".

The newcomer raised his brows. The whites of his eyes showed alarmingly in the light of the flames.

"Like that, eh? Wot'd 'e give yer the sack for?"

Gilbert started as if he had been hit. This assumption on the part of the shabby stranger of the relationship between him and Coburn, this making of him into an inferior—he all but choked with fury. A wild impulse seized him to hit out with his club. Then the heat left his brain, and a swift flood of cunning rushed in. How much *had* the stranger seen? What gave him the confidence to be so familiar?

"I don't know what you mean", he said, as steadily as he could. "I've never been here before".

"I see. Just club mates, you and 'im. Ascot—Royal Enclosure. I get yer".

Gilbert's dry lips stretched in a grin. "You won't believe me, of course. But I do know him. And he never employed me—much less gave me the sack. Still, it doesn't matter whether you believe me or not, does it?"

"No. And it don't matter whether you was usin' that little stick to pick yer teef wiv. Oh, all right, mate—don't look crooked. What you're doin' is no business o' mine. What I'm doin' is no business o' yours. I only thought, seeing we was both 'ere, we might 'ave a look together, like".

"What are you looking for?"

It was a silly question, but the stranger did not seem to mind.

"Well, you know—when a thing like this 'appens, yer might find a tin o' this layin' about, or a jar o' that. No good to the people wot lived 'ere; quite useful to the likes o' you and me. Pity to leave it layin' about, to be picked up by chaps as mightn't want it partic'lar".

"I see".

"Wot say—shall we 'ave a look round?"

"I don't think so. I'm not interested in—er—tins and jars. Don't let me stop you, though".

"*I'm* not interested in wot's in blokes' pockets: but don't let me stop *you*."

Gilbert opened his mouth to speak, and shut it again. He *had* taken a lighter from Coburn's pocket, even though he had put it back again. How much had the fellow seen?

"All right. I'll help you, if you like".

He hadn't intended to say that. It slipped out.

"Don't put yerself out".

The stranger was exploring now, kicking at heaps of debris, testing piles of rubble, brushing dust aside with a sweeping motion of his sleeve.

"Now then. You two want anything?"

A Special. He'd loomed up from nowhere. The firelight leaped and danced, made him look bigger than he was. Gilbert coughed and stammered. Before he could find anything to say, the stranger had replied.

"Yes, Guv'nor. We're lookin' for a nice smooth plank. A bit o' floor-boardin' 'd do".

"What d'ye want that for?"

"'Orace". He jerked his thumb at the figure on the ground. The constable started. He hadn't seen Coburn. Gilbert spoke.

"A warden was along here just now, and he thought the man was dead. So did I. But he isn't".

"Oh".

It was plain the constable did not believe them, but could not quite make up his mind what to do. He made a rumbling sound in his throat, as a preparation for speech, when suddenly Gilbert saw, passing close behind him in what remained of the street, the man he had pulled out of the wreckage—how long before?—he couldn't say: the man, with the woman holding the child's hand.

"Hullo!" he called. "You all right now?"

The man turned, and stared vaguely. He couldn't see against the light. He seemed shocked still, and bewildered.

"Excuse me", Gilbert said, and pushed past the Special. "Is he all right?" he asked the woman loudly.

"Yes. Yes. We're all right now—thanks to you". She saw the constable, and pointed to Gilbert. "He's a brave chap, he is. Pulled Fred out from under all sorts. Ought to 'ave the George Medal".

The constable was suddenly convinced. "He's found another here", he said.

"That's like 'im", said the woman. "Ought to 'ave the George Medal. Come on, Fred. It ain't far now".

"I'll see if I can find a stretcher-bearer". The constable gave a nod, and moved off after the trio.

"Nice work". Gilbert's associate in misdemeanour was bending over Coburn. "Your college chum 'ere 'as opened 'is little eyes. Come and see if 'e reckonises yer".

Gilbert came to where Coburn lay, and bent down. The handsome face was foolish with returning consciousness.

"Go on. Arsk 'im if 'e knows yer", said the stranger, mockingly.

"Well, Coburn. Know me?"

"Can't say I—oh yes. Good Lord! Moss!"

"Yes. Moss."

"Good. Nice to see a familiar face".

"You think so, do you."

"Decidedly. Come on—lend a hand, there's a good chap".

"I don't think I will." He turned to the stranger, who was watching with narrowed eyes. "Do you know what this man did to me? Shall I tell him—Coburn? I will".

Continued by Inez Holden; see *1606*. For Part 1, see *1558*.

1575. To Martin Armstrong
[16 October 1942?]

Martin Armstrong wrote to Orwell on 15 October asking for precise details of the five-part story to which he was to contribute the fourth instalment on 30 October 1942. His letter is annotated by Orwell, 'Answered 16.10.42.' This telegram seems to be that response. See also Orwell's letter to Armstrong of 17 October, *1581*. The Monday referred to in the telegram was the 19th.

INSTRUCTIONS AND SCRIPTS WILL REACH YOU MONDAY
ORWELL BROADCASTS

1576. To Eric Barnard[1]
16 October 1942   PP/EB/NP

Dear Sir,
I am enclosing a copy of a talk by Dr. Franklin Kidd, on the subject of dehydrated food. The talk, which was recorded yesterday, is scheduled to be broadcast on Tuesday next, October 20th.
I should be most grateful if you will let me know whether the talk is satisfactory as it stands, or whether you would like to suggest any changes.

Yours truly,
Eric Blair
Talks Producer
Indian Section

1. Dr. Eric Barnard (1891–1980; DSO, 1917; CB, 1951) served as Deputy Secretary, Department of Scientific and Industrial Research, 1945–55. He replied to Orwell on 17 October, stating that the Department had no changes it wished to propose. When he wrote, Orwell did not know Barnard's first name.

1577. To J. C. Drummond
16 October 1942   PP/EB

Dear Professor Drummond,
You may remember that you suggested to me that Dr. Franklin Kidd might be willing to give a talk in the Indian Service of the BBC, on the subject of dehydrated food. Dr. Kidd very kindly agreed to do the talk, which was

recorded yesterday. He tells me that you wish to have a copy of the script, which I am enclosing herewith. This talk will be broadcast on Tuesday next, October 20th. I should be most grateful if you will let me know whether the talk is satisfactory as it stands, or whether you would like to suggest any changes.[1]

Yours sincerely,
Eric Blair
Talks Producer
Indian Section

1. Professor Drummond replied on 17 October 1942 that he had already told the Department of Scientific and Industrial Research that the talk was satisfactory as it stood.

1578. To T. S. Eliot

16 October 1942   PP/EB/NP

Dear Eliot,

I wonder if you would like to take part in a programme on Tuesday November 3rd. We have a magazine number once a month which is called "Voice" and pretends to be a magazine in broadcast form. Where it is possible we try to get poets to read their own work. We usually arrange each number round a central theme and we think next time of having an American number. You are I think the only American poet at present in England, though there may perhaps be others, in which case I should be glad to hear about them. In any case we would like it very much if you would take part and read something of your own, either one or two poems taking anything up to five minutes in all. The other people who will probably be taking part are Herbert Read, William Empson, myself, and Mulk Raj Anand, though we will try to dig up some American writers if we can. Please do this if the date is at all possible for you. It will only mean giving up the morning of that particular day.

Yours sincerely,
George Orwell
Talks Producer
Indian Section

1579. News Review, 44

17 October 1942

Although not marked 'As broadcast,' the typescript for this commentary bears both censorship stamps; the censor's initials are unreadable. There are no changes to the typescript. The script was read by Homi Bode.

After a lull of some days the German attacks on Stalingrad have been resumed and appear to have made some progress. The German High Command seem to have realised that they cannot take the town by direct infantry assault, and to have been waiting until they could bring up more artillery and dive-bombers in order to make a preliminary bombardment. Evidently they are now using the very big guns which they used in the capture of Sebastopol. The effect of artillery such as this is worse even than air bombing and the heroic defenders of Stalingrad may have before them an even more terrible ordeal than that of the last two months. On the other hand, two facts should be mentioned which justify some degree of optimism. The first is that the Russian defenders of Stalingrad are in a very much better position than those of Sebastopol since they have not got their backs to the sea and can fairly easily be supplied and reinforced. The other is the fact demonstrated in the last war that it is difficult even for the heaviest concentration of artillery fire to drive out defenders who have had time, as the Russians have had in this case, to fortify their position thoroughly. It is possible that Stalingrad may yet fall, but the German change of plan so late in the year is a confession of at least partial failure.

Evidence accumulates that the Germans are now thinking in terms of a merely limited victory. They are talking of their impregnable position on the Atlantic coast and of the power Europe has to be self-sufficient in food and raw materials when scientifically organised. The picture which is being drawn by German journalists and broadcasters is of Europe as a vast fortress containing in itself all the necessities of life and invulnerable to any attack from outside. Within this fortress, of course, the German people will be the master race, and the other European peoples will be reduced to varying degrees of serfdom. No doubt the main object of this new turn in German propaganda is to reconcile the German people to a prospect of endless war and at the same time to persuade the Allies that further attacks are useless. It must be admitted, however, that the picture of Europe as a huge self-contained slave camp is not altogether fanciful. Such an arrangement could be made to work, always provided that it were not assailed from the outside and that there were no serious resistance within. But the ever-increasing British air attacks, the growing strength of the Allied Armies and the increasing discontent and sabotage among the conquered peoples suggest that both these expectations will be disappointed. During this week there has been news of fresh trouble for the German invaders in France, Norway and Jugoslavia.[1] In the latter country guerilla fighting is continuous and all attempts to crush the Serbian patriot forces under General Mihailovitch[2] have failed. In Norway, the quisling administration has been a miserable failure and it is hardly even pretended that it represents the will of the people. In France, the attempt to get together a large draft of volunteers to work in Germany has also failed; the Germans demanded 150,000 men, and though as a bribe they offered to release a corresponding number of war prisoners, only a few thousands have volunteered.[3] The conquered people of Europe have by this time fully grasped the hollowness of the so-called 'New Order', and though the Germans may still hold millions of men as slaves, they have probably lost all chance of obtaining their willing cooperation.[4]

As we foretold earlier the Japanese are making very determined efforts to recapture the islands in the Solomons occupied by the Americans. They are directing their attacks particularly against the island of Guadalcanal, where the Americans hold a port and an airfield from which they can attack Japanese shipping with land-based aeroplanes. During the past week the Japanese have landed various detachments of men on the south side of Guadalcanal under cover of darkness. Four days ago they attempted a landing on a large scale and received very severe damage in a naval action. A Japanese cruiser and four destroyers were sunk. Other warships were damaged and the United States losses were only one destroyer. On the following day the sinking of another Japanese cruiser by submarine action was announced.[5] Since then, however, the Japanese have made a fresh landing and appear to have succeeded in bringing artillery ashore. Fierce attacks both from land and sea are being made on the American-held airfields. The Americans expect to be able to hold their positions, but do not disguise the fact that there is a hard struggle ahead. The Australian advance in Central New Guinea is still continuing and for some time past little opposition has been met with. No one knows why but it is thought possible that the Japanese are withdrawing troops from this area in order to use them in the Solomons. The Americans meanwhile have occupied two more small islands in the Solomons group. So long as the Americans are there, the Japanese position in New Guinea and indeed their whole position in the Southern Pacific, is in great danger and we must therefore expect further heavy fighting in this area. The Americans have also occupied another island in the Aleutian Archipelago, without encountering opposition.

The Germans have renewed their heavy air attacks on Malta, and during the past week no less than 103 German planes have been shot down there. The probable reason for this renewal of the attacks on Malta is that the successful work of the R.A.F. and the allied submarines in the Eastern Mediterranean makes it difficult for the Germans to use the ports of Tobruk and Benghazi. They are once again compelled to bring their supplies from Italy to Tripoli and it is necessary from their point of view that Malta should be immobilised if possible. The fact that they are willing to lose aeroplanes at the present rate suggests that they are bringing, or are about to bring, large reinforcements to Africa. In any case a renewal of fighting on the Egyptian front is to be expected in the near future. Three Axis supply ships have been sunk in the Mediterranean during the past week, and several others damaged.

950 French soldiers from the garrison of Madagascar have joined General de Gaulle. Those taken prisoner were given the alternative of joining de Gaulle or of being repatriated to Vichy France. Only a very few chose the latter alternative, the great majority preferring to continue the fight at the side of the Allies. This is yet another sign of the contempt and loathing in which the Vichy regime is held by nearly all classes of Frenchmen.

German propagandists in the Press and on the wireless are putting out persistent rumours that the British and Americans are about to attack Dakar in French West Africa. The Vichy wireless has just announced that the commander of the French air forces at Dakar has been killed, probably in a reconnaissance flight over British territory. These rumours should not be altogether ignored, because they probably mean that the Germans are seeking a further pretext for aggressive action against French West Africa, on which they have had designs for years past.

1. There were also disturbances in Denmark. On 11 October the arrival on leave of Danish Nazi volunteers from the Russian front led to protests in Copenhagen. Troops opened fire and eleven people were injured. See *1343, n.1.*
2. Draža Mihailović (1893?–1946) led Serbian guerrillas (the Chetniks) against Axis forces in World War II. The Yugoslav government-in-exile promoted him to general and made him Minister of War, but he was opposed by Marshal Tito and his guerrilla forces (the Partisans). Accused of collaborating with the Axis, he was dismissed by King Peter of Yugoslavia, and Allied support was withdrawn. Captured by the Partisans in 1946, he was tried for treason and executed, 17 July, despite worldwide protests, in which Orwell was to join.
3. In Lyons, only 15 of 700 workers selected for shipment to Germany had volunteered, and on 15 October, 3,000 workers struck in protest. On 17 October, a general strike was threatened to protest against German recruitment policy.
4. Some 130,000 Frenchmen were conscripted into the Wehrmacht in the summer of 1942. They were called the *malgré-nous*, the unwilling soldiers. Most fought on the Russian front. Some 20,000 were killed, 15,000 captured. Most of the latter suffered extreme privation and many died at Camp 188, Tambov, some 300 miles south of Moscow. Survivors were returned to France (mainly to Alsace and Lorraine) in the autumn of 1945, and suffered another year of detention. See Pierre Rigoulet, *La Tragédie des Malgré-Nous* (Paris, 1990).
5. At night on 11 October 1942, the U.S. Navy caught a Japanese naval force by surprise off Savo Island in the Solomons (the Battle of Cape Esperance). It was claimed at the time that three Japanese cruisers and five destroyers were sunk in half an hour. In fact, Japanese losses were one cruiser and one destroyer; the United States lost one destroyer, as Orwell reports.

1580. News in Bengali,[1] 14

17 October 1942

The English original was written by Orwell. No script has been traced.

1. This title is an error for the usual 'Newsletter'; the news proper was prepared and transmitted by a separate division of the Overseas Service. Though generally reliable, the PasBs cannot be depended upon implicitly.

1581. To Martin Armstrong

17 October 1942   PP/EB

Dear Mr. Armstrong,
I send you herewith the three previous instalments of the story. I'd have sent them a day or two earlier, but I was hesitating about the third one,[1] which does not seem to be very good, and it does not carry on the story or rather gives it a twist in another direction. However, as you say you work slowly I thought it better to send them along at once, rather than get this instalment re-written. Your instalment is the fourth and should therefore bring the story within sight of a climax. You will see that both the second and the third

contributors have passed on the baby by not explaining what was the cause of the quarrel, between the two men introduced in the first chapter. I don't want of course to dictate what you are to say, but I think your contribution should certainly make this clear and then end in some way that will make a climax possible. You are on[2] October 30th, so if I can have yours by the 25th at the very latest, I should be obliged.[3] The time is 13½ minutes, which generally means about 15 hundred words. On the day of the broadcast will you come to 200, Oxford Street at 11.30 which will give us time for rehearsal before the broadcast which is at 12.15.

Yours sincerely,
George Orwell
Talks Producer
Indian Section

1. By Inez Holden.
2. on] 'on the on' *was typed*
3. Armstrong sent his section, Part 4, on 22 October, and on 27 October he sent a revised version, cut to time.

1582. To Stevie Smith

17 October 1942   PP/EB

Dear Stevie[1]

I don't know what you are grizzling about! I told you a long time back that we hoped you would take part in that programme and gave you the date verbally. We then picked the poems you were to read and you typed out a copy and sent it to me. A few days before the broadcast, my secretary sent a P.C. reminding you of the date and time, to the only address of yours which she had. I suppose the fact was that the address which you had previously given us was actually Inez's. My secretary did not know that you worked at Newne's°until I told her so on the actual morning of the broadcast. I assumed that you knew all about it and merely sent the P.C. as a formality.

I am sorry about this, but the programme went off all right and Read read your poem quite nicely.

Yours
Eric Blair
(Talks Assistant)

1. Stevie Smith (Florence Margaret Smith, 1902–1971), poet, novelist, essayist, and friend of Orwell, was to have read her own work in 'Voice,' 3, 6 October, but did not appear for the broadcast. On 14 October, she sent Orwell poems in proof with a comic-irate note expressing her annoyance that she had not been informed about the broadcast. This is Orwell's reply; it brought an angry response which said that Orwell was 'the most persistent liar and these fibs are always coming back to me from other people.' She also said she had not been given the broadcast date, Orwell had not breathed a word about her reading her own poem, and that she had not given him Holden's address 'as she was on the point of leaving.' Her letter is included in *Me Again: Uncollected Writings*, edited by Jack Barbera and William McBrien (1981, 284). Their biography, *Stevie*, was published in 1987, and her *Collected Poems*, edited by James MacGibbon, in 1975; reprinted, Penguin Twentieth-Century Classics, 1985.

1583. War-time Diary

17.10.42: Heard a "Jew joke" on the stage at the Players' theatre last night—a mild one, and told by a Jew, but still slightly anti-Jew in tendency.
More Second Front rumours. The date this time is given as October 20th, an unlikely date, being a Tuesday.[1] It seems pretty clear that something is going to happen in West or North-west Africa, however.

1. A Tuesday, but 6 June 1944, was the day of the Normandy landings (D-Day).

1584. 'Answering You,' 65

BBC, London; Mutual Broadcasting System, New York; 18 October 1942

The extracts from this two-way broadcast give only Orwell's contributions, in context. There are gaps in the transcript (represented by ellipses) where, presumably, what was said could not be heard to be transcribed; there is no indication that the censor cut anything. The programme was purportedly repeated on 19 October in North American and Eastern Services, but not recorded in PasB.

NEW YORK STUDIO	LONDON STUDIO
Master of Ceremonies	Master of Ceremonies
Peter Donald, radio	Colin Wills
raconteur "Can you top this?"	
Speakers	*Speakers*
Howard Dietz, playwright	George Strauss, M.P.
Madame Lee Ya Ching,	George Orwell, author of
Chinese woman pilot	"Down and Out in Paris and London"
Pat Mulhearne, editor of	Commander Pauline Gower, A.T.A.
'Hobo News'	Aircraftwoman Dean, W.A.A.F.
	W. Vaughan Thomas of "John Londoner"

ANNOUNCER: This is London, England. And you're about to hear the British programme "Answering You" — 65th edition. Again questioners in a New York Studio address themselves directly to speakers in London and they are ready and waiting with our Master of Ceremonies, Mr. Colin Wills, Australian War Commentator.

After the introductions, Pat Mulhearne asked the first question:

MULHEARNE: After the first war General Pershing said that the American hobo was one of the best fighters under his command. He said that they can march further with a pack on their back, they could go for days without anything to eat, they could sleep in a 'bus, car or a trench—it didn't make any difference. And what is the British military opinion of this?

WILLS: Well Pat we haven't got any British military leaders right here in the studio but we've got a fellow who's a Sergeant in the Home Guard—you know what that is. This Sergeant is George Orwell. He's also a bit of a poet and he's been a bit of a hobo in the English way. So George, will you tell him how the British hobo—if you can define such a person— gets on in the war.

ORWELL: Well you've got to remember that in England the whole set-up is a bit different. There isn't that big hobo community here that you've got in America. The reason is at bottom that England's a very small country—I suppose it's only about as big as one of the smaller American States. It's very thickly populated, there's a policeman at every corner, you can't live that sort of wild, free life found in . . . novels and so on. Of course that type exists in England but they generally tend to emigrate to Australia or Canada or somewhere. You see, people going on the road—as they call it here in England—is generally a direct result of poverty, particularly unemployment. The time when that population on the road was biggest in England was during the slump years when I suppose there were not less than a hundred thousand people living that sort of life in England. But I'm afraid that by American standards you'd find it a very peaceful, harmless, dull existence. They're extremely law-abiding and their life really consists of going from one casual ward to another, eat a very unpleasant meal of bread and margarine, sleep on a hard bed and go on to the next.

MULHEARNE: But how about their fighting qualities?

ORWELL: Well it's quite true that some of the best regiments in the British Army, particularly the Highland regiments—the Scotch regiments—are recruited from very poor quarters of big towns such as Glasgow. But not, I should have thought, from what you could possibly call the derelict community.

DONALD: Well any more questions on that theme?

MULHEARNE: Question number two. The American hobo you know is basically a skilled migratory farm worker, or what you'd call an apple-knocker. Now are the English hobos skilled in farm work? And what part are the English hobos playing in this war? Are they digging up a lot of scrap over there and so forth?

WILLS: Well, George here will answer that one too I think.

ORWELL: Well I think the chief fact about them as a result of the war is that they've diminished in numbers very much—they have sort of got jobs or are in the army. There is in England that nucleus of skilled or semi-skilled migratory farm labour. For instance hop-picking, potato-picking, even sheep-shearing is done largely by that type of labour. But very largely by the gypsies. Or apart from the gypsies there's other people who are not gypsies by blood but have adopted that way of life. They travel around from farm to farm according to the seasons, working for rather low wages. They're quite an important section of the community. But I think that's been somewhat interfered with by the war because now there's all sorts of voluntary labour, also Italian prisoners, schoolboys and whatnot.

Later, Dietz asked about the democratizing effect of the war. Strauss replied at length on the theme that 'war is a great leveller,' and he quoted figures given by the Chancellor of the Exchequer that, whereas in 1938 there were 7,000 people with an income of over $24,000 net per year, there were only 80 in 1942. He concluded, 'Those modifications will go on, and as the war goes on, will get more level.' Orwell was asked to respond.

ORWELL: Well, I can't altogether agree with Strauss about the decrease in big incomes, I know that's what the statistics say but that's not what I see when on occasion I put my nose inside an expensive hotel.

WILLS: You ought to put your nose inside a British restaurant.[1]

ORWELL: . . . war, two years during which at any rate there has been a good . . .[2] in people's thoughts, is that people are still thinking in terms of what they call going back to normal after the war. For example, it's a fact that the average man working in a factory is afraid of mass unemployment after the war. I do agree with what you might call mechanical changes that have been brought about by war rationing and lack of consumption goods and so on, but that to have any real deep effect without any structural changes is dependent on the war going on for some years. I think we must conclude that a change is happening in England but it's happening in a very peaceful manner—sort of twilight sleep.

1. He was referring to officially sponsored restaurants, often in temporary quarters, which provided a basic hot meal at a very modest price.
2. The transcript is defective here.

1585. To Mulk Raj Anand

18 October 1942   EB/NP

Dear Mulk,
I am sending you a copy of the talk for Friday. I am afraid it is a bit late, but as you know, we have been very busy this week.
    I shall expect you in my office at 11.30 on Friday next.

Yours,
George Orwell
Talks Producer
Indian Section

1586. Gujarati Newsletter, 34

19 October 1942

The English original was written by Orwell. No script has been traced. PasB gives timing as approximately 10 minutes.

1587. To Desmond Hawkins

19 October 1942   PP/EB/NP

Dear Hawkins,
This is to confirm that you are doing our Anniversaries feature for us. I think we arranged this verbally. The broadcast this time is on Tuesday November 3rd, so it should be the anniversary of something occurring in November. We have looked through the list and the two which seem to me most promising are the opening of the Suez Canal in 1869 and Stanley finding Livingstone in 1871. These are the 16th and the 10th respectively. Will you let me know your ideas about this pretty soon, and we should want the script not later than October 30th. We did agree, I think, that it would be better to do a programme of this type on one event rather than on a number.

Yours,
George Orwell
Talks Producer
Indian Section

1588. To Mr. Nash

19 October 1942   PP/EB/NP

Dear Mr. Nash,[1]
This is to confirm that Sir Ramaswami Mudaliar[2] will be broadcasting in

English in the Eastern Service on Saturday, November 14th, at 12.15 B.S.T. We should like him to come to 200, Oxford Street at 11.45 a.m., which will give him time to rehearse the talk for timing before he goes on the air.

If you can let us have the script of his talk by Friday, so much the better, otherwise it will be perfectly all right if we get it by about 10.30 a.m. on the day of the broadcast.

I wonder whether Sir Ramaswami would have any objection to supplying us with some information about himself which we could use for publicity purposes. We can of course compile this ourselves, but wherever possible, we like our speakers to provide the material themselves. If he agrees, we should like to have this material by Monday, November 2nd.

We should also like to have Sir Ramaswami photographed in the studio, if he has no objection. Perhaps you will let us know about this a few days before the broadcast.

Yours sincerely,
Eric Blair
Talks Producer
Indian Section

1. Not identified.
2. A. Ramaswami Mudaliar (1887–1976; Kt., 1937), onetime Vice-Chancellor of Travancore University, held many posts of responsibility in India, among them: adviser to the Secretary of State for India, 1937–39; Commerce Member, Governor-General's Executive Council, 1939–42; representative of India at War Cabinet and Pacific War Council in London, 1942–43; member of Viceroy's Executive Council, 1942–43. He led the Indian delegation to the United Nations Conference in San Francisco in 1945, and to its first General Assembly meeting, 1946.

1589. BBC Talks Booking Form, 19.10.42

Clemence Dane: 'Women Generally Speaking'; two 13-minute talks on More Books and Reading; recorded 26.7.42 (both); broadcast 5 and 20.8.42; fee £15.15s each talk. Signed: M Blackburn for I.P.O. Remarks: 'I am sorry that the booking slip for these two talks was over-looked. Please note that the dates given above for reproduction are correct — it was originally decided to use the talks on 29.7 & 5.8 but this had to be altered.'

1590. BBC Talks Booking Form, 19.10.42 [?]

[Marked as received by Talks Booking Manager 20.10.42.] Gujarati News-letters, 32 and 33; written by E. Blair, translated and read by R. R. Desai; broadcast 5 and 12.10.42; fee £5.5s + 17s 0d expenses. Signed: M Blackburn for I.P.O.

1591. BBC Talks Booking Form, 19.10.42[?]

[Marked as received by Talks Booking Manager 20.10.42.] Gujarati Newsletter, 34; written by E. Blair, translated and read by R. R. Desai; broadcast 19.10.42; fee £5.5s + 12s 0d fare. Signed: M. Blackburn for I.P.O.

1592. To Mulk Raj Anand

20 October 1942   PP/EB

Dear Mulk,

I have written to the first four speakers in your series "A Day in My Life", confirming that they will be giving the talks, and telling them that if they can't come on the day, they can record the talk beforehand. I have also asked them to send me some publicity about themselves. You will probably be able to supplement this.

I imagine that you will write the scripts with them, and let me have a copy. In each case, we shall want the script *not later* than a week before the broadcast—in the case of Keidrich Rhys[1] and Bill Balcome,[2] we'd like the scripts earlier, because they have to be sent to the War Office and the Ministry of War Transport respectively.

When are you going to let me have the names of the other speakers? I should like some of them at least as soon as you can let me have them.

Yours,
George Orwell
Talks Producer
Indian Section

1. Keidrych Rhys (1914–1987), poet, journalist, and broadcaster, edited a number of volumes of poetry—two of servicemen's poetry and several of Welsh poetry. His *The Van Pool and Other Poems* was published in 1942. After the war he directed the Druid Press. See *1989* for his correspondence with Orwell in *Tribune* about Welsh nationalism.
2. Not identified, but see *1594*.

1593. To Herbert Read

20 October 1942   PP/EB/NP

Dear Read,

We are having another number of Voice on Tuesday, November 3rd, and would like you to take part as usual, if you will. We want to make this a number devoted to American poetry. I have written to Eliot, suggesting that he might like to take part, but he has not answered yet. I have not yet decided what we shall use, but will let you know as soon as I do. If you are able to take part, I am afraid it will mean giving up most of the morning again—we should like you to be here at about 10.30 as usual.

Yours sincerely,
George Orwell
Talks Producer
Indian Section

1594. BBC Talks Booking Form, 20.10.42

Mulk Raj Anand: 'A Day in My Life,' weekly series; 'arranging and producing 13 minute talks with war workers, in which Mr. Anand interviews his speakers'; broadcast 6, 13, 20, 27.11.42 and 4, 11, and 18.12.42; fee: £10.10 each programme, 'to cover the usual work in arranging talks, contacting speakers & interviewing them at the microphone.' Signed: M Blackburn for I.P.O. Remarks: 'Presumably Mr. Anand will receive the same fee for these talks as he did for the series MEET MY FRIEND, which was done in the same way.'

1595. BBC Talks Booking Form, 20.10.42

Mulk Raj Anand: 'History of Fascism', 5, The Spanish Civil War; broadcast 3.12.42; fee £8.8s. Signed: M Blackburn for I.P.O.

1596. BBC Talks Booking Form, 20.10.42

Ritchie Calder: 'Science and the People,' 2; 12-minute talk on microfilms; broadcast 17.11.42; fee £8.8. Signed: M Blackburn. Remarks: 'Mr. Calder is attached to P.I.D.,[1] but I understand that a non-staff booking slip is issued to him as a rule.'

1. P.I.D. was at the Foreign Office, Bush House, Aldwych.

1597. BBC Talks Booking Form, 20.10.42

Gujarati Newsletters, 32, 33, 34 (two forms); written by E. Blair, translated and read by R. R. Desai; broadcast 5, 12, 19.10.42; fee £5.5s + 12s 0d each broadcast, + 17s 0d subsistence for 5 and 12 October to stay overnight in order to listen to All-India Gujarati broadcasts. Signed: M Blackburn for I.P.O.[1]

1. These forms presumably correct or clarify 1590 and 1591.

1598. BBC Talks Booking Form, 20.10.42

R. R. Desai: 'History of Fascism,' 3, The June Purge; broadcast 19.11.42; fee £8.8s + 12s 0d fare. Signed: M Blackburn for I.P.O. [Fee should have been £9.9s but was revised down on 18 November 1942; the fare was deducted because it was paid on the Newsletter contract.]

1599. BBC Talks Booking Form, 20.10.42

Cedric Dover: 'History of Fascism,' 1, The March on Rome; broadcast 5.11.42; fee £8.8s. Signed: M Blackburn for I.P.O.

1600. BBC Talks Booking Form, 20.10.42

E. M. Forster: 'Some Books,' monthly series; 13-minute talk on books; broadcast 11.11.42, 9.12.42, 6.1.43, and 3.2.43; *his* usual fee.' Signed: M Blackburn for I.P.O.

1601. BBC Talks Booking Form, 20.10.42

Lady Grigg: 'Women Generally Speaking'; broadcast 4, 11, 18, and 25.11.42; fee £8.8s each broadcast. Signed: M Blackburn for I.P.O.

1602. BBC Talks Booking Form, 20.10.42

Princess Indira of Kapurthala: 'The Debate Continues'; broadcast 2, 9, 16, 23, and 30.11.42; fee £10.10s each talk. Signed: M Blackburn for I.P.O.

1603. BBC Talks Booking Form, 20.10.42

Dr K. S. Shelvankar: 'History of Fascism,' 2, Rise of the Nazi Party; 7, The Invasion of the USSR; broadcast 12.11.42 and 17.12.42; fee £8.8s for each talk. Signed: M Blackburn for I.P.O.

1604. BBC Talks Booking Form, 20.10.42

Noel Sircar: Film Commentary; 13-minute talk on films being shown in India at the time of the broadcast; broadcast 17.11.42 and 15.12.42; fee £9.9s each talk. Signed: M Blackburn for I.P.O.

1605. BBC Talks Booking Form, 20.10.42

Shridhar Telkar: 'Behind the Headlines,' weekly series on news of the week; broadcast 4, 11, 18, and 25.11.42; fee £9.9s[1] for each talk. Signed: M Blackburn for I.P.O.

1. The fee was originally set at £8.8s. When Telkar queried this on 27 October, it was raised to £9.9s. He was told on 29 October that the lower fee had been offered because it was mistakenly thought 'these talks were slightly shorter than the previous ones.'

1606. Story by Five Authors
Through Eastern Eyes, 23 October 1942

Part 3 by Inez Holden

For those of you who have not heard or will not remember the two earlier instalments of this serial, Part I by George Orwell and Part II by L. A. G. Strong—Gilbert Moss finds himself alone in a blitzed house during a London Air Raid, he sees an unconscious man lying near him, a reflected light from burning buildings shows him that it is his old enemy Coburn. He decides to take advantage of the circumstances to commit a murder which will be written off as the results of enemy action. The unconscious Coburn carries in his two pockets a gold cigarette lighter and a plain tinder-lighter. Moss takes the gold lighter and looks at it to revive bitter memories of how Coburn had wronged him, thereby justifying in his own mind the action he is about to commit. As he swings a club high to deal the death blow he suddenly sees that a sneak thief is calmly watching him. Coburn recovers consciousness. Moss threatens to tell the thief the reason for their enmity—there Mr. Strong left off, and I go on. . . .[1]

Coburn came slowly to consciousness. He was not really aware of Moss or his henchman from the bombardment. Even his own identity eluded him—as if the various parts of his nature, his associations and memories were groping to join hands through a thick fog.

Coburn was aware only of wanting something to steady his nerves. Perhaps a cigarette could do this. He felt in the left-hand pocket of his trousers, and took out the tinder-lighter; he had left the gold lighter with his initials C.J.K.C. on it in his right-hand pocket. He took some Virginian cigarettes from his breast pocket and lit one. The tinder-lighter was very useful in the blackout, because it only gave out a spark, and on these cold nights the wind soon flicked it into a steady glow. Coburn could remember the time, during the Spanish war, when the Republicans had gone up to the front line with the ropes of these tinder-lighters tied round their waists. Once Coburn had worn his round his neck, like a halter. His cigarette wasn't really alight. He held the tinder in his hand and, with his thumb, turned the wheel back to make a spark.

It was this that set Coburn's memories on the move. It seemed as if his whole mind, with all its elaborate machinery, clocked into reverse, and then went ticking and somersaulting along, backwards.

Something of this sort had happened to Coburn once before. That was the day Mary came to see him in the hospital in Paris. He had a long conversation with her—or so she told him afterwards—yet he hadn't recognised her, and when he checked up on it, with her help, some weeks later, after he had got well, he realised that his speech had been automatic while his mind was elsewhere.

Now again his mind was working at a good speed, but in another direction.

He was lying in his bed in the slovenly French hospital again trying to recover from his wound, and watching the cockroaches crawling along the floor. They made dark smudges; the ceilings were smudged, too, but there was no movement on the ceiling, only small cells of accumulated dirt; and all around Coburn men were dying. Sometimes their comrades called out to the long-robed, funereal nuns: "Numero-quinze"—or "Numero quatre là!—" pointing to the men who had got away early because their lives had gone from them.

The cockroaches were still moving slowly along the floor; Coburn had heard that there was cockroach-racing at the back of restaurants in Paris, and that the spectators would bet a few francs on their favourites. It might be so—he had never seen this himself. Anyhow, these cockroaches didn't hurry. Some of them had stopped moving altogether. He thought that if they could be enlarged they would be like crocodiles sleeping in the sun. Well, —he was like them; powerless, unable to move. Suddenly the sun came into the hospital ward. There was a ray right across Coburn's bed. He was warmed by it and again there came to him the question, like an immense word shooting out in a caption from a film: "WHY?"

He answered this in action. He was not weak any more, he wanted to get going and away from here. It didn't take him long to dress. His leg was not well, but he did not drag it after him as he limped out of the ward, instead he seemed to use his wounded leg to propel himself along at greater speed. No one tried to stop him.

He was back on the road to Spain. "That's strange—I thought the war was over". But he wasn't going back the way he had gone in. He was taking the route he had followed to come out, and with him the same refugees who had streamed over the frontier after the fall of Barcelona. They rose up all around him and travelled back.

He put his hand in his pocket for a cigarette, and remembered the gold lighter. He didn't really like that lighter—it reminded him too much of 1920 days. "C.J.K.C."—those awful initials! Charles Joachim Kallahan Coburn. Charles, after his blustering, fox-hunting uncle of whom he had said: "He may be good to hounds, but he's no good to me!" But if he was honest, he had to admit that it had taken him some years to work up to this witticism. There had been a time when he had been quite proud of Uncle Charles, and boasted to the boys of his "prep" school that he came from this family of hard-riding land-owners. Of course the boys were all little snob-brats. "I suppose it was the system of society that made them like this! Anyhow snobbishness was a harmful thing which boys absorbed up like blotting paper".

Joachim, the second name, was worse. That was after a Spanish Duke that used to come down to his father's place to play polo, an "absento-landlord" with a grandiose manner.

Kallahan, the third name, could pass all right. It was his mother's surname. There was really nothing much wrong with Kallahan.

Well, the gold lighter had gone. Coburn's brain cleared and suddenly, with piercing understanding, he knew where it was. A pick-pocket had taken it from him a few moments ago in a London air-raid. His thoughts were back now, pivoting themselves on to the moment of living.

He knew several things at once—that the cigarette he had lighted a little while ago was now burning his fingers; that the Spanish cause had been lost; that the German bombers were over London and the narrow-eyed, light-fingered fellow facing him at this second of existence, had got the gold lighter with the initials "C.J.K.C." branded on it.

All the time in unconsciousness he had been living in reverse, like a film put on backwards. Sometimes they did this in the cinemas with the sports films, just to show you, the diver comes up right out of the swimming-pool into the air and back on the spring-board; the fallen horse rises up and leaps backwards over the hedge unhurt again, the jockey goes from the ground over the horse's head, safe in the saddle once more. —Just put the actions in reverse and the man you knocked down becomes the one you pick up, the refugees are drawn back into Spain; the pick-pocket presents you with a gold lighter with your own initials on it. Coburn thought. "That's what we want in life. Some careful cutting as in a film, the sequence altered here and there—" — he sighed, and said aloud: "A New Order!" Or a new "New Order"!

The pick-pocket said: "Cor, Mister, he's come to—he's speakin'. I never thought he wouldn't speak no more after I seen him pass clean out like that!"

There was a lull in the air-raid; the bombers had been driven off but soon another wave of them would be coming over. They usually kept it up until dawn.

The pick-pocket, taking advantage of this opportunity, ran out like a rat, he didn't want to be caught with the gold lighter on him.

Coburn said: "You see, he doesn't want to hear the old story of rights and wrongs, Moss, but I do, — so why don't you tell me?" Why couldn't Moss get going on his story? He'd been so anxious to talk a little time ago. Of course, it must be a bit disconcerting for him, not to have an audience. It reminded Coburn of trying to talk to his father at home—it was always the same, after he'd got out a sentence or two, Father began shouting at the dogs under the side-board: "Lie down, Foozle! Stop scratching, Boozle!" Well, the sideboard was there still—or bits of it. But it was so splintered up that you had to have known it from childhood to be able to recognise it now. It wouldn't be worth much, so there need never be any trouble about who it should come to. Good-bye to inherited property—and not such a bad thing either!

"What did I do, Moss?"

A fire engine rushed through the streets, its bells clanging. Coburn saw the firemen standing up to attention on either side of a long ladder in the centre of the car.

"Speak up, Moss," he said. "I am waiting to hear!"

Continued by Martin Armstrong; see *1623*. For Parts 1 and 2, see *1558* and *1574*.

1. This summary is presumably by Holden. In his letter to E. M. Forster of 30 October 1942 (see *1624*), Orwell asks him if he would write a summary of the preceding instalments. See also *1628*. Summaries for the second and fourth instalments have not been traced. The summary refers to a 'plain tinder lighter;' this is not mentioned in the earlier instalments. The expression 'Moss takes the gold lighter' is misleading because Moss put back that lighter, if reluctantly.

1607. Venu Chitale to Eileen Blair

23 October 1942

Dear Mrs. Blair[1]

Thank you very much for your letter, and the recipes you sent me.

I am sure this is the sort of thing we want to use for India, and I know that anything which has to do with Pancakes or fritters will of course be most welcome. Scones and biscuit things made on top of the heat sound simply ideal. Any recipes in that line are just the sort of thing an Indian housewife would like to try out, so will you choose the ones you think useful to our purpose, and send them to me at your leisure.

It is really kind of you to take all this trouble for us, but I know that you are the person to whom I can come to get the right line of things we want for our broadcast.

Thanking you again,

Your sincerely,
[Initialled] V.C.
V. Chitale.
Indian Section

1. Miss Chitale wrote to Eileen Blair at the Ministry of Food, where she worked.

1608. Weekly News Review, 45

24 October 1942

There is only one slight amendment to this script and that, though only faintly to be perceived in the microfilm, seems to be in Orwell's hand. The script carries both censorship stamps; the censor was probably Thavenot. Orwell has written at the top of the first page, 'As broadcast 13' 7" E.A.B'. The script was read by Shridhar Telkar.

The battle for Stalingrad has now lasted for more than two months and the issue is still uncertain. During all this period the fighting has never slackened for more than a few days, and though accurate figures are hard to obtain, the Russian High Command considers that the German casualties in this battle alone exceed a quarter of a million. During the past week the German attacks have not made much progress, and the latest reports seem to indicate that the Germans have again abandoned direct infantry assault and are relying on artillery bombardment. There has been heavy rain, and the mud has no doubt slowed down the German tanks. From the other Russian fronts there is not much to report.

On the island of Guadalcanal in the Solomon Islands, the Japanese have made no new attacks on the American airfield during the past four or five days, but they are known to have powerful naval forces in the neighbourhood and heavy fighting must be expected in the near future. The Americans have also been reinforced on land and sea, and their commanders speak confidently about the forthcoming struggle although admitting that it is certain to be a hard one. At present it is largely a struggle of air power against sea power. The Americans have superiority in the air and have the advantage of possessing the Guadalcanal airfield, but storms and foggy weather have aided the Japanese warships, which are waiting their opportunity to cover another Japanese landing. The latest news is that American Flying Fortresses have scored hits on 10 Japanese warships and are believed to have sunk a cruiser and a destroyer. The Americans themselves have lost 2 destroyers during the current week. In New Guinea, the Allied advance has continued, though slowly because of the difficult nature of the mountain and jungle country through which our troops are moving. The Australian forces are now not far from Kokoda, the last Japanese stronghold before their sea and air bases on the coast of New Guinea.

October 21st was the anniversary of the battle of Trafalgar. This battle 137 years ago occupied rather the same place in the Napoleonic War as the Battle of Britain in 1940 occupied in the present one. The French Emperor, Napoleon, a man who had many points in common with Hitler, had assembled a powerful invasion army at Boulogne opposite the coast of Britain. Could he have got his army across the Channel he would almost certainly have conquered Britain, in which case the other European nations would in all probability not have gone on fighting. Europe would have been given over to military dictatorship and its development would have been set back by many years. However, it was impossible for Napoleon to bring his army across without obtaining command of the sea, and the fleet with which he had tried to lure away and destroy the British Navy was utterly destroyed off Cape Trafalgar on the coast of Spain. Thereafter, the danger of invasion hardly existed, and though it took another ten years to win the war, it was at any rate certain that Britain could not be conquered at one blow. In just the same way in 1940 the Germans only needed command of the air to attempt the invasion of Britain, and with their defeat in a battle which lasted several weeks and in which they lost between two and three thousand aeroplanes, the danger of invasion passed, at any rate for the time being.

We draw attention to the anniversary of Trafalgar because the naval side of the war is ultimately the most important though it is the most easily forgotten. The whole struggle of the Allied Nations in the Far East, in Australia, in Africa and even on the plains of Russia, is finally dependent on the command of the sea which allows men and materials to be freely sent to and fro. Very appropriately, the Admiralty marked the anniversary of Trafalgar by announcing that two new battleships of the King George V class have been put into commission. These ships, which *are each of* [1] 35,000 tons, are about the most powerful vessels now afloat. This makes five new battleships Britain has launched since the outbreak of war, of which one, the Prince of Wales, has been lost. In almost all classes of warship, the British Navy is stronger than it was at the outbreak of war and the long slow struggle against the Axis submarines is being gradually won. During the past week, two facts which gave great encouragement in this connection have been revealed. One is that convoys crossing the Atlantic can now by means of a series of patrols be given air protection the whole way. The other fact revealed in a statement made a few days ago by the First Lord of the Admiralty is that since the outbreak of war the British and Americans have sunk or damaged no less than 530 Axis submarines. This is in addition to any submarines sunk or damaged by the Russians. This achievement is important not so much because of the submarines destroyed—for submarines can be fairly rapidly built—but because their crews are highly trained men whom it is difficult to replace. In the last war, the struggle at sea took a rather similar course for a long time: the German submarines enjoyed great success and there was a period in 1917–1918 when the shipping situation of the Allies was desperate. In the long run, however, the German naval effort was worn down by the killing or capture of their best submarine crews and in the later months of the war it deteriorated quite suddenly so that towards the end the Allied convoys could sail the seas almost unmolested.

On October 17th, a very heavy daylight raid was carried out by British bombers on the Schneider arms factories in Occupied France. After Krupps factories at Essen, these are probably the biggest arms works in Europe, and it is known that they were working at full pressure for the Germans. 94 of the heaviest British bombers, each of which can carry eight tons of bombs, made an attack and only one bomber failed to return. The damage is known to have been tremendous. This is the second big raid within about 10 days that Allied forces have carried out in daylight. Two days ago, British bombers also carried out a heavy raid on Genoa in Italy. This involved a flight of fifteen hundred miles, and it also involves flying over the Alps, which are almost as high as the Himalayas. At present the Germans are only countering the British raids in a very petty way by single raiders or small groups which machine-gun civilians somewhere near the coast and hurriedly make off again. Their bombing fleet is too busy on the Russian front to do more than this, and the success of the British and American daylight raids suggests that the Germans no longer have sufficient fighter planes to guard every corner of their territories.

The struggle of Laval, the French Quisling, to force Frenchmen to work for Germany is continuing, without much success. The Germans want 150,000 workers and have held out the bribe that a corresponding number of war prisoners will be released. In spite of this, it is known that not more than 30,000 volunteers[2] at most have come forward, and the time-limit for enrolment has had to be extended several times. It is of course in the power of the Germans to apply compulsion, but that is not very satisfactory from their point of view; it means dropping once and for all the pretence that the New Order has been willingly accepted by the peoples of Europe. Almost simultaneously with this the German 'protector',[3] as he is called, of Czechoslovakia has announced that reprisals are going to be taken against the relatives of Czech exiles in Britain and also that the Czech universities which were closed for a period of three years in 1939 are not going to be re-opened. The reason, he said, was that the Czech intelligentsia have shown themselves irreconcilable. Many similar events could be reported from other parts of Europe and indeed they are a weekly occurrence. We could if we wished completely fill this newsletter every week with news of civil war, rioting, sabotage, strikes and executions from occupied Europe. But we merely pick out from time to time one or two instances to remind our listeners of the utter failure of the New Order and the growing understanding among the European peoples of the evil nature of Fascism.

Field-Marshal Smuts,[4] President of the Union of South Africa, spoke on October 21st in London to a gathering of the members of both Houses of Parliament. His speech excited great interest and has been broadcast and published all over the world. General Smuts reviewed the progress of the war up to date and paid high tribute to the gallant peoples of Russia and China, both references being loudly cheered by the audience. He also said that we must never forget the year during which Britain fought alone and probably saved the world by doing so. Although preferring not to discuss future military operations, he said that the time had now come when the United Nations were able to take the offensive, and emphasised the fact that our strength was constantly growing while that of our enemies was beginning to decline. After the war he looked forward to a more stable society in which poverty and political oppression would be abolished and internationalism would be a reality. General Smuts, who is now aged 72, fought with distinction against the British in the South African War of 40 years ago. He afterwards became completely reconciled to Britain and was one of the most brilliant and influential members of the British War Cabinet in the war of 1914–1918. Few modern statesmen are more respected in Britain. His speech was wound up by Mr Churchill and introduced by his former chief, David Lloyd George.

1. *are each of*] weigh
2. West: *Commentaries* records that at the time the Ministry of Information was circulating a figure of 18,000 to the press; Vichy announced that the 80,000th man had recently volunteered: 'Orwell provides his own average' (171).
3. Karl-Hermann Frank (1898–1946), a leader of the Sudeten German Nazi Party, was, from 1939, Secretary of State to the Protectorate of Bohemia and Moravia. After the assassination of Reinhard Heydrich in 1942, he ordered revenge killings in Czechoslovakia, including the

massacre at Lidice (see Orwell's War-time Diary, *1218, 11.6.42*). He was publicly hanged by the Czechs in May 1946.

4. Jan Christiaan Smuts; see *1116, n. 15*. He maintained the stance he had adopted after the Boer War at the conclusion of World War I, unsuccessfully arguing at Versailles for moderation towards Germany. He also supported the formation of the League of Nations.

1609. Bengali Newsletter, 15

24 October 1942

The English original was written by Orwell. No script has been traced. PasB gives timing as 13′ 32″.

1610. To E. M. Forster

24 October 1942   PP/EB

Dear Forster,

You remember my asking whether you would like to wind up the serial STORY BY FIVE AUTHORS, each instalment of which was written by a separate person. I am sending you herewith the first four instalments. I am afraid it was an unsuccessful experiment, the second and third writers having failed to carry on the story as it should have been. The fourth instalment, which is quite good, really does what the second instalment ought to have done. Nevertheless the germ of a story is there and it might amuse you to wind it up in some way or even if you like simply to comment on it, saying it might end this way or it might end that way and in my opinion the following would be the best ending. It would, however, be necessary to manufacture *some* kind of denouement. The only thing is I would like to know pretty promptly whether you can do this, because if not, we shall have to arrange for somebody else. But I would of course like you to do it if you feel equal to it. The date of the broadcast is November 6th, at 12.15.

Yours,
George Orwell
Talks Producer
Indian Section

1611. BBC Talks Booking Form, 24.10.42

R. R. Desai: Gujarati Newsletter, 35; broadcast 26.10.42; fee £5.5s + 12s 0d fare + 17s 0d subsistence (see *1567, n. 1*). Signed: M Blackburn for I.P.O.

1612. Gujarati Newsletter, 35

26 October 1942

The English original was written by Orwell. No script has been traced. PasB gives timing as approximately 12 minutes.

1613. To Keidrych Rhys

27 October 1942   PP/EB

Dear Rhys,

I think Mulk Raj Anand has approached you about a broadcast we would like you to do in the Eastern Service (to India) on 13th November. This series is called "A Day in My Life" and is done in the form of interviews with war-workers of various descriptions who describe how they spend their time and what work they are doing. We should like you to speak in the capacity of a soldier. Mulk will ask the necessary questions and you give the answers. You can be reasonably honest in broadcasts in this service. I hope you will undertake this. Please let me know as soon as possible, and then if you are willing I will get Mulk to come and do his stuff. You must get the permission of your Commanding Officer in writing to do this, but that is only a formality and there is never any difficulty as a rule. The time of the broadcast is 12.45, which means coming to 200 Oxford Street at 12 o'clock to rehearse, but if you can't manage that we can record it some time beforehand.

I am sorry we haven't yet been able to arrange for you to take part in our monthly poetry programme "Voice", but we shall have other numbers coming on later and perhaps you will contribute some time.

Yours sincerely,
George Orwell
Talks Producer

1614. To Henry Treece

[27 October 1942?]

NOVEMBER THIRD SUITABLE WRITING[1]

ORWELL BROADCASTS.

1. 3 November was a Tuesday, which tallies with the P.S. to Orwell's letter; see *1615*.

1615. To Henry Treece

27 October 1942   Top and carbon copies   PP/EB

Dear Treece,

Many thanks for your telegram. I will arrange a recording time for you on Tuesday afternoon, if this will suit you. I think we can arrange for you to record between 3 and 4 that afternoon, but I'll let you know definitely before Tuesday.

As it happens, we are doing the fourth number of Voice on that day—it is a number devoted to American poetry. If you'd care to come along and listen we'd be very pleased to see you—it goes on the air at 12.15.

We should be glad if you would get permission from your Commanding Officer to record some of your poems—this is just a formality, of course. It is best to have it in writing.

You should come to 200, Oxford Street, on the corner of Great Portland Street—Mr. Schimanski[1] knows where it is.

Yours sincerely,
[Signed] Geo. Orwell
George Orwell
Talks Producer
Indian Section

P.S. Recording from 2.45–3.45 on the 3rd. Is this O.K.?[2]

1. Stefan Schimanski had edited *Kingdom Come: The Magazine of War-Time Oxford* with Henry Treece and Alan Rook in 1941; he and Treece edited the annual *Transformation*, Nos. 1–4, 1943–47. Schimanski edited sections of Orwell's War-time Diary for *World Review*, June 1950.
2. The postscript does not appear on the carbon copy. See also *1614*.

1616. BBC Talks Booking Form, 27.10.42

Mulk Raj Anand: 'Voice,' 3; 'half hour programme of poems etc. with discussions lasting about 5 mins. Mr. Anand helped to put the programme together & took part in the discussions'; broadcast 6.10.42; fee £5.5 'to cover part in discussion and general assistance in the prog.' Signed: M Blackburn for I.P.O. Remarks: 'I'm afraid this contract got overlooked. We have apologised to Mr. Anand. He should receive his usual fee for this programme.'

1617. Memorandum to B. H. Alexander, Programme Copyright

28 October 1942   EB/NP

Copy to Empire Programme Executive

Story by Five Authors:
Serial for Eastern Service

Thank you for your memo. of 27th October.

We have heard from E. M. Forster that he will do the final instalment in this series. The date of the broadcast is November 6th, at 1115 GMT (1215 BST), and the length of the broadcast is 13½ minutes. I should be glad if you would kindly arrange terms with Forster.

I am sending a booking slip to Talks Bookings, so that they may book Forster for the reading of the material.

[Signed] Eric Blair
(Eric Blair)

1618. Extract from Minutes of Eastern Service Meeting

28 October 1942

COMPETITIONS

Sub-committee's report recommending a monthly competition for critical essays in English on the English programme approved in principle. Sub-committee to compile simple and short rules, consider procedure for short-listing entries in New Delhi and draw up list of possible judges well known as being competent.

Orwell initiated and was to organise this competition.

1619. To G. M. Young

29 October 1942

This letter, giving details of when Ezra Pound's broadcasts from Rome might be heard, is reproduced in West: *Broadcasts* (225). It is *not* from Orwell, but from Lanham Titchener.

1620. BBC Talks Booking Form, 29.10.42

Mulk Raj Anand: 'Voice,' 4; 'taking part in discussions and helping compile the programme — 13 min. programme'; broadcast 3.11.42; fee £5.5, 'to cover part in discussion and assistance in compiling prog.' Signed: M Blackburn for I.P.O.

Remarks: 'Mr. Anand will presumably receive his usual fee for helping with this programme.'

1621. BBC Talks Booking Form, 29.10.42

E. M. Forster: 'Story by Five Authors,' 5; 'reading of fifth & last instalment of this serial story (copyright for writing this being covered by Miss Alexander.) 13½ mins'; broadcast 6.11.42; 'Presumably E. M. Forster will NOT receive his usual fee, as this is for *Reading only*'; fee 'usual,' £21 changed to £5.5; Talks Booking Manager entered 'No reply. No fee paid.' Signed: M Blackburn for I.P.O.

1622. BBC Talks Booking Form, 29.10.42

Herbert Read: booked for 'Indian — Empire' [changed in ink from typed 'Eastern']; 'Voice,' 4; 'reading poem by T. S. Eliot (Prufrock) for about 5 mins. and taking part in discussions'; broadcast 3.11.42; 'presumably Mr. Read will receive the same fee as before for taking part in VOICE'; fee £4.4 'to cover reading & part in discussion.' Signed: M Blackburn for I.P.O.

1623. Story by Five Authors
Through Eastern Eyes, 30 October 1942

Part 4 by Martin Armstrong

Gilbert Moss stood gazing incredulously at his old enemy. Coburn still lay in exactly the same position, still a dead man except that his eyes were now open and alive. But were they? Wasn't it simply the effect of the glare and flicker of the blazing rubbish? But he had spoken too. "Come on, Moss," he had said: "I'm waiting to hear". But no; that was impossible. It wasn't Coburn who had said that. Nobody had said it. The whole exhausting business was simply a dream. Moss felt suddenly as weak as a kitten and gave it up, stood there motionless and speechless, waiting. If he waited patiently, something would happen; a moment of confusion, then clearness, daylight, and the old alarm-clock rattling on the mantelpiece, telling him that it was time to get up and go to the lab. But what roused him at last was not the alarm-clock, but Coburn's voice again: "I say, old man, do give me a hand. This isn't a bit comfortable. I can't move: some damned thing's wedging my shoulder".

How amazingly familiar and attractive the voice was, recalling old times, happy times. Incredible that a few minutes ago he had been on the point of beating the fellow's brains out. And why? Why, because . . . but no; his mind refused to focus itself. And then, for the first time, he noticed that the raid was over. All round him hung a blessed silence, broken only by the spasmodic crackle of burning beams. Not only that. Against a silvery-green background of luminous sky he could see clearly and steadily the jagged walls of the great hollow tooth in which he was standing. He clambered over to where Coburn lay. A joist, one of its ends buried in bricks and rubble, lay across his left arm and shoulder and in half a minute or so Moss had dragged it back.

With a sigh of relief Coburn sat up, then got on to his feet, steadying himself for a moment with a hand on Moss's shoulder. "Come on", he said, "let's get out of this". He glanced round him with an attempt at a smile. "Sorry not to give you a better reception". Moss didn't understand. "You mean to say . . . ?"

"Exactly; that this is our town house. In point of fact it was just through there that you and I . . ."

Moss cut him short. "You don't want to have a look round for the others?"

"The others? O, I see what you mean. No, there aren't any others. The house was empty. I was simply spending the night here. Come on".

They scrambled out into the street. In the half-light of early morning it looked surprisingly unchanged. Coburn's house seemed to be the only one whose front had gone. The rest faced each other sedately across the roadway, though, here and there, pavements and road were littered with broken glass and splintered woodwork and here and there a gaping window betrayed that behind that respectable screen lay, not the gloom of domestic privacy, but the vacancy of open sky. Coburn slid his arm through Moss's and steered him across the street.

"Where are we off to?" Moss asked.

"To a seat in the Park, till there's a chance of breakfast somewhere. You're going to tell me, you know, what I did to you".

Moss breathed out a long sigh. "O damn all that", he said. "I don't know. I can't remember". He had no energy left. When Coburn had taken his arm he had been aware of an immense relief. What a rest to give up all responsibility of thought and action and submit obediently to be led.

Coburn steered him across another road. "But you must", he said. "Here's the Park. As soon as we can find a seat you must tell me all about it. You see, I've never understood".

It was this fatuous assumption of innocence, that restored Moss's energies. With a sudden movement he shook his arm free and let fly. "O no, of course you know nothing. You're as innocent as an unborn lamb, aren't you? Well, here's a seat for you. Sit down. If you want to have it, you shall have it".

Coburn sat down. "Yes", he said, "tell me what I did to you and, when you've done, I'll tell you what you did to me".

Moss was too wrapped up in his old grievance to notice the final phrase. He sat down and turned to Coburn. "And look here", he said, "if you want me to tell you, *let* me tell you. Don't butt in with excuses, or I stop and clear out".

"I see", said Coburn; "as you did last time".

"Exactly. Just as I did last time, and as I ought to have done the very first time I met you, if I'd had any sense, instead of letting you get round me. Yes, you're a wonderful chap for getting round people, aren't you, Coburn? Still, I was easy game in those days: any fool could have got round me. When Challenor asked me round and introduced me to his little set, I was simply delighted. I thought I'd got into the Kingdom of Heaven. And there were you, handsome, son of a lord, going to be a lord yourself some day, simply lousy with money, and yet interested in my views and treating me as your equal. Yes, you took me in properly. I believed you and I was enormously grateful, silly ass that I was. I danced round you and wagged my tail and let you put a collar round my neck and lead me on a string. Whenever you whistled I came galloping up, only too delighted to obey. I thought you the most wonderful chap I'd ever met. I simply adored you. Why, good lord, you transformed my whole life from top to bottom. Before I met you, I'd never had a soul to talk to about all the things that mattered. Nobody talked to me at the lab, where I did my bottle-washing as you politely called it one day. Lancaster, my boss, despised me and they all thought me a little worm not worth bothering about. And so I was. If I hadn't been a worm, I wouldn't have let *you* get round me. But you said[1] how useful I might be. You'd found out that I was methodical, and that I had a natural gift for organising and had read a devil of a lot of science and history, even though I was only a bottle-washer. Just the chap you wanted to do the jobs no one else could do on your precious new monthly magazine. Good God, how excited I was when you explained the scheme to me. A marvellous monthly review, dealing with art, literature, history, science, from a brand-new left-wing point of view. A sort of crusade. A six guineas a week salary for me. I shall never forget the evening we finally fixed it up. I'd been feeling rotten. Lancaster had given me a terrific ticking-off about some blessed experiment that somebody else had mucked up, and I'd taken it lying-down, because I was frightened of losing my job. You laughed when I told you about it. 'Never mind about that', you said. 'Tomorrow morning, when you go to work, ask to see Lancaster, tell him exactly what you think of him, and walk out. Then come round to our place for lunch and we'll fix up about moving into our office on Thursday. All's clear. My people are out of town'.

"Yes, Coburn, that was very convenient, wasn't it? His lordship and her ladyship were out of town, so there was no fear of them running across the scruffy little worm you'd taken into your employment. That didn't strike me at the moment. It was the first time you'd asked me round to your place and I was so fatuously delighted that nothing else mattered. Well, there it was. Next morning I had a gorgeous row with Lancaster and cleared out. Then I went home and spruced myself up a bit and presented myself at your front door. I was a bit intimidated when that striped flunkey of yours opened the door and showed me into the library; but I was also pretty pleased with myself, dropping in for a bit of lunch at the house of a lord. However, I was kept waiting about twenty minutes in the library and that cooled me down a bit. Then you came in. How well I remember your face on that occasion, Coburn, all embarrassed and hesitating. I hardly knew you. You began to explain. Your people had turned up unexpectedly the previous evening and you and I couldn't lunch together after all. The flunkey would bring me *my* lunch, there in the library. Ha! You were in an awful hurry to get away from me. The lord and lady couldn't be kept waiting for their grub, still less be exposed to the company of the scruffy little worm. However, you were awfuly nice about it; O awfully nice. You patted me on the shoulder and told me to come back at tea-time.

"At first I couldn't speak. Then I said I didn't want lunch; I had a lot of things to do; I preferred to go at once. That upset you a bit, and you mumbled something about being sure I wouldn't misunderstand you. Ha! you were right there, Coburn. I didn't misunderstand you any longer. I'd seen through you at last. Then you had a brain-wave. You got out a wallet, fished a bit of paper out of it and handed it to me. It was a ten-pound note. 'What's that for?' I asked you. 'Some cash in advance', you said. 'Thought you might be needing it'. Lovely, wasn't it? Ten pounds. More than enough to soothe the feelings of a worm. Well, *you* know the rest. I tore up your blasted ten-pound note and chucked it in your face, and told you I didn't want your dirty money, and then I told you one or two things about yourself and all the rest of your kind. And then I told you I was done with you. That made you sit up, didn't it, Coburn? Your face—I remember it still—turned suddenly white. But you didn't forget your manners. O dear me, no. You remained the perfect gentleman and your voice was perfectly calm. 'I see', you said; 'I see. Well, if you really feel like that, there's nothing more to be said'.

"It was simple enough for you, wasn't it? But it wasn't quite so simple for me. I'd dished myself for good and all at the lab, and there was I, on the rocks. Still, that was a minor detail. O yes, I mean it; a minor detail compared with what you'd done to my . . . well, to my mind, my self-respect, my . . . my feelings. That's where you did me in. It was as good as murder. Worse, in fact; far worse. When a man's murdered, he thinks no more about it.

"Well, there you are. You're not going to deny all that, are you?"

Concluded by E. M. Forster; see *1638*. For Parts 1, 2, and 3, see *1558*, *1574*, *1606*.

1. Typescript has 'say.'

1624. To E. M. Forster
30 October 1942   PP/EB

Dear Forster,
Many thanks for agreeing to do the final instalment of the serial story.[1] I'm afraid it didn't turn out quite as I had hoped.

Thanks very much for sending the voucher for your ticket for the Indian ballet. We have sent in a claim for the money, and I shall let you have it next week when you come.

I wonder if you could write a sort of resume of "the story so far", to preface your instalment? We have done this as a rule, and I think it helps people who may have missed an instalment, or who haven't been listening to it before. It only needs to be a few lines.

I am enclosing a letter from Gangule which was sent to you from this address.

> Yours,
> George Orwell
> Talks Producer
> Indian Section
>
> Dictated by George
> Orwell and despatched
> in his absence by:
> [No name on carbon copy]

1. The carbon copy shows that a false start was made to this letter. It originally began, 'Mr. Orwell has asked me to thank' and then breaks off. Evidently Orwell wanted the letter written as from him. Whether a precise form of letter was dicated is open to question (here and elsewhere).

1625. Weekly News Review in English, 46

31 October 1942

Typed at the head of the first page of this script is 'written by E. Blair' in parentheses and at the top of this page Orwell has written, 'As broadcast 11′ 20″ E.A.B'. However, the single change to the text is not in Orwell's hand. The script carries both censorship stamps; the censor may have been C. Lawson-Reece, the Eastern Service Organizer. The script was read by Bahadur Singh.

A week ago the Allied forces in Egypt opened up a large-scale attack,[1] and since then fighting has been almost continuous. In the opening stages of the attack, the Allies broke into the enemy positions and took considerable numbers of prisoners. The Germans then counter-attacked and there were some clashes between armoured formations, but the ground gained was all successfully held. This morning's news is that the Allies have made a further advance and taken another large batch of prisoners. It is worth noting that the prisoners taken in this second advance are mostly Germans—a sure sign that the Axis forces are doing their best to hold to their positions, as it is usual to put Germans rather than Italians in any place when hard fighting is expected.

As yet we prefer not to predict the outcome of the battle in Egypt, but we can point to one or two factors likely to govern it. One is that any advance in the area where the fighting is now going on is likely to be slow. The battle area is a narrow space between the sea and the QUATTARA° Depression, a marshy area, where tanks cannot operate. Consequently, the only method of advance is direct frontal attack, which is a slow process since it means assaulting a series of strongly fortified positions and carefully clearing minefields, without which the tanks cannot advance. In this sort of fighting, therefore, an advance of two thousand yards, such as that reported this morning, means more than an advance of many miles in the open desert. Secondly, the outcome of such a battle is largely a question of supplies, and the fact of the Allies having attacked first is probably a good sign. Arms and reinforcements for the Allied army in Egypt have to travel much further than those destined for the Axis forces, but the Axis line of communications from Italy to Tripoli and thence up the coast to the Egyptian front is liable to sea or air attack almost the whole way. During recent weeks the Axis losses on this supply route have been very heavy, and a recent Admiralty statement revealed that during this year the Axis have had no less than six hundred thousand tons of shipping sunk or damaged in the Mediterranean. This is the background of the present fighting in Egypt in which both sides fight under considerable difficulties. It is evident that the Allies are stronger in the air. Which side is stronger in tanks and other fighting vehicles we cannot yet say. *The main body of our troops comes from Britain, but*[2] Australian, South African, New Zealand, Indian, Free French and Greek troops are all taking part. We shall be able to report more fully on the Egyptian campaign next week. It is now evident that the heavy RAF raids on Genoa and Milan in Northern Italy, the first of which we reported last week, were a preliminary to the attack in Egypt. Axis supplies and reinforcements for the Egyptian front are largely despatched from Genoa, and the disorganisation caused by these raids will make itself felt on the battlefield.

During the past week there has been heavy fighting in the Solomon Islands and some anxious moments for the Allies. It was clear that the Japanese had a powerful fleet in the neighbourhood of Guadalcanal, and they had also been able to land enough troops on the island to outnumber the Americans who hold the all-important airfields. The Americans were being shelled by warships every night besides having to beat off land attacks by forces which included tanks. At the same time there were a number of sea and air engagements in which both sides had ships sunk and damaged. However, this morning's news is that the Japanese fleet has retired again and that all the land attacks have been successfully resisted.[3] Colonel Knox, the United States Navy Secretary,[4] has just announced that the Americans still hold all the territory which they captured from the Japanese at the beginning of August. This does not mean, however, that the fighting in the Solomons has ended. The Japanese are certain to renew their attacks, partly because of the importance of the Guadalcanal airfield, partly because of the loss of face if they fail to drive the Americans out after promising confidently to do so. As Colonel Knox put it, the first round has gone to the Americans but the defenders of Guadalcanal are waiting for the second round to start.

The battle for Stalingrad continues and both sides have suffered heavy casualties during this week. The German attacks have made little or no progress. It is now more than a month since the speeches in which Hitler and Ribbentrop promised the capture of Stalingrad within a few days. As yet, apparently, the German people cannot be allowed to learn what enormous numbers of their sons and brothers have gone to their deaths in vain attacks on Stalingrad. But such facts cannot be kept secret for ever, and the heavy and more or less futile casualties of this year's campaign are likely to have their effects on morale, later in the winter.

News was released a few days ago that the new military road known as the Alaska High Road[5] has been opened. This road runs from the United States through Canada and Alaska and makes it possible to supply any force operating in the Aleutian Islands much more rapidly than could be done before. The Aleutian Islands are the point at which Allied territory is nearest to Japan, and also the point at which America is nearest to Soviet Russia. The strategic importance of this new road is therefore very great. It was completed in an astonishingly short time, although for much of the way it runs through virgin forests which had previously hardly been explored.

We are able to give a few more details about the new British bombing plane, the Mosquito, which made its first official appearance two or three weeks ago. This was the first front line plane in this war to be built entirely of wood. Its body is therefore easily manufactured and is probably cheap. Its great feature is its extremely high speed, which rivals that of fighter planes. It is also powerfully armed, carrying 20-millimetre cannons as well as machine-guns. It has been used very successfully for several daylight raids on the continent.

We will end by giving an extract from The Times of two days ago,[6] which has some up-to-date information about the behaviour of the Japanese in Java.

A young Dutch officer who escaped from Java several weeks ago and is now in Australia reports that the attitude of the people in Java towards the Japanese invaders is one of passive hostility. During the early days of the occupation the Japanese took cruel measures against looters. Dead Malays were often seen hanging from trees in Batavia. The Japanese military police still habitually beat up persons from whom they want information. These repressive measures have cowed the Javanese people, who, though sympathetic towards Europeans, are afraid of offending their temporary military masters.

All the sympathy they may feel towards the Europeans is really suppressed by the fear, so it is quiet sympathy.

The production of rubber, tea, tobacco, and other commodities in which Java is so rich has been drastically curtailed. There is a great deal of unemployment in the country.

Groups of Allied soldiers are still at large in the mountains, but they are unable to maintain any effective resistance. Wounded Japanese soldiers from those regions are still brought occasionally to hospitals in Batavia.

1. The Second Battle of El Alamein began on 23 October 1942. (The first had taken place at the beginning of July 1942.)
2. *The main body . . . Britain, but*] British. *Passages added or substituted are in italic.*
3. This followed the Battle of Santa Cruz, 26–27 October 1942. Though large fleets were

engaged, the battle was fought entirely by aircraft, the fleets never coming within range of one another. The United States lost the aircraft carrier *Hornet* and had several ships seriously damaged. The Americans lost 74 planes; the Japanese, about 100. In the short term this was a success for the Japanese, but the Americans temporarily paralysed Japanese movement by sea and stopped reinforcements for Guadalcanal (*2194 Days of War*, 303).

4. William Franklin (Frank) Knox (1874–1944) was Secretary of the Navy, 1940–44. He had been one of Theodore Roosevelt's 'Rough Riders' during the Spanish-American War, publisher of the Chicago *Daily News*, and vice-presidential candidate in 1936.

5. The Alaska Military Highway (later called the Alaska or Alcan Highway), built mostly by U.S. troops, March to September 1942, ran 1,523 miles, from Dawson Creek, B.C., to Fairbanks, Alaska.

6. West: *Commentaries* notes that in taking the following from *The Times* of 29 October, Orwell omitted the concluding sentence: 'Japanese military discipline has been good and no cases reported of white women being molested' (175, n. 300).

1626. Bengali Newsletter, 16

31 October 1942

The English original was written by Orwell. No script has been traced.

1627. Gujarati Newsletter, 36

2 November 1942

The English original was written by Orwell. No script has been traced. PasB gives timing as 10′ 35″.

1628. To E. M. Forster

2 November 1942   PP/EB/NP

Dear Forster,

Thanks for your letter of November 1st. I am sending you the resume° to the third instalment, because Armstrong's script was rather on the long side, and we didn't have time for him to give a resume.[1]

We should like to have your script some time on Thursday, if possible. It would be quite all right if you brought it here in the afternoon or early evening, as long as you can let us know when it will be coming. I'm sorry about this, but it has to be censored first thing on Friday morning.

Yours sincerely,
George Orwell
Talks Producer
Indian Section

1. It is not clear whether a resumé was written but not broadcast, or not written.

1629. BBC Talks Booking Form, 2.11.42

R. R. Desai: Gujarati[1] Newsletter, 36; broadcast 2.11.42; fee £5.5s + 12s 0d fare + 17s 0d subsistence, so he could hear All-India Radio Gujarati Bulletin monitored in London on 1 November. Signed: M Blackburn for I.P.O.

1. It was only from this point that Mary Blackburn spelt 'Gujarati' with an 'a' after the 'j' and not an 'e.' In headings and talks booking forms the correct spelling has been given in this edition.

1630. 'Voice,' 4: A Magazine Programme
3 November 1942

'Voice,' 4 is reproduced from a typescript used for the broadcast, as amended by Orwell. Unlike the first three editions of 'Voice,' it is not marked 'As broadcast,' though it is marked as passed for Security and Policy. The script looks as if it had been typed on a BBC typewriter, and since the typing is not of professional standard, it may be Orwell's work. From the original typescript it is plain that Louis MacNeice should have taken part. From the way that the pages have been numbered and renumbered it is apparent that the extracts were initially typed separately. Texts of passages quoted are as given in the typescript; cuts have been restored but are indicated in the notes. The following names, probably in Orwell's hand, are written in capitals at the top of the first page of the script: 'Herbert Read, Una Marson,[1] Mulk Raj Anand, Wm: Empson.'

ANNOUNCER: This is London calling. Today we present the fourth number of VOICE, our monthly radio magazine. Here is George Orwell introducing it.

ORWELL:[2]   Good evening everybody. This month we have decided that VOICE shall be devoted to American poetry and American literature generally. It's a big subject and we can only hope to cover it in an impressionistic way of picking out a characteristic fragment here and there. Thinking it over we came to the conclusion that the best way is to start at the end and work backwards. I mean, to start off with contemporary American writers and end up with the pioneering period. We shan't have time to go further back than that. Now, I wonder who is the most representative modern American writer?

ANAND:[3]   T. S. Eliot.

ORWELL: We'll have something of Eliot, of course, but I think we ought to start off with someone a bit more American. Eliot's an American by origin, but he's a British subject and rather Europeanised. Who else is there?

READ:[4]   Archibald MacLeish, or Marianne Moore, or Hemingway, or John Steinbeck.[5]

[EMPS]ON: I think MacLeish is the most representative. For instance there's that poem about the immigrant labourers who built the trans-American railway. It's called "The Burying Ground by the Ties", I think.

ORWELL: All right, we'll start with that one. Here it is. The Burying Ground by the Ties, by Archibald MacLeish.[6] This is Wm. Empson[7] reading it.

EMPSON: BURYING GROUND BY THE TIES, by Archibald MacLeish.[8]

Ayee! Ai! This is heavy earth on our shoulders:
There were none of us born to be buried in this earth:
Niggers we were Portuguese Magyars Polacks:

We were born to another look of the sky certainly:
Now we lie here in the river pastures:
We lie in the mowings under the thick turf!

We hear the earth and the all-day rasp of the grasshoppers:
It was we laid the steel on this land from ocean to ocean:
It was we (if you know) put the U.P. through the passes

Bringing her down into Laramie full load
Eighteen mile on the granite anticlinal
Forty-three foot to the mile and the grade holding:

It was we did it: hunkies of our kind:
It was we dug the caved-in holes for the cold water:
It was we built the gully spurs and the freight sidings:

Who would do it but we and the Irishmen bossing us?
It was all foreign-born men there were in this country:
It was Scotsmen Englishmen Chinese Squareheads Austrians . . .[9]

Ayee! but there's weight to the earth under it:
Not for this did we come out—to be lying here
Nameless under the ties in the clay cuts:

There's nothing good in the world but the rich will buy it:
Everything sticks to the grease of a gold note—
Even a continent—even a new sky!

Do not pity us much for the strange grass over us:
We laid the steel to the stone stock of these mountains:
The place of our graves is marked by the telegraph poles!

It was not to lie in the bottoms we came out
And the trains going over us here in the dry hollows . . .

ORWELL: That speaks for the immigrants and for the American labourers generally. It's a pity we haven't time for a short story by Steinbeck[10] or one of the I.W.W.[11] songs of the last war, or something from James Farrell.[12] But now we've got to represent expatriate America. That's where Eliot comes in. I still think his earlier poems are his best.

ANAND:[13] And surely the best of the early poems is[14] "The Love Story of Alfred J.° Prufrock"?

ORWELL: All right, we'll have that one. Here it is. "The Love Story of Alfred J.° Prufrock". This is Herbert Read reading it.

READ: THE LOVE SONG OF J. ALFRED PRUFROCK
by T. S. Eliot

Let us go then, you and I,
When the evening is spread out against the sky
Like a patient etherised upon a table;
Let us go, through certain half-deserted streets,
The muttering retreats
Of restless nights in one-night cheap hotels
And sawdust restaurants with oyster-shells:
Streets that follow like a tedious argument
Of insidious intent
To lead you to an overwhelming question. . .[15]
Oh, do not ask, 'What is it?'
Let us go and make our visit.

In the room the women come and go
Talking of Michelangelo.

The yellow fog that rubs its back upon the window-panes,
The yellow smoke that rubs its muzzle on the window-panes,
Licked its tongue into the corners of the evening,
Lingered upon the pools that stand in drains,
Let fall upon its back the soot that falls from chimneys,
Slipped by the terrace, made a sudden leap,
And seeing that it was a soft October night,
Curled once about the house, and fell asleep.

And indeed there will be time
For the yellow smoke that slides along the street
Rubbing its back upon the window-panes;
There will be time, there will be time
To prepare a face to meet the faces that you meet;
There will be time to murder and create,
And time for all the works and days of hands
That lift and drop a question on your plate;
Time for you and time for me,
And time yet for a hundred indecisions,
And for a hundred visions and revisions,
Before the taking of a toast and tea.

In the room the women come and go
Talking of Michelangelo.

And indeed there will be time
To wonder, 'Do I dare?' and, 'Do I dare?'
Time to turn back and descend the stair,
With a bald spot in the middle of my hair—
(They will say: 'How his hair is growing thin!')
My morning coat, my collar mounting firmly to the chin,
My necktie rich and modest, but asserted by a simple pin—
(They will say: 'But how his arms and legs are thin!')
Do I dare
Disturb and universe?

In a minute there is time
For decisions and revisions which a minute will reverse.

For I have known them all already, known them all—
Have known the evenings, mornings, afternoons,
I have measured out my life with coffee spoons:
I know the voices dying with a dying fall
Beneath the music from a farther room.
    So how should I presume?

And I have known the eyes already, known them all—
The eyes that fix you in a formulated phrase,
And when I am formulated, sprawling on a pin,
When I am pinned and wriggling on the wall,
Then how should I begin
To spit out all the butt-ends of my days and ways?
    And how should I presume?

And I have known the arms already, known them all—
Arms that are braceleted and white and bare
(But in the lamplight, downed with light brown hair!)
Is it perfume from a dress
That makes me so digress?
Arms that lie along a table, or wrap about a shawl.
    And should I then presume?
    And how should I begin?

. . . . .

Shall I say, I have gone at dusk through narrow streets
And watched the smoke that rises from the pipes
Of lonely men in shirt-sleeves, leaning out of windows? . . .

I should have been a pair of ragged claws
Scuttling across the floors of silent seas.

. . . . .

And the afternoon, the evening, sleeps so peacefully!
Smoothed by long fingers,
Asleep . . . tired . . . or it malingers,
Stretched on the floor, here beside you and me.
Should I, after tea and cakes and ices,
Have the strength to force the moment to its crisis?
But though I have wept and fasted, wept and prayed,
Though I have seen my head (grown slightly bald) brought in upon a platter,
I am no prophet—and here's no great matter;
I have seen the moment of my greatness flicker,
And I have seen the eternal Footman hold my coat, and snicker.
And in short, I was afraid.

And would it have been worth it, after all,
After the cups, the marmalade, the tea,
Among the porcelain, among some talk of you and me,
Would it have been worth while,
To have bitten off the matter with a smile,
To have squeezed the universe into a ball
To roll it toward some overwhelming question,
To say: 'I am Lazarus, come from the dead,

Come back to tell you all, I shall tell you all'—
If one, settling a pillow by her head,
   Should say: 'That is not what I meant at all.
   That is not it, at all.'

And would it have been worth it, after all,
Would it have been worth while,
After the sunsets and the dooryards and the sprinkled streets,
After the novels, after the teacups, after the skirts that trail along the floor—
And this, and so much more?—
It is impossible to say just what I mean!
But as if a magic lantern threw the nerves in patterns on a screen:
Would it have been worth while
If one, settling a pillow or throwing off a shawl,
And turning toward the window, should say:
   'That is not it at all,
   That is not what I meant, at all.'
  . . . . .

No! I am not Prince Hamlet, nor was meant to be;
Am an attendant lord, one that will do
To swell a progress, start a scene or two,
Advise the prince; no doubt, an easy tool,
Deferential, glad to be of use,
Politic, cautious, and meticulous;
Full of high sentence, but a bit obtuse;
At times, indeed, almost ridiculous—
Almost, at times, the Fool.

I grow old . . . I grow old . . .
I shall wear the bottoms of my trousers rolled.

Shall I part my hair behind? Do I dare to eat a peach?
I shall wear white flannel trousers, and walk upon the beach.
I have heard the mermaids singing, each to each.

I do not think that they will sing to me.

I have seen them riding seaward on the waves
Combing the white hair of the waves blown back
When the wind blows the water white and black.

We have lingered in the chambers of the sea
By sea-girls wreathed with seaweed red and brown
Till human voices wake us, and we drown.

ORWELL: Again, we ought to have a bit of prose from Henry James to balance that. But we haven't time. Before we go on to 19th Century writers we must have something to represent the negro writers.

MARSON: Well, there are James Weldon Johnson, Counteè Cullen,[16] Paul Lawrence Dunbar[17] . . .

ORWELL: But we'd like you to read something of your own. We're lucky having a negro writer with us in the studio today, Una Marson her name is. What do you think you could read us?

MARSON: Well, I've one here called "The Banjo Boy" that might do. It's only short, though.

ORWELL: All right, go ahead. Here it is. "The Banjo Boy". This is Una Marson, the West Indian writer, reading it.

MARSON:
Black boy,
How you play that banjo!
Gee—it goes right to my toes,
I could dance all night
And through the day again.
How your face beams.
Do you love it?
I'll say you do.

Where did you get that rhythm?
That swing and that motion,
That bubbling laughter
With which you punctuate
Your songs? I have it too,
I can feel it going through me,
But I cannot express like you do.

You know it's good to be alive,
Don't you, as long as the sun shines
And the banjo is in your hands?
Maybe you are hungry,
Maybe your shirt is going,
Maybe you are not worth a gill,
But what do you care?

There's your banjo, the boys come
And sing and hum and dance
Round you—they share in your joy,
They respond to your songs—
Those banjo songs that call me.

ORWELL: Now we must start on the 19th Century writers. We'll have something from Walt Whitman presently. I think it's time now we had a bit of prose.

EMPSON: Well there's Poe & Hawthorne & Emerson. But if we're sticking to the pioneering period and leaving the New England writers out,[18] the best of all is Mark Twain's "Life on the Mississippi. Or "Roughing It" and "The Innocents at Home". These two books give you the disorderly side of the pioneering period, which Whitman rather leaves out. There's also a wonderful atmosphere in "Tom Sawyer" and "Huckleberry Finn".

ORWELL: Unfortunately Mark Twain is difficult to quote from because he never talks about the same subject for more than half a page at a time.

READ: What about Herman Melville? Something from "Moby-Dick" for instance.

ANAND:[19] Or "White-Jacket". That gives a picture of life aboard an American ship in the 'forties. It's about the time when Melville was a seaman in the American Navy.

146

EMPSON: The passage I like best in it is Melville's description of falling off the mast into the sea.

READ: Very well, let Orwell read that. Here it is. A passage from "White-Jacket",[20] by Herman Melville.

ORWELL: With the end of the line in one hand, I was mounting the topmast shrouds, when our captain of the top told me that I had better take off my jacket; but though it was not a very cold night, I had been reclining so long in the top, that I had become somewhat chilly, so I thought best not to comply with the hint.[21]

Having reeved the line through all the inferior blocks, I went out with it to the end of the weather-top-gallant yard-arm, and was in the act of leaning over and passing it through the suspended jewel-block there, when the ship gave a plunge in the sudden swells of the calm sea, and pitching me still further over the yard, threw the heavy skirts of my jacket right over my head, completely muffling me. Somehow I thought it was the sail that had flapped, and, under that impression, threw up my hands to drag it from my head, relying upon the sail itself to support me meanwhile. Just then the ship gave another sudden jerk, and, head foremost, I pitched from the yard. I knew where I was, from the rush of the air by my ears, but all else was a nightmare. A bloody film was before my eyes, through which, ghost-like, passed and repassed my father, mother, and sisters. An unutterable nausea oppressed me; I was conscious of gasping; there seemed no breath in my body. It was over one hundred feet that I fell—down, down, with lungs collapsed as in death. Ten thousand pounds of shot seemed tied to my head, as the irresistible law of gravitation dragged me, head foremost and straight as a die, toward the infallible centre of this terraqueous globe. All I had seen, and read, and heard, and all I had thought and felt in my life, seemed intensified in one fixed idea in my soul. But dense as this idea was, it was made up of atoms. Having fallen from the projecting yard-arm end, I was conscious of a collected satisfaction in feeling, that I should not be dashed on the deck, but would sink into the speechless profound of the sea.

With the bloody, blind film before my eyes, there was a still stranger hum in my head, as if a hornet were there; and I thought to myself, Great God! this is Death! Yet these thoughts were unmixed with alarm. Like frost-work that flashes and shifts its seared hues in the sun, all my braided, blended emotions were in themselves icy cold and calm.[22]

So protracted did my fall seem, that I can even now recall the feeling of wondering how much longer it would be, ere all was over and I struck. Time seemed to stand still, and all the worlds seemed poised on their poles, as I fell, soul-becalmed, through the eddying whirl and swirl of the maelstrom air.

At first, as I have said, I must have been precipitated head foremost; but I was conscious, at length, of a swift, flinging motion of my limbs, which involuntarily threw themselves out, so that at last I must have fallen in a heap. This is more likely, from the circumstance, that when I struck the sea, I felt as if some one had smote me slantingly across the shoulder and along part of my right side.[23]

As I gushed into the sea, a thunder-boom sounded in my ear; my soul seemed flying from my mouth. The feeling of death flooded over me with the billows. The blow from the sea must have turned me, so that I sank almost feet foremost through a soft, seething, foamy lull. Some current seemed hurrying me away; in a trance I yielded, and sank deeper down with a glide. Purple and pathless was the deep calm now around me, flecked by summer lightnings in an azure afar. The horrible nausea was gone; the bloody, blind film turned a pale green; I wondered whether I was yet dead, or still dying. But of a sudden some fashionless form brushed my side— some inert, coiled fish of the sea; the thrill of being alive again tingled in my nerves, and the strong shunning of death shocked me through.

For one instant an agonising revulsion came over me as I found myself utterly sinking. Next moment the force of my fall was expended; and there I hung, vibrating, in the mid-deep. What wild sounds rang in my ear! One was a soft moaning, as of low waves on the beach; the other wild and heartlessly jubilant, as of the sea in the height of a tempest. Oh soul! thou then heardest life and death: as he who stands upon the Corinthian shore hears both the Ionian and the Aegean waves.[24] The life-and-death poise soon passed; and then I found myself slowly ascending, and caught a dim glimmering of light.

Quicker and quicker I mounted; till at last I bounded up like a buoy, and my whole head was bathed in the blessed air.

I had fallen in a line with the main-mast;[25] I now found myself nearly abreast of the mizen-mast, the frigate slowly gliding by like a black world in the water. Her vast hull loomed out of the night, showing hundreds of seamen in the hammock nettings, some tossing over ropes, others madly flinging overboard the hammocks; but I was too far out from them immediately to reach what they threw. I essayed to swim towards the ship; but instantly I was conscious of a feeling like being pinioned in a feather bed, and, moving my hands, felt my jacket puffed out above my tight girdle with water. I strove to tear it off; but it was looped together here and there, and the strings were not then to be sundered by hand. I whipped out my knife, that was tucked at my belt, and ripped my jacket straight up and down, as if I were ripping open myself. With a violent struggle I then burst out of it, and was free. Heavily soaked, it slowly sank before my eyes.

Sink! sink! oh shroud! thought I; sink forever! accursed jacket that thou art!

'See that white shark!' cried a horrified voice from the taffrail; 'he'll have that man down his hatchway! Quick! the *grains*! the *grains*!'

The next instant that barbed bunch of harpoons pierced through and through the unfortunate jacket, and swiftly sped down with it out of sight.[26]

Being now astern of the frigate, I struck out boldly toward the elevated pole of one of the lifebuoys which had been cut away. Soon after, one of the cutters picked me up. As they dragged me out of the water into the air, the sudden transition of elements made my every limb feel like lead, and I helplessly sunk into the bottom of the boat.

Ten minutes after, I was safe on board, and, springing aloft, was ordered to reeve anew the stun'-sail halyards, which, slipping through the blocks when I had let go the end, had unrove and fallen to the deck.

The sail was soon set; and, as if purposely to salute it, a gentle breeze soon came, and the Neversink once more glided over the water, a soft ripple at her bows, and leaving a tranquil wake behind.

EMPSON:[27] It's a very ornate piece of prose, isn't it? And in a way very English. Quite unlike a modern American writer. I think you notice about the earlier American writers that they are much more deeply under European influence than the modern ones, even when they're very proud of not being Europeans.

ORWELL: Since we're trying to cover the pioneering period we ought to have something by Bret Harte. He's best known for his comic poems, but I should like something that brings in the Western mining camp motif.

READ: A very suitable piece[28] from Bret Harte would be the poem he wrote after Dickens's death. That has the mining camp background, and it illustrates what you were saying just now—the cultural dependence of America on Europe at that date.

ORWELL: All right, let's have that. Here we are then. "Dickens in Camp", by Bret Harte. This is William Empson reading it.

EMPSON: DICKENS IN CAMP by Bret Harte

Above the pines the moon was slowly drifting,
    The river sang below;
The dim Sierras, far beyond, uplifting
    Their minarets of snow:

The roaring camp-fire, with rude humour, painted
    The ruddy tints of health
On haggard face and form that drooped and fainted
    In the fierce race for wealth;

Till one arose, and from his pack's scant treasure
    A hoarded volume drew,
And cards were dropped from hands of listless leisure
    To hear the tale anew.

And then, while round them shadows gathered faster,
    And as the fire-light fell,
He read aloud the book wherein the Master
    Had writ of "Little Nell".

Perhaps 'twas boyish fancy — for the reader
    Was youngest of them all —
But, as he read, from clustering pine and cedar
    A silence seemed to fall;

The fir-trees, gathering closer in the shadows,
    Listened in every spray,
While the whole camp, with "Nell" on English meadows
    Wandered and lost their way.

And so in mountain solitudes — o'ertaken
    As by some spell divine —
Their cares dropped from them like the needles shaken
    From out the gusty pine.

Lost is that camp, and wasted all its fire;
    And he who wrought that spell? —
Ah, towering pine and stately Kentish spire,
    Ye have one tale to tell!

> Lost is that camp! but let its fragrant story
>> Blend with the breath that thrills
> With hop-vines' incense all the pensive glory
>> That fills the Kentish hills.
>
> And on that grave where English oak, and holly,
>> And laurel wreaths entwine,
> Deem it not all a too presumptuous folly —
>> This spray of Western pine!

ORWELL: We're getting near the end of our time, and we must have something from Whitman. Which bit shall we have, I wonder.

READ: Again, the best are unfortunately the longest. Poems like "Seadrift" & "When Lilacs Last in the Dooryard Bloom'd".[29]

ANAND:[30] We haven't touched on the American civil war yet. We ought to bring that in.

MARSON:[31] Then why not have "O Captain! My Captain"? It'll bear repeating.

ORWELL: I tell you what. We'll have "O, Captain! My Captain!", and then to finish up with we'll have the poem about Ann Rutledge from the "Spoon River Anthology" of Edgar Lee Masters,[32] which goes with it in a way. I suggest that as they're both short poems we read them straight off without a break between. Read, will you read the Whitman, and Empson, will you read the bit from the "Spoon River Anthology"? Here they are, then. "O Captain! My Captain!", by Walt Whitman, and "Ann Rutledge" by Edgar Lee Masters.

READ: O CAPTAIN! MY CAPTAIN!

O Captain! My Captain! our fearful trip is done,
The ship has weather'd every rack, the prize we sought is won,
The port is near, the bells I hear, the people all exulting,
While follow eyes the steady keel, the vessel grim and daring;
    But O heart! heart! heart!
        O the bleeding drops of red,
            Where on the deck my Captain lies,
                Fallen cold and dead.

O Captain! My Captain! rise up and hear the bells;
Rise up—for you the flag is flung—for you the bugle trills,
For you bouquets and ribbon'd wreaths—for you the shores a-crowding,
For you they call, the swaying mass, their eager faces turning;
    Here Captain! dear father!
        The arm beneath your head!
            It is some dream that on the deck,
                You've fallen cold and dead.

My Captain does not answer, his lips are pale and still,
My father does not feel my arm, he has no pulse nor will,
The ship is anchor'd safe and sound, its voyage closed and done,
From fearful trip the victor ship comes in with object won;
    Exult O shores, and ring O bells!
        But I with mournful tread,

Walk the deck my Captain lies,
Fallen cold and dead.

EMPSON: ANN RUTLEDGE by Edgar Lee Masters

Out of me unworthy and unknown
The vibrations of deathless music;
"With malice toward none, with charity for all."
Out of me forgiveness of millions toward millions,
And the beneficent face of a nation
Shining with justice and truth.
I am Ann Rutledge who sleep beneath these weeds,
Beloved of Abraham Lincoln,
Wedded to him, not through union,
But through separation.
Bloom forever, O Republic,
From the dust of my bosom.

ANNOUNCER: That is the end of the fourth number of "Voice", our monthly radio magazine. Those taking part were Herbert Read,[33] Una Marson, George Orwell, Mulk Raj Anand, and William Empson. The next number of "Voice" will be on Tuesday, December 1st.

The first reading is that of the text as amended by Orwell for the broadcast; the second reading is that of the original typescript, except that passages cut from readings have been restored (for easier reading) but the extent of the cut is noted.

1. Una Marson (1905–1965), a West Indian poet, was at this time working as West Indian Programme Organiser in the BBC Overseas Service; see 1706.
2. ORWELL:] GEORGE, written in after ORWELL:
3. ANAND] SOMEONE
4. READ] SOMEONE
5. John Steinbeck] even Gertrude Stein
6. The Burying Ground by the Ties, by Archibald MacLeish.] manuscript insertion
7. Wm. Empson] Louis MacNeice; similarly adjusted for next speaker
8. Typescript has 'Read by: L. MacNeice,' which is not amended.
9. The ellipses, for indications of omission, are as in the script.
10. Steinbeck] Jack London
11. or something from James Farrell] manuscript interlinear insertion
12. The Industrial Workers of the World (Wobblies), a revolutionary industrial union founded in Chicago in 1905, one of the aims of which was the overthrow of capitalism. The main period of its strength was in the years before the United States entered World War I.
13. ANAND] SOMEONE. There is a large asterisk written against Anand's name.
14. And surely the best of the early poems is] Then what about having
15. The ellipses and lines of five periods are as in the original poem. Spaces have been inserted after lines 12 and 72 that were not in the typescript. There are large asterisks in the margin beside lines 98–99 and 110–11, perhaps to ensure that the reader did not miss them. The typescript has 'And for a hundred indecisions,' after 'And yet time for a hundred indecisions.' This comes at the end of a page of typescript and is probably a false start for the next line. It is not reproduced here.
16. Countee Cullen] manuscript interlinear insertion
17. James Weldon Johnson (1871–1938), American poet, editor, and lawyer, helped found the National Association for the Advancement of Colored People; his fictional Autobiography of an Ex-Colored Man was published in 1912; his actual autobiography, Along This Way, in 1933. Countee Cullen (1903–1946) was a leading poet of the Harlem Renaissance; his works include Copper Sun (1927), The Ballad of the Brown Girl (1927), The Black Christ and Other

Poems (1929), and *The Medea and Some Poems* (1929). Paul Laurence Dunbar (1872–1906) was of an earlier generation of black poets; his *Lyrics of Lowly Life* (1896) had an introduction by William Dean Howells. He also wrote four novels.

18. Well there's Poe . . . writers out,] *manuscript interlinear insertion*
19. ANAND] SOMEONE. *The typescript has* a wonderful picture *but* wonderful *has been crossed out.*
20. A passage from "White Jacket",] From chapter . . . of "White Jacket". *The passage is from ch. 92, 'The Last of the Jacket.' Orwell's typescript has* The thousand *for* Ten thousand *in the second paragraph; the ship's name,* Neversink, *is not marked for italicisation in the last paragraph. Some additional hyphenation in the typescript has not been changed; it may have been an aid to delivery. Orwell did not hyphenate the title.*
21. With the end of the line . . . comply with the hint.] *cut from broadcast*
22. With the bloody, blind film . . . cold and calm.] *cut from broadcast*
23. At first . . . my right side.] *cut from broadcast*
24. What wild sounds . . . the Aegean waves.] *cut from broadcast*
25. A large asterisk has been written in the margin against this line.
26. Heavily soaked . . . out of sight.] *cut from broadcast*
27. EMPSON] SOMEONE
28. A very suitable piece] Much the most suitable thing
29. READ: Again, the best . . . Dooryard bloom'd".] *interlinear insertion. Slight styling errors in the titles have been silently corrected.*
30. ANAND] SOMEONE
31. MARSON] SOMEONE ELSE
32. by Edgar Lee Masters,] *interlinear insertion.* Edgar Lee Masters (1869–1950) is remembered particularly for his *Spoon River Anthology* (1915), which, in free verse, characterises the secret lives of those living in a small Midwest town. Ann Rutledge (1813?–1835) was the daughter of Abraham Lincoln's landlord in New Salem, Illinois. After her death, an unsubstantiated story of Lincoln's love for her became the basis for a persistent myth.
33. The name Louis MacNeice followed Read but was crossed through.

1631. To K. K. Ardaschir

4 November 1942   PP/EB

Dear Ardaschir,

Your talk on President Inonu is on November 11th, sometime between 12.15 and 12.30, so if you are here at 11.45 that will be O.K. The talk may be a minute or so on the long side, but if so we can easily shorten it when we rehearse it. I am returning the two talks on neutrality and "The History of the Huns". I am afraid I cannot use these because not only is my schedule very full up, as you know—in fact it is now full up until some time into next year—but the second one in particular is politically very doubtful from our point of view. I don't of course mean that there is nothing in what you say, but we have a certain propaganda line, which we cannot depart from very widely without seeming to falsify ourselves. I am sorry about this. We are broadcasting your recorded talk on Byron on November 17th. You have asked for me° private address: it is 10A, Mortimer Crescent, N.W. 6.

I should be very glad to buy another pullet if you come across one.[1]

Yours sincerely,
Eric Blair
Talks Producer
Indian Section

1. Despite his reviewing and work at the BBC, as well as his Home Guard duties, Orwell was evidently still active as a smallholder. See his War-time Diary, *1345*, *1.8.42*, where he records he is making a hen-house.

1632. To T. S. Eliot

4 November 1942   PP/EB/NP

Dear Eliot,
We were sorry you could not take part in yesterday's production of "Voice", so we are giving you plenty of notice about the next one. It will be on December 1st, which is a Tuesday. We will let you have further details later, but if you are free on that morning, roughly speaking between eleven and one (we usually begin rehearsing at 10.30) we should like it very much if you would take part.

> Yours sincerely,
> George Orwell
> Talks Producer
> Indian Section

1633. To L. F. Rushbrook Williams

4 November 1942   Original; EB/NP

PROPOSED TALK BY SIR RAMASWAMI MUDALIAR

I shall be grateful if you could cover through the proper channels the proposed broadcast in English, of 13½ minutes duration, by Sir Ramaswami Mudaliar, Cabinet Minister. The date of the proposed broadcast is Saturday 14th November, 1115–1130 GMT, in the Eastern Service (Red Network).[1]

> [Signed] Eric Blair
> (Eric Blair)

1. On the same day, Mary Blackburn (on Bokhari's behalf) wrote to Boswell of Talks Booking explaining payment arrangements for Sir Ramaswami Mudaliar: 'He is a Cabinet Minister and we understand, therefore, that no Contract is issued, but that a fee is offered, which Sir Ramaswami Mudaliar can either accept or pass on the fee to a charity. Will you kindly arrange this in the usual way. We understand that a fee of twelve guineas would be suitable.' The fee typed in was ten guineas, but was changed to twelve.

1634. BBC Talks Booking Form, 4.11.42

S. K. Das Gupta: to translate and read Bengali Newsletters; written in English by E. Blair; broadcast 7, 14, 21 and 28.11.42; fee £5.5s each. Signed: M Blackburn for I.P.O.

1635. BBC Talks Booking Form, 4.11.42

Flying Officer Henry Treece: 'recording 6 of his own poems — total duration 5 mins. approx';[1] recorded 3.11.42; broadcast not fixed; fee £2.2s. Signed: M Blackburn for I.P.O. Remarks: 'Copyright being covered through Miss Alexander.'

1. In the space provided to give the series title there is simply a number of dashes. Owing to the problems Treece faced in getting leave to broadcast in a particular programme at a particular time, Orwell was having him record some poems against their future use.

1636. To Henry Treece

5 November 1942   Original and carbon copies   PP/EB/NP

Dear Treece,

I forgot to ask you for a copy of the two poems which you read from manuscript. They are called "Love Song" and "Through Seven Days and Seven Nights". We have got them on the record of course, but we had better have a written copy as well. Can you let me know, at the same time, whether these two have been published yet, or not, as I want to get the Copyright covered.

You will get the written authorisation from your Commanding Officer, won't you? There is no immediate hurry, because I don't expect to be able to use these till about January.

Yours,
[Signed] Geo. Orwell
George Orwell
Talks Producer
Indian Section

1637. 'Imaginary Interview: George Orwell and Jonathan Swift'

Recorded, 2 November 1942; broadcast, BBC African Service, 6 November 1942; *The Listener*, 26 November 1942, as 'Too Hard on Humanity'

It is not a simple matter to present Orwell's 'Imaginary Interview' with Swift in the form he might have preferred were he now seeing the text through the press. In West: *Broadcasts* is a version of the typescript which differs considerably from that given here, though West notes that 'Additions or corrections made by Orwell in his own hand to a typed script have . . . been incorporated' and he does not claim to 'provide any alternative readings written by third parties' (68). In a footnote, he states that this broadcast was printed 'in a censored form' in *The Listener* (7). That the text in *The Listener* is shorter is true, but it also has portions added to it which West does not include. Censorship seems doubtful. There are other possible reasons for this version. Paper was in very short supply at this time; even after the war, articles had to be cut to get sufficient variety into a journal. A more probable reason was that it followed necessary shortening of the typescript for the broadcast. The full text would probably have taken a little over 16 minutes to read, given that the typescript lacks a passage to be quoted; this was included in *The Listener* but not in West. Presumably the broadcast, with its accompanying announcements, lasted for 15 minutes. Invariably Orwell asked his speakers to write a script that would run for 13½ minutes. It is impossible to know how quickly this script was read, yet, as cut and, perhaps, with the addition found at the end of *The Listener*, a time of 13½ minutes would be about right. Censorship can finally be ruled out, surely, not only by the content of the talk, but also because of the appearance of two bold rubber stamps (unmentioned by West) indicating that the interview was passed for Policy and Security. These clearances, which are signed, were given on 1 November 1942.

The typescript seems to have been prepared by Orwell himself. The typewriter face looks like his and 'today' is unhyphenated, unlike BBC secretarial practice. There are quite a number of manuscript changes (most incorporated in *The Listener*) and Orwell had indicated by stress lines, indications in the margin, and by hyphenating 'clergymen-who-thought,' how the text was to be read. These may, of course, have been prompted by his producer. The script is marked in yellow, green, and red crayon, as well as in pencil. Here, indications of how the text should be spoken are indicated by italicising the words underlined (leaving in roman the titles of books, which Orwell does not underline in his typescript), and adding what might be described as 'stage directions' in italics in square brackets for indications as to tone of voice provided by Orwell in margins or interlineated in the typescript. Typed directions are in roman type.

It is noticeable that the long section omitted from *The Listener* (from 'SWIFT: "The king was struck . . .' to 'SWIFT: . . . true wisdom or true refinement?') is scarcely marked at all for spoken delivery. Two words are lightly underscored, 'impotent' and 'grovelling' (given in italics here), and attention to them is directed by crosses in the margin. This lends weight to the suggestion that this passage, and possibly a few other lines, were cut to save time at the broadcast.

The text in *The Listener* probably follows reasonably closely what was broadcast. The obvious exceptions are the expansion of colloquial forms (so that, for example, 'I've' becomes 'I have') and giving the correct place described by Swift in the poem quoted. The latter might well be a correction made for *The Listener* only. Since Orwell would probably have willingly accepted it had it been pointed out (and he might have seen proofs), that change has been incorporated. Colloquial forms have been retained. Quotations are as Orwell typed them; significant variations from the kind of eighteenth-century edition he purported to have used are noted and the blatant error, left unchanged till now, which refers to a nonexistent Part V of *Gulliver's Travels* has been corrected. The passage at the end in *The Listener* has been added. The aim has been to reproduce the text Orwell wished to broadcast, with the indications for how the text was to be spoken (in square brackets) and the final printed addition, which might or might not have been included in the broadcast. Differences in readings and readings for which the substitutions are included in the text are noted. The many differences between West: *Broadcasts* and this edition are not noted.

It is not always possible to produce a text with which everyone will agree. That is especially so at the point Orwell refers to a passage having to be cut out.

What followed in Swift would certainly have been omitted (it is given in the notes), but I suspect the awkwardness of Swift's continuing to quote from *Gulliver's Travels* required a cut by Orwell on the grounds of clarity and that cut I have maintained (see *n. 45*).

On the verso of the last seven pages of typescript, Orwell has written two telephone numbers for Wickham Steed: 'Freeland nr Witney 254' and (probably) 'Park 4115.' Steed lived in Lansdowne Park in London and at Wootton, near Woodstock in Oxfordshire. The telephone number of the latter was Tackley 2430, so presumably Steed was staying at Freeland. In addition to the programme Steed did for Orwell with Hamilton Fyfe on 7 August 1942, he also took part in 'Imaginary Interview: William Pitt the Younger' on 18 December 1942.

It must be reiterated that, as with the texts of many of Orwell's books, no claim is being made that a definitive text has been—or can be—produced. A very narrow path has to be trodden between Orwell's intentions for his broadcast, what he did with it on the day of broadcasting, how he modified the text for publication, changes agreed to and made silently, and errors introduced in printing. Because the typescript is marked 'Not checked with broadcast' and so, though amended, does not purport to include all changes—indeed, since no text is given for Swift to read from 'A Lady's Dressing Room,' the typescript cannot wholly represent what was broadcast—reliance must be placed on *The Listener* for some readings.

The idea for a series of Imaginary Interviews might have come from Walter Savage Landor's *Imaginary Conversations* (1824–29), some of which are in dramatic form.

ORWELL: My edition of Swift's works was printed some time between 1730 and 1740.[1] It's in twelve small volumes, with calf covers a bit the worse for wear. It's not too easy to read, the ink is faded and the long S's are a nuisance, but I prefer it to any modern edition I've seen. When I open it and smell the dusty smell of old paper[2] and see the woodcut illustrations and the crooked capital letters, I[3] almost have the feeling that I can hear Swift speaking to me. I've a vivid picture of him in my mind's eye,[4] with his knee-breeches and his three-cornered hat, and the snuff box and the spectacles he wrote about in Gulliver's Travels,[5] though I don't believe I've ever seen a portrait of him.[6] There's something in his way of writing that seems to tell you what his voice was like. For instance, here's one of his "Thoughts on Various Subjects": "When a true Genius[7] appears in the world . . ."

SWIFT [*with contempt*]: "When a true Genius appears in the world, you may know him by this infallible sign: that all the *Dunces* are in Confederacy against him".[8]

ORWELL: So[9] you *did* wear a wig, Dr. Swift.[10] I've often wondered.

SWIFT: So you have[11] the first collected edition of my works?[12]

ORWELL: Yes. I bought them for five shillings at a farmhouse auction.

SWIFT: I[13] warn you to beware of all *modern* editions, even of my Travels. I have suffered from such damned dishonest editors as I believe no other writer ever had. It has been my especial misfortune to be edited usually by clergymen-who-thought[14] me a disgrace to their cloth. They were tinkering with my[15] writings long before Dr. Bowdler was ever born or thought of.

ORWELL: You see, Dr. Swift, you have put them in a difficulty. They know you are our greatest prose writer, and yet you used words and raised subjects that they couldn't approve of. In a way I don't approve of you myself.

SWIFT: I am desolated, sir.[16]

ORWELL: I believe Gulliver's Travels has meant more to me than any other[17] book ever written. I can't remember when I first read it, I must have been eight years old at the most, and it's lived with me ever since so that I suppose a year has never passed without my re-reading at least part of it.

SWIFT: I am vastly gratified.[18]

ORWELL: And yet even[19] I can't help feeling that you laid it on a bit too thick. You were too hard on humanity, and on your own country.[20]

SWIFT: H'm![21]

ORWELL: For instance, here's a passage that has always stuck in my memory—also stuck in my gizzard, a little. It's at the end of Chapter VI in the second Book of Gulliver's Travels. Gulliver has just given the King of Brobdingnag a long description of life in England. The King listens to him and then picks him up in his hand, strokes him gently and says—wait a moment, I've got the book here.[22] But perhaps you remember the passage yourself.

SWIFT: Oh, ay. "It does[23] not appear, from all you have said, how any one virtue is required toward the procurement of any one station among you; much less that men were[24] ennobled on account of their *virtue*; [*voice up*] that priests were[25] advanced for their *piety* or *learning*, soldiers, for their conduct or valour; judges, for their integrity; senators, for the love of their country; or counsellors for their wisdom . . .[26] [*Quieter*] By what I have gathered from your own relation, and the answers I have with much[27] pains wringed and extorted from you, I cannot but conclude the bulk of your natives to be the most pernicious race of little odious vermin that nature [*crescendo*] ever suffered to crawl upon the surface of the earth"

ORWELL: I'd allow you 'pernicious' and 'odious' and 'vermin', Dr. Swift, but I'm inclined to cavil at 'most'. 'The *most* pernicious'.[28] Are we in this island really worse than the *rest* of the world?

SWIFT: No.[29] But I know you better than I know the rest of the world. When I wrote, I went upon the principle that if a lower kind of animal existed than you[30] I could not imagine it.

ORWELL: That was 200 years ago. Surely you must admit that we have made a certain amount of progress since then?

SWIFT: Progress in quantity, yes. The buildings are taller and the vehicles move faster. Human beings are more numerous and commit greater follies. A battle kills a million where it used to kill a thousand.[31] And in the matter of great men, as you still call them, I admit[32] that your age outdoes mine. Whereas previously some petty tyrant was considered to have reached the highest point of human fame if he laid waste a single province and pillaged half a dozen towns, [*with ironic pleasure*] your great men nowadays can devastate whole *continents* and condemn[33] entire races of men to *slavery*.[34]

ORWELL: I was coming to that. One thing I feel inclined to urge in favour of my country is that we don't produce great men and don't like war. Since your day something has appeared called totalitarianism.

SWIFT: A new thing?[35]

ORWELL: It isn't strictly new, it's merely been made practicable by[36] modern weapons and modern methods of communication. Hobbes and other seventeenth-century writers predicted[37] it. You yourself wrote about it with extraordinary foresight.[38] There are passages in Part III of Gulliver's Travels that give me the feeling that I'm reading an account of the Reichstag Fire trial. But I'm thinking particularly of a passage in Part IV[39] where the Houyhnhnm who is Gulliver's master is telling him about the habits and customs of the Yahoos. It appears that each tribe of Yahoos had a Dictator, or Fuehrer and this Dictator liked to surround himself with yes-men. The Houyhnhnm says:

SWIFT [*quiet*]:[40] "He had heard, indeed, some curious Houyhnhnms observe, that in most herds there was a sort of ruling Yahoo,[41] who was always more *deformed* in body, and *mischievous* in disposition, than any of the rest. That this leader had usually a [*tenderly*] favourite, as like himself as he could get, whose employment was to lick his master's feet[42] and [*licorously*][43] drive the female Yahoos to his *kennel*; for which he was now and then rewarded with a piece of ass's flesh. This favourite is hated by the whole herd, and therefore, to protect himself, keeps always near the person of his leader. He usually continues in office till a worse[44] can be found; but the very moment he is discarded, his successor, at the head of all the Yahoos in that district, young and old, male and female, come in a body, and—"

ORWELL: We shall have to leave out that bit.

SWIFT: Thank you, Dr. Bowdler.[45]

ORWELL: I remember that passage whenever I think of Goebbels or Ribbentrop, or for that matter Monsieur Laval. But looking at the world as a whole, do you find that the human being is *still* a Yahoo?

SWIFT: I had a good view of the people of London on my way here, and I assure you that I could remark very little difference. I saw round me[46] the same hideous faces, unshapely bodies and ill-fitting clothes that could be seen in London two hundred years ago.[47]

ORWELL: But the town had changed, even if the people had not?

SWIFT: Oh, it has grown prodigously. Many a green field where Pope and I used to stroll after dinner on summer evenings is now a warren of bricks and mortar, for the kennelling of Yahoos.[48]

ORWELL: But the town is a great deal safer, more orderly,[49] than it was in your day. One can walk about nowadays without the fear of getting one's throat cut, even at night. You ought to admit some improvement there, though I suppose you won't. Besides, it's cleaner. In your day there were still lepers in London, not to[50] mention the Plague. We have baths fairly frequently nowadays, and women don't keep their hair up for a month at a time and carry little silver goads to scratch their heads with. Do you remember writing a poem called "A Description of a Lady's Dressing Room"?[51]

SWIFT: 'Strephon, who found the room was void
And Betty otherwise employed,
Stole in, and took a strict survey
Of all the litter as it lay:
Whereof, to make the matter clear,
An inventory follows here'.

ORWELL: Unfortunately I don't think the inventory is suitable for broad-casting.

SWIFT: Poor Dr. Bowdler!

ORWELL: But the point is, would you sign[52] that poem nowadays? Tell me candidly, do we stink as we used to?

SWIFT: Certainly the smells are different. There was a new one I remarked as I came through the streets—(sniffs)—

ORWELL: It's called petrol. But don't you find that the mass of the people are more intelligent than they were, or at least better educated? How about the newspapers and the radio? Surely they have opened people's minds a little? There are very few people in England now who can't read, for instance.[53]

SWIFT: That is why they are so easily deceived. [*Voice up*] Your ancestors two hundred years ago were full of barbarous superstitions, but they would not have been so credulous as to believe [*gentle*][54] your daily newspapers. As you seem to know my works, perhaps you will remember another little thing I wrote, an "Essay upon Genteel and Ingenious Conversation?"

ORWELL: Of course I remember it well. It's a description of fashionable ladies and gentlemen talking—an appalling stream of drivel which goes on and on for six hours without stopping.

SWIFT: On my way here I looked in at some of your fashionable clubs and suburban coffee shops,[55] and listened to the conversation. I half believed that that little Essay of mine was being parodied.[56] If there was any change, it was only that the English tongue had[57] lost something of its earthy[58] natural quality.[59]

ORWELL: How about the scientific and technical achievements of the last two hundred years—railway trains, motor cars, aeroplanes and so forth? Doesn't that strike you as an advance?

SWIFT: I also passed through Cheapside on my way here. It has almost ceased to exist. Round St. Paul's there is only an acre of ruins. The Temple has been almost wiped out, and the little church outside it is only a shell. I am speaking only of the places I knew, but it is the same all over London, I believe. That is what your machines have done for you.

ORWELL:[60] I am getting the worst of this argument, but I still feel, Dr. Swift, that there is something deeply deficient in your outlook. You remember what the king of Brobdingnag said when Gulliver described cannons and gunpowder to him?

SWIFT: "The king was struck with horror at the description I had given of those terrible engines, and the proposal I had made. He was amazed, how so *impotent* and *grovelling* an insect as I (these were his expressions) could entertain such inhuman ideas, and in so familiar a manner as to appear wholly unmoved at all the scenes of blood and desolation, which I had painted as the common effects of those destructive machines; whereof, he said, some evil genius, enemy to mankind, must have been the first contriver. As for himself, he protested, that although few things delighted him so much as new discoveries in art or in nature, yet he would rather lose half his kingdom than be privy to such a secret, which he commanded me, as I valued my life, never to mention any more."

ORWELL: I suppose the king would have spoken even more forcibly about tanks or mustard gas. But I can't help feeling that his attitude, and yours, show a certain lack of curiosity. Perhaps the most brilliant thing you ever wrote was the description of the scientific academy in part III of Gulliver's Travels. But after all you were wrong. You thought the whole process of scientific research was absurd, because you could not believe that any tangible result would ever come out of it. But after all the results have come. Modern machine civilisation is there, for good or evil. And the poorest person nowadays is better off, so far as physical comfort goes, than a nobleman in Saxon times, or even in the reign of Queen Anne.

SWIFT: Has that added anything to true wisdom or true refinement? Let me remind you of another saying of mine: "The greatest Inventions were produced in the Times of Ignorance; as the use of the Compass, Gunpowder and Printing; and by the dullest nations, as the Germans."

ORWELL: I see now where it is that we part company, Dr. Swift. I believe that human society, and therefore human nature, can change. You don't. Do you still hold to that, after the French Revolution and[61] the Russian Revolution?

SWIFT: You know very well what is my final word. I wrote it on the last page of Gulliver's Travels, but I will speak it again. "My reconcilement to the Yahoo kind in general might not be so difficult if they would be content with those vices and follies only, which nature has entitled them to. I am not in the least provoked at the sight of a lawyer, a pickpocket, a colonel, a fool, a lord, a gamester, a politician, a whore-master, a physician, an evidence,[62] a suborner, an attorney, a traitor, or the like: this is all according to[63] the due course of things: but when I behold a lump of deformity and diseases both in body and mind, smitten with *pride*, it immediately breaks all the measures of my patience; neither shall I be ever able[64] to comprehend how such an animal . . ." [*voice fading*]

ORWELL: Ah, he's fading out! Dr. Swift! Dr. Swift! Is that your last word?

SWIFT [*voice a little stronger then finally fading out*]: Neither shall I ever be able[65] to comprehend how such an animal and such a vice could tally together. And therefore I here entreat those who have any tincture of this absurd vice, that they will not presume to come[66] in my sight.

ORWELL: He's gone. I didn't get much change out of him. He was a great man, and yet he was partially blind. He could only see one thing at a time. His vision of human society is so penetrating, and yet in the last analysis it's false. He couldn't see what the simplest person sees, that life is worth living and human beings, even if they're dirty and ridiculous, are mostly decent. But after all, if he could have seen that I suppose he couldn't have written Gulliver's Travels.[67] Ah well, let him rest in peace in Dublin, where, in the words of his epitaph, 'Savage indignation can no longer lacerate his heart'.

SWIFT: *Ubi saeva indignatio ulterius cor lacerare nequit.*

TS = typescript; *L* = *The Listener*; *om.* = omitted from; where notes indicate a ms insertion in TS and this is followed by '*and L*' it is, of course, the text that is to be found in *L*, not the mode of insertion.

1. The edition, like the interview itself, seems to be imaginary. A list drawn up after his death shows Orwell possessed 'SWIFT, J. Miscellanies. 1, 2, 3, 4, 5, 6, 7, 8, 9, 10, 13. 1738–1744,' and it is probably to this (which is not the first edition; see Swift's second speech) to which he refers. He also had the Nonesuch, one-volume edition of *Gulliver's Travels and Selected Writings* (1944), but that was not given to him until 1946 (by Paul Potts). There were editions of Swift's works published in 4 vols. (1735), 6 vols. (1738), 8 vols. (1746), 6 vols. (1755), 12 vols. (1755), 9 expanded to 14 vols. (1755–75), 12 expanded to 16 vols. (1755–65), among others. The reference to woodcuts may be no more than a loose reference to printers' ornaments.
2. old paper] old paper—that's an intoxicating smell if you're fond of books—, TS, *but crossed through; om.* L
3. I] *L; om.* TS
4. vivid picture] vivid imaginative picture, TS, *inserted interlinearly*; in my mind's eye] *crossed through in* TS; *restored in* L
5. and the snuff box . . . Travels,] *added in* L
6. him.] him. Sometimes I half expect that he'll step out of the printed page and answer me, TS, *but crossed through; om.* L
7. Above 'a true Genius' is written 'published in' in TS, but crossed through. Orwell may have begun to add detail he then thought superfluous, or he may not have been able to check the date conveniently.

8. 'Genius,' 'Dunces,' 'Confederacy': *some editions also capitalise* 'World' *and* 'Sign,' *but not* 'Confederacy'
9. So] *preceded by* 'He's materialised after all! I knew it would happen sooner or later. How do you do, Dr. Swift.' *in TS, but crossed through; om. L*
10. Dr. Swift] *interlinear insertion in TS; om. L*
11. So you have] Did you say that you possessed, *handwritten substitution in TS; also in L.*
12. See *n. 1 above.*
13. I] You were lucky I *in TS, but crossed through; om. L*
14. clergymen-who-thought] *hyphens inserted by hand in TS* (*as aid in reading to convey correct sense?*); *om. L*
15. with my] with your, *ms. substitution in TS*; with] at *in L*
16. SWIFT: I am desolated, sir.] *ms. marginal insertion in TS and L*
17. other] *ms. insertion in TS and L*
18. SWIFT: I am vastly gratified.] *ms. marginal insertion in TS*; I am gratified, *in L*
19. even] *added in L, perhaps following omission of* 'even' *when last sentence was cut* (*see n. 20*).
20. country.] country. You even preferred Louis XIV's France, which is almost like preferring Hitler's Germany today *in TS, but crossed through; om. L. This comparison was perhaps not tactful in a broadcast beamed to Africa, where he might be heard in French territories.*
21. SWIFT: H'm!] *ms. marginal addition in TS; om. L*
22. —wait a moment, I've got the book here] *om. L*
23. does] doth *in most editions*
24, 25. were] are *in most editions*
26. wisdom . . .] TS, *as amended*; wisdom.] L; TS *originally had:* 'wisdom. As for yourself (continued the king), who have spent the greatest part of your life in travelling, I am well disposed to hope you may hitherto have escaped many vices of your country. But
27. much] so much, L
28. 'The *most* pernicious'.] *ms. insertion in TS and L*
29. No. But I know] L; TS *has ms. insertion,* 'Not at all. But' *and adds* 'I know' *after* 'better than'
30. existed than you] than an Englishman existed, *amended in TS and L*
31. Orwell: That's true.] *marginal ms. interjection in TS, but crossed through; not in L*
32. admit] must admit, TS
33. condemn] *ms. substitution for* 'reduce' *in TS and L*
34. *slavery*] *ms. substitution for* 'the status of slaves' *in TS and L*
35. SWIFT: A new thing?] *marginal ms. insertion in TS and L*
36. by] *ms. substitution for* 'owing to,' TS *and L*
37. predicted] L; TS *has* 'forecast' (*change made to avoid initial rhyme resulting from next alteration?*)
38. foresight] L; *ms. substitution for* 'prescience,' TS
39. Part IV] *editorial emendation*; TS *and L have* 'Part V,' *but* Gulliver's Travels *has only four parts, and it is to* Part IV *that Orwell refers*
40. '[quiet]' *is written well above the top line in TS and over* 'observe.' *There are brackets around the first eight words of the speech, indicating that it is these that are to be spoken quietly.*
41. Yahoo] Yahoo (as among us there is generally some leading or principal stag in a park, TS, *but crossed through*
42. *Gulliver's Travels has* 'feet and posteriors.'
43. 'licorously' *is written in yellow crayon and is uncertain; originally* 'contempt' *was written in the margin in red crayon, but this was crossed out in yellow.*
44. worse] worse one, L (*printing error?*)
45. We shall have to leave out that bit.] *lightly crossed out in TS. and later restored. It appears in L, followed by* 'SWIFT: Thank you, Dr. Bowdler.' *In TS, Swift originally said:* 'But how far this might be applicable to our courts, and favourites, and ministers of state, my master said I could best determine.' *This is amended in TS by a ms. insertion,* 'continued one Gentleman' *after* 'courts,' *but this, with the whole passage, is crossed out, and does not appear in L. It may have struck Orwell or his producer that to continue quoting after stating a passage had been omitted could confuse the listener. The passage might have been cut on grounds of taste, however. It reads:* 'and discharge their excrements upon him from head to foot' (*chap VII*). *See n. 51 for another interpolation referring to Dr. Bowdler.*
46. round me] all round me, TS, *but* 'all' *is heavily crossed through with what looks like an arrowhead directing the reader to the next line;* 'all' *om. L*

47. In London two hundred years ago] two hundred years ago in London, or in any other city, for that matter, TS, *which marks transposition of* 'in London' *and crosses out last eight words; similarly amended in L*

48. after dinner . . . Yahoos] after dinner on summer evenings is now a wilderness of bricks and mortar,' TS, *but* 'after dinner' *crossed through,* 'warren' *substituted for* 'wilderness.' *Full point after* 'mortar' *changed to comma and* 'for the kenneling° of Yahoos' *added in ms. L restores* 'after dinner' *but otherwise follows amendments (as given in this edition), allowing for Orwell's second thoughts.*

49. safer, more orderly] safer and more orderly, *amended in TS; L*

50. TS duplicates 'to.'

51. Dressing Room] L; 'Bed–Chamber,' TS. *The correct title is* 'The Lady's Dressing Room.' *A blank line is left after* SWIFT, *TS; L has passage reproduced here, including the reference to Bowdler, presumably what was read.* 'Strephon,' 'Betty,' *and* 'inventory' *are italicised in the 1766 edition.*

52. ORWELL: Unfortunately . . . would you sign] That's the one. But would you sign,' TS; *L reads as reproduced here. The* 'inventory' *thought unsuitable begins,* 'And, first a dirty smock appeared / Beneath the arm-pits well besmeared . . .' *and describes in disgusting detail what underlies a lady of fashion's toilette when she, in Society,* 'all her glory shows.'

53. for instance] *added in L*

54. '[*gentle*]' *is added in manuscript margin of TS, to be applied to* 'your daily newspapers.' TS *has* 'in your,' *but* 'in' *is crossed through.*

55. looked in . . . coffee shops] L; looked in at the Savoy Grill and at some of your fashionable clubs in Pall Mall, TS, *but amended*

56. parodied.] *followed in TS by* Even many of the cant phrases were still the same.; *om. L*

57. had] has, *altered in TS and L*

58. its earthy] the earthy, *altered in TS; L has* 'its earthly,' *a printer's error*

59. quality] quality it once had, TS, *but crossed through; om. L*

60. This speech, the next two speeches, and the first sentence of Swift's next speech are crossed through in TS, om. L. The cut was probably made to save transmission time—hardly a result of censorship.

61. and] L; *om.* TS

62. 'an evidence': *OED*, 7 gives 'One who furnishes testimony or proof; a witness'; also as 'an evidencer' (the form given in West: *Broadcasts*, 116). *OED* also gives an example contemporaneous with Swift from *The Gentleman's Magazine*, 1731: 'The Lady Lawley was sentenced to be imprisoned one month for spiriting away an evidence.'

63. From here to the end of Swift's speech there is a line in the margin down the side of the text; in yellow crayon is a word that appears to be 'grad'—perhaps indicating a gradual fading of the voice level (typed as instruction at the end of the speech).

64. shall I be ever able] L; TS *omits* I

65. ever be able] TS, L; *should read* 'be ever able' *as at n. 64*

66. come] TS, L; *most editions have* 'appear'

67. The TS text and West: *Broadcasts* conclude here. The last five lines of TS are squeezed into the small available space. L adds the final three lines given in this edition, but they may not have been broadcast.

1638. Story by Five Authors

Through Eastern Eyes, 6 November 1942

Part 5 by E. M. Forster

This is a serial by five authors, and to–day I have to finish it. Here are a few reminders of what has been happening in previous instalments. The scene is London during the Blitz, and Gilbert Moss, a disgruntled intellectual, finds an unconscious man lying in a ruined house, and recognises his old enemy, Coburn. He decides to take advantage of the circumstances to commit a murder which will be written off as the results of enemy action. He swings a club high—then realises that a pick-pocket is watching him. Coburn recovers consciousness. Moss threatens to tell the thief the reason for their enmity. But the fellow makes off—taking with him Coburn's gold cigarette lighter, which Moss has been handling. Coburn, who, unknown to Moss has fought in the Spanish Civil War, now takes him outside to talk things over, and they sit in the Park, waiting for the morning to come. Moss pours out his grievances in a passionate speech, showing that Coburn in the past has lost him his job and insulted his feelings. He ends up "You're not going to deny all this, are you." Now I start.

. . . .

Stan—even pick-pockets and touts have names, and this one had been registered at birth as Stanley Barnes—Stan was creeping back across the Park in search of further booty. He had not done badly with the gold cigarette lighter, and his old Ma, to whom he had passed it, advised him to attempt no more until the Jerries were over again and breaking things up. The present raid was in control now, the police, the A.R.P., the A.F.S.[1] were all busy, and it really wasn't safe. But Stan, though cunning, was not always wise, nor could he ever keep still: he was always sliding and darting over the ruins, he was a creature of burning doorways, crashing beams, rubble heaps and spouting drains; he was half-lizard, half-rat; his sort has haunted London ever since the foundation of the city, and 1940 seemed bringing it into its own. So he crept back across the Park towards the ruins in Mayfair, and on his way he came to the bench where Coburn and Moss sat. He recognised Moss's voice— They were talking, talking, talking. What about? He dropped on the grass behind them, to find whether the talk would do him any good.

Moss—the one who called himself the poor one—talked most. Christ, 'ow he fancied the sound of his own voice, that Moss. Talking, talking about his feelings. Seemingly Coburn, the rich one, had once give Moss ten quid not to come to lunch, and did Moss take the money? No. He tear it up. He says 'my feelings is murdered'. He says "Your not going to try to deny all that, are you?"

Then Coburn starts. Coburn's turn. Coburn says no, he's not going to deny it, still he did go to Spain. That seems to please and satisfy Moss no end. 'Spain! what! you fought in Spain?' he squawks. 'Spain! I never knew. 'Oo sent you there?' Coburn he says 'You did. You when you told me what you thought of me and made me see how worthless I was. You've changed my life.' And then they shook 'ands and started shouting and laughing like a pair of kids.

Stan made nothing out of this. To him both of them sounded completely crackers. If he was given money, he didn't give it away, and if there was a war he tried to dodge it. However he never criticised people—that is a pastime for the educated—he merely watched them in case they were any use. His big hope, when he crouched behind the seat, was to do a spot of blackmail. Moss had for sure been going to club Coburn in the burning house, they had for sure exchanged angry words, and where there are troubled waters Stan knew how to fish. But the hope faded. Blackmail was no use now that they were jabbering about Spain and what you did for me and what I did for you, and oh yes and oh no and wonderful.

Presently their voices dropped. Stan had to crawl nearer and he heard Coburn say "Moss, I should like you to meet my woman—Mary. She's wonderful. I suppose you'll refuse after the way I've treated you, still I should have liked it."

Moss he raised no objection. Moss's turn now. Moss he say "Coburn, I should like you—to meet a woman whom I shall never meet again perhaps myself, someone whose very name I don't know. She has kissed me, she has saved my life and more than life."

There was nothing to be done now that they had started about their Judies. He had wasted his time, and it was now too light to work any more bombed houses. Out in the east, far behind Mayfair was a glow of fire— they had got the docks again—and in the direction of Westminster was another glow, faint, and dirty, which proceeded from the neglected sun. A new day was dawning on God's Earth, and Stan regretted it. Still one can't have everything, things being what they are, the night cannot last for ever, and a gold cigarette lighter is better than nothing.

"Well, what about breakfast? Let's see if my Club still exists" said Coburn, stretching himself and suddenly rising. "Brr . . . it's good to be alive at the worst of times. —Hallo, what's that?"

Moss, who felt happier than he had been for years, recognised the pickpocket and pounced. "It's the little worm I saw in your burning diningroom" he cried.

"Oh, let him go!"

"He's got your lighter on him still. I can feel it."

"I ain't, I never pinched it, I worn't there. Who was there? You was, I seed you" spat Stan. The two educated men laughed: seemingly he had said the wrong things.

"I've got it—no I haven't—its—whatever is it?" Moss extracted a flat metal object, fan-shaped, and pierced with four holes. It was a simple and inexpensive contraption for causing pain, it was a knuckle duster. Moss held it on the palm of his hand.

"Gimme that—that's mine". Stan had acquired the knuckle duster while he was employed by the British Fascists. It had been a happy episode— plenty of food, a bed to sleep in at the local centre, and ten shillings a week. "We will cleanse this city of London" he had been told. "We will hack our way through to power". Well, and why not? And he had taken part in one or two purity drives, and had hit one or two people whose noses were the wrong shape, upon the head. British Fascism had not come to a great lot, there hadn't been enough money behind it, it had never gone full steam ahead as in Germany, still, it had been better than nothing, and the knuckle duster was a memento.

"Gimme that back".

Moss tried it on, slipping his four fingers into the holes, and clasping the base in his palm. It fitted comfortably, and gave him a sense of power. The treacherous and primitive little gadget, made in some back alley, was a forerunner of the expensive bombs which had made a rubbish heap of Mayfair and a bonfire of the Docks. "We'll keep this," he told Coburn, who laughed cheerfully, and they turned to go. Chaos became visible: it looked as if civilisation would never creep back, but Coburn, who had seen similar destruction in Spain, knew that this wasn't the case, and that a city can rise again and again to her knees. They spoke of matters pleasant to them: Moss realised that he had indeed been his friend's salvation, and had turned him from a dilettante aristocrat to a gay and selfless hero. The Coburn he had always longed for and loved was a reality—and then—then he got a blow on the back of the head.

It was a badly directed one, he staggered, turned round, and swiped and caught Stan hard. Stan fell like a twig on to the grimy grass and lay motionless.

"My God, it's that pick-pocket" again cried Coburn. "Why won't he leave us alone. Come along Moss, don't wait about. If he's dead, we can't do anything, and if he's alive he'll get up."

"Do you suppose I've killed him?" said Moss doubtfully, for the fallacy of Liberalism, that belief in the preciousness of human life, still vexed him at times.

"It can't matter either way. Poor lad, he has nothing to contribute. I have seen too many of his type."

"And probably no one to care for him."

"Oh, one can't go in for that—it gets one all mixed. He may be greatly loved, who knows? Throw his knuckle duster away. It shows signs of use."

"By Jove, you're right. I'm afraid you're always going to be right." He dropped it into the trunk of a shattered elm. Then they turned down the Mall and up the steps by the Duke of York's column, looked at the closed German Embassy and the statue of Captain Scott, and reached Coburn's Club. It was in fair working order. A wash would be possible, even a bath, and presently they sat drinking coffee. Moss did not feel touchy or shy any more. They had helped each other, they had made good, and it seemed to be his club too. How decent Coburn was, and when he was exasperating again, as he would be, it would be bearable. They talked of their plans for the future, and of their hopes of helping to pull the world through; no doubt they would crash themselves, but they had seen what needs doing, and would help each other. Presently their voices dropped again, and Moss recurred to the woman—the woman in overalls who had kissed him, and as it were blessed him. There is something in a universe where such encounters can happen.

They gave no further thought to the mean-minded little pick-pocket, lying on his back in the dirt of the Park, nor to old Ma Barnes wondering where he was. They did not realise that the world might be his not theirs, that the future might be for the rat, the lizard, the night prowler who have patiently been awaiting their turn ever since civilisation started, that the spirit of anarchy may be stealing out of the craters our science has made, and nesting in the ruins we have provided.

. . . .

So that's how I've wound up this serial by five authors. I've shifted the interest from Coburn and Moss to the pickpocket, and I've tried to show how their fine sentiments would appear to that sort of man. He doesn't care about snobbery or outraged feelings or moral redemption or heroism in Spain, or hopes for the world's future. He can't see either why the two mugs quarrelled or why they make it up. And when they punish him—which they do pretty thoroughly—they can't see that he too has a way of life, and a way which, in our present chaos, may possibly flourish. I expect that there are better endings to the story, and in particular that something more ought to have been done with that woman in overalls. But I could not work her in, and since the scenery prescribed was falling houses and the blitz, I turned to the character which best typifies destruction, and named him Stan Barnes. Did Stan's own knuckle-duster kill him? I don't know, but I hope not, because I believe in the importance of individual life. Coburn and Moss don't know and don't care.

For the earlier parts of this story, see *1558, 1574, 1606,* and *1623.*

1. A.R.P., Air Raid Precautions, was the title used for the service manned by air raid wardens and other air raid workers. The A.F.S. was the Auxiliary Fire Service.

1639. To Norman Marshall

6 November 1942   PP/EB

Dear Mr. Marshall,[1]

I am sending you a long and, I'm afraid, rather formidable document dealing with your first broadcast. Mr. and Mrs. Sahni have gone to some pains to give a picture of your probable listeners, which I think will turn out to have been worth while. After this, they append a list of the questions, your answers to which will make up the bulk of the talk. I am rather against starting off the first talk with a lot of generalities however, and suggest therefore that you answer questions one and two rather shortly and spread yourself on questions three and four. The whole of your talk, including the questions which, of course, amount only to a few words, should come to about 1500 words. When the script is written, it may perhaps be well to break it up a bit with further short questions and interjections. Can you be kind enough to let me have the script not later than Wednesday, November 11th, at the latest?

Yours sincerely,
George Orwell
Talks Producer
Indian Section

Dictated by George Orwell & despatched in his absence by: [No name given]

Enclosed with Orwell's letter:

LET'S ACT IT OURSELVES

Description of the town:

About 50,000 people. It is not an industrial town but the industrial civilisation has made inroads. Therefore it is more accurate to divide the citizens into classes rather than castes or religions.

Majority are very poor, labourers, cart-drivers, petty shop-keepers, etc. They are ignorant and uneducated. Therefore they are constant prey to communal and opportunist propaganda. In riots etc. these poor people pay dearly.

But they also realise that they are too poor to observe the religious rites and taboos and middle class morality. In fact in their lives they are more progressive out of sheer necessity. Whether they are Hindus, Moslems or untouchables they live and eat alike. Their women must work so cannot keep Purdah.

● The middle-Class. Not parallel to middle class here. Much poorer. But outlook similar. This class consists of traders, Government petty officials, moneylenders etc. This class is in ferment. On one side the religious fanatacism is much greater among them. Because he who *has* money thinks God has given it. On the other hand education has brought speculation and skepticism. The older generation is keen on sex taboos, purdah, religious rites, caste etc. But the younger generation among them is rebellious. But this younger generation of students etc. is rebellious without direction. Through western education it has lost its own and has not imbibed any real culture. Also it depends on the older generation for livelihood and influence for getting jobs. So, frustration.

But there is a nucleus of a few young men and women who have a purpose. Their purpose is:

1. Break down the barriers of money, caste, creed, and make them realise that they are one nation.
2. That all these people must be made to see that superstition and ignorance must go if progress is to be achieved.

To bring about this awareness they think of the theatre as means of propaganda.

The old theatre has been killed by the films. The home-made talkie, which is purely escapist. The talkie avoids discussion of every social[2] problem.

There is a westernised college in town which puts on western plays. But they have no social value, because they are too foreign. And also the performance of students is too raw.

This nucleus wants to revive the theatre tradition. Wants to get new social plays written and produce them on modern lines. But they haven't enough stage knowledge. Several attempts have failed. They meet the expert, and ask:

1. Do you think the theatre has social importance in other countries?

2. In our villages, and even in our town, the old kind of religious plays, like your miracle plays, is done. Very very simply. Bare stage, sometimes even without curtain. But rhetoric acting and plenty of singing. Do you think we should adapt that kind of play to newer needs or should we break completely away and start on Naturalistic stage?[3]

3. Perhaps we overcome the above difficulty by having both kinds of plays. One to interest the educated audience and the other the uneducated audience. Now *you* tell us what a modern stage is like.

4. What are the bare essentials which an amateur society must possess?

From this point Mr. Marshall can dictate his own policy. He can command what questions he likes to be put to him, because he is now building the society.

Roughly we have thought of dividing the discussions under the following six headings.

1. General—description of setting—local colour—and problems—the necessity of reviving theatre etc. and the first practical requirements.

2. Selection of play—copies—cast—producer—stage-manager—rehearsals when and where.

3. Make-up—lighting—costumes.

4. Business side. Box-office—advertising.

5. Properties—steward—general management. Co-ordination, dress rehearsal. Last tips by producer before—

6. Curtain goes up. Here we may actually act a one act play with Indian voices. Why not get a one-act play specially written say Mulk Raj Anand?

1. Norman Marshall (1901–1980; CBE, 1975), play producer, was responsible for many successful West End presentations, including *Victoria Regina* (1937), *Of Mice and Men* (1939), *The Petrified Forest* (1942), *Uncle Vanya* (1943). After serving in the army, 1940–42, he was Head of Drama for Associated-Rediffusion Television, 1955–59, and Chairman, British Council's Advisory Committee on Drama, 1961–68.

2. 'Social' was typed as 'spcial'.

3. Many months later, the Sahnis wrote to Orwell to express their sympathy following the death of Eileen Blair in March 1945. In that letter they tell Orwell that they are touring Indian villages presenting plays. Balraj Sahni was a colleague of Orwell's in the Indian Section; his wife, Damyanti, had worked at the Shakespeare Memorial Theatre; see *861, n. 1*.

1640. BBC Talks Booking Form, 6.11.42

R. R. Desai: Gujarati Newsletter, 37; broadcast 9.11.42; fee £5.5s + 12s 0d fare. Signed: M. Blackburn for I.P.O.

1641. Weekly News Review, 47

7 November 1942

The typescript has only one change: the word 'heavily' is marked by Orwell to be inserted into the second paragraph. The script carries both censorship stamps, and Orwell has written at the top of the first page, 'As broadcast 9' 22 E.A.B'. The reader was Noel Sircar. This was the last Newsletter to be read on Orwell's behalf. There was no broadcast on 14 November. From 21 November until this series ended on 13 March 1943, Orwell read his own scripts; see *1571*.

The Battle in Egypt has developed into a great victory for the United Nations. The Axis forces are not yet destroyed, but they are in great danger, and for three days they have been in disorderly retreat, with wave after wave of Allied bombers attacking them as they go. Something over three hundred Axis tanks have been destroyed or captured. Prisoners taken by our forces amounted yesterday to 15,000—but there will be many more within the next few days. The commander of the Afrika Corps has been taken prisoner, together with a number of other German and Italian senior officers.

It is clear from the reports that have come in during the last two days that when once the Axis positions in the narrow neck of land between the sea and the Qattara Depression had been broken, the enemy had no choice but to fall back as rapidly as possible and attempt to make another stand somewhere in the neighbourhood of the Egyptian frontier. We do not care to predict as yet whether they will be able to do this. Now that the mine-fields round El Alamein have been cleared, the Allied tanks have raced ahead, and together with the R.A.F. are pounding the retreating Axis columns along the coastal road. It is clear that the Allies possess almost complete supremacy in the air, and the retreating enemy must be losing *heavily* all the time in tanks, transport, and men. Nevertheless, the German commander may be able to extricate sufficient tanks and anti-tank guns to make a stand in the strong positions at Halfiya and Sollun,[1] on the border between Libya and Egypt. The most recent news is that our forces have captured the airfield at Fuka, seventy miles west of El Alamein, and fighting is taking place at Mersa Matruh, another fifty miles to the west. Large numbers of Axis troops, chiefly Italians,[2] have been left behind in the Southern part of the battle-field, and these will be almost entirely destroyed or captured. Six Axis supply ships have been sunk by our submarines in the Mediterranean during the past few days.

It is certain that by next week we shall have further news to report about the Egyptian campaign, and possibly sensational news. Meanwhile it is too early to say that the Axis armies in North Africa have been destroyed, but it can at least be said that the threat to Egypt has been removed.

The Japanese landed some reinforcements on the island of Guadalcanal, in the Solomons, four days ago, but have not renewed their attack. There has been some land fighting, in which the Americans have gained a little ground. The Japanese are certain to make further efforts to recapture Guadalcanal, but for the moment they have evidently lost too many planes and warships to continue without a pause for refitting. On the island of New Guinea, the Australian forces have made another advance and captured the Japanese-held village of Kokoda, with its airfield.

Throughout most of the week there has been heavy fighting at Stalingrad, but little or no change in the position. In the south, the Caucasus area, the Germans have made an advance within the last few days.[3] They appear to be trying to get possession of the northern approaches of the main roads over the Caucasus mountains. At this time of year, to cross the mountains is probably not practicable, but they may be thinking of the spring, as well as of securing defensible positions for the winter. In Ukrainia, the Germans are making great efforts to organise the captured territories and exploit them in order to feed their home population. In the German press and on the radio, it has been explained in the frankest way that the Germans intend to plunder these territories for their own advantage, without regard to the interests of the inhabitants, and that they intend to break up the collective farms which the Russian peasants had built for themselves, and to hand the land over to individual German owners. It is clear, however, that this process is not proceeding so smoothly as the Germans would like to pretend. The farming of this important cornland depended almost entirely on oil-driven tractors, and when the Russians retreated they took care to destroy such machinery as they could not remove. It is impossible for the Germans to supply fresh agricultural machinery in anything like the quantities required, and it will probably be difficult for them even to muster sufficient labour. During the last war it will be remembered the Germans also had possession of the Ukraine, and tried then, as now, to plunder it for their own benefit, but in fact they got very little out of it. It looks very much as though the same story were going to be repeated this time.

Premier Stalin broadcast to the Soviet people last night on the eve of the 25th birthday of the U.S.S.R. The keynote of his speech was his confidence in the complete victory of the United Nations. Although, he said, the Germans had been able to take the offensive this year because of the absence of a second front in Western Europe, and the Red Army had had to face the onslaught of 240 German divisions, the main strategy of the Germans had failed. They had sought to outflank Moscow from the south and then capture it, and simultaneously to capture the oilfields of Baku. Both dreams had failed to materialise.

Stalin contrasted the aims of the Fascist nations, who attempt to exterminate and subjugate other peoples, with those of the Allies, who have no wish to subjugate anybody and are fighting only to destroy the so-called New Order and kill off the comparatively small cliques of people responsible for it. He also ridiculed the idea that political and economic differences were any obstacle to collaboration between Britain, Soviet Russia and the United States. In the fight against slavery, he said, it is possible even for nations with very different ideologies to have a common programme, and the events of the past year prove conclusively that the members of this great coalition are coming nearer and nearer to one another.

The hostilities in the island of Madagascar have been brought to a close, the French Governor-General having asked for and received an Armistice. Although the campaign in Madagascar was only a side-show and involved little fighting, it has had its importance as the possession of Madagascar was necessary for the command of the sea approaches to Egypt, and the Middle East. The victory of Egypt has only been made possible by the fact that the Allies were able to build up there a substantial force of tanks and aeroplanes, which they could not have done unless the sea-routes round Africa were reasonably safe. At a press conference two days ago, President Roosevelt disclosed that only a minority of the armaments used in Egypt were of American manufacture, the great bulk of them being British. It has taken a long time and continuous journies by great fleets of ships to build up this force, and the seizure of Madagascar and consequent cutting off of Axis submarine bases—which existed or were always liable to exist while Vichy remained in control of this island—has played its part in the campaign.

1. Halfiya Pass and Sollum.
2. Liddell Hart summed up the result of El Alamein and its immediate aftermath: 'The Eighth Army, besides killing several thousand, had captured some 10,000 Germans and over 20,000 Italians . . . together with some 450 tanks and over 1,000 guns.' Only some 5,000 Germans and 2,500 Italians escaped, with 21 tanks and a little more than 100 guns. Of Rommel's most senior officers, General von Stumme died of a heart attack after his armoured car was hit, and the commander of the Afrika Corps, General Ritter von Thoma (who had commanded the German tanks in the Spanish civil war), was captured. The Eighth Army suffered 13,500 casualties (History of the Second World War, 312, 317, 320; U.S.: 299, 301, 305, 307).
3. This was as far east into the Caucasus as the Wehrmacht under General Field Marshal Ewald von Kleist penetrated. His men failed to take either Grozny or Ordzhonikidze and by the end of 1942 he was directing a retreat. Kleist (1881–1954), dismissed by Hitler in 1944, was captured by British troops in 1945 and tried by the Yugoslavs for war crimes. He was released in 1949 and handed over to the Russians, who imprisoned him for war crimes. He died in captivity. Although the Germans failed to take Grozny in 1942, it fell to the Russians in 1995 after Chechenya declared its independence of the Russian Federation.

1642. Bengali Newsletter, 17

7 November 1942

The English original was written by Orwell. No script has been traced.

1643. To Leonard Moore

7 November 1942   Typewritten

10a Mortimer Crescent London   NW 6

MAI[da Vale] 4579   (This is my permanent address)

Dear Mr Moore,
I don't think I would press the diary on Gollancz if he doesn't want it. At the same time I should say it is worth publishing, so we might perhaps try it on

someone else. How about Cape, for instance? Someone told me recently that he is anxious to get hold of something of mine, and though this is only a slight thing he might be willing to publish it by way of ground-bait as it were. No doubt there are several others we could approach. If it falls through I will lay the book by for a few years. It is in my opinion worth printing as it records a good deal which is already half forgotten.

Among the last press-cuttings you sent me was one which said that "Shooting an Elephant" had been included in a book called "Modern Essays" (Macmillan).[1] Did we give them permission to do this? I don't remember doing so, but I may have.

I enclose the readers' reports Gollancz sent.

Yours sincerely
Eric Blair

1. *Modern Essays, 1939–1941*, edited by A. F. Scott, was published by Macmillan in July 1942; reprinted in Scholar's Library series, 1944. The essay was included in a section entitled 'Life and Letters.'

1644. Gujarati Newsletter, 37

9 November 1942

The English original was written by Orwell. No script has been traced. PasB gives timing as approximately 10 minutes.

1645. From Laurence Brander to L. F. Rushbrook Williams

9 November 1942   Copy to Mr Davenport[1]

RESILIENCE IN PROGRAMMES

1. Today we can have every set in India tuned in to the BBC.[2]

For the first time since the Blitz we have a monopoly in News. If we fail to take this opportunity we add to the list of our defeats. I listened to our taking the biggest hiding in broadcasting history in May and again in August. All listeners sympathetically said: "When you have a couple of victories you can talk". During the next few days and weeks we may have these victories, and with victory talk becomes the best form of entertainment.

2. Listeners will tune in to London for the latest news. The news is of victory. Respect for us will grow. The mood of India will be modified. Listeners will be prepared for listening to us on their own problems. Therefore now is the time to demand guidance from the highest quarters on propaganda policy for the near future on internal Indian affairs. With success in Africa the whole atmosphere of the Indian situation will change so that settlement will become possible. The generosity of our offers will at last be recognised — but we must work quickly.

3. But certain talks in our schedule become completely irrelevant in the
   entirely new atmosphere which success in Africa will bring. Irrelevant
talking now is irritating to the listener. We must catch up with the mood that
the moment will produce. We carry a lot of stuff which has become dead
wood today:—

> *Monday*:   "The Debate Continues" (only necessarily today)
> *Tuesday*:   "Everybody's Scrapbook" — unless it be scrapped and
> rescrapped.
>
> "Here in Britain" — adjustable.
> *Wednesday*:   "Behind the Headlines" — President Inonu (*that* will follow
> "Some Books"   the news!)
> "Women Generally Speaking"
> "Six points for Playwrights" (on a day when Indians at last
> may be thinking we are worth cooperating with)
> *Thursday*:   "Story of Fascism" — (is the script revised to tell?)
> "Behind the Battlefront" — in Britain!
> *Friday*:   "A Day in My Life".
> *Saturday*:   No change.

4. In general, it is clear that the programmes need heavy revision in these
   items. Most of them would do with up-to-the-minute reviewing, but
even so they would be very second best. To obtain victory in this wireless
war we must use our big guns, — As well as Wickham Steed, Vernon Bartlett
and the best of our Service Commentators on events in Africa.

5. We may congratulate ourselves that we have so much music and light
   entertainment in the Eastern Transmission that News Flashes can come
in very easily.

6. We must remember that on our side we only have AIR, not very resilient
   and now far behind us with the news; and that after the morning paper
most of our listeners have no means but wireless for hearing news and
commentaries. Now is the time to talk.

1. J. H. Davenport attended Eastern Service meetings and sometimes reported on Brander's
behalf.
2. Operation Torch, the Allied invasion of Morocco and Algeria, began on 8 November 1942.

1646. BBC Talks Booking Form, 10.11.42

Jon Kimche: 13-minute talk on war strategy, The Plan Unfolds in Africa;
broadcast 10.11.42; fee £8.8s. Signed: M. Blackburn for I.P.O. The form is
marked RETROSPECTIVE.[1]

1. The form may have been restrospective because it had been overlooked, but it is possible that,
in the light of Brander's comments on the need for relevancy (see *1645*), this topical talk was
hastily arranged. PasB states that Kimche gave a 'Talk on French North Africa' and he was
announced as 'Military Correspondent of the London *Evening Standard*.' See also *1651*. Jon
Kimche had worked as an assistant, with Orwell, at Booklovers' Corner in Hampstead,
1934–35; see *212, n. 8*.

1647. To R. R. Desai
[11 November 1942?]

CAN YOU RECORD 4.45 TO 5.45 MONDAY NEXT EXPECTING SCRIPT BY SATURDAY MORNING AT LATEST[1]

BLAIR BROADCASTS

1. Saturday, 14 November 1942.

1648. To R. R. Desai
11 November 1942   PP/EB/NP

Dear Desai,

I understand from Miss Blackburn that you are recording Gujarati Emergency announcements[1] on Monday until 4.30, so I have arranged for you to record, from 4.45 to 5.45 on that day, your talk in the series "The Story of Fascism" for 19th November. I hope that you will send me the script so that it reaches me on Saturday morning at the very latest.

If you aren't able to record at the time mentioned above, I think we shall have to ask you to come down from Cambridge again and do it live, unless you can record some time on Tuesday. If you do want to change the day of the recording, I should be glad if you will let me know immediately, as it is very difficult to book a studio at a moment's notice.

Yours sincerely,
Eric Blair
Talks Producer
Indian Section

1. Desai did not record these announcements, and Mary Blackburn wrote to him on 17 November 1942 asking him whether he would be prepared to record them on 23 November.

1649. To the Officer Commanding E Battery, RMA[1]
11 November 1942   EB/NP

Dear Sir,

I am sending you herewith a copy of a talk to be broadcast in the Eastern Service of the BBC on Friday November 13th. The writer, Gunner Keidrich Rhys, was previously serving in your battery but has now been discharged from the Army. As he is no longer a soldier it is not technically necessary for him to get your permission for the broadcast, but we thought that you might like to see a copy of the talk. It has already been passed for censorship in the normal way. Should you wish to make any changes, could you be kind enough to ring me up at Euston 3400, Ext. 208. If we do not hear from you we will assume that you have no alterations to suggest.

Yours truly,
Eric Blair
Talks Producer
Indian Section

1. Royal Military Academy.

1650. Extract from Minutes of Eastern Service Meeting
11 November 1942

COMPETITIONS

Mr. Blair submitted arrangements and publicity leaflet proposed by the sub-committee for essay competitions. Agreed Mr. Brander to draft telegram explaining the scheme to the Government of India and requesting that a copy be passed to Ahmed Ali:[1] to write Ahmed Ali fully requesting his suggestions re payment of judges, short-listing, etc. by cable: announcement of the starting date postponed: reference to forthcoming competitions to be made in programmes: leaflet to state that judges will be distinguished Indians: one judge to adjudicate one competition.

1. Ahmed Ali was BBC Listener Research Director, New Delhi, 1942–45; see *1103, n. 3.*

1651. BBC Talks Booking Form, 11.11.42

K. K. Ardaschir: French North Africa; 13½-minute talk; broadcast 13.11.42; fee £9.19.6d.[1] Signed: M Blackburn for I.P.O. Remarks: 'Miss Boughen's office suggests that this speaker should receive 10/6d. in addition to normal fee because he was only asked to do the talk to-day and as we need the script to-morrow[2] night for special censorship he has volunteered to come up to London specially to bring the script.'

1. The fee was to be the 'usual' one–9 guineas (£9.9s)—but was altered to 'Special fee,' and 9½ guineas (£9.19s.6d) was paid.
2. These forms originating from 'Eric Blair' were most probably typed by a secretary, perhaps Mary Blackburn. That Orwell did not himself type them is almost certainly indicated by the hyphenated forms of 'to-day' and 'to-morrow'; he preferred the unhyphenated forms.

1652. BBC Talks Booking Form, 12.11.42

R. R. Desai: Gujarati Newsletter, 38; broadcast 16.11.42; fee £5.5s + 12s 0d fare + 17s 0d expenses, to stay overnight to listen to All-India Radio Gujarati bulletin.

1653. BBC Talks Booking Form, 12.11.42

Norman Marshall: 'Let's Act It Ourselves,' 1 to 6; 'six 13½ minute talks on how to start up amateur dramatic societies etc. With Balraj Sahni (staff) as questioner'; broadcast 13, 20, and 27.11.42 and 4, 11, and 18.12.42; fee £9.9s each broadcast. Signed: M Blackburn for I.P.O. Remarks: 'Mr. Marshall was until recently a member of the staff of the BBC, but I understand he has now left, & therefore does not require a staff contract.'

1654. To Leonard Moore

13 November 1942   Typewritten

10a Mortimer Crescent   London   NW 6

Dear Mr Moore,

Don't press the diary on Gollancz if he doesn't want it. Send it back to me and I will decide whether to try elsewhere with it or to lay it by for a few years.[1]

Yours sincerely
Eric Blair

1. In a letter Inez Holden wrote to Ian Angus, 21 May 1967 (see *1443*, *n. 1*), she said she supposed Gollancz turned down Orwell's diary because he was afraid of offending people. See also *1326, n. 1* and *1514*.

1655. 'Let's Act It Ourselves,' 1

13 November 1942

This series, as the supporting correspondence shows, was organised by Orwell, but he seems to have participated in only the first broadcast. The series is a good example of his concern to promote active participation in creative work.

Norman Marshall Interviewed by Balraj and Damyanti Sahni
Introduced by George Orwell

Introduction by Orwell: This is a new series of talks, or interviews I should rather say. It is addressed to people who are interested in the stage, not simply interested in it as spectators, but interested in actual dramatic production. There are going to be six of these talks and in them we hope to tackle a whole series of concrete technical questions in such a way as to give people who are interested in amateur dramatic production some idea of how to go to work. Well, we are doing this by getting Mr. Norman Marshall, who has had very long experience as a producer, to tell us all about it. He will be interviewed by Balraj and Damyanti Sahni, who will put to him all the questions they think want answering. By the way, curiously enough, Balraj and Damyanti Sahni and Mr. Marshall were all born in Rawalpindi in the Punjab. Now here's Balraj Sahni . . .

The script is typewritten except for the final two speeches, which are in Orwell's hand, though they do not read as if he composed them.

D. Sahni: Well, we've said a lot about the preliminaries, but we haven't said anything yet about the plays we are going to act.
B. Sahni: I'm afraid we shan't have time for that now, we shall have to discuss it next. Meanwhile, thank you very much, Mr Marshall, for the hints you have given us.

1656. Weekly News Review, 48

14 November 1942

This regular Weekly News Review was not given. Instead, Sir Ramaswami Mudaliar gave a talk in English; see *1588, n.2*.

1657. Bengali Newsletter, 18

14 November 1942

The English original was written by Orwell. No script has been traced. From PasB a timing of 10′ 5″ can be implied.

1658. War-time Diary

<u>15.11.42:</u> *Church bells rung this morning—in celebration for the victory in Egypt.[1] The first time that I have heard them in over two years.*

1. Following the attack launched at El Alamein on 23 October 1942, the Eighth Army cleared Egypt by 11 November 1942; Tobruk, in Libya, was retaken on 12 November. Allied forces landed in Morocco and Algeria on 8 November, and by 12 November were close to the western Tunisian border. Final victory in North Africa, however, was not to come until mid-May 1943.

This concludes Orwell's War-time Diary.

1659. Gujarati Newsletter, 38

16 November 1942

The English original was written by Orwell. No script has been traced. PasB gives timing as approximately 10 minutes.

1660. To T. S. Eliot

16 November 1942   PP/EB/NP

Dear Eliot,

Many thanks for your letter of the 11th. There would not be any need for you to come up to London on Monday, 30th November, and on Tuesday morning it would really do if you could come in any time before 12. The programme goes on the air actually at 12.15, and we are rehearsing from 10.30 onwards, but if you are only reading something, there is not much rehearsal needed. We have not yet picked the stuff for this programme, but the idea of this number is to be the influence of Oriental literature on English literature. I suppose we shall make use of some direct translations, but we shall also use poems where it is only a case of direct or indirect influence. I don't know whether you have anything which you feel comes under this heading in your own work. We should certainly like you to read something of your own if possible. Perhaps "What the Thunder Said" from *The Waste Land*?[1] But we will let you know more about the make-up of the programme later. I certainly hope you will be there, in any case, and as you say you come up to town on Tuesday mornings, perhaps it won't mean wasting very much of your time.

Yours sincerely,
George Orwell
Talks Producer
Indian Section

1. This, the final section of *The Waste Land* (1922), concludes with a quotation from the *Brihadaranyaka, Upanishad*, 5.1: 'Datta. Dayadhvam. Damyata' (for which Eliot provides a translation: 'Give, sympathise, control') and the thrice-repeated 'Shantih.'

1661. To Norman Marshall

16 November 1942   Original   EB/NP

Dear Mr Marshall,

I am afraid you are getting these questions for this week's talk at rather short notice. There are nine questions here, but perhaps 4 and 5 are less important than the others. However, I would like you to spread yourself on whichever ones you think most important. I don't quite see how nos. 1 and 2 hook up. The talk for this week really starts at No. 2 and No. 1 merely seems to be a sort of preliminary to remind people what was said last week. I should think you might answer it by simply saying, "Well, the next thing is to choose a play", after which No. 2 follows fairly naturally. Could we have your script some time on Thursday? I am sorry that you should have to do this in such a rush. I understand from the Sahnis that they will be free at 4 p.m. on Thursday, so if you'd like to come over and go over it with them, perhaps you'll let me know.[1] Unfortunately they are both very busy on Friday morning, so it's no good asking you to come earlier and go over it with them then.

Yours sincerely,
George Orwell
Talks Producer Indian Section
Dictated by G. Orwell & despatched in his absence by:
[Signed] N. A. Parratt.

Enclosed with Orwell's letter:

QUESTIONS FROM MR. AND MRS. SAHNI[2]

(For 20.11.42.)

1. Let us presume that we have now got a hall, a stage, and curtains arranged as suggested by you and lighting—although I must say that lighting is by no means a small problem for us—now, what is to be done next?

2. What sort of play do we want? Well, I explained to you that our audience is thirsting for knowledge—for a frank discussion of social problems. We don't want escapist plays because talkies do that. Can you suggest some English play which our friends can read as a sort of illustration. Perhaps they would like to translate it and act it. For purposes of this discussion we shall take it for granted that they will read it and act it. Which plays do you suggest?

3. Which must be decided first, selection of the play or selection of the producer?

4. One thing more. I hear that in Moscow the entire responsibility of production, direction, almost everything except the business side lies with the producer. That is, each theatre is known by its regisseur or producer? It is true?° If so, what is the difference between Regisseur and producer?

5. Will a regisseur be more necessary for us or will a producer do?

6. What are the qualifications of a producer?

7. How far is he a dictator and how far a democrat?

8. Who is a stage manager? What is his function?

9. What else must be decided before the rehearsals begin?

1. I understand . . . let me know.] *crossed through (by Nancy Parratt?)*
2. Against each question a figure has been lightly written: 41 for the first; for the others, 85, 15, 47, 12, 7, 10, 10, 10. These are, presumably, timings, but if they are minutes, which seems likely, they allow far too much time; if seconds, far too little.

1662. BBC Talks Booking Form, 16.11.42

Keidrych Rhys: 'A Day in My Life,' 2; 13-minute talk on his life as a soldier; broadcast 13.11.42; fee £6.6s (amended from £8.8s). Signed: M Blackburn for I.P.O. Remarks: 'We were not able to send in a booking slip earlier because Mr. Rhys, having just been discharged from the Army, apparently has no address.'

1663. Memoranda on News Commentaries in English for Malaya

On 16 November 1942, the Eastern Service Director, L. F. Rushbrook Williams, wrote to Rowan Davies[1] about the English Period on the Malayan Band. In addition to expressing the hope that uncertainties about the "Malayan Band" (his quotation marks) were being cleared up, he wrote: 'If you agree, I will get "George Orwell" to write a script,[2] which can be read for him, for this period. He has kindly agreed to do this.'

Davies replied on the same date, annotating the memorandum sent him: 'Yes: I am sure Blair would do it admirably. 2. May I take it that he will write the script for Friday 20th? 3. Who will read the script for him? Mrs Lee[3] or an other°. If the latter—I must explain to Mrs Lee why her Contract is being cancelled.'

Both memoranda are handwritten. There is no figure '1' for the first of Davies's points.

1. E. Rowan Davies is shown on a typed staff list of the 'Empire Department Eastern Service,' probably dated 27 November 1941 (File R13/154/2A) as a Transcription Assistant in the same section as Orwell. In the Staff List dated 21.8.43 he was shown as School Broadcasting Manager in the Home Division.
2. Presumably a News Commentary; see *1669*.
3. Probably Mrs. H. C. Lee, who wrote and read the first seven News Commentaries in English broadcast to occupied Malaya; see *1669*.

1664. To Desmond Hawkins

17 November 1942   Original and carbon copies   EB/NP

Dear Hawkins,

The anniversaries for December seem somewhat thin. I suggest one of the following:

Sir Isaac Newton, born December 25; Milton, born December 9; Nostradamus, born December 17; Kepler[1] born December 27; Tycho Brahe, born December 14; Karel Kapek, died December 25; Sibelius, born December 8; Richelieu, died December 4.

That seems to be about all, unless one puts in war things, which I rather want to avoid in this programme. The Aswan Dam was completed on December 10th 1902, but [as] we have just had one dealing with Egypt, it might be better to select one from the others I have given you. There seems to be rather a preponderance of astronomers this month, but there is one astrologer if you prefer that. Let me know which of them you choose.

We shall want the script by November 26th if possible. The broadcast is on December 1st, at 1145 GMT, and we hope to get Malcolm Baker-Smith to produce it again.

Yours,
[Top copy signed] Geo. Orwell
George Orwell
Talks Producer
Indian Section

1. Typed as 'Kapler' but corrected in ink on top copy. The 'e' looks more like Nancy Parratt's than Orwell's.

1665. To E. M. Forster

18 November 1942   PP/EB/NP

Dear Forster,

I don't know if you have heard about Narayana Menon's book on W. B. Yeats?[1] It will, I think, be suitable to mention in your next talk. It is also being pubished in India. He tells me he is going to send you a copy. If he doesn't, we can get one for you.

Have you finished with "Conditions of Peace"?[2] We don't want to hurry you, but there seems to be a considerable demand for it, so perhaps you could post it, when you have finished with it.

Yours,
George Orwell
Talks Producer
Indian Section

1. Reviewed by Orwell, in *Horizon*, January 1943; see *1791*.
2. One of the books that Orwell had sent Forster to provide material for his monthly broadcasts on recent books; see *1561* and *1600*. The books were needed by the BBC's library.

1666. To V. E. Yarsley

18 November 1942   PP/EB/NP

Dear Dr. Yarsley,

Mr. Ritchie Calder has suggested to me that you might be willing to do a talk in one of our series. We have a series called "Science And the People" in which we get experts to discuss new discoveries and processes which are of importance to ordinary people. Mr. Ritchie Calder himself has just done us one on Micro-films. We should like you very much, if you would, to do one on Plastics. These talks are for the English-speaking Indian audience and should be rather simple and non-technical, though one can assume that one is talking to a well-educated audience. These take 13½ minutes, which usually means about 15 hundred words. The date of this talk will be Tuesday December 15th, at 12.15, and we would like to have the script by about December 8th at the latest. Would you be kind enough to let me know whether you would like to undertake this?

Yours truly,
Eric Blair
Talks Producer
Indian Section

1. Dr. V. E. Yarsley (1901–) was engaged in developing non-flammable cine film. He had held a Research Fellowship in Germany and on returning to England was for many years a consulting chemist specialising in plastics. With E. G. Couzens, he wrote *Plastics* for Penguin Books. Orwell gives a more detailed account of his life in his memorandum to Anthony Weymouth, 7 December 1942; see *1724*. See also *1725*, for Norman Collins's reaction to this booking.

1667. To A. R. Bell, Programme Accounts
18 November 1942   EB/NP

RECORDING BY DAME MYRA HESS AND SCOTT GODDARD

On Monday, 16th November 1942, in Studio 4 at 200 Oxford Street, Dame Myra Hess[1] recorded a 13½ minutes programme, consisting of about six minutes of speech in the form of question and answer (interviewer being Mr. Scott Goddard), and about 7 minutes of pianoforte playing.[2] Dame Myra Hess's contract was arranged with Music Booking Manager, and that of Scott Goddard with Talks Booking. The programme was successfully recorded and it is in order for Dame Myra Hess and Mr. Scott Goddard to receive their fees.

The date of reproduction is Wednesday 25th November 1942 from 200 O.S. at 1145–1200 GMT in the Eastern Service (Red Network) in Lady Grigg's programme Women Generally Speaking. The discs (DOX: 6984) will go to R.P. Library Oxford Street.

[Signed] Eric Blair
(Eric Blair)

On 18 November, Mary Blackburn wrote this Private & Confidential note in Bokhari's name to the Empire Music Supervisor:

We understand that Dame Myra Hess has on certain occasions received a maximum fee of 75 guineas, but this is not the case for a 13½ minute programme. She has previously (and very kindly) broadcast for us in the Eastern Service at a very much smaller fee—even as low as 15 guineas! The question of payment to Dame Myra is being dealt with by Mr. Wynn (Music Booking manager).

Your point regarding the similarity of voice, in the case of Scott Goddard and Dr. Sargent is most pertinent, but Lady Grigg (who arranges these programmes in the series "Women Generally Speaking") feels that arrangements have gone rather too far ahead for any alteration to be made now. We have spoken to her about the similarity of voices, and she says she will try to see that sufficient difference is maintained for short-wave broadcast.

1. Dame Myra Hess (1890–1965), distinguished and much-loved concert pianist. When most of the National Gallery's pictures were removed to Wales for safety during the war, she organised a long-running series of lunch-hour concerts. She can be seen playing in one such concert in the film *Listen to Britain* (1942).

2. Rushbrook Williams had written to Dame Myra on 7 November confirming arrangements for this programme. He expressed gratitude to her for sparing the time and told her, 'I know [the programme] will be listened to in India with the greatest appreciation and interest.'

1668. Background of French Morocco

Tribune, 20 November 1942

United States forces landed in French Morocco on 8 November 1942. The Resident-General, M. Noguès, surrendered on 11 November. It was this that prompted Orwell's article. Following the Casablanca Conference attended by Churchill, Roosevelt, and de Gaulle in January 1943, Churchill persuaded Roosevelt to spend a short time with him in Marrakech (which Churchill called 'the Paris of the Sahara'), where Orwell had spent the winter of 1938–39.

As you travel in the train from Spanish into French Morocco you pass for a while through a strip of territory which resembles my own mental picture of the Russian collective farms. Black earth, with here and there a tractor plough crawling across it, stretches away to the horizon on either side of the line, and every few miles there is a neat cluster of limewashed cottages and agricultural buildings. This is the fertile coastal belt, watered by the winds from the Atlantic and producing a million tons of wheat annually. Needless to say, the Arabs do not own an inch of it. It is all owned by a French syndicate which works it with gang labour. The Arabs, the vast majority of whom are small peasants, cultivate a dried-up, treeless soil on which they grow barley, lucerne and various fruits and vegetables. They live chiefly on barley and the milk of miserable goats which graze on cacti, and whose daily yield is a quarter of a pint per head.

The general poverty of the country is startling, and probably worse than anything to be seen in India. Beggars are as common as flies. Children are herding goats or sheep by the time they are six, and are often doing a full day's work at carpentering or blacksmithing when they are twelve. Most of the transport of the country is done by tiny donkeys, which cost ten shillings each and are worked to death within a few years. Bigger than England in size, Morocco barely supports a population of seven millions, and even if not under alien rule it would still be desperately poor, because of its lack of water. There are no considerable rivers, and until you come to the Atlas Mountains there are no wild trees at all, except in a few areas where the French have started reafforestation. The French settlers cultivate the land successfully and grow first-rate oranges and olives and a rather inferior wine, but this depends on having sufficient capital to dig wells and storage tanks. Apart from its agricultural and animal products the country has not much in the way of natural wealth, though the Atlas Mountains, which are not fully explored, no doubt contain minerals.

There are some 200,000 Europeans in Morocco, French or Frenchified Spanish. The seaport of Casablanca has a white proletariat of perhaps 70,000. Of the rest of the population about 5 millions would be Arabs, 100,000 Jews, and the rest chiefly Chleuh, a rather primitive Berber people inhabiting the

Atlas. Except for Casablanca the big towns are really enormous villages where the peasants come to sell their beasts and buy cooking pots, nails, etc. Everything is made by hand with tools which have not altered since Biblical times. The Moroccan handicrafts, especially the pottery and the blankets, are some of the finest in the world, and have held their own against European or Japanese imports because of the miserable wages paid to the people who make them. A highly-skilled potter or carpenter earns round about a penny an hour. Except for agriculture the Jews do the same work as the Arabs, and seem on average to be somewhat poorer.

I may have seemed to paint a picture of general misery, but I must record that in 1938 and 1939 the people in Morocco struck me as being happier than, for instance, the people in London. One saw everywhere the most shocking destitution and drudgery, but also, on the whole, one saw happy faces and magnificent bodies. The Chleuh, even poorer than the Arabs of the plains, were one of the most debonair peoples I have seen. One must remember that Morocco is still almost entirely in the feudal stage, barely touched by industrialism with its conveniencies and its discontents. The French took the country over in 1906, but they did not complete its conquest till 1934. The Arabs are not French citizens (for them this has the advantage that military service is not compulsory), and the country is ruled indirectly, through the Sultan, who is the creature of the French but towards whom the Arabs have a feudal loyalty. The excellent motor roads have carried a thin trickle of French culture from the Mediterranean shore to the southern slopes of the Atlas, but the mass of the people are untouched by it. Hardly any Arabs speak French correctly and few Frenchmen bother to learn Arabic.

The European population is made up of three quite distinct strata. At the top there are the well-to-do business men, bureaucrats and army officers, forming a society similar to that of Anglo-India, but probably stupider and certainly more reactionary. Then there are the small settlers, shopkeepers and minor officials, who look down on the Arabs and treat them as children; and then the white prolateriat, who do not perhaps despise the Arabs but tend to keep aloof from them. Even very petty official jobs are done by Frenchmen, so that there are probably more white officials in Morocco, with its 7 million inhabitants than in India, with its 350 millions. The normal French attitude towards the Arabs is patronising, though not unkindly. Even in 1939 the country was ripe for Fascism. Almost the whole of the Press was pro-Franco—one of the principal papers was run by Doriot's party—*Gringoire* and *Candide*[1] were the favourite reading of the army officers, and the petite bourgeoisie were anti-Semitic. The left-wing parties had little footing in the country, even in Casablanca. The attitude of the Arabs towards the French occupation was rather difficult to gauge. Although the conquest was comparatively recent it seemed to have left no scars behind, and the absence of race-hatred was very striking. Wherever one went one met with friendliness, though no servility—even the beggars were not really servile. The Arabs have probably transferred some of their feudal feeling to the French régime, and the French have found it easy to recruit an excellent mercenary army of the colonial type. But towards the poorer classes of

French the attitude of the Arabs appeared to have an undercurrent of good natured contempt. They were very much nicer human beings than these petty functionaries and shopkeepers, and perhaps they were aware of it. It would be absurd to expect a revolutionary movement of anything like the European type to arise in Morocco, but a violent nationalist movement, non-existent three years ago, could probably arise quite suddenly. The French defeat by Germany may have paved the way for it.

It now seems as though the United Nations are going to have control of Morocco, and what they ought to do with it is clear enough in general terms.[2] A country like Morocco cannot be genuinely independent, because it cannot defend itself; it must be under some kind of tutelage, and it must have the loan of European technical experts; but to free the Arabs from economic exploitation would be very simple, and would hurt nobody except a few wealthy men in Paris and Casablanca. There is no need to interfere with the small French settler, who improves the soil and does little harm. But the big syndicates which have absorbed all the best land and given themselves a monopoly of the wine and tobacco trades should be expropriated forthwith. Above all, that strip of fertile soil down the west coast should be given back to the peasants. The buildings and the machinery for collective farms are already there; but even if the land were split up into small holdings the possession of it by the Arabs themselves would raise the standard of living perceptibly. It would be very easy for us and the Americans to do this, our own interests not being directly involved. Such a deed would echo round the world and cause convulsions in Franco's colony next door. But when one tries to imagine it actually happening, and then looks at the faces of the people who rule us, one remembers rather sadly that the age of miracles is over.

A shortened version of this article appeared in *World Digest*, February 1943, 'by permission of the author.' The chief omissions were the last sentence of paragraph 2; the section in paragraph 5 from 'Even in 1939 . . .' to '. . . even in Casablanca'; and all of the last paragraph. There is some evidence of change in tone—for example, the omission of 'Needless to say' at the beginning of the fourth sentence of the first paragraph.

1. For Jacques Doriot, see *662, n. 4. Gringoire* and *Candide* had circulations in the 1930s of over 600,000 and 350,000 respectively. They were described by Eugen Weber as virulent, right-wing publications, anti-semitic and sympathetic to Mussolini (*The Hollow Years*, pp. 105 and 128). See also *1913*.
2. On 4 December, *Tribune* published a letter from Cecily Mackworth arguing that Morocco should be treated no differently from France's other possessions in Africa and that the French had 'a better chance of bringing peace and prosperity to Morocco than the impersonal government of the United Nations.' Compare *1702*.

1669. News Commentary in English for Malaya, 8

20 November 1942

This was written and read by George Orwell. No script has been traced. The News Commentaries in English for Malaya began on Friday, 2 October 1942.

They were first written and read by Mrs. H. C. Lee. The first three (2, 9, 16 October) were called 'English News Commentary'; the next four (23, 30 October, 6, 13 November) had the title 'News Commentary in English for Malaya.' This was the title used for Orwell's scripts, which he read himself; see *1663* for the proposal that Orwell take over this work. The series ran until 2 July 1943 (No. 40), and most were written and read by Orwell and broadcast by him by that name. From 9 July, he broadcast a Newsletter to Indonesia. When he was ill from 20 January to 11 February 1943, 17 was read by someone else and 18, 19, and 20 were written and read by others; 25 was written by Orwell but read by someone else. Details are given at the appropriate dates. Thus, Orwell was responsible for writing 30 of the 40 scripts and for reading 28 of them.

A Newsletter in Malay (usually given by Richard Winstedt[1]) was also transmitted on Fridays. Orwell's English-language broadcast went out at 1130 GMT and that in Malay at 1430. The Malay-language broadcast continued when Orwell's Newsletter was directed to Indonesia from 9 July 1943.

Orwell believed few people, if anyone, heard his Newsletters, and his fear was supported by Miranda Wood. Mrs. Wood typed a version of *Nineteen Eighty-Four* and, in a private memoir kindly given to the editor (see Appendix 12, *3735*), she says that in 1946 Orwell asked her if she had heard any BBC Overseas Service broadcasts when she was living in Japanese-occupied Java. Though not a prisoner, being technically a German citizen then, she told Orwell she 'had done no radio listening in the Japanese occupation at all' because it was far too dangerous. 'Orwell said he had thought as much.' A rare chance has brought to light a diary from 1943 kept by a civilian internee in Bangkok, Albert Gentry, then aged forty-two. The prisoners, it says, had access to news and were able to listen regularly to All-India Radio and from time to time to BBC broadcasting from London. From his diary, it would seem he heard straight news bulletins, but it is possible that on 18 June 1943 he heard Orwell's commentary; see *2139, n. 1*. From the diary and from reports made available to the editor by the then protecting powers (Sweden and Switzerland), it is clear that consular officials in Bangkok regularly listened to BBC broadcasts (as might be expected). One or two entries from this diary (indicated by 'Gentry') are reproduced where they may help to elucidate events.[2]

On 17 September 1984, a Women's Royal Army Corps officer, Barbara Rigby, wrote to Tom Hopkinson about Orwell's broadcasts to Malaya. She had by chance picked up an old copy of *Cornhill* in which, in an article about Orwell, he wondered whether Malayans had heard Orwell's broadcasts.[3] When she had been in Malaya in 1983 she had helped collect toys for orphans cared for by Roman Catholic nuns. One nun, Sister Margaret, a Scot 'in her seventies, if not more,' spoke of the privations suffered during the Japanese occupation. She said that they had relied on the BBC and had walked many miles in their heavy clothing in the hot sun to smuggle reports of what they had heard. Sister Margaret described 'how they had been cheered by George Orwell—"we used to bless that good man", she said. . . . I told her that he had died of consumption, and she was most distressed.' She concluded her letter to Hopkinson: 'I thought you might be pleased to know that what must have seemed thankless work to the man himself was eagerly awaited, as cheering in unpleasant conditions.'

1. Sir Richard Olof Winstedt (1878–1966) rose from an inspector of schools in Perak state in 1902 to the post of Director of Education for what is now Malaysia and Singapore. He was very successful in improving vernacular education, though he was criticised for showing little enthusiasm for educating Malays to participate in management and government. He was an

authority and published much on Malay language and history. He retired in 1935 and from 1937 to 1947 was Reader in Malay at the University of London.

2. For a short account of this diary, with illustrations, see P. Davison, 'Bangkok Days: Orwell and the Prisoner's Diary,' *Manuscripts*, XLI, No. 4 (Fall 1989), 303–10. The diary was deposited in the Imperial War Museum in 1992.

3. 'George Orwell—Dark Side Out,' *Cornhill*, Summer 1953, 450–70.

1670. Review of *The British Way in Warfare* by B. H. Liddell Hart

The New Statesman and Nation, 21 November 1942

This collection of revised and reprinted essays written from about 1932 onwards, is largely a history of the development of the British army in the years between the two wars. Its opening chapters, however, contain a survey of Britain's "traditional grand strategy" which is the most interesting and provocative part of the book and the most important at this moment. The battle for mechanisation has been won, at any rate on paper, but the controversy over the Second Front is still raging, and Captain Liddell Hart's theories are extremely relevant to it.

What is the "traditional strategy" which we have abandoned and which Captain Liddell Hart implies that we should return to? Briefly, the strategy of indirect attack and limited aims. It was practised with great success in Britain's predatory wars of the eighteenth century and only dropped in the decade before 1914, when Britain entered into an all-in alliance with France. Its technique is essentially commercial. You attack your enemy chiefly by means of blockade, privateering, and sea-borne "commando" raids. You avoid raising a mass army and leave the land fighting as far as possible to continental allies whom you keep going by means of subsidies. While your allies are doing your fighting for you you capture your enemy's overseas trade and occupy his outlying colonies. At the first suitable moment you make peace, either retaining the territories you have captured or using them as bargaining counters. This was, in fact, Britain's characteristic strategy for something like two hundred years, and the term "perfide Albion" was thoroughly justified except in so far as the behaviour of other States was morally similar. The wars of the eighteenth century were waged in a spirit so mercenary that the normal process is reversed, and they seem more "ideological" to posterity than they did to the people who fought in them. But in any case the "limited aims" strategy is not likely to be successful unless you are willing to betray your allies whenever it pays to do so.

In 1914–18, as is well known, we broke with our past, subordinated our strategy to that of an ally, and lost a million dead. Commenting on this Captain Liddell Hart says: "I can find in the conditions of the war no satisfying explanation of our change. . . . No fundamental cause for a change of historic policy seems to appear. Hence one is inclined to find it in a change of fashion—in the military mode of thought inspired by Clausewitz." Clausewitz[1] is the evil genius of military thought. He taught, or is supposed to have taught, that the proper strategy is to attack your strongest enemy, that nothing is solved except by battle, and that "blood is the price of victory". Fascinated by this theory, Britain "made her navy a subsidiary weapon, and grasped the glittering sword of continental manufacture".

Now there is something unsatisfactory in tracing an historical change to an individual theorist, because a theory does not gain ground unless material conditions favour it. If Britain ceased, at any rate for four years, from being "perfide Albion," there were deeper reasons than Sir Henry Wilson's[2] tie-up with the French General Staff. To begin with it is very doubtful whether our "traditional" strategy is workable any longer. In the past it really depended on the balance of power, more and more precarious from 1870 onwards, and on geographical advantages which modern technical developments have lessened. After 1890 Britain was no longer the only naval power, and moreover the whole scope of naval warfare had diminished. With the abandonment of sail navies became less mobile, the inland seas were inaccessible after the invention of the marine mine, and blockade lost part of its power owing to the science of substitutes and the mechanisation of agriculture. After the rise of modern Germany it was hardly possible for us to dispense with European alliances, and one of the things allies are apt to insist on is that you do your fair share of the fighting. Money subsidies have no meaning when war involves the total effort of every belligerent nation.

The real shortcoming of these stimulating essays, however, lies in Captain Liddell Hart's unwillingness to admit that war has changed its character. "Limited aims" strategy implies that your enemy is very much the same kind of person as yourself; you want to get the better of him, but it is not necessary for your safety to annihilate him or even to interfere with his internal politics. These conditions existed in the eighteenth century and even in the later phases of the Napoleonic wars, but have disappeared in the atomised world in which we are now living. Writing in 1932 or thereabouts, Captain Liddell Hart is able to say, "Has there ever been such a thing as absolute war since nations ceased to exterminate or enslave the defeated?" The trouble is that they haven't ceased. Slavery, which seemed as remote as cannibalism in 1932, is visibly returning in 1942, and in such circumstances it is impossible to wage the old style of limited profit-making war, intent only on "safeguarding British interests" and making peace at the first opportune moment. As Mussolini has truly said, democracy and totalitarianism cannot exist side by side. It is a curious fact, not much remarked on, that in the present war Britain has, up to date, waged the kind of war that Captain Liddell Hart advocates. We have fought no large-scale continental campaign, we have used up one ally after another, and we have acquired territories far larger and, potentially, far richer than those we have lost. Yet neither Captain Liddell Hart nor anyone else would argue from this that the war has gone well for us. Nobody advocates that we should simply wipe up the remaining French and Italian colonies and then make a negotiated peace with Germany because even the most ignorant person sees that such a peace would not be final. Our survival depends on the destruction of the present German political system, which implies the destruction of the German army. It is difficult not to feel that

Clausewitz was right in teaching that "you must concentrate against the main enemy, who must be overthrown first", and that "the armed forces form the true objective", at least in any war where there is a genuine ideological issue.

To some extent Captain Liddell Hart's tactical theories are separable from his strategic ones, and here his prophecies have been all too well justified by events. No military writer in our time has done more to enlighten public opinion. But his justified war with the blimps has perhaps overcoloured his judgment. The people who scoffed at mechanisation and still labour to reduce military training to a routine of barking and stamping are also in favour of mass armies, frontal attacks, bayonet charges and, in general, meaningless bloodshed. Disgusted by the spectacle of Passchendaele,[3] Captain Liddell Hart seems to have ended by believing that wars can be won on the defensive or without fighting—and even, indeed, that a war is better half-won than won outright. That holds good only when your enemy thinks likewise, a state of affairs, which disappeared when Europe ceased to be ruled by an aristocracy.

1. Karl von Clausewitz (1780–1831), Prussian general and director of the War College, Berlin, 1818–30, set out the doctrine of total war in his famous *Vom Kriege (On War)* (3 vols., 1833).
2. Sir Henry Wilson (1864–1922), Field Marshal, was Chief of the Imperial General Staff and, in the final stages of World War I, principal military adviser to Prime Minister Lloyd George. As Director of Military Operations at the War Office, 1910–14, he advocated supporting France in a war against Germany. He was closely associated with Marshal Foch personally and militarily.
3. Passchendaele was the scene of particularly bloody and futile infantry fighting on the Ypres sector of the Western Front. The British suffered heavy casualties, 31 July to 4 November 1917, advancing through torrential rain on a fifteen-mile front. After more than three months of fighting, the small town of Passchendaele was taken. The Germans recovered the whole area in the spring offensive of 1918. The Belgians finally reoccupied Passchendaele in September 1918. The 'mud of Passchendaele' became symbolic for the British of the futility of war and of the fighting on the Western Front in particular, as did Verdun for the French.

1671. News Commentary, 48

21 November 1942

This was the first weekly Newsletter in English for India written and read by Orwell; on the previous day he had read his first Newsletter to Malaya; see *1669*. The new arrangements are confirmed in Orwell's letters to Bahadur Singh, Noel Sircar, and Shridhar Telkar of 21 November; see *1674* to *1676*. See also Venu Chitale's Programme Preview, 24 November, *1683*. The script is headed 'News Commentary' and is marked, in Orwell's hand, 'As b'cast   13' 15"   E.A.B'. PasB states, 'News Review by George Orwell.' West omits this broadcast, assuming that Orwell began reading his own Newsletters from 28 November 1942 (West: *Commentaries*, 179, n. 307).

It so happens that this news commentary wasn't delivered last week, so that it's now a fortnight since a discussion of the war situation has been broadcast in this service. During that fortnight the whole face of the war, one might say, the face of the world, has altered. It's hardly necessary for me to recapitulate in detail the news from North Africa and the Pacific. But let me just run over the main items, which may help us to get the situation into focus.

Last time this news commentary was broadcast the Eighth Army was at Mersa Matruh, about a hundred and twenty miles west of el Alamein. Now they are [almost] at Benghazi, several hundred miles inside Libya, and the latest figures give the Axis losses at a minimum of seventy-five thousand men, mostly prisoners. A fortnight ago there were rumours of Allied warships gathering at Gibraltar, and it was possible to infer that something was going to happen in West Africa.[1] Now the whole of Algeria and Morocco are under Allied control, and the British First Army is advancing into Tunisia and has made contact with the Axis forces there.[2] A fortnight ago we knew nothing about the situation in the Solomon Islands except that land fighting was going on and the Japanese were probably planning another naval attack. Now the Japanese have had a shattering naval defeat in which between ten and twenty of their warships have gone to the bottom, besides transports carrying not less than twenty thousand men.[3] I mention the Solomons battle not only because it's important in itself, but because—as you can see easily enough if you look at a map of the world—it links up with events in Africa and both have their effect on India.

Now let me try to get the situation into its right perspective. It's important to see it objectively and not expect too much. In particular, one ought to guard against hoping that the campaign in Africa will be all over in a few days, or even a few weeks.

The biggest achievement of the American seizure of North Africa, coinciding with the British victory in Egypt, was to rob the Germans of the initiative and drive them on to the defensive. For the time being the Germans have to move in response to our moves, and not the other way about, as has been happening throughout most of the war. [The Germans can't, in fact, counter our move in North Africa without weakening their forces elsewhere and throwing their strategy out of gear. On the other hand they can counter pretty vigorously, and are already doing so. It's important to keep in mind that all the commanders on the spot, British and American alike, have emphasised that there is a tough fight ahead before the Axis armies in Africa are destroyed and the Mediterranean is under our control.]

What counter-move can the Germans make? They have already occupied the whole of what used to be Unoccupied France, and also Corsica.[4] That was to be expected sooner or later, and it's doubtful whether it will do the Germans much good. It's not even at all certain why they have done it. But beyond that, it is clear that the Germans are going to gamble [heavily] on holding on to Tunisia and perhaps on making a come-back in Libya. [If you look at the map you can see that Tunisia, especially the naval base of Bizerta, is strategically of great importance. If the Germans could hang on to Bizerta and its airfields— with Sicily less than a hundred miles away—they could cork the central Mediterranean entirely.] Within a few days of the American landings in North Africa the Germans were flying troops into Tunisia; others have come by sea, and others may have moved in overland from Tripoli.

They are probably in possession of Bizerta already, and they can be counted on to consolidate their position very rapidly. Meanwhile the British First Army, with American support, has crossed the border from Algeria and already clashed with the Axis forces, and two days ago British and American parachute troops captured two airfields somewhere deep into Tunisia. *There was news this morning that British advanced units had made contact with the Germans only 30 miles from Bizerta.* But for the moment the situation in Tunisia may favour the Axis, because we can't altogether prevent them from ferrying reinforcements across from Sicily, and on the other hand bad communications may hold up the Allied advance for some days. The northern tip of the Atlas Mountains runs down to the sea near the Algeria-Tunisia border, and the railway communication is not good. The Allied armies *are evidently entering*[5] Tunisia in two columns, one near the coast and one further south, via Tebessa. But they can't move without air support, which means acquiring airfields and moving ground-staff, and for some days their progress may slow down. If it does, we can count on the Axis broadcasters to make the most of the fact. In the long run, however, the chances are against the Germans being able to hold on to Tunisia; and no doubt they know this and are attempting what is really a delaying action. If they are going to lose Tunisia in the end, the more men and tanks they pour into it now, the greater their loss in the long run. On the other hand, if they can hold us up in Tunisia they may save what is left of the Afrika Corps in Libya, and that is probably the meaning of their manoeuvre.

The remains of the Afrika Corps is now somewhere west of Benghazi. *The Germans announced that they had evacuated Benghazi yesterday. They*[6] may by this time have received reinforcements from over sea, or perhaps from Tripoli. General Alexander, who should know, considers that the Germans will make their next stand at el Agheila, about 50 miles west of Benghazi. This is a marshy area favouring defensive tactics, and it was here that the Germans made their comeback in the campaign of last winter. It is unlikely that they will be able to turn the tables on us as they did that time. Every eyewitness account that has come in in the past few weeks has emphasised the tremendous losses the Germans and Italians have suffered, not only in men, but in tanks, guns and transport. They have also been heavily outmatched in the air all through the battle. It isn't likely that they can reinforce the Afrika Corps to the extent needed for a successful counterattack, especially when they are trying to hang on to Tunisia as well. More probably they mean to fight a rearguard action which will allow the bulk of General Rommel's army to escape over sea, or fall back on Tripoli.

I believe we are destined to see the whole southern shore of the Mediterranean pass into Allied hands. But it may take months, if only because of the vast distances involved. During the last few weeks the Eighth Army has advanced faster than any army at any stage of the war, but even at that pace they couldn't reach Tripoli before the New Year. We mustn't lose sight, also, of the other countermoves the Germans might possibly make. They might make an airborne attack on some point in the Middle East or conceivably even on the British Isles, or they might violate Spanish neutrality and attack Gibraltar. The Spanish Government has ordered partial mobilisation, and this must have some meaning. Probably, also, we shall suffer heavy losses at sea until all the African coastline is ours. No figures have been published yet, but we do know that in the first week of the Mediterranean operations the Axis lost thirteen submarines, which means that they are making very big efforts to attack our shipping. But on the whole the prospects are good, and it needs to be emphasised that even if the strategic situation in the Mediterranean remained as it now is, it would have shifted enormously in favour of the Allies. The range of airfields now open to us is enormously greater, Italy is within easy reach of our bombing planes, and the Germans are cut off from Dakar in French West Africa, on which they undoubtedly had designs. More important yet, they have lost the vast quantity of imports—foodstuffs, vegetable oils, raw rubber, wool and various minerals—which they were previously drawing from French Africa. And incidentally we have acquired two or three hundred thousand tons of merchant shipping which was in the North African ports.

The political situation in North Africa is less satisfactory—at best, it is confused. The one thing that is certain *is* that there is virtually no support for the Axis in North Africa, either among the French or the Arabs. In Morocco and Algeria the French put up only a token resistance to the American landings, and in Tunisia they are already fighting against the Germans. But the support we are getting from the local French authorities has its liabilities. Most of the local French military and naval commanders seem to have come over to the Allied side, including some who were strong supporters of Vichy and the policy of so-called collaboration. In particular Admiral Darlan, who only a little while ago was one of the most anti-British of the Vichy gang, appears to have changed sides and also appears to have been confirmed in some kind of position of command in French North Africa. [We don't know how long this unsatisfactory state of affairs will last.] The Fighting French National Committee under General de Gaulle has very naturally washed its hands of the whole affair and refused to cooperate with any of the supporters of Vichy. It has evidently done this with the full understanding of the British Government. President Roosevelt has stated that all present arrangements are merely provisional. He has also asked the French authorities in Africa to open up the concentration camps where anti-Fascist refugees—25,000 of them— were interned, and to revoke the anti-Jewish laws which the Germans had forced on Vichy. We may hope that this will happen quite soon. Meanwhile the political set-up in North Africa is of a temporary kind, and we perhaps ought to suspend judgment on it till the Axis armies are destroyed.

At the other end of the world, down in the South Pacific, the Japanese have had their heaviest blow since the battle of Midway Island. In the main battle this week they lost no less than eleven warships, including a battleship, and five subsequently; also a number of transports which would involve the death of not less than twenty thousand men. There is no need to answer the lies which the Japanese have published, because the facts speak for themselves: the Japanese fleet has retreated from the Solomon Islands. In New Guinea the Australian and American forces have been advancing steadily, and the

Japanese hold on the eastern part of the island is now confined to a small area round Buna. There is some reason to think that the Japanese may evacuate their remaining troops by sea. I said earlier that the campaigns in North Africa and the Pacific are connected, and if you look again at the map you'll see that the point of their intersection is India. India is the spot where the two main Axis partners hope sooner or later to join hands. Well, every Allied victory in the Mediterranean or in the Pacific helps to make that impossible. If the North African campaign succeeds, the Mediterranean is opened up and communication between Britain and India becomes comparatively safe and rapid. If the Japanese continue to lose ships at the speed they have been doing, they can't get naval control of the Bay of Bengal, and without that they are unlikely to attempt the invasion of India.

While all this has been happening in Africa & the Pacific, the situation at Stalingrad has remained much as it was in spite of renewed German attacks, & in the Central Caucasus the Germans have evidently had a serious reverse. This week I have had to talk chiefly about the North African campaign, because events there have outweighed everything else and it was necessary to bring this news commentary up to date after a week's interval. Next week I hope to be able to deal with the other fronts as well.

1. Operation Torch, the landing of Allied forces in Morocco and Algeria on 8 November 1942.
2. British paratroops engaged German forces in Tunisia on 17 November 1942.
3. The naval Battle of Guadalcanal, 12–15 November 1942, involved large U.S. and Japanese fleets and some 270 American and 215 Japanese aircraft. The United States lost the light cruisers *Atlanta* and *Juneau* and seven destroyers; the Japanese lost the battleships *Hiei* and *Kirishima*, the heavy cruiser *Kinugasa*, two destroyers, and seven of eleven transports carrying 10,000 reinforcements for Guadalcanal. Only about 4,000 men were landed (*2194 Days of War*, 313).
4. The Germans marched into Unoccupied France on 11 November 1942. Pétain broadcast a protest that night, and a week later Pierre Laval was given absolute power.
5. *are evidently entering*] will probably enter
6. *They*] It

1672. Bengali Newsletter, 19

21 November 1942

The English original was written by Orwell. No script has been traced.

1673. To T. S. Eliot

21 November 1942   PP/EB/NP

Dear Eliot,

Thank you for your letter of the 18th. I should like it very much if you would read "What the Thunder Said", on December 1st. It will be quite all right if you are at 200 Oxford Street by 11.30 on that day.

I am rather anxious to arrange for the speakers in that particular programme, who will include Mulk Raj Anand and Narayana Menon, to be photographed. I hope you will have no objection to this.

Yours sincerely,
George Orwell
Talks Producer
Indian Section

1674. To Bahadur Singh

21 November 1942   PP/EB/NP

Dear Mr. Bahadur Singh,
It has been suggested that we should make a slight change in the presentation of the Weekly News Review, which you have so kindly helped us with. As I write the script myself, I have been asked to read it as well, so we are trying this out, with effect from to-day. I believe I told you about this last time I saw you. This means that for the time being, at least, we shall not be asking you to read the News Review, but I am most grateful to you for the help that you gave us. I hope that we shall be able to ask you to broadcast for us again later on.

Yours sincerely,
Eric Blair
Talks Producer
Indian Section

1675. To Noel Sircar

21 November 1942   PP/EB/NP

Dear Mr. Sircar,
I think I may have told you last time you were here that we are making a slight change in the presentation of our Weekly News Review. It has been suggested that I should broadcast the script as well as write it, and so we are trying this out with effect from to-day. This means that for the time being, at least, we shall not be asking you to read the News Review, but I am very grateful for the help that you gave us with it.

Yours sincerely,
Eric Blair
Talks Producer
Indian Section

1676. To Shridhar Telkar

21 November 1942   PP/EB/NP

Dear Telkar,
I think I told you a week or so ago that we are making a slight change in the presentation of our Weekly News Review. It has been suggested that I should broadcast the script as well as write it, and so we are trying this out with effect from today. This means that for the time being, at least, we shall not be asking you to read the News Review, but I am very grateful to you for the help that you gave us.

Yours sincerely,
Eric Blair
Talks Producer
Indian Section

1677. To V. E. Yarsley

21 November 1942   PP/EB/NP

Dear Dr. Yarsley,
Thank you for your letter of 20th November, and for agreeing to do the talk on Plastics. The lines you suggest are just what we want, and I shall very much look forward to seeing your talk.

Please do not bother to send us a copy of your other talk; we are asking the Schools Department to let us have one, and I expect we shall receive it by Monday next.

Yours sincerely,
Eric Blair
Talks Producer
Indian Section

1678. BBC Talks Booking Form, 21.11.42

R. R. Desai: Gujarati Newsletter, 39; broadcast 23.11.42; fee £5.5s + 12s 0d fare + 17s 0d subsistence, in order to listen to All-India Radio bulletin in Gujarati. Signed: M Blackburn for I.P.O.

1679. Gujarati Newsletter, 39

23 November 1942

The English version was written by Orwell. No script has been traced.

1680. To Norman Marshall

23 November 1942   EB/NP/np°

Dear Mr. Marshall,

I enclose another list of questions, supplied by Mr. and Mrs. Sahni. Mr. Sahni asked me to tell you that the questions are tentative, and that you should not consider yourself bound by them. You can add new ones and delete any or all of these, if you like.

Perhaps you will give me a ring and let me know if you would like to come and go through the script with the Sahnis, or if not, when I may expect the script.

Yours sincerely,
Eric Blair
Talks Producer
Indian Section

Enclosed with Orwell's letter:

LET'S ACT IT OURSELVES

No. 4—Friday, 4th December

Question: Last time, Mr. Marshall, you talked to us about the producer's
1   work at the early rehearsals and the importance of the prompter. Now today I suggest that you should tell us something about the art of acting on the stage.

Marshall: I shall gladly do so, but I thought your actors did not act the performance in the English language, so I do not know whether what I say will be very helpful to them.

Question: I should not worry much about that because we need to impress
2   on our listeners very strongly that it [is] no use staging plays in English. They will fail. It is also of no use to imitate the conventions in many of the productions of the western stage. These talks are just to let them know about the western stage. They can take what suits their genius and their circumstances. It is from that point of view that I want to ask you about the actors here and their conventions.

(Mr. Marshall may say a few words in agreement and speak about the unbroken tradition of acting in England—it did not have much respect as a profession in the early days but today it's an important and respected profession etc.)

Question: In one discussion you told us about talking [over] the play.
3   Would it not be better in an amateur society where the producer may not be so far superior to the rest of the company in talent and experience to have one or two preliminary discussions about the play, the different characters, the author's meaning etc?

Question: What are the accomplishments of a good actor? Is he born or
4   made? If made, how? Are there any acting schools in England?
Question: Is it necessary to be good looking to be a successful actor or
5   actress?
Question: What is "ham" acting? Is it necessarily bad?
6
Question: Should the actors be natural? Some people say there is no such
7   thing as natural acting, what do they mean?
Question: What is meant by tempo and movement?
8
Question: What is meant by grouping?
9
Question: How long before the dress rehearsal should the actors know
10   their parts thoroughly?

1681. BBC Talks Booking Form, 23.11.42

S. K. Das Gupta: to translate and read Bengali Newsletters written in English by
E. Blair; broadcast 5, 12, 19, and 26.12.42; fee £5.5s each. Signed: M Blackburn
for I.P.O. Handwritten addition: '[Mrs R. Ghosh will do 2 mins in this period].'

1682. To K. K. Ardaschir

24 November 1942   PP/EB/np

Dear Mr. Ardaschir,
As Mr. Blair is away today, he has asked me to write and thank you for the
Philippines synopsis that you sent him; he would like to keep it as we
might be able to use something along those lines sometime.
    I believe you are coming to London towards the end of the week, and
Mr. Blair would like to see you then, if possible, about the Tunis script.
Perhaps next time you are in London you will ring up and we can arrange a
time to suit you both. There is no space in the schedule for this talk now,
but it *might* be fitted in if Tunis comes very much into the news.

Yours sincerely,
Secretary to Mr. Blair

1683. Extract from Venu Chitale's Programme Preview

24 November 1942

You have, of course noticed the change in the NEWS REVIEW period on
Saturdays. I mean the fact that George Orwell, novelist and journalist,
author of *Burmese Days* and other books, now reads the weekly news

commentary written by himself. Those who know him through his books will now have the opportunity of hearing him regularly on Saturdays.

1684. BBC Talks Booking Form, 24.11.42

Mulk Raj Anand: 'Voice,' 5 '(in conjunction with Dr. Menon)'; Oriental influence on English Literature; 'half hour programme of poems etc. with discussions lasting about 5'. Mr. Anand helped to put the programme together & will take part in discussions'; broadcast 1.12.42; fee £4.4s. Signed: M Blackburn for I.P.O. Remarks: 'As Dr. Menon is helping in this prog. as well, Dr. M. R. Anand should receive slightly less than his usual fee.'

1685. BBC Talks Booking Form, 24.11.42

Gujarati Newsletters, 40–44; English version written by E. Blair, translated and read by R. R. Desai; broadcast 7, 14, 21, and 28.12.42; fee £5.5s + 12s 0d fare + 17s 0d expenses (in order to listen to All-India Gujarati broadcasts[1]).

1. The listening-in was cancelled, and, more important, Desai was to recast Newsletters 43 and 44, as a 'trial run.' Thereafter he composed and read the Gujarati Newsletters, and these are no longer included here. For Orwell's guidance of Desai, see his letter of 19 December 1942, 1753.

1686. BBC Talks Booking Form, 24.11.42

Lady Grigg: 'Women Generally Speaking'; broadcast 2, 9, 16, 23, and 30.12.42; fee £8.8s each broadcast. Signed: M Blackburn for I.P.O.

1687. BBC Talks Booking Form, 24.11.42

Princess Indira of Kapurthala: 'Favourite Moments'; 'four 30-minute programmes comprising 5–7 mins. speech & the rest gramophone records'; 'script written by Hubert Foss (separate contract)'; 'reading only'; broadcast 5, 12, 19, and 26.12.42. Though initially signed by Mary Blackburn, her signature was crossed out, the form was left incomplete and marked 'Example—for Miss Savage to see.'

1688. BBC Talks Booking Form, 24.11.42

Princess Indira of Kapurthala: 'The Debate Continues'; broadcast 7, 14, 21, and 28.12.42; fee £12.12s each talk. Signed: M Blackburn for I.P.O.

1689. BBC Talks Booking Form, 24.11.42

Narayana Menon: almost identical details as those for Mulk Raj Anand in *1684*.

1690. BBC Talks Booking Form, 24.11.42

Herbert Read: 'Voice,' 5; 'reading poems and taking part in discussions in this 30 minute programme'; broadcast 1.12.42; fee £4.4s. Signed: M Blackburn for I.P.O. Remarks: 'Mr. Read should receive his usual fee for taking part in this programme.'

1691. BBC Talks Booking Form, 24.11.42

Shridhar Telkar: 'Behind the Headlines'; broadcast 2, 9, 16, 24, and 31.12.42; fee £9.9s each talk. Signed: M Blackburn for I.P.O. Remarks: 'As from December 24, Mr. Telkar will b'cast on Thursday instead of Wednesday.'

1692. BBC Talks Booking Form, 24.11.42

Dr. V. E. Yarsley: 'Science and the People,' monthly; 3, Plastics; broadcast 15.12.42; fee £9.9s. Signed: M Blackburn for I.P.O. Remarks: 'Dr. Yarsley is an expert on this subject, & I suggest he should receive the same fee as Dr. Kidd & Ritchie Calder, who gave the first 2 talks in the series.'

1693. To L. F. Rushbrook Williams

24 November 1942   Handwritten annotation

On 22 November, Chinna Durai sent the Eastern Service Director a script which he had earlier discussed with him. It was designed to promote a 'Commonwealth consciousness' that would encourage India to stay within the Empire. Durai thought there was an opportunity that should be taken to project Britain in a favourable light to India following the success of the Eighth Army in Libya. Rushbrook Williams circulated it to Orwell, A. L. Bakaya, and Balraj Sahni, but all turned it down. Its only new point, Bakaya thought, was 'Britain looks forward with confidence to invading Europe.' Neither Bakaya nor Orwell could fit it into their talks' schedules; Sahni was willing to meet Durai. Orwell wrote:

E.S.D.
I'm afraid we simply can't find space for this without cutting our schedule up.

Eric Blair   24.11.42

1694. To Herbert Read

[26 November 1942?]

DONT FORGET EXPECTING YOU 10.30 TUESDAY[1]

ORWELL

1. 'Voice,' 5, in which Read was to participate, was broadcast on Tuesday, 1 December 1942.

1695. To Bahadur Singh

26 November 1942   PP/EB

Dear Bahadur Singh,
Thanks for your letter. I am sorry, but I don't think I can arrange to do anything on Christmas Day itself, as we have more or less Christmas items on the 23rd and also the 29th. We have a new series coming on in January in which I think you could take a hand occasionally. This is a series called "In The Public Eye" which will be short character sketches of prominent personalities of the week, and probably in most cases adapted from the Profiles in the Observer, which you may have seen. This will be a weekly item, done by different people, and there is no reason why you would not cover this item from time to time.

Yours sincerely,
Eric Blair
Talks Producer
Indian Section

1. Singh had replied to Orwell's letter of 21 November expressing his willingness to contribute scripts and immediately offered a talk for Christmas Day. Orwell annotated Desai's letter, 'Answered 25.11.42'—not 26, as on the letter sent to him.

1696. To Stevie Smith

26 November 1942   PP/EB/np

Dear Stevie,
I'm sending herewith the proof copies of the two books, and also the manuscripts you lent me. I'm sorry I have kept them for so long.
Thanks very much for your suggestions for a Christmas number of Voice. I think we could make an excellent programme, based on those ideas, but I am inclined to think that it would mean devoting far more time to it than we can possibly spare at the moment. However, we are hoping to have the

Christmas number of December 29th, and we may find that there is more time in hand by then.[1]

Yours
George Orwell
Talks Producer
Indian Section

1. The meaning of this paragraph is unclear. A special Christmas number of VOICE *was* broadcast on 29 December (*1778*); see also *1786*.

1697. News Commentary in English for Malaya, 9
27 November 1942

This was written and read by George Orwell. No script has been traced.

1698. Weekly News Review, 49
28 November 1942

Marked in Orwell's hand, 'As B'cast 12′ 15″ E.A.B'. Intermediate timings have been written at the foot of each page of the script. They are shown here in italic within square brackets. The cumulative totals do not quite tally with the timings for individual pages of the script.

At the end of my commentary last week, I promised that this time I might be able to give some news from the other fronts, particularly the Russian front. Well, the news has come, and it is just as sensational as the African move of a week or two earlier.

Six days ago, the Russians opened an offensive north-west and south of Stalingrad. Almost immediately there was news that the northern attacking forces had broken through, made a fifty mile advance and captured thirteen thousand prisoners. Since then, however, it has gone very much further. The attacking Russian army has circled round to the south and captured in all something over sixty thousand prisoners and an enormous amount of material.[1] The latest Russian reports speak of driving the enemy eastward over the Don, which can only mean that they have circled right round to the rear of the enemy forces and that a very much larger body of Germans than those taken prisoner already is in danger of being cut off if they don't get out quickly. Even in the German communiques it is possible to deduce the fact that the present position of the German army before Stalingrad is very shaky, and I think in any case we are safe in saying that the long siege of Stalingrad has now been definitely raised.

I don't care as yet to predict too much about the results of this Russian offensive. If the German position is as precarious as it looks on the map they may not only have to lose very much more heavily in men and material, but they may even have to make a big retreat and go back to somewhere about the line they occupied last winter. But however that may be, I want to emphasise two facts about the Russian offensive. The first is its probable effect on German morale and Axis morale in general. It will now be very hard indeed to conceal from the German people the fact that the [*3' 10"*] German[2] campaign in Russia in 1942 has been a failure. The objectives of that campaign were first of all to get to Baku and the oil fields, secondly in all probability to capture Moscow by an encircling movement from the south, and thirdly quite certainly to get to Astrakhan on the Caspian Sea and thus cut the Russian communications running North and South. Well, not one of those objectives has been achieved, and the prime cause of the failure has been the heroic Russian defence of Stalingrad. It is impossible that the German common people should not recognise how important Stalingrad is, because it has been in the news for too long. Indeed, so long as they felt confident of taking it the German military spokesmen emphasised the importance of Stalingrad for all they were worth. It is now something over three months since the siege began, and something over two months since Hitler solemnly promised that it would be taken. A month or so later, when Stalingrad hadn't been taken, Hitler explained that after all, it was not of very great importance because even if the Russians were still in possession of the city itself or what was left of it, the Germans were in a position to prevent Russian traffic moving up and down the Volga. Well, now that almost certainly the Germans will be forced to retreat from Stalingrad even that claim can't be made any longer. The German propagandists, therefore, will be in the unenviable position of having to admit that their military commanders have poured out lives and material on an enormous scale for an objective which finally wasn't achieved. The effects even on German morale must be bad, and on Germany's so-called Allies they may be disastrous. The war has already lost most of its meaning from the Italian point of view, and it will not make the Italians any happier to know that tens of thousands of their sons are being frozen in Russia for absolutely nothing, at the same time as their African Empire is slipping away from them and their cities are [*2' 20"=5' 30"*] being bombed to pieces.

The other thing I'd like to point out about this Russian campaign is its co-relation with the North African campaign. Through a great part of this year the Russians have had to fight almost alone against the biggest army in the world. Now Russia's allies have managed to stage a diversion elsewhere and the effects make themselves felt almost immediately on the Russian front. For there can't be much doubt that the Russian success is partly due to the Germans' having to withdraw part of their air strength in order to rush as many planes as possible south in hopes of retrieving the situation in Africa.

Since last week French West Africa has fallen into line with the other French colonies and entered into collaboration with the Allies. The only bit of French African territory still nominally neutral is French Somaliland with the port of Jibouti, which no doubt will come over in the near future. French West Africa coming into the Allied sphere of influence is not merely important because of the valuable products—raw rubber, vegetable oils and various food stuffs—which we shall now be able to get from those territories. It is also important because of the great naval base of Dakar which has docks big enough to take battleships and which is only sixteen hundred miles from Brazil. With nearly the whole of the West African coast line under our control, it is much easier to deal with the U-boats in the South Atlantic and also with the ports further north which we now hold we have a much safer supply route to the Central Mediterranean than we have had hitherto. There is road and rail communication all the way from Casa Blanca° almost to Tunis and if the North African campaign succeeds completely it will be possible to travel from Gibraltar to Suez by a comparatively short route without once entering in the range of the Axis aeroplanes. French West Africa came over quite amicably without any fighting and is under the general [*2' 25"*= *7' 53"°*] control of Admiral Darlan. I repeat what I said last week, that we must regard the present political set-up in French Africa as merely temporary and likely to come up for revision when the military part of the campaign is settled. We may not like the past record of some of the Vichy commanders who have now come over to our side, but the fact of their coming is at any rate a good symptom—it means that with their *much* greater inside knowledge of events in Europe than we ourselves *can* possess at present—they have decided that the Nazi ship is sinking. [*And no doubt Hitler's treacherous attack on Toulon,*[3] *and his breach of his solemn promise given only two weeks ago will further strengthen the resistance to the Axis of many Frenchmen who have hitherto held aloof from the United Nations. The scuttling of the French fleet to prevent it falling into German hands was a defiance worthy of French valour.*][4]

There hasn't been a great deal of development on the two battlefronts in Libya and Tunisia. The 8th Army entered Benghazi almost a week ago—in all probability this will be the third Christmas they have spent there—and they have also occupied Jedabya, fifty miles south on the coastal road, and are in contact with the enemy near El Agheila. Probably the Germans intend to make a stand here and it may take the 8th Army some days more to get their heavy equipment into position for a fresh attack. If the Germans decide not to stand at El Agheila, they will probably have to go back to Misurata, another two hundred miles along the Libyan coast. The Allies have also occupied the Jalo oasis, two hundred miles south in the desert, which safeguards them against any out-flanking movement. On the other side, in Tunisia, the First Army is evidently getting into position for a direct assault on *Tunis or* Bizerta. Their movement has been slowed up no doubt partly by the fact that much of their material still has to come all the way from Casablanca, but partly also by the evident fact that the Axis are for the time being stronger in the air on this front. It isn't easy for the Germans to reinforce their army in Tunisia on any big scale with men or heavy equipment, but they can reinforce their air strength more quickly than we can; and this advantage may remain with them for some days to come. In the long run, however, it is unlikely that the Germans will get the [*2' 20"*=*10' 16"*] better of the air battle, even on this front, because the total air strength of the Allies is now greater and is getting increasingly more so. In any case, any air reinforcements they send to Tunisia is weakening some other front, especially the Russian front. Meanwhile, their air losses have already been heavy and even if they successfully fight a delaying action which allows the bulk of Rommel's army to escape by sea, they may turn out not to have gained much in the process.

There is not very much news from the South Pacific. The Japanese succeeded in bringing their forces at Buna some small reinforcements by sea, but it is not expected that they will be able to hold on to Buna much longer. The Allies have captured Gona, a few miles along the coast, and the Japanese are being heavily bombed besides being attacked on the ground. If they are driven out altogether from the Eastern part of New Guinea, this, along with the stronger American hold on the Solomons after their naval victory, will make it possible to launch an attack on Rabaul, which is the most important Japanese base in this area. [*11' 37"*]

Addition to News Review.[5]

Hitler has broken his pledge to Marshal Petain° and occupied Toulon. The French commanders have scuttled the French fleet and destroyed the naval arsenal and ammunition dumps. Hitler has ordered the demobilisation of what is left of the French Army. I give these items of news very baldly because it is too early to comment on them adequately. We don't know yet whether any of the French ships escaped to join the Allies, though we do know that none of importance have fallen into the hands of the Germans. I hope to comment on this next week. Meanwhile, just let me point out two things. One is that this marks the end—and from our point of view the successful end—of Hitler's two and a half years of intrigues to get hold of the French Fleet. The other is that it is the final death blow to the New Order. Any chance of French collaboration with the Nazis has now gone for good.

[*No timing marked*]

1. On 22–23 November, a Russian pincer movement closed at Kalach, trapping more than a quarter of a million German soldiers and five Romanian divisions. Although the German commander, von Paulus, was promised air support, this proved impracticable. Friedrich von Paulus (1890–1957), Commander-in-Chief of the Sixth Army, was created General Field Marshal the day before surrendering his wretched surviving troops on 31 January 1943.
2. German] *typed as* German's
3. The German SS took over Toulon naval base on 27 November 1942. Admiral Jean de Laborde ordered the French fleet to be scuttled, and two battleships, a battle-cruiser, seven cruisers, 29 destroyers, two submarines, and other ships were sunk; four submarines escaped (*2194 Days of War*, 319).
4. This passage was added in manuscript by Orwell, but then crossed through. It was presumably added not long before the news review was transmitted. It was then replaced by 'Addition to News Review,' see *n. 5*.
5. This addition replaces the shorter account of this incident added in Orwell's hand above but crossed through (see *n. 4*). From the timings it must have been spoken at the end of the broadcast although it is marked with an 'A' in Orwell's hand as if it were to be an insert. The last timing marked is 11 minutes 37 seconds. The timing of the whole broadcast is given as 12 minutes 15 seconds, and this addition would roughly account for that additional 38 seconds.

1699. Bengali Newsletter, 20

28 November 1942

The English original was written by Orwell. No script has been traced. From PasB a timing of 8′ 30″ may be implied.

1700. To Miss McCallum

28 November 1942   PP/EB

Dear Miss McCallum[1]

I understand from Miss Blackburn that you are kindly helping us by suggesting a speaker for our series of talks "A Day in My Life" (A Canteen worker). We shall be most grateful if you will approach Lady Peel[2] and find out from her if she will be willing to do this talk, in the form of an interview with Dr. Mulk Raj Anand. Dr. Anand is arranging this series of talks and is interviewing each speaker in the series. He has already interviewed a Munition worker, a Soldier, a Seaman and a Nurse. For Lady Peel's information, we enclose a copy of one of the broadcasts. The whole interview should take 13½ minutes. The date of broadcast is Friday, 18th December and the actual time of the broadcast is from 12.45 to 1.0 p.m. BST. If the time and date are not convenient to Lady Peel, it will be possible to arrange for the talk to be recorded in advance.

We shall be grateful if you can telephone us as soon as possible, so that we may arrange for Dr. Anand to meet Lady Peel and discuss their interview together.

Yours sincerely,
[Initialled] E.A.B
Eric Blair
Talks Assistant

1. Miss McCallum was Warden of the Victoria League Club, which was run especially for servicemen from overseas. Orwell, in his notes to Anthony Weymouth on 'Speakers for Week 51,' 7 December 1942, stated that 'many Indians serving in the forces in England go there regularly when on leave'; see *1724*.
2. In 'Speakers for Week 51' Orwell describes Lady Peel as the wife of Sir William Peel, onetime Governor of Hong Kong; she was 'one of the oldest commandants and workers of the Victoria League Club,' organising three midday shifts of meals each week.

1701. Notes

c. 28 November 1942

On 27 November 1942, T. S. Eliot wrote to Orwell asking him to ensure Eliot's right of entry to the BBC in order to participate in the 'Voice, 5' broadcast; no ticket of admission had been sent him. He concluded: 'I wish I could get you for lunch some time.'

On the verso of this letter, in Orwell's writing, are the following notes:

<u>Talbot</u>

"One of the most difficult"
. . . "successful party"

<u>Kharkov</u>

"Under the famous 5 year plans". . . .
"building up a new life"

1702. In the Darlan Country

The Observer, 29 November 1942

Before the war French Morocco, like much of North Africa, lived partly on its picturesqueness, ultimately traceable to poverty. Except for the climate, every feature that attracted the tourist really depended on the fact that the average human being's earnings were round about a penny an hour.

The most striking thing in Morocco is its barrenness. Of its seven million inhabitants the great majority are small peasants, cultivating a soil which is little better than desert. Down the Atlantic coast there is a strip of fertile land where a million tons of wheat are grown annually, but this is owned by a French syndicate which works it with gang labour. The Arab peasant stirs his dried-up soil with a primitive plough drawn by a cow and an ass yoked together, and grows crops of weed-infested barley and lucerne. For a few months there are fitful storms of rain, and then the streams swell, the grass springs up and the miserable domestic animals put on a little flesh, but for the rest of the year water is precious enough to be a cause of feuds and murders. Just as in Biblical times, landmarks are moved and streams suddenly diverted in the middle of the night. Part of the trouble is the lack of trees.

There are date palms, pomegranates, and, where the French have settled, groves of oranges and olives, but except in the Atlas Mountains there are no wild trees at all. This is the result of hundreds of years of goat-grazing. Even in the thinly-populated Atlas, where there are forests of oak and fir, the mountain-side round each village is bare as a slag-heap, thanks to the goats.

Morocco differs from the majority of French colonies in that it has only recently been conquered (the fighting did not really end till 1934), and French cultural influences have barely touched it. Very few Moroccan Arabs speak French otherwise than in a sort of barbarous pidgin. In the way of education the French have done very little, and there are no universities and no class corresponding to the English-speaking intelligentsia of Egypt or India. In 1939, at any rate, there was no vernacular Press or Arab-owned French Press, nor any nationalist movement worth bothering about. The social relationship between French and Arabs is complicated by the fact of Morocco being so near Europe. Excellent motor roads run all the way from the Mediterranean shore to the desert beyond the Atlas; and the French lorry-driver, carrying with him the atmosphere of Marseilles, is as ready to sit down in the wayside bistro with an Arab as with a European.

In Casablanca there is a large French proletariat, drawing low wages, and everywhere there are small traders and shopkeepers living among the Arabs, but reproducing as well as they can the life of provincial France. On the other hand, the business community, the bureaucracy, and the army officers live in a more lordly, Anglo-Indian style, and there is a general tendency to treat the Arabs as charming but rather naughty children. Everyone tu-toies them, and the newspapers refer to them patronisingly as "les indigènes" ("natives"). But the fact that the French working class have little colour prejudice—so that, for instance, French conscripts do not mind being put in the same barracks as African troops—makes for a friendly atmosphere, and has no doubt played its part in damping down nationalist feeling.

There are some 200,000 Europeans in Morocco, all French-speaking, though some of them are of Spanish origin. Since 1940 few Englishmen can have seen the interior of Morocco; and one can only guess at subsequent political developments, but in 1939, at any rate, the prevailing outlook among Europeans was semi-Fascist. The loyalties of the local Press ranged from Daladier to Doriot, and the Fascist weeklies, "Gringoire," "Candide," "Je suis Partout,"[1] and the rest of them, were on sale everywhere. The Left-Wing parties had no foothold, even in Casablanca. During the Munich crisis the general apathy and cynicism, even among army officers, were very striking. Anti-semitism was common, although the Moroccan Jews, who live in self-contained communities and are mostly petty craftsmen, present no real problem. Some nationalist feeling may also have increased among the Arabs as a result of the French defeat and the consequent slump in French prestige.

Morocco is now under the control of the United Nations, and merely to govern it, in the sense of preventing rebellion, is not likely to be difficult. The French have successfully ruled it through the phantom Sultan, who has already transferred his allegiance to ourselves. But whether Morocco can be brought actively into the war is another question, not answerable during the political interregnum. At present we appear to have guaranteed Admiral Darlan, and if that means that we have guaranteed the existing régime, then Morocco will remain what it has always been—stagnant, feudal, and desperately poor. The long-term needs of the country are obvious enough. It needs more trees, more irrigation, better agricultural methods, better breeds of animals, more schools, more hospitals. All this means foreign capital and, inevitably, foreign protection for a weak and backward country like Morocco cannot be genuinely independent.

But it would be a great pity if a positive short-term policy, capable of enlisting the Arabs on our side, cannot be evolved. Morocco is obviously important in the strategy of the war. The road and rail communication running from Casablanca to Tunis gives us a supply route far safer than we have had hitherto, and at the worst the possession of Casablanca would partly offset the loss of Gibraltar. In spite of its poverty Morocco can export several valuable foodstuffs, and at need it could also produce at least 100,000 soldiers of the highest quality. The peace-time strength of the colonial army in Morocco was 50,000, of whom perhaps half would be Arabs. They were long-term volunteers, the Moroccan Arabs, unlike the Algerians or the Senegalese, not being French citizens and therefore not liable to conscription. The equipment of these troops was and probably still is old-fashioned, but as human material they would be hard to beat.

It seems unlikely, however, that Morocco will enter fully into the war effort unless the war can somehow be given a meaning from the Arab point of view. Basically it is a matter of economic restitution. The French exploitation of Morocco has not been particularly gross, but still it is exploitation, and any thinking Arab must be aware of this. Nearly all of the most fertile soil of the country, and all the modern industries, are in foreign hands.

Moreover, if Italian Libya is conquered and some fairly generous settlement arrived at there, it must have repercussions among the Western Arabs. The grosser injustices could be wiped out without interfering with the small French settler, though not, indeed, without bumping up against the big capitalist interests. If we want the Arabs on our side we have got to promise them either autonomy or a higher standard of living, or both. And there is also the local French working-class, whose interests are approximately the same as those of the Arabs. Whether the existing French authorities, whom we have so hastily guaranteed, will lend themselves to any genuine programme of reform seems very doubtful. But it is certain that in Morocco, as in so many other places, the mass of the people will not and cannot be actively with us unless we are ready to make deep changes in the status quo.

1. *Je Suis Partout*: an extreme right-wing journal with a circulation of some 60,000 copies, xenophobic and anti-semitic. See *1668, n. 1* for *Gringoire* and *Candide*.

1703. Gujarati Newsletter, 40

30 November 1942

The English original was written by Orwell. No script has been traced. PasB gives timing of approximately 9 minutes, and this is also given in Mary Blackburn's letter of 4 January 1943. However, the implied timing from the PasB data is 8' 35".

1704. To Norman Marshall

30 November 1942   PP/EB/np

Dear Mr. Marshall,

I am enclosing herewith the questions provided by Mr. and Mrs. Sahni. Mr. Sahni asked me to emphasise that, although [he] has divided the questions into two sets, it rests entirely with you which lot you take first, and so on. He also says that if you don't like the questions and would prefer to make your own, please do!

As you know, you will be recording the 5th discussion on Saturday, 6th December, from 5.45 to 6.45 p.m. at 200 Oxford Street. We shall expect you on Thursday next, at about 6 o'clock, as usual.

Yours sincerely,
George Orwell
Talks Producer
Indian Section

Enclosed with Orwell's letter:

LET'S ACT IT OURSELVES
No. 5—Friday, 11th December (recording Saturday, 6th December)

Question 1: In this fifth discussion let's take up stage work, lighting, music etc. and if there is time the business side. Suppose an amateur society is putting on a play like "The Enemy of the People." How many people will the stage manager require to assist him? What will be their duties?

Question 2: Should settings aim at reality or suggestion? Would suggestion not be preferable in a small theatre?

Question 3: What is meant by a pre-dimensional [three-dimensional?] setting?

Question 4: Are foot-lights absolutely necessary? How do they get rid of shadows on the stage?

Question 5: If an experienced stage electrician is not availabe are there any very simple hints for amateur lighting?

Question 6: Is make-up necessary, if so why?

Question 7: If a company has to travel about can you give any practical advice from your experience?

Question 8: When we came off the air last time you said that the secret of good production is "right emphasis", what did you mean?

Question 9: What is the minimum capital required for starting an amateur theatrical society in an English provincial town?

Question 10: Do various dramatic societies help each other? How?

Question 11: What is the stage generally built of in this country? Is it always made of wood or is it ever a solid platform?

Question 12: Should music be used during the intervals of a performance?

1705. 'Voice,' 5
1 December 1942

An illustration of the participants of 'Voice,' 5 appears in *London Calling*, No. 175, 22 (programmes for 14–20 February 1943). The caption reads: 'Here is a picture taken during the broadcasting of "Voice", a radio magazine programme of modern poetry for English speaking India, in the B.B.C.'s Eastern Service. From left to right, sitting, are: Venu Chitale, a member of the B.B.C. Indian

Section; M. J. Tambimuttu, a Tamil from Ceylon, editor of "Poetry (London)";
T. S. Eliot; Una Marson, B.B.C. West Indian Programme Organiser; Mulk Raj
Anand, Indian novelist; Christopher Pemberton, a member of the B.B.C. staff;
Narayana Menon, Indian writer. Standing: George Orwell, author, and
producer of the programme; Nancy Parratt, secretary to George Orwell;
William Empson, poet and critic. It is hoped that "Voice" will return to the
Eastern Service in the spring of this year [1943].' It did not continue after 'Voice,'
6, 29 December 1942. The illustration is reproduced as Plate 2, West, *Orwell:
Broadcasts*.

1706. 'Voice,' 5: A Magazine Programme

1 December 1942

The script for this programme has not been traced but the PasB gives some
details which enable an outline to be reconstructed. The theme was 'Oriental
Influence on English Literature.' Those who participated were George Orwell,
William Empson, Una Marson, T. S. Eliot, Narayana Menon, Mulk Raj
Anand, M. J. Tambimuttu, and Christopher Pemberton (see *1705*). The first
three people, BBC staff members, were marked as receiving no fee.

The programme included: 'Brahma' by R. W. Emerson (12 lines); 'What the
Thunder Said,' part V of *The Waste Land*, by T. S. Eliot (113 lines), read by the
author; extract from 'The Rubaiyat of Omar Khayyam' (36 lines); 'The Indian
upon God' by W. B. Yeats (20 lines); 'The Mark' by W. B. Yeats (15 lines);
'Mohini Chatterjee' by W. B. Yeats (20 lines); passages from 'The Secrets of the
Self' by Sheikh Muhammed Iqbal (40 lines); passages from 'Confessions of an
English Opium-Eater'[1] by De Quincey (360 words). Herbert Read was to have
read some of his poems, but he was not able to be present.

1. Orwell's father had been a sub-deputy agent in the Opium Department of the Indian Civil
   Service.

1707. To E. W. D. Boughen, Talks Bookings

1 December 1942   EB/WMB

We had arranged for Herbert Read to take part in VOICE No. 5, on December
1st, 1942, from 11.15 to 11.45 GMT. Unfortunately, he was prevented from
coming and therefore did not take part in the programme. I expect he will
return the contract in due course.

Dictated by Eric Blair and
despatched in his absence by
[Signed] Winifred Bedwell[1]

1. This appears to be the first communication typed for Orwell by his new secretary, Winifred
   Bedwell. 1 December was a Tuesday, so she evidently overlapped with Nancy Parratt for
   about two weeks. Many letters do not have the initials of either, but Miss Bedwell did not
   indent paragraphs, whereas Miss Parratt did. The last letter that can be identified as Miss
   Parratt's is dated [Monday], 14 December 1942, though she typed and signed a memorandum

of 21 December (see *1758*). Miss Bedwell typed her last letter for Orwell on Friday, 23 July 1943. Miss Parratt, who left to join the WRNS, wrote to Orwell just before he died; see *3713*.

1708. BBC Talks Booking Form, 1.12.42

Lady Peel: 'A Day in My Life,' 7; '13 minute interview with Mulk Raj Anand (who arranges the series) on her life as a canteen worker'; broadcast 18.12.42; fee £8.8s. Signed: M Blackburn for I.P.O.

1709. BBC Talks Booking Form, 1.12.42

M. J. Tambimuttu: 'Voice,' 5; 'half hour programme. Made one or two remarks in the discussion but came primarily out of interest in the programme'; broadcast 1.12.42; fee 'usual' £2.2s. Signed: M Blackburn for I.P.O. Remarks: 'I suggest he should receive a small[1] token fee.'

1. 'small' was inserted in manuscript by Mary Blackburn, and underlined.

1710. To T. S. Eliot

2 December 1942   PP/EB[1]

Dear Eliot,

It was very kind of you to take part in the ramshackle programme yesterday.[2] I hope you may later take part in one of these programmes which will have rather more natural unity. The next one comes off on December 29th, and I think we are going to make it a Christmas number, probably with carols interspersed. You might like to take part in that one and you could, at any rate, keep the date in mind. I will let you know particulars of the programme later. For this type of programme you don't really need to be here except on the morning itself.

Meanwhile, I am hoping that you will do one of the talks in another series, which begins in the last week of this year. We are going to have seven talks on American writers, so as to try to put American literature a bit more on the map in India, as we have previously done with English, Russian and Chinese literature. I am going to get Herbert Read to more or less run the series and he will, I think, do the opening talk on Hawthorne. The ones following are Poe, Melville, Mark Twain, Jack London, O. Henry, Heminway.° You could take any of these you like but above all I should like you to take the one on Poe. The scheme of the programme is this. First there is a 13½' talk on the author in question. Then an interlude of music and then five minutes reading from the chosen author's work. This should be quite easy to select in the case of Poe. You might let me know about this and we could talk it over.

I don't know how often you are in town. You could, perhaps, have lunch with me one day next week, or come to my place in the evening, whichever you prefer. We could always put you up for the night as we have spare rooms.

Yours sincerely,
George Orwell
Talks Producer
Indian Section

1. There is no third set of initials for the reference; the typing suggests the work is not that of a trained typist.
2. Orwell's diffident response to this programme is akin to his reaction to the performance of his *Charles II (155)*.

1711. To George Woodcock

2 December 1942   Handwritten

On 18 November 1942, George Woodcock wrote to Orwell:

I have just read the controversy in the Partisan Review,[1] and I feel one reference in your letter calls for some kind of reply. I mean, of course, the B.B.C. Indian broadcasts.

As you know, I had the opportunity of observing one from the inside.[2] What I heard (and found myself saying) certainly surprised me and made me feel that, if I had heard a fair sample of the Indian broadcasts, I might in the past have been a little too angry about them. I don't think the broadcast I heard was even remotely likely to "fox the Indian masses", because (1) it would reach only the educated crust and (2) it contained no propaganda likely to alter the ideas of a disaffected Indian. This, however, does not alter the fact that the intention behind Indian broadcasts conducted under the auspices of a British imperialist government is, admittedly, to keep India out of the clutches of the Fascists, but, equally certainly, to keep it in the clutches of the British nabobs. I do not mean that this is *your* intention — in fact I am sure it is not — but I fear it is the intention these broadcasts will unwillingly serve.

I should explain my own motives in taking part in the broadcast. Of course, I suspected immediately that your offer was a trap of some kind[3] but I decided to accept because of my curiosity to see what went on inside. I was reasonably rewarded! In case you should think I had any mercenary motive ("financially profitable back-scratching" etc), if you enquire at the B.B.C. contract office you will see that I did not return the contract and have taken no payment.[4]

I don't wish to enlarge on this matter, as I imagine this kind of haggling is probably unpleasant to you. I'd like to discuss your ideas on the younger writers, and particularly this business of "financial profit" (I earn most of my money growing cabbage plants and tomatos°!), but I don't feel this is quite the occasion.

Yours sincerely
George Woodcock

Orwell replied on 2 December 1942:

10a Mortimer Crescent   NW 6

Dear Woodcock,

I'm sorry I didn't get round to answering your letter earlier, but I'm very busy these days. I am afraid I answered rather roughly in the "Partisan Review" controversy. I always do when I am attacked—however, no malice either side, I hope.

I can't help smiling at your (a) not accepting the fee after doing a broadcast for the BBC & (b) "suspecting a trap" when asked to b'cast. As a matter of fact it was Mulk's[5] idea to ask you. That particular b'cast is a bit of a private lunacy we indulge in once a month & I would be surprised if it is listened-in to by 500 people. In any case there is no question of getting to the Indian *masses* with any sort of b'cast, because they don't possess radios, certainly not shortwave sets. In our outfit we are really only b'casting for the students, who, however, won't listen to anything except news & perhaps music while the political situation is what it is.

I am sorry that what I said about "financially profitable" rankled—I didn't mean it to apply to you or any of the others personally, merely to the whole process of literary racketeering about which doubtless you know as well as I do.

As to the ethics of b'casting & in general letting oneself be used by the British governing class. It's of little value to argue about it, it is chiefly a question of whether one considers it more important to down the Nazis first or whether one believes doing this is meaningless unless one achieves one's own revolution first. But for heaven's sake don't think I don't see how they are using me. A subsidiary point is that one can't effectively remain outside the war & by working inside an institution like the BBC one can perhaps deodorise it to some small extent. I doubt whether I shall stay in this job very much longer, but while here I consider I have kept our propaganda slightly less disgusting than it might otherwise have been. I am trying to get some of our b'casts for the Indian section published in book form.[6] If this goes through you may see from the book that our b'casts, though of course much as all radio stuff is, aren't as bad as they might be. To appreciate this you have to be as I am in constant touch with propaganda Axis & Allied. Till then you don't realise what muck & filth is normally flowing through the air. I consider I have kept our little corner of it fairly clean.

Yours
Geo. Orwell

1. September–October 1942 issue; see *1270*.
2. 'Voice,' 2, broadcast 8 September 1942.

3. 'Of course . . . some kind' is underlined (by Orwell?) and there is an exclamation mark in the margin.
4. See BBC Talks Booking Form, 7 September 1942, *1461*.
5. Mulk Raj Anand had helped put together 'Voice,' 2; see *1449*.
6. Published as *Talking to India*, edited by George Orwell, in 1943.

1712. To Edmund Blunden

3 December 1942   Top[1] and carbon copies

Dear Mr. Blunden

I think Brander will have rung you up before this letter reaches you. We would like it very much if you would compere a series of talks for us and deliver one in the series yourself. I should warn you, however, that it is all rather short notice and it is very important to get all the scripts in by the end of this month.

I will explain the reason. We are proposing to have a series of six talks covering some of the set books in the B.A. course in the° English literature at Calcutta University. This will be more or less similar to the series you took part in before, but we propose this time to publish the six talks in the form of a pamphlet in Calcutta, so as to appear before the University examinations. This will mean that the scripts will have to be despatched from England early in January at latest, though some of them will not actually go on the air until a few weeks later. The six subjects are:—

1) Shakespeare, with special reference to JULIUS CAESAR.
2) Milton, with special reference to the shorter poems.
3) Hardy, with special reference to FAR FROM THE MADDING CROWD.
4) HAZLITT—with some remarks about English essays in general.
5) Shaw—with special reference to ARMS AND THE MAN.
6) The Book of JOB.

The speakers I have projected are E. M. Forster, F. L. Lucas, yourself, George Sampson, Bonamy Dobree and T. S. Eliot, respectively. Of course you could alter this list as much as you wished, but the all important thing is to get things moving quickly. The first talk would be actually delivered on the 25th December (it can be recorded beforehand of course) but I should want to have all six manuscripts in by about that date.

These are 15 minute talks, which means approximately 1500 words.

Can you please let me know, as early as possible, whether you can undertake this.

Yours sincerely
[Signed] Geo. Orwell
George Orwell
Talks Producer
Indian Section

1. The original of this letter has been annotated by Edmund Blunden. Above the BBC letterhead address is written '6.15 Wed. 16th meet L.B. at Reform Club. Write I.R.   B.B.C. Fridays to India, & ?Jan. 8 for me.' L. B. would be Laurence Brander; I. R. has not been identified. In the

left margin are the proposed dates for the talks with, against the fourth, 'before Christmas'—the day the talk was to be broadcast—'—fix a day.' In the right margin are the initials or names of those who might speak. For the first four talks these are EMF, G. S., EB. and D.N.S.—the initials of those given in Orwell's memorandum to Miss Playle on 21 December; see *1758*. The fifth and sixth talks presented problems, and were given by Orwell and W. J. Turner, whose names were written in by Blunden. For the fifth he had crossed out H. M. Tomlinson and what is probably intended for E. W. Gillett (the 'W' is unclear), Professor of English, Raffles College, Singapore, 1927–32, literary editor and broadcaster; and, for the final talk, TSE, W. de la Mare, and la Billière were crossed out.

1713. Venu Chitale to Sarup Mukerjee

3 December 1942   PP/VC/np

Dear Sarup,

We are recording an adaptation of an Indian play for our programme which will be transmitted to India on January 12th 1943, in our series "*Indian Play*".

The recording is fixed up for Monday, December 14th, and we would need you here from about 2.30 onwards. If it is suitable for you to be in London on the 14th, I want you to do the part of Madhav in the play "Malti and Madhav" in Bhavabhuti.[1] Lilla Erulkar will play opposite you.

Please let me know by return of post if you will be able to take part in the recording, so that I can inform the Contract Department. As soon as I know that you will be taking part, I shall send you a roneo-ed copy of the script.

Yours sincerely,
Venu Chitale
Talks Assistant
Indian Section
(Mr. Blair's Office)

1. This is a little confused. The correct title is *Mālatī Mādhava*; 'in Bhavabhuti' reads as if this were a language, but it is the dramatist's name. Bhavabhūti lived in the eighth century and was an outstanding Sanskrit writer. Only an excerpt of this ten-act domestic drama must have been given. See *1742, n. 1*.

1714. To V. E. Yarsley

3 December 1942   PP/EB/WMB

Dear Dr. Yarsley

I am sending you the scripts you asked for and as these are the only copies we have I should be glad if you would kindly return these when you have finished with them.

I received your talk and script yesterday and thank you very much for sending them in such good time.

It was very kind of you to give us all the details about yourself over the telephone yesterday and our Publicity section were very pleased with it.

Would you be good enough to be here at 200 Oxford Street on December 15th, the day of the broadcast, at 11.30 a.m. This will give you time to rehearse.

Yours sincerely
[Initialled] E. A. B
Eric Blair
Talks Producer
Indian Section

1715. 'The End of Henry Miller'

Tribune, 4 December 1942

No more that is of any value will come out of Henry Miller. Fruit trees past bearing continue to put forth leaves, and writers never stop writing, but Miller is one more instance of the fact that even the best writer has only a limited number of books in him. Since his work is autobiographical, he might well have produced only one book worth reading, but in fact he produced two, or possibly three, and it is of these that I would like to speak, rather than his latest pot-boiler.[1] For it is something to have written even one book that remains memorable after seven years, and for a variety of reasons Miller's early work has never had its due in this country.

Miller's best book is *Tropic of Cancer*, published in 1935. It might seem useless to recommend anyone to read it, since the Nazis in Paris and the police in this country have seen to it that there are not many copies in circulation, but I would back it to survive. Books which are worth reading always become respectable sooner or later. Meanwhile there is no harm in drawing attention to its existence; also *Black Spring* and *Max and the White Phagocytes*, which belong to the same period.

Tropic of Cancer was excluded from this country because it contained unprintable words and dwelt on unmentionable subjects. It is by no means a book of pornography, but the dirty words are integral to it and no expurgated edition would be possible, because it is a straightforward attempt to describe life as it is seen and lived by the average sensual man. I emphasise "straightforward," because Miller is in a sense not attempting very much. If one wants to describe life as it really is, there are two main difficulties to be got over. The first is that our language is so crude compared with our mental processes that communication between human beings is chancy at best. The second is that so much in our lives is normally considered unprintable that the most ordinary words and actions, once they get on to paper, are given a false emphasis. Joyce in *Ulysses* was dealing with both of these problems, but primarily with the first; Miller is only dealing with the second, and dealing with it by pretending that it does not exist. In *Tropic of Cancer* there is nothing resembling the complex pattern of *Ulysses*, nor the desperate effort to convey differing states of consciousness by means of linguistic tricks. There is only

Henry Miller, an out-at-elbow American of exceptional intelligence, but of average morals and opinions, talking about his everyday life. Granted that he is a brilliant prose-writer, Miller writes as the average man talks. The great charm of *Tropic of Cancer* is that it is a good-tempered book, the book of a man who enjoys the process of life and, unlike Joyce, is not struggling against a Catholic upbringing or a Swiftian horror of the body. It is obscene, but less so than the average conversation you would overhear in a Nissen hut, and the facts it recounts are mostly sordid, but not more sordid than the things one had to do in the nineteen-twenties and 'thirties in order to earn a living.

Miller was a highbrow American novelist living in a Paris backstreet, and to that extent his circumstances were abnormal, but in writing *Tropic of Cancer* he was filling a gap that existed in the over-political literature of the nineteen-thirties. The book has no moral, it offers no programme, no key to the riddle of the universe. It speaks for the common man whose aim is, first, self-preservation, and secondly, a "good time." Is the common man heroic? Not consciously. Is he anxious to die for a Cause? No. Does he want to be faithful to his wife? No. Does he even want to work? Not very much. This side of human nature Miller expressed admirably, because he not only shared it but, as a lumpenproletarian intellectual, a man who for many years had walked the narrow tightrope between starvation and honest work, possessed it in a hypertrophied form. Most current enthusiasms struck him as sheer lunacy. What did it matter, for instance, whether or not Hitler ruled the world? The great thing was to stay alive. He was particularly proud of the clever way in which he had dodged military service in the last war. The shortlived periodical which he edited, the *Booster*, expressly rejected "purpose" of every kind, its nearest approach to a political statement being, immediately after Munich, to print a full-page advertisement which read: DRINK PILSNER—IT'S STILL CZECH.

After *Tropic of Cancer* there came *Black Spring*, which partly continued the tale of Miller's life in Paris, but also included a flash-back of his boyhood in New York, and *Max and the White Phagocytes*, a collection of essays and sketches. Thereafter the particular vein that he was working seemed to peter out. He was at his best in writing about the unheroic, and we live in what is, however unwillingly, a heroic age. One thing that is noticeable about Miller's books is how strongly they smell of the nineteen-twenties—a point in their favour, simply as books, for the 'twenties were pleasanter to live in than the 'thirties. The Latin Quarter of Paris, with its population of artists, bugs, prostitutes, duns and lunatics, was his spiritual home.

But that kind of world could not endure for ever, and when the period of wars and revolutions reopened Miller's contacts with contemporary life became less intimate. This is very noticeable in his latest book, *The Colossus of Maroussi*. It is a book about Greece, and it barely rises above the level of the ordinary travel book; indeed, it has all the normal stigmata of the travel book, the fake intensities, the tendency to discover the "soul" of a town after spending two hours in it, the boring descriptions of conversations with taxi-drivers, etc. The reason is probably that in a period like the present a contempt for politics and a regard for one's own skin lead one almost automatically away from any place where anything interesting is happening. *The Colossus of Maroussi* consists quite largely of rhapsodies on Greece and diatribes against England and America, which Miller declares he never wants to set eyes on again. One naturally assumes that Miller has remained with the Greeks in their hour of agony. But no, it appears that he is now in New York. He had, in fact, left for Greece when war became imminent in northern Europe, and left for America when war became imminent in Greece. If war should come to the United States one feels reasonably certain that he will be in Argentina, or perhaps Central Asia. What a book he might have written, with his mastery of words and his disillusioned eye, about life in Paris under the Germans! But then, if the Germans were in Paris Miller would inevitably be somewhere else, and therein lies his limitation.

A writer's work is not something he takes out of his brain like tins of soup out of a storeroom. He has to create it day by day out of his contacts with people and things, and he is not likely to do his best when the kind of world he understands and enjoys has passed away. In *The Colossus of Maroussi* Miller notes sadly that the war will destroy everything that he himself regards as valuable. Indeed, it is certain that whatever survives this war, the kind of society that Miller described in *Tropic of Cancer* will not. Never again in our time will human beings be so free or, probably, so insecure. But Miller was a true chronicler of that society while it lasted, and since men with either the daring or the good temper to write about life as it is are not common, *Tropic of Cancer* has its place in the short list of twentieth-century novels that are worth reading.

On 18 December 1942, *Tribune* published the following letter from the poet Nicholas Moore, who had taken issue with Orwell in the January–February 1942 *Partisan Review*, see 854.

I hardly dare quarrel with Mr. Orwell again, because last time I did it in an American magazine, he accused me of wishing to usurp his place as political correspondent, and this time I suppose he will accuse me of wishing to become a reviewer in *Tribune*. However, that appears to be an attitude integral to his state of mind, and I'm afraid I can't help that. His article on Henry Miller contains once again his insolent air of know-all and tell-all, which, coupled with his excellent style and show of intelligence, is capable of persuading innumerable readers that what he says is true.

The generalisations in Mr. Orwell's first paragraph are amazing. I can assure your readers that it is no more true that "No more that is of any value will come out of Henry Miller" than it is that "writers never stop writing." His view must simply be based on prejudice and lack of knowledge. Admittedly, perhaps, he couldn't be expected to know it—but then, if he doesn't, he shouldn't make such remarks—but Henry Miller has been writing concurrently with *The Colossus of Maroussi* a novel called *The Rosy Crucifixion*,[3] which I see every reason to believe will be just as good as *Black Spring*, if not better. I am willing to agree that *The Tropic of Cancer* is the best, but that does not help prove any point for Mr. Orwell, since he included *Black Spring* in Miller's best work.

I suggest that Mr. Orwell would do better in attempting to put an end to himself rather than to other more creative writers before their time. And I suggest that he would have done better to concentrate on reviewing the book before him rather than parade his knowledge in support of an extremely silly generalisation. For the *Colossus of Maroussi* is not as bad as all that, and, if it is a potboiler, it is a very remarkable one. Even Shakespeare wrote potboilers, but that did not mean he never wrote another good play.

I strongly advise no one to be led too acquiescently by Mr. Orwell's nose, for it is extremely sensitive to all sorts of odours that to another nose are not there. What he will smell in this letter I don't know. I leave it to him. Something dirty, beyond all doubt.

[Mr. Orwell writes: It seems a pity to waste space over this kind of thing in a time of paper shortage, so I will answer as briefly as possible.

(1) I "paraded my knowledge" (i.e. wrote in general terms about Henry Miller) instead of reviewing *The Colossus of Maroussi* because that was what the Editors of the *Tribune* asked me to do.

(2) As to "prejudice" and "lack of knowledge," I have studied Miller's work with some care, and I was the first person in this country to draw attention to it in print.[2] When *Tropic of Cancer* was published in 1935 my review of it was the first that appeared, and Miller and his publisher were so excited by the review as to reprint it in the form of a leaflet—or so Miller told me. From that time onwards I have done what I could to give Miller's work publicity, in print and even over the air. None of this alters the fact that Miller's later work, beginning with *Tropic of Capricorn*, is poor stuff. If *The Rosy Crucifixion* turns out to be any good I think I can be trusted to recognise this, since I "spotted" Miller a long time before Mr. Moore did.

(3) I did not accuse Mr. Moore of "wishing to usurp my place as political correspondent." That is merely a lie (*vide* correspondence in the *Partisan Review*). But he is quite right in saying that I smell something dirty in his letter, and so no doubt will your readers. That "something" is pathological envy and desire for self-advertisement, and a very dirty smell it is:—Eds., *Tribune*.]

1. *The Colossus of Maroussi*.
2. Orwell reviewed *Tropic of Cancer* on 14 November 1935 (see *263*) and *Black Spring* on 24 September 1936 (see *325*). See also his letter to Henry Miller, 26–27 August 1936, *323*. The first section of 'Inside the Whale' (see *600*) is largely devoted to Miller's work.
3. Although the first part of the trilogy, *Sexus*, appeared in 1949, *Plexus* and *Nexus*, were not published until 1953 and 1960, some years after Orwell's death.

1716. News Commentary in English for Malaya, 10
4 December 1942

This was written and read by George Orwell. No script has been traced.

1717. To T. S. Eliot

4 December 1942   PP/EB

Dear Eliot,

Thanks for your letter of December 3rd. All right, let's make it lunch on Friday the 18th. You will hear from Read about the American talks, but we are, I think, postponing this series for six weeks, so the matter is not so urgent as it seemed when I wrote.

If you would like, I should like you to do one talk in the series preceding the American ones. Do you think you could do a talk on the Book of Job? This series is probably being looked after by Edmund Blunden, and I have already suggested your name to him as the speaker for this particular talk. Blunden will get in touch with you about this, but I should warn you that this script is wanted by about 25th December, because we propose to publish all the talks in the form of a pamphlet in Calcutta[1]—the talks cover some of the set books in the B.A. course in English literature at Calcutta University.

Yours sincerely,
George Orwell
Talks Producer
Indian Section

1. It was published as No. 3 in the B.B.C. Pamphlets series as *Landmarks in American Literature,* Oxford University Press, Bombay, 29 October 1946.

1718. To Herbert Read

4 December 1942   PP/EB/WMB

Dear Read

About the talks on American literature. It isn't after all, so urgent as I thought when I spoke to you, as we have decided to postpone this series for six weeks so that the first will be on February 6th. The authors I suggested having the talks on (subject to your revision are):—
   1. Hawthorne
   2. Poe
   3. Melville
   4. Mark Twain
   5. Jack London
   6. O. Henry
   7. Hemingway
These, I think are a representative selection, though not in all cases necessarily the *best* authors. They also all, except perhaps Mark Twain, have the advantage of being quotable in fairly short extracts.

The way we have decided to do the programmes is this. First, perhaps, two minutes (at most) from you, introducing the speaker. Then 11–12 minutes talk on the chosen author, then a 7 minutes interlude of music which will be selected by Narayana Menon, and then a 5 minutes reading from the chosen author. In the case of Poe, London and Hemingway, at any rate, this should be easy enough. I shall have to leave most of the work to you as I'm very busy.

Please let me know what you think about this.

Yours
George Orwell
Talks Producer
Indian Section

1719. Weekly News Review, 50

5 December 1942

The text has not been traced, but it is recorded in PasB as being written and read by George Orwell.

1720. Bengali Newsletter, 21

5 December 1942

The English original was written by Orwell. No script has been traced. From PasB a timing of 11' 30" may be inferred, of which Mrs. Renu Ghosh contributed 1' 30" 'of News interest to Bengali women' (PasB for 26 December 1942; see *1681*).

On 28 November 1942, Mary Blackburn, writing on the I.P.O.'s behalf, requested that a cable be sent to Ahmed Ali[1] in New Delhi to advise him that personal greetings would be included in vernacular news commentaries from recently arrived Bevin Boys[2] and Indian students. These would be in the same language as the news commentary. Those in Bengali were to be included in the programmes transmitted on 5, 12, and 19 December and there were to be messages in Marathi on 10, 17, and 24 December, and in Gujarati, for which no dates were given.

1. Ahmed Ali was Listener Research Director in the BBC New Delhi Office, 1942–45. See *1103*, *n. 3*.
2. These were young Indians sent to Britain for technical training (and are to be distinguished from young British conscripts, also called 'Bevin Boys' who were conscripted to serve in British coal mines instead of serving in the armed forces; see *949, n. 2*).

1721. To Edmund Blunden

5 December 1942   Top and carbon copies   PP/EB/np

Dear Mr. Blunden,
Brander tells me that he has spoken to you on the phone and that though very much occupied you have kindly agreed to undertake our special series of talks

to students. You have a list of the subjects and suggested speakers. Of course you can arrange with whatever speakers you like, but I have already written to Eliot asking him to do the talk on Job and I would like that arrangement to stand if Eliot is willing.[1]

The way we thought of doing the talks was this. First you do about two minutes introducing the speaker, then the speaker does his stuff for 15 minutes or thereabouts—say not more than 1700 words—then there is an interlude of music which we will be responsible for choosing, and then five minutes reading from the works of the author who is the subject of the talk. In some cases this can be done by the speaker. Where it is a case of a play, we shall have to act a scene of it, but that will be quite easily arranged.

The idea, as I have already explained to you, is to have these six talks making about 10,000 words published in book form in India in time to appear before the Calcutta University examinations. That is the reason for the haste with which the manuscripts are needed.

The talks will be actually going on the air between December 25th and January 29th inclusive. I am afraid I shall have to leave most of the dirty work to you, including making the speakers produce their stuff on time. Please let me know any further particulars you want. I should be glad if you would also let me know the names of the speakers you choose if you depart from the list I suggested, as we have to do publicity about them. If anyone cannot do his talk on the day appointed, they can always be recorded beforehand.

Yours sincerely,
[Signed] Geo Orwell
George Orwell
Talks Producer
Indian Section

1. Eliot declined; see Orwell to Blunden, 10 December 1942, *1727*.

1722. Gujarati Newsletter, 41

7 December 1942

The English original was written by Orwell. No script has been traced. Broadcasts on 7, 14, and 21 December included greetings from Bevin Boys and Indian students who had recently arrived in Britain; see *1720*.

1723. To Noel Sircar

7 December 1942   PP/EB/WMB

Dear Sircar,

Confirming our telephone conversation, the first IN THE PUBLIC EYE talk, which I want you to do is on December 29th at 1215 GMT. It takes 8 minutes or possibly a little less, which roughly means 1200 words. We obviously cannot fix who is the celebrity of the week more than a week in advance, which means you probably don't get your cue till Monday, but I suppose that will be time enough. In the case of our making use of THE OBSERVER column,[1] as I suggested, very little work is required.

Yours
Eric Blair
Talks Producer
Indian Section

1. This was the feature 'Profile,' devoted to someone currently in the news.

1724. Memorandum to Anthony Weymouth, Talks Assistant, Eastern Service

7 December 1942   EB/WMB

SPEAKERS FOR WEEK 51

Copies to Mrs Archer, Langham Hotel[1]
E.S.D.   I.P.O.   E.T.M.[2]

On Sunday, the 13th December as usual, the Brains Trust will answer questions sent in by listeners. Those taking part will be Dr. Malcolm Sargent, Leslie Howard, Dr. C. E. M. Joad,[3] the guest speakers being Captain F. J. Bellanger,° M.P.[4] and Dr. C. H. Waddington. Dr. Waddington has already broadcast a talk in the series LITERATURE BETWEEN WARS, on science and literature, and also took part in a discussion with Professor J. B. S. Haldane, on the subject of scientific research in the series "I'd like it explained" in the Eastern Service.

On Monday, the 14th, at 1115 GMT, Princess Indira, continues her usual weekly review of events in Parliament THE DEBATE CONTINUES. This is followed by RADIO THEATRE, in which John Burrell presents a selection from NELSON, featuring Leslie Howard.

On Tuesday, the 15th, we have the third in the series SCIENCE AND THE PEOPLE, dealing with PLASTICS, the new synthetic substances which have revolutionised the light industries all over the world. The talk is delivered by Dr. V. E. Yarsley. After the last war Dr. Yarsley graduated in the Honours School of Chemistry, at Birmingham University and was awarded a Research Fellowship by the Salters Institute of Industrial Chemistry which he held at the Eidgenossische Technische Hochschule in Zurich. Returning to England he was engaged as Chief Chemist in the manufacture of non-inflammable cinefilm, and had the somewhat unique experience of producing this film right from the raw cotton minters to the production on the screen. 12 years ago commenced practice as an independent consulting chemist, specialising in cellulosic plastics and products. Was Chairman of the Plastics Group of the Society of Chemical Industry and a member of the Council of the Institute of Plastics Industry, having particular interest in the establishment of schemes for education in plastics. Dr. Yarsley is co-author with a colleague (E. G. Couzens) of PLASTICS, in the Pelican series, which is published by Penguin Books Ltd. This talk will, we hope, be followed at 1145 GMT by Noel Sirkar's° film commentary in which he tells listeners in India about films shortly to be released.

On Wednesday, the 16th, at 1115 GMT, Shridhar Telkar is at the microphone, as usual, with BEHIND THE HEADLINES, in which he explains to listeners the importance of some or other current event which may have escaped general notice. This is followed by quarter of an hour of violin solos by F. Grinke,[5] and then by Lady Grigg's usual Wednesday programme WOMEN GENERALLY SPEAKING. The speaker will be Mrs. Eugenie Fordham, and the title of her talk is TESSA—A POLISH BABY. Mrs. Eugenie Fordham is Assistant Director of British Survey at the British Association for International Understanding. She read law at Cambridge, is married to a barrister and has a son aged 8.

On Thursday, at 1115 GMT, Dr. Shelvankar will give the Seventh and last talk in the series THE STORY OF FASCISM and will deal with the Nazi invasion of Soviet Russia. Dr. Shelvankar has been a frequent speaker in this service and has usually talked about Russian and central Asian affairs.

At 1130 GMT the feature programme BEHIND THE BATTLEFRONT appears as usual.

On Friday, the 18th, at 1115 GMT, listeners will hear an imaginary interview between William Pitt, the younger, Britain's Prime Minister during the darkest days of the Napoleonic war and Wickham Steed. Wickham Steed is a frequent broadcaster in this service and is almost too well known to need any introduction. He was for many years Editor of the Times and is probably the most respected figure in British journalism. This is followed at 1130 GMT by the Sixth and last interview in the series LETS° ACT IT OURSELVES, when Norman Marshall, the well-known theatrical producer answers questions on stage technique put to him by Balraj and Damyanti Sahni.

At 1145 GMT Mulk Raj Anand conducts the Seventh and last interview in his series A DAY IN MY LIFE in which he interviews war workers of various kinds. This time the speaker is a canteen worker, Lady Peel. Lady Peel is the wife of Sir William Peel who is a member of the Club Committee (Victoria League Club Committee) and also a member of the Victoria League Central Executive Committee. He was a Governor and Commander in Chief Hong-Kong. Lady Peel herself is one of the oldest commandants and workers of the Victoria League Club. She has been with the Victoria League Club since it opened. She looks after and organises entirely three midday shifts of meals a week, one of the busiest times of course which the Club has to cope with. The Victoria League is run entirely for the benefit of men from overseas and many Indians serving in the forces in England go there regularly when on leave.

On Saturday, the 19th, at 1145 GMT, George Orwell, gives his usual weekly NEWS COMMENTARY. This is followed by Princess Indira's musical programme, FAVOURITE MOVEMENTS. This week she's presenting a selection from various French composers.

[Signed] Eric Blair
(Eric Blair)

1. The Langham Hotel faces Broadcasting House and it served as offices for the BBC until its restoration as a hotel in the late 1980s.
2. The Eastern Service Director (L. F. Rushbrook Williams); Indian Programme Organizer (Z. A. Bokhari); Empire Talks Manager (Norman Collins). For Anthony Weymouth, see 635, n. 2.
3. Dr. Malcolm Sargent (1895–1967; Kt., 1947) was a distinguished and popular orchestral conductor with a gift for discussing musical and general issues on radio. He trained as an organist and led many choral societies in the thirties and forties, was conductor of the Liverpool Philharmonic Orchestra, 1942–48, and chief conductor of the BBC Symphony Orchestra, 1950–57. Leslie Howard (1893–1943), actor, film star (Ashley Wilkes in *Gone With the Wind*, Professor Higgins in *Pygmalion*), and film director (*Pimpernel Smith* and *The First of the Few*, in both of which he starred). He was killed when the civil plane in which he was travelling from Portugal to Ireland was shot down by the Germans over the Bay of Biscay. For C. E. M. Joad, philosopher and writer, see 497, n. 4.
4. Captain Frederick John Bellenger (1894–1968), Labour M.P. for Bassetlaw, Nottingham, from 1935, had served in the army, 1914–19, and was evacuated from Dunkirk in 1940. In the Labour government, he was Under-Secretary, then Secretary of State for War, 1945–47.
5. Frederick Grinke (1911–1987), Canadian concert violinist and Professor of Violin, Royal Academy of Music, London. He led the Boyd Neel Orchestra for ten years and then pursued a distinguished career as a soloist.

1725. Norman Collins, Empire Talks Manager, to L. F. Rushbrook Williams, Eastern Service Director

8 December 1942

Norman Collins and Orwell had crossed swords when Collins was Deputy Chairman of Victor Gollancz Ltd.; see 267. This is his reaction to Orwell's memorandum.

MR. BLAIR'S SPEAKERS IN THE EASTERN SERVICE

A copy of Mr. Blair's memo of the 7th December (of which you have been sent a copy) has just reached me. I notice one thing in it which suggests that Blair is working rather too independently of the existing organisation.

On Tuesday, the 15th December there is a talk on Plastics by Dr. Yarsley:[1] on Monday of this week there was a talk on the same subject by C. F. Merriam. It may well be that Dr. Yarsley's talk is better than C. F. Marriam° (or vice-versa), but it certainly seems extravagant from the point of view of the Corporation that we have paid for two talks on the same subject within little more than a week.

I wonder if the situation could be met by someone from Mr. Blair's department attending the Daily Talks meeting. I had thought that Mr. Weymouth would cover such points, but I gather that° now that Blair does not refer his arrangements to him.

Similarly, Blair's note of the 5th December regarding the new series of talks to cover the set books in the B.A. course in English literature at Calcutta University mentions T. S. Eliot and refers to fixing up other speakers. To avoid duplication and approaches made I suggest that Blair should fall in with the usual procedure whereby talks producers refer to my office to know if anyone else is approaching these speakers round about the same time. (I know you will understand that this is simply not red tape, but to prevent one speaker from getting two letters from the Empire Service on the same day).

1. For Orwell's letter to Yarsley, see *1666*.

1726. BBC Talks Booking Form, 8.12.42

Miss Lilla Erulkar: Indian Play, 1, 'Malati Madhav'°; 15 minutes; recorded 14.12.42; broadcast 12.1.43; fee £4.4s. Signed: M Blackburn for I.P.O. Remarks: 'Important woman's part. Roughly same as S. Mukerji.'

1727. To Edmund Blunden

10 December 1942   07/ES/EB/WMB[1]

Dear Mr. Blunden

Eliot says he cannot do the talk on THE BOOK OF JOB as he is too busy. This is a pity but no doubt you could think of someone else. Forster says he can do the first one on SHAKESPEARE and I think it would be a good idea to stick to him for this talk as his name carries weight in India.

I hope all is going well with the series and that we shall not be behind time.

I shall make arrangements to record the whole of the first talk so that no-one need be here on Christmas Day.

Yours sincerely,
[Signed] Geo. Orwell
George Orwell
Talks Producer
Indian Section

PS. The dates of the talks are December 25th, January 1st, 8th, 15th, 22nd and 29th, at 12.15 to 12.30 BST.

1. 'ES' presumably stands for Eastern Service, replacing 'PP,' for Portland Place. It is also used by Nancy Parratt.

1728. To E. C. Bowyer

10 December 1942   07/ES/EB/WMB

Dear Mr. Bowyer

I wonder if you would like to undertake some more talks for us or, if not, to advise us who would be a suitable speaker. We have got a series beginning on January 22nd called MODERN AIRCRAFT, the idea of which is to give listeners in India some general information about the functions of different kinds of planes, such as, heavy bombers, fighter planes, dive bombers, etc. etc. There is probably a public for this kind of thing among the younger generation in India, but one cannot assume so much knowledge as one could with the English public so the talks would have to be on the elementary side.

I am arranging these talks partly with a view to supplementing our News Commentaries so that our listeners can get a clearer idea than they probably have at present of what distances planes can fly, of the bomb load they can carry, what they need in the way of ground staff and so forth.

Your previous talks were so good that I should like you to undertake, at any rate, some of these if you would but if not you might perhaps be kind enough to suggest other names to me. Could you let me know about this and I will let you have full particulars.[1]

Yours sincerely
[Initialled] G. O.
George Orwell
Talks Producer
Indian Section

1. Bowyer replied on 12 December saying that he was willing to be included in this series. At the foot of the letter Orwell wrote, in pencil, 'Answered. File' and, in ink, 'P.T.O.' On the verso he wrote, in ink, 'Dear Mr Bannan, Many thanks for your letter'; in pencil, he then crossed out 'Bannan' and wrote 'Bowyer' above it. The whole draft is crossed through in pencil.

1729. Confidential Memorandum to E. W. D. Boughen, Talks Bookings

10 December 1942   EB/NP

CONTRACT FOR TALK BY DR. ANAND
Copy to Empire Programme Executive.

Dr. Mulk Raj Anand was commissioned to write a talk on "The Spanish Civil War"—the fifth talk in the series STORY OF FASCISM, to be broadcast as above.

Mr. Anand submitted the script, but it was not passed by the censor. I suggest that as Dr. Anand had taken a good deal of trouble over his talk, he might be paid a proportion of the fee. You will realise that this subject is a particularly delicate one at the present time, and we decided that rather than alter the whole angle of the talk, it would be better to abandon it altogether. A fill-up talk was therefore used.[1]

[Signed] Eric Blair
(Eric Blair)

1. The broadcast was to have been made on 3 December. The Programme Contracts Director wrote to Anand on 11 December explaining the position. He offered a fee of five, instead of eight, guineas. However, since eight guineas had already been paid, it was suggested that three guineas be deducted from his next fee, which would be for 'A Day in My Life,' to be broadcast on 18 December.

1730. To R. R. Desai

10 December 1942   Handwritten draft and typed carbon copies
07/ES/EB/WMB

Dear Desai

Thanks for your letter of Tuesday (only just received). I am always anxious to know *anything* that listeners say about our broadcasts, especially the newsletters. I should be very obliged if you could let me know what has been said, either favourable or unfavourable. There is no need to give your correspondents' names or give away their identity in any way, and you can send in the actual letters, or quotations, or a general account of what is said, just as you like.

Yours
[Initialled] E. A. B
Eric Blair
Talks Producer
Indian Section

1731. News Commentary in English for Malaya, 11

11 December 1942

This was written and read by George Orwell. No script has been traced.

1732. To Norman Marshall

11 December 1942   07/ES/EB/np

Dear Mr. Marshall,

I am enclosing the last batch of questions for you. Unless we hear to the contrary, we shall expect you at about 6 o'clock next Thursday, to go over the script with Mr. and Mrs. Sahni.

We all hope that everything went off well in Liverpool.[1]

Yours sincerely,
Eric Blair
Talks Producer
Indian Section

QUESTIONS FOR "LET'S ACT IT OURSELVES" NO. 6

1.   I was talking the other day to Dr. Mulk Raj Anand. He has gone through our previous scripts and some of our discussions he has heard while they were on the air. His opinion is very encouraging. He thinks we have hit the nail on the head all the time, and even if our discussions do not appeal to the highbrow listener they would certainly stimulate the young enthusiasts of the theatre.

MARSHALL: I am very glad to hear that . . . etc. . . .

D.S. I have been thinking of asking you a question, but it may sound rather trivial to you and so I have hesitated. May I ask it now?

MARSHALL: Go ahead etc. . . . . .

D.S. Is there still any prejudice in this country about women taking up the stage as a profession?

B.S. Could you run through the different stages of the rehearsals? I remember we talked at some length about the early rehearsals but not so much about the later rehearsals. Which is the most difficult period?

D.S. Are there any rules about grouping? What is the triangle system, or is there any such system?

B.S. I remember you once said the essence of good production is correct emphasis. What exactly do you mean?

D.S. What attracted you to a stage career Mr. Marshall?

B.S. Is there any different technique for producing comedy:

D.S. What is meant by conscious and unconscious movement? Do tell us something about entrances and exits as well.

Last: When are you going to let us watch the rehearsals of THE PETRIFIED FOREST . . . etc. ?

1. Orwell probably refers to a pre-London production of Robert Sherwood's *The Petrified Forest*, which Marshall produced at the Globe Theatre, London, 16 December 1942, with Constance Cummings and Owen Nares.

1733. To Ramaswami Mudaliar

11 December 1942   07/ES/EB/WMB

Dear Sir Ramaswami
We thought you might perhaps like a copy of the photograph which was

taken of you on the occasion of your broadcast, and I am enclosing one herewith.

Yours sincerely,
[Signed] Eric Blair
Eric Blair
Talks Producer
Indian Section

1734. English News Commentary, 51
12 December 1942

PasB records that this 'News Review' was written and read by George Orwell. The script has no timing and is not marked 'As broadcast,' but PasB gives a timing of 13 minutes. It was passed for Policy and Security by A. F. N. Thavenot. The passage omitted (given here within square brackets) was evidently cut in two stages. Although each line is crossed through, bold square brackets mark off the first sentence ('Here I will mention . . . in this country'). Whereas the first sentence might have been cut on grounds of policy, that would hardly apply to the second sentence, giving Cordell Hull's opinion.

Since last week both the Russian offensives have slowed down somewhat, owing to stiffening German resistance and also, on the southern front, to the soft snow that has been falling. We can't, I imagine, expect any further big move on this front for the time being, and this week the chief interest has centred in North Africa, where it has become even clearer than before that there's a hard struggle ahead.

It is just a week since the Germans counterattacked west of Tunis and retook Tebourba and Jedeida, the two points which it's necessary for the Allies to control before they assault Tunis itself. The Germans have delivered another attack since, but they don't appear to have got any further, and our main positions round the Tunis-Bizerta area stand firm. It's become clear from the reports that are coming in that the Germans are stronger in the air and are likely to remain so for some time to come. They possess the airfields of Bizerta and Tunis, besides having their air bases in Sicily and Sardinia only a hundred miles away, while the Allies don't at present hold any air field nearer than Bone, 120 miles away along the Algerian coast. They can and, of course, will prepare landing grounds in the forward area, but this takes time, especially as equipment, ground staff and probably even labour have to be brought from places far to the west, over poor roads and one ill-equipped railway. At present, therefore, the strategic picture in Tunisia is something like this. The Allies, whose ultimate strength is much greater, are building up a striking force as fast as they can, but they have to do it in the face of dive-bombing and with insufficient cover from fighter planes. The Germans, who probably have only about 20,000 men in Tunisia and not a great supply of heavy tanks or large-calibre guns, but who possess temporary air superiority, are doing their best to slow up the Allied concentration and to build up their own forces in Tunisia by air and sea. Further south, in the neighbourhood of

Sfax and Gabes on the Tunisian coast, another struggle is going on for the control of the coastal road which leads southward in the direction of Tripoli. There isn't at present much news from this area, where the fighting seems to have been chiefly between parachutists and airborne troops from both sides; but it doesn't appear that any Allied Force has yet reached the sea. All in all, the Germans only control the eastern strip of Tunisia, but they are in a strong position so long as they can keep up the stream of supplies from Sicily and Sardinia.

However, the air superiority of the Germans is likely to be a wasting asset. The reserves they have near at hand aren't inexhaustible, and the ultimate source of supply is Germany itself, which is a long way away and is connected with the battle area by railway communications which are none too good. It's here that the RAF bombing of northern Italy, through which all supplies for the African fronts have to pass, is important. The Raf° have delivered very heavy raids on Italy during the last week—Turin for instance was heavily bombed twice in 24 hours—and have evidently done very severe damage. One can infer this from the broadcasts of the Italians themselves. All this adds to the difficulties of the Germans, who are already fighting a long way from their main base on a front they didn't willingly choose. Moreover, the more they strive to[1] build up their force in Tunisia, the harder it is for them to reinforce their other army in Libya—and it's there, in all probability, that the next big move will come.

During the last week there have only been reports of patrol activity at el Agheila, west of Benghazi, but it looks as though the new British attack were about to start. I should expect it to have started before I broadcast my next news commentary—and once again my reason for saying this is the Axis radio propagandists, who are already talking about the forthcoming British attack and don't sound over-hopeful about the possibility of General Rommel holding on. Long before the British Eighth Army got to Benghazi it could be foreseen that the Afrika Corps would make its next stand at el Agheila, which is a naturally strong position—a neck of land with the sea on one side and impassable marshes on the other—rather like the position it formerly occupied at el Alamein. Before General Montgomery could make a new attack he had to bring up his heavy equipment—over a distance of hundreds of miles, remember, and with in effect only one road. The last few weeks, therefore, have been a race to bring up supplies—the British bringing it from Egypt, the Germans from Tripoli. At el Agheila the Germans are actually further from their nearest port of supply—that is Tripoli—than they were at el Alamein in Egypt, when they could use Tobruk. It looks from the German communiques as though the British have been winning the race for supplies, and the Germans expect to have to fall back again to avoid destruction. They appear to be preparing German public opinion for something of this kind, as they are beginning to claim that Rommel's Army in Libya was never intended to do more than create a diversion. It's only 3 or 4 months since Rommel himself was announcing in Berlin that he had come to Africa to conquer Egypt and that he already had Egypt in his grasp. But perhaps the German public have forgotten that—or at least the official broadcasters hope they have. If the fresh British offensive at el Agheila takes place and is successful, it won't have an immediate repercussion on the Tunisia front, but it must do so within a few weeks.

An agreement has now been signed between the United States government and General Boisson, the French commander at Dakar in French West Africa, for the use of the port and airfields at Dakar by the Allies. That will be of great value in dealing with the U-boats in the South Atlantic. There is still much that is unexplained about the precise political situation in North Africa and the relation between General° Darlan and ourselves. This matter has now been debated in Parliament and I think we may expect an official pronouncement on it in the not too distant future. [Here I will mention only two relevant facts. General Catroux,[2] the Free French leader, has uttered a protest against the tie-up between the United States military commanders and General° Darlan, which has been given a good deal of publicity in this country. Mr. Cordell Hull,[3] the American Foreign Secretary, has given his opinion that by entering into agreement with Admiral Darlan, and thus taking over North Africa peacefully, the United States saved the lives of about 20,000 men.]

Japanese airplanes attacked a convoy in the Bay of Bengal about a week ago, and two days ago they carried out a small bombing raid on Chittagong—the first bombs to fall on Indian soil for many months. It's too early to say what this means, but one can say now that a Japanese invasion of India, which seemed so likely a year or 6 months ago, is now very improbable. The Japanese have been so hard hit in the Southern Pacific that they have in all probability lost their chance of gaining naval control of the Bay of Bengal. During this week, on the anniversary of the Japanese attack on Pearl Harbour, the United States government published the first full account of the attack and its after-effects, and gave some revealing figures of their own and the Japanese shipping losses during the year. It now appears that the unexpected Japanese attack was very damaging indeed—no less than 8 battleships were damaged in varying degrees—but that all except one of the ships damaged has since been put back into service or is in process of being so. Ever since then the Japanese losses at sea have been very much higher than those of the Allies. In the Solomons area alone they have lost 135 ships, warships and merchant ships, sunk or damaged, and over 600 airplanes. The Japanese are very much less able to bear these losses than the Allies, because their industrial capacity is very much less. They are also at least as dependent on sea-borne supplies as the British Isles are. Meanwhile during the current year the Americans have turned out over 40,000 airplanes of all types, and built 8 million tons of merchant shipping. The American ship-building programme called for 8 million tons in 1942 and 15 million tons in 1943, and the 1942 construction at any rate is up to schedule. They have also built large numbers of warships, including a new battleship of over 50,000 tons launched during this week.[4] Add to all this the fact that the Japanese have lost certainly 4 and probably 6 of their largest aircraft carriers sunk, and it becomes clear why they aren't likely after all to attempt the invasion of India. They appear to have given up, at any rate for the time being, their attempts to drive the Americans off Guadalcanal in the Solomon Islands. At Buna, on the coast of New Guinea, they are still holding on to a small area and have fought with great courage, but they are not expected to hold their position there much longer. The threat to Port Moresby, and hence to Darwin in Australia, which seemed so imminent a few months ago, is probably at an end. Mr Curtin,[5] the Australian Prime Minister, however, has warned his country-men that the Japanese might make an attempt further west on the North Australian coast, using the Island of Timor as their jumping-off place.

The Polish Government has just published the full facts about the systematic massacre of the Jews in German-occupied Poland. The Polish Government's statement is not propaganda. It is verified from many sources, including the pronouncements of the Nazi leaders themselves. For instance, in March of this year Himmler, the head of the Gestapo, issued a decree calling for the "liquidation"—remember that in totalitarian language liquidation is a polite name for murder—of 50 per cent of the surviving Polish Jews. It seems as if his programme is being carried out successfully. The Polish Government's figures show that of something over 3 million Jews living in Poland before the war, well over a third—that is, *well over one million human beings*[6]—have been killed in cold blood or died of starvation and general misery. Many thousands of them, men, women and children, have been deported to Russian territory, sealed up in cattle trucks without food or water for journeys that may take weeks, so that when the trucks were opened sometimes half the people inside are dead. This policy, which Hitler himself has proclaimed over and over again as his chosen one in speeches both before and after the war, is carried out wherever the Germans are in control. Already, now that they have taken over the whole of France, they are putting the anti-Jewish laws into operation there and French Jews are being deported to the East. And France, be it remembered, is the country where for 150 years—ever since the Great Revolution—there have been no legal disabilities against Jews whatever. I don't mention this persecution of the Jews simply for the sake of repeating horror stories, but because this kind of cold-blooded, systematic cruelty, utterly different from the violences committed in battle, brings home to us the nature of Fascism, the thing we are fighting against.

1. to] the *in typescript*
2. George Catroux (1879–1969), for a short time in 1956 Governor-General of Algeria, also served as French ambassador to the Soviet Union.
3. Cordell Hull (see *908, n. 3*) was the U.S. Secretary of State at this time.
4. The USS *New Jersey*, 57,450 tonnes; served in the Pacific (and in the Mediterranean, off Lebanon, 1983–84).
5. John Joseph Curtin (1885–1945), leader of the Australian Labour Party, 1934–45, and Prime Minister and Minister of Defence, 1941–45.
6. Italic in the original – not an insertion.

1735. Bengali Newsletter, 22

12 December 1942

The English original was written by Orwell. No script has been traced. Mrs.

Renu Ghosh participated with S. K. Das Gupta in reading this Newsletter. PasB implies a timing of 14′ 30″.

1736. Gujarati Newsletter, 42

14 December 1942

The English original was written by Orwell. No script has been traced. PasB gives timing as approximately 11′ 5″.

1737. To Edmund Blunden

14 December 1942   07/ES/EB

Dear Blunden,

I am glad our series of talks seems to be going ahead. We have asked Forster to come here and record his talk on Tuesday December 22nd. This is about as late as we can safely leave it and also we have to take what recording dates we can get, owing to the Christmas rush. If so be that you can't yourself come on that day to do your introduction of Forster, it would be possible to record it separately, but it is simpler to do it all in one go. Forster is to record at 12 o'clock. He is supposed to bring his script on Monday to be typed, but probably won't bring it till Tuesday morning. With the other five speakers it is not quite equally urgent, but I would like to have all their scripts during Christmas week.

When you send us the list of your speakers, could you let me have their addresses at the same time, so that we can have their contracts sent on?

Yours sincerely
[Signed] Geo. Orwell
George Orwell
Talks Producer
Indian Section

1738. To E. M. Forster

14 December 1942   07/ES/EB/np

Dear Forster,

I have just sent you a telegram,[1] to the effect that I have been able to arrange a recording session on Tuesday December 22nd, from 12 to 12.45, at 200, Oxford Street, and I suggest that you rehearse from 11.30–12.00 approximately. I do hope this arrangement will suit you, because it is extremely difficult to fix up recordings so close to Christmas. I hope that Blunden will be able to come at the same time, but if he can't manage it, we can record his introduction to your talk separately.

We really arranged Tuesday because I thought you might like to bring your script in on Monday for typing, or on Tuesday morning first thing, at the latest.

Yours,
George Orwell
Talks Producer
Indian Section

1. Not traced.

1739. To E. M. Forster

14 December 1942

Forster replied to Orwell's telegram on 14 December, saying that he could not manage 22 December but could come on the following day. Orwell evidently then sent this telegram, to which Forster replied 'YES,' also on 14 December. See West: *Broadcasts*, 236.

WILL TWENTYTHIRD SUIT AT TEN THIRTY A.M.

ORWELL BROADCASTS

R/P. 9d.[1]

1. Reply paid up to nine old pence.

1740. BBC Talks Booking Form, 14.12.42

Edmund Blunden: 'Calling All Students,' 1–6; 'arranging and compèring six talks on English literature — speaking for about 2 minutes each time. (15 min. talks plus 5 mins reading)'; broadcast 25.12.42, 1, 8, 15, 22, and 29.1.43; fee £8.8s + £1.1s expenses + travel vouchers. Signed: M Blackburn for I.P.O. Remarks: 'Mr. Blunden is fixing up and contacting all speakers himself, on advice from E. Blair.'[1]

1. 'on advice from E. Blair' was added in Mary Blackburn's hand. Venu Chitale, in her monthly preview of forthcoming programmes, said, on 22 December 1942: 'These talks are going to be about the set books in the English literature B.A. series at Calcutta University. We chose Calcutta University because we thought that would be helpful to the biggest number of students but some of the books in the series also appear in the B.A. course at Lahore and other Indian universities.' Combined with the publication of some of these talks by Oxford University Press in India, these broadcasts are an early example of 'distance teaching' as developed by the Open University more than twenty-five years later.

1741. BBC Talks Booking Form, 14.12.42

E. M. Forster: 'Calling All Students', 1; 15-minute talk on Shakespeare; recorded 22.12.42;[1] broadcast 25.12.42; fee £21. Signed: M Blackburn for I.P.O.

1. Changed to 23 December; see *1739*.

1742. BBC Talks Booking Form, 15.12.42

Princess Indira of Kapurthala: Indian Play, 'Malati and Madhav'°; 15 minutes; 'She had a fairly large part'; recorded 14.12.42; broadcast 12.1.43; fee £4.4s. Signed: M Blackburn for I.P.O.[1] Remarks: 'This contract was not issued previously because Princess Indira was ill and we did not know if she would be back in time to do the recording.'

1. In her programme preview broadcast on 22 December 1942, Venu Chitale said: 'Talking about plays there is another one scheduled for Tuesday, January 12th. It is an "Indian Play" . . . "Malati and Madhav°" by Bhavbhuti° of the 8th century. I must say it was a bit of a job too, to condense a 10 act Sanskrit play into a 13-minute radio feature. The cast consists of actors from the BBC Repertory and some Indian artists in this country. Some of the music was specially recorded for this feature. This is the first Indian play ever produced on the BBC in English for Indian listeners. It will be a regular 4-weekly programme, so look out for "Indian Play" every fourth Tuesday.'

1743. To Edmund Blunden

[c. 16 December 1942]

The date could be any between 15 and 23 December inclusive, but on 23 December Orwell acknowledged receipt of Turner's[1] script on 'The Book of Job', so the telegram was probably sent at the start of this period. The 16th was a Wednesday.

TURNER AGREES TO DO JOB STOP CAN DO SHAW IF UNAVOIDABLE BUT MUST KNOW MONDAY AS TUESDAY ONLY DAY FREE FOR WORK[2]

ORWELL BROADCASTS

1. Walter J. Turner (1889–1946), poet, novelist, and music critic, had been drama critic of the London Mercury, 1919–23, and literary editor of the Daily Herald, 1920–23, and of The Spectator, 1942–46. He was also editor of the series, Britain in Pictures, from 1941, to which he contributed English Music (1941), and Orwell contributed The English People (1947), see 2475.
2. This is an indication of Orwell's work schedule; but that Tuesdays in all weeks were free for work cannot be assumed. The two-day Christmas holiday may have restricted days available for work. One shilling was prepaid for a reply to the telegram.

1744. For Z. A. Bokhari to P. Chatterjee

16 December 1942   07/ES/ZAB/ED[1]

Dear Sir,
I am writing to ask whether you would be interested in helping us with our broadcasts in Bengali. These broadcasts are in the form of a weekly newsletter which goes out on Saturdays from 3.30 to 3.45 p.m. The

newsletter is usually written in English by a member of the staff, and then translated into Bengali and read at the microphone by a Bengali Announcer/Translator, who comes to this office to do his translation on Saturday morning.

If you would be interested in doing some of these newsletters for us, perhaps you would care to ring up and make an appointment to come along and see us, when we could show you one of the newsletters, and when you could perhaps do a trial translation of one.[2]

Yours faithfully,
[Initalled] MB[3]
for Z. A. Bokhari
Indian Programme Organiser

1. 'ED' is possibly Miss E. Dunstan, who signed talks booking forms for Sircar (see *1750*) and for Desai (see *1754*). She is listed as secretary to the Overseas Presentation Director, Staff List, 21.8.43.
2. Chatterjee took over from Das Gupta on 6 February 1943 and evidently prepared the Newsletters without benefit of an English version written by Orwell, at least from the spring of 1943; see Orwell's letter to him of 23 March 1943, *1967*. He was commissioned in the Indian Army in August 1943, and Dr. H. C. Mukerji took over; in December 1943, Das Gupta was back. See also *858, n. 2* and *2269, n. 1*.
3. The initials only approximate roughly to Mary Blackburn's full signature, but the follow-up letter of 28 December 1942 is clearly initialled by her.

1745. To R. R. Desai

16 December 1942   07/ES/EB

This letter marks an important change in Orwell's duties. Although he drafted the English versions of Gujarati Newsletters 43 and 44, Desai recast them and thereafter prepared them in both languages. See Orwell's letter of 19 December for his brief to Desai, *1753*.

Dear Desai,

I have fixed it all up for you to compose your Monday Gujarati newsletter yourself. You can use the Library at Broadcasting House (not 200 Oxford Street) on Sunday. It is open until 6 p.m. You will find almost all British and many American periodicals there.

I shall have to have the English version of your script some time on Monday morning. I think, probably at any rate at first, I shall have to give you some kind of brief. I don't want to dictate what you are to say but sometimes there will be some special line which it is our policy to emphasize and, in any case, I ought to warn you whenever there is some subject which must be avoided as it is no use writing something which the censorship is going to cut out.

Perhaps the best arrangement would be for me [to] leave a note for you which you can pick up at the Reception Desk at Broadcasting House when you get there on Sunday.

Yours
[Signed] Eric Blair
Eric Blair
Talks Producer
Indian Section

1746. To C. K. Ogden

16 December 1942   07/ES/EB

Dear Mr. Ogden[1]

Many thanks for your letter.[2] We didn't have any response to that talk on Basic English given by Miss Lockhart but that doesn't necessarily mean anything because we get very little response indeed to all our broadcasts and I understand that even in India, Indians are not very strong on writing to broadcasters to give criticisms or suggestions.

When we did Miss Lockhart's talk my idea was, if possible, to follow this up sometime later by a series of talks giving lessons in Basic English which could perhaps afterwards be printed in India in pamphlet form. I still have not given up this project but I must tell you that it has come up against a great deal of discouragement and opposition, some of which I understand and some not. You, no doubt, know the inner workings of this controversy better than I do. If, at any time, it seems possible to do something about Basic English on the air again I will of course get in touch with you.

I am sorry not to be more helpful at this moment.

Yours sincerely,
George Orwell[3]
Talks Producer
Indian Section

1. Charles Kay Ogden (1889–1957), psychologist and teacher, developed Basic English in the 1920s (in part as a result of discussions with I. A. Richards) and published several books setting out the system. Churchill formed a Cabinet Committee on Basic English in 1943, and in June 1946 Ogden assigned his copyright to the Crown for £23,000. A Basic English Foundation was established by the Ministry of Education in 1947.
2. Ogden asked if there had been any response to Leonora Lockhart's talk broadcast on 2 October 1942 (see Orwell's letter to her, 18 August 1942, *1393*). He also asked if Orwell had been in touch 'with Paxton, who has been using Basic for the Arab educational talks' and whether Orwell had seen a report on Basic by the British Association in *The Advancement of Science*, October 1942, 256–57. On 17 December Ogden replied at length to Orwell's report of discouragement and opposition. He outlined the problem of introducing something new and asked for specific details of the sort of opposition Orwell had experienced.
3. The carbon copy is signed 'Geo. Orwell' but the signature may not be Orwell's.

1747. Rushbrook Williams to Orwell

16 December 1942

L. F. Rushbrook Williams, the Eastern Service Director, sent Orwell this copy of a memorandum he had prepared for Joanna Spicer, the General Overseas Service Programme Planner. He asked Orwell to see whether Professor Lyell could be used by the Eastern Service.

I had a long talk with Mr. Lyell yesterday. He is a nice and well-preserved gentleman; but he is a microphone man and not an administrator. Moreover, he has acquired his microphone technique very late; and although he seems to have made a great success of it, he cannot afford me the technical guidance regarding local conditions for which I am looking in a Far East Programme Organiser. He knows practically nothing of China, and has scarcely met any Chinese. He is very fond of the Japanese—which makes it a little awkward at the moment! When one probes down sufficiently deeply, one discovers that he is fundamentally an enthusiastic and stimulating teacher of English literature, who has had considerable success along these lines in the Far East. I think he has one or two very good "stories" in him; and that he could give a fascinating talk or series of talks about Japan to schools. I will myself find out if we can use him in the Eastern Service for talking about English literature to Indians. I am asking Mr. Blair to get in touch with him in this connection.

Mr. Blair Mr. Lyell has done a good deal of broadcasting for the Shanghai shortwave station XGDN. Among other things he prepared, organised, and broadcast an English Language and Literature Course. His address is: 30 Moore Street, Lennox Gardens, S.W.3.

Orwell wrote to Lyell on 21 December: see *1756*.

1748. To E. C. Bowyer

17 December 1942   07/ES/EB

Dear Mr. Bowyer

Many thanks for your letter. I will tell you some more about the proposed series of talks. We planned 6 talks on the following subjects:—

    1. Bombing planes
    2. Fighter planes
    3. Dive bombers and torpedo bombers
    4. Naval aircraft
    5. Gliders
    6. Transport planes

It might be better to alter the arrangement and I would welcome suggestions, except that I think the first two talks (Bombing planes and fighters) should stand, as they have been scheduled.

These talks (of 13½ minutes or 1500–1600 words) should be on the elementary side, giving a clear idea of the function of each type of plane and what performance in the way of range etc., can normally be expected. I think also each talk should enumerate the principal types now in use (of ourselves and the Axis—but with the emphasis on British planes) with perhaps a few hints as to how you can recognise them from the ground.

If you could undertake all or any of these talks I would like that very much. Failing that you could perhaps help me by suggesting suitable speakers. The first talk is due in mid January, so we ought to get the thing swinging pretty soon.

Yours sincerely
[Initialled] E A B
George Orwell
Talks Producer
Indian Section

1749. News Commentary in English for Malaya, 12

18 December 1942

This was written and read by Orwell. The script has not been traced.

1750. BBC Talks Booking Form, [18.12.42?]

Noel Sircar: 'In the Public Eye,' 1; weekly 8-minute talk on the outstanding personality of the week; broadcast 23 and 30.12.42; fee: 'This broadcast is normally an adaptation of a newspaper article not involving very much work & I suggest that £3.3.0 would be a suitable average rate for the 8 minutes (I.P.O.). Signed: E. Dunstan.

1751. English News Commentary, 52

19 December 1942

The typescript is marked, in Orwell's hand, 'As b'cast 12' 5'° E.A.B.'; PasB has 'News Review—a Commentary. By George Orwell' and gives a timing of 12' 50". Unusually, there is an announcer's note that six minutes into the transmission a News Flash interrupted the reading and that this lasted 1' 29". The total timing for the programme was given as 13' 45" (which would include the announcer signing on and off), making a curious combination of timings. The subject of the News Flash is not noted, though allowing for time differences it might just have referred to the bombing of Calcutta on 20 December by the Japanese, which is, surprisingly, no more than touched on in the Newsletter of 26 December. For the first time, Orwell was announced in *London Calling* as presenting this Newsletter. Manuscript changes are in Orwell's hand.

During this week there hasn't been much news from any front except the North African one. In Russia both the Russian offensives and the attempted German counterattacks have been slowed down, no doubt chiefly because of the weather. There is bound to be a sort of pause on the Russian fronts at about this time of year, when the snow is falling but hasn't yet frozen hard. *But* the position of the German armies before Stalingrad and in Rzhev, on the Moscow front, isn't enviable, and the Russians have reported impressive captures of war materials during this week, [but it looks as though the Germans can hold on in their present positions, if they want to.] Down in the South Pacific the Japanese have succeeded in landing a few men—it's not known exactly how many, probably a few hundreds—north-west of Buna in New Guinea. The object, probably, is to bar the way to an Allied advance westward when Buna itself has been mopped up by the Allies. The Japanese lost heavily in men and landing craft. They haven't yet renewed their attempts to drive the Americans out of Guadalcanal in the Solomon Island[s]. Japanese planes have, however, again bombed Chittagong, the second time[1] in about 10 days. It's too early yet to be quite certain what this means, but it's not impossible that the Allies are contemplating some fresh move in the area of the India-Burma frontier. The main news of this week has been the fighting in Africa, and it's that that I want to devote most of my commentary to.

Last week I suggested that there would be renewed activity very shortly on the Libyan front, and sure enough, it has happened. Five days ago the news broke that the Germans had abandoned their strong defensive position at el Agheila, 50 miles west of Benghazi, and were retreating rapidly westward. Evidently the German plan was to get their main force away as rapidly as possible, while holding up the pursuit of the British Eighth Army by small rearguard actions and by sowing anti-tank mines. However, there has evidently been a hitch in the plan already. The day before yesterday the news came in that an advance detachment of the Eighth Army had made a big outflanking movement, circling round through the desert and then reaching the sea again at a place called Matratin, about 60 miles west of el Agheila. The Axis rearguard *was*[2] cut off and [is being] attacked from both sides, *& appears to have been scattered.* How many men are involved isn't yet known, but it is probable that the Axis force which *was* cut off included[3] considerable numbers of tanks and guns. To see the full significance of this one has got to relate it to the probable German plan, and to the North African campaign as a whole.

It doesn't appear as though the Germans intend making another stand in Libya, except perhaps in defence of Tripoli itself. Having abandoned el Agheila, the most natural place to make another stand would be at Misurata, about 150 miles east of Tripoli. This is another natural defensive position, with the road leading up to it flanked on one side by desert and on the other by a marshy area probably lending itself to ambushes, and with several streams forming natural obstacles. Misurata also has a small seaport and is within fairly easy road distance of Tripoli. However, the tone of the German communiques rather suggests that their plan is to abandon Libya altogether and transfer Rommel's army to Tunisia, or, possibly, to get it away by sea. For the first few days the Axis radio commentators refused to admit that any retreat was going on. Then they suddenly changed their tone and switched over to claiming that the retreat was a clever prearranged manoeuvre which had completely thrown the British strategy out of gear. To read the German communiques of this moment you'd think that retreating was the whole art of war, and certainly some of their phrases are most ingenious. We have all heard of "strategic withdrawals" and "elastic defence", but the German commentators have thought of better ones than that. Their best phrase to describe a rapid retreat is "We have successfully increased the distance between ourselves and the enemy"; another is "We have compelled the British to advance westward"—also, of course, that by choosing to retreat General Rommel "retains the initiative". You will have noticed that when a dog is chasing a rabbit, the rabbit retains the initiative. But this phraseology is worth noticing, because it makes clear that the Germans are preparing their home public for bad news. They don't, in all probability, expect[4] to be able to turn the tables this time, and the best they can hope is to slow down the British advance while the other Axis force consolidates its position in Tunisia.

That is where the importance of the *defeat*[5] of the Axis rearguard comes in. At best it is difficult for the Eighth Army to advance rapidly, because the distances to be covered are enormous, and moreover they are now entering the desert of Sirte, which is about 200 miles wide. Most of their water will have to be brought from the rear, either by road or in barges along the coast. The function of the Axis rearguard was to hold up the Allied advance by destroying such wells as exist, and by anti-tank mines. When these are buried in the ground they blow up any vehicle which passes over them, and the army as a whole can't advance till special troops have gone ahead and dealt with the mines, which often take a long time to find. The outflanking move which has cut off the Axis rearguard will probably have disrupted these delaying tactics considerably. Meanwhile the main enemy force is being pursued westward, along a narrow coast [road?] where it's difficult for them to disperse to avoid air attacks. All the reports that have come in show that the Allies are greatly superior in the air on the front.

But now look at the Libyan front in relation to the other front in Tunisia. There the Allied attack on Tunis and Bizerta is still held up, and evidently by the same cause as before—German superiority in the air. The Germans are still better supplied in the matter of air fields, and probably they are being fairly rapidly reinforced—in men, that is—by air from Sicily and Sardinia. They haven't, however, been successful in their new attacks since their capture of Tebourba and Jedeida. The British First Army is still holding on to Medjes el Bab, west of Tunis, in spite of several German attacks. The main Allied position, behind which they are building up their striking force, hasn't been breached. If the Eighth Army gets to Tripoli or thereabouts, that will weaken the German position in Tunisia just as much as heavy reinforcements on the other side. The Germans will be subjected to air attack from both east and west, and also from Malta, which it has already been possible to reinforce. It's probably safe to say that with the Allies both in Tripoli and in Algiers the Germans couldn't hold on in Tunisia, though from the amount of reinforcements they have thrown in already it looks as if they mean to gamble on it—perhaps partly for prestige reasons.

Admiral Darlan has issued a fresh statement in his capacity as High Commissioner for French North and West Africa. He has said that the French warships at the various African ports will operate on the side of the Allies. These include the warships which were at Dakar and Casablanca, and also those which were interned in Alexandria when France went out of the war. These will make a big addition to the Allied fleets, though perhaps not an immediate one. Besides several heavy cruisers and a number of destroyers and smaller vessels, they include two battleships, both of them at present damaged—the Richelieu, which was hit by a British torpedo soon after the armistice in 1940, and the Jean Bart, which was more heavily damaged in the fighting at Casablanca. These will take time to repair and the vessels which were interned were partly disarmed. But the smaller ships, it is thought, will be able to start in service almost immediately. The fate of the French fleet is now finally settled, after more than two years of uncertainty, and the Allies have come immensely better out of the bargain than the Germans.

[Certain points about Admiral Darlan's position have still not been made clear. In his statement to the press, however, he said two things which have caused widespread satisfaction. One was that all Frenchmen in North Africa who had been interned or imprisoned by the Vichy authorities for activities against the Axis are to be released, just as President Roosevelt requested. It isn't absolutely clear whether this covers the various other anti-Fascist refugees, chiefly Germans and Spaniards, who had been shut up in concentration camps under the Vichy regime. We may hope it does—at any rate it should be possible to get confirmation on this point in the near future. The other thing Admiral Darlan announced—this had also been requested by President Roosevelt—was that the anti-Jew laws in North Africa, which had been forced on Vichy by the Germans, are to be abolished.]

I spoke last week about the fresh German persecution and massacre of the Jews in Poland. Even after three years of war, when people inevitably grow callous, this has caused the most profound horror all over the world. I believe there is not a newspaper in this country that has not commented on it with indignation, it has been debated in both houses of Parliament, and many intercession services have been held in which Jews and Christians have taken part together. Mr Anthony Eden has given a solemn promise on behalf of the British Government that after the war those responsible for these cold-blooded massacres will be punished—and not merely the little clique at the top of the Nazi party, but also those who have actually carried out their orders. The International Federation of Trade Unions has called on the German working class to demonstrate, before it is too late, that they are not at one with those who rule them. Until the war is won that is about all that it is possible to do. There is, however, just a slight chance that something positive can be done even now to save at any rate some of the victims of persecution. A move is on foot to evacuate Jewish children from German-occupied

Europe under the supervision of some neutral power. It may not come to anything, but on the other hand it is just possible that it may.[6] The Germans have shown that they are not more merciful to children than to adults, but because of their food problem it might seem to them worth while to get rid of some of their unwanted population. Even so there are many and obvious difficulties in the way of such a scheme. But we may earnestly hope that it will be put into operation, and the fact that it is at least put forward and receives popular support shows that the people of this country have not forgotten what cause they are fighting for.

1. West: *Commentaries* points out that this was the third such raid, 186, 188, ns. 321, 330.
2. *was*] has been
3. *was* cut off include*d*] is cut off includes
4. expect] except *in typescript*
5. *defeat*] encirclement
6. Orwell may have had in mind the attempt to take 1,000 Jewish children from Vichy France. On 6 November 1942 the Secretary of State for the Colonies, Lord Cranborne, was told by the British High Commissioner for Palestine and Transjordan that 1,000 children would be admitted. The German occupation of Vichy France on 11 November put a stop to this rescue attempt.

1752. Bengali Newsletter, 23

19 December 1942

The English original was written by Orwell. No script has been traced. PasB notes that although Das Gupta as usual read the body of the Newsletter, Mrs. R. Ghosh read its conclusion. Das Gupta's section was timed as 9' 20".

1753. To R. R. Desai

19 December 1942   07/ES/EB

Dear Desai

Just a few notes as promised about your News Review. I don't want to dictate what you're to say but would like to make a few general indications.

First of all, we are going to follow the policy of making these talks rather more in the nature of commentaries on the weeks° news and not a Newsletter, as we find it difficult to keep up with the news in an item which only happens once a week, and particularly when we are dealing with people, most of whom read newspapers. No doubt we shall get the formula better worked out within a few weeks.

As to the North African campaign, I think you can plug the German retreat and the destruction of their rearguard pretty hard. It is not known what numbers are involved but it does look as if the rearguard has been scattered or destroyed. It seems unlikely that the Germans can make any comeback east of Tripoli.

If you can, using all discretion, bring in something about the renewed persecution of the Jews in Poland and its repercussions in this country, I should like it. I know the subject of Jews is full of thorns and you will be the best judge of the re-actions of your audience, but I don't think this matter should go unnoticed and it is not impossible that within the next few weeks there may be some move to evacuate large numbers of Jewish children from Europe and it is important to make sure, in advance, that this is not represented in the east as a sort of Jewish invasion of other countries. This is best done by making clear what sort of persecution of Jews has been going on during recent weeks in Poland and other places.

I don't think I have any other suggestions for this week.

It is O.K. for you to use the Broadcasting House Library up to 6 p.m. on Sunday.

Yours
Eric Blair
Talks Producer
Indian Section

1754. BBC Talks Booking Form, 19.12.42

R. R. Desai: Gujarati Newsletters, 43 and 44; 'Gujarati Newsletter to be written in Gujarati by Mr. Desai and read at the microphone, and an English version supplied to us by Mr. Desai'; broadcast 21 and 28.12.42; fee £9.9s + 12s 0d fare + 17s 0d expenses. Signed: E. Dunstan for I.P.O. Remarks: 'Will you please amend Mr. Desai's present contract for the 21st & 28th Dec. as Mr. Desai is going to write the Newsletters himself, not just translate.'[1]

1. The original contract was issued on 24 November 1942 (see *1685*). Desai's fee was raised and he was informed of this in a separate letter from the Programme Contracts Director on 21 December 1942. No further booking forms will be reproduced for this series, because Orwell was no longer directly involved. Desai unwittingly failed to leave a typed copy of the English script, and he was informed by Mary Blackburn on 30 December of the proper procedure for censorship and production of typescripts: 'I have noticed that as there was no time to make a typed copy of your Gujarati Newsletter, your script in your own handwriting was submitted for censorship. I'm afraid this is quite contrary to the Corporation's practice, and except in very rare cases all scripts are typed before they are handed to the censors. I shall be glad if you will kindly help us in this matter in future, either by leaving a copy of your script at the Reception Desk at 200 Oxford St. on Sunday nights so that we can get it typed first thing on Monday mornings, or, if that is not convenient to you, could you come in soon after 9 o'clock on Monday mornings and dictate the English version of your script to a secretary, who will take it down straight on to the typewriter? If you will be kind enough to send me a line, saying which of these suggested arrangements will suit you best, I will make the appropriate arrangements at this end.'

1755. Gujarati Newsletter, 43

21 December 1942

The English original was written by Orwell; it was recast and translated by R. R.

Desai, who took over fully from No. 45. No script has been traced. PasB has the Newsletter as translated and read by Desai. The timing is given as approximately 8′ 35″.

1756. To T. R. G. Lyell

21 December 1942   07/ES/EB/WMB

Dear Mr. Lyell

Mr. Rushbrook Williams has spoken to me about you and thinks you might like to do some broadcasts on the India Service. I cannot arrange anything just at this moment as our schedule will be full up until some time in February but after that we might be able to fix up something.

I wonder if you would be kind enough to make an appointment to come and see me at some time convenient to yourself, and we might then decide what subjects you could talk on.[1]

Yours truly
Eric Blair
Talks Producer
Indian Section

1. Orwell's letter was the first of three invitations to Professor Lyell which were made within a few days of one another from different directions within the BBC. Only one came to immediate fruition, but one that did not gives important details of attitudes to the Japanese at the time and the lengthy saga illuminates what went on behind the scenes when new speakers were recruited. On 23 December, Edgar Blatt, the Transcription Manager, recommended Lyell to Hilton Brown of the Home Talks Service. Brown met Lyell and on 4 January 1943 and sent the following proposal to G. R. Barnes, Director of Talks for the Home Service, who passed it to H. R. Cummings, the Deputy Foreign Adviser:
I had a long talk with Professor Lyell on Friday, 1st January. I am of the opinion he could give us an excellent 9.20 [talk] on "Young Japan". It would not, however, proceed on the popular lines of abusing or belittling the young Japanese—quite the contrary. The rough outline would be . . . the young Japanese student (comment on the extraordinary spread of education in Japan) is an excellent chap in himself, (anecdotes about the rugger matches etc.), but they are all extraordinarily young, childish and unbalanced for their age and they have the intense emotionalism of all Eastern peoples. This childishness and emotionalism is systematically played upon by the militarist authorities as soon as the men join the army, whether from the student class at ages 25–27 or from the peasant class at 21. Brutality is systematically inculcated and stimulated with alcohol, drugs, etc., none of which the Japanese youth can "take".
Professor Lyell is, however, convinced that while young Japan has a real veneration for the figure of the Emperor, they could easily be made to see the truth about these brutal militarist autocrats and would, in the end, gladly turn against them. There is nothing, fortunately, like the Hitler Jugend in Japan and the brutality is purely a matter of their military service.
All this would be brought out by anecdote and illustration from Professor Lyell's experiences rather than laid down as statements of fact. The moral of the whole thing would be, not that the Japanese is a miserable creature who must be crushed or exterminated, but the much better and more encouraging one that young Japan has good stuff in it and if it could be freed with its own consent from those who are at present leading it astray, we might find it an associate well worth having when peace comes.
Cummings replied on 6 January to say that the proposal did not strike him as very timely but he 'thought it well to consult the Foreign Office' and it confirmed his doubts:
They say it is not quite the picture to be given at the moment—complicated, as you know, by

the atrocity and shackling questions. It might be a little misleading to the general listener, for whom it is more important to rub in the fact that Japan is a very formidable enemy which must be crushed. There is no hope whatever from the young Japanese, or any other Japanese, so long as the war lasts. When Japan is beaten, or on the point of being beaten, then it might be useful to hear Professor Lyell's view that it is possible to hope for something from the young generation.

Hilton Brown wrote to Lyell on 7 January regretting his proposed talk could not be broadcast. That very day, Rushbrook Williams circulated a memorandum saying that the Ministry of Information, in consultation with P.W.E., 'have decided that it would serve the ends of H.M.G.'s policy if the anniversary of the Tokyo Military Rebellion of 1936 were well "played up" on February 26th.' The theme was to be that this was the moment when 'dangerous thoughts' gave way to 'danegrous° Actions' and when 'the "New Structure" idea, which led to the present war, first came into practical operation.' Two names were proposed of people who had been in Tokyo at the time: Lyell of the Reference Section, Ministry of Information and Vere Redman of the Ministry's Far East Section. The talk was organised by Anthony Weymouth, Talks Producer for the Overseas Service, and Lyell was invited to speak in a letter dated 12 January 1943. A talks booking form was issued on 15 January, and the talk was broadcast in the Overseas Eastern Service on 26 February; Lyell was paid £12.12s.

1757. To George Bernard Shaw

21 December 1942   07/ES/EB/WMB

Dear Mr. Shaw[1]

I am writing to ask whether you will give your permission for a short passage from ARMS AND THE MAN to be broadcast to India on the 21st January 1943. I will explain the circumstances.

We are broadcasting a series of six talks on English literature covering the set books in the B.A. course in English literature at Calcutta University. The fifth subject in the series is yourself and the book specially chosen for study is ARMS AND THE MAN. The series is being managed by Edmund Blunden, with speakers for each talk, and I am doing the one on ARMS AND THE MAN myself. The way we do these talks is to have fifteen minutes by the chosen speaker then an interlude of about seven minutes of music and then a five minutes reading from the author in question. In the case of plays we like to get a scene acted and that is what I want to do in this case. The passage I had picked on is from Act I of ARMS AND THE MAN, beginning—THE MAN: "A narrow shave" . . . . down to RAINA: — . . . . "to whom I am betrothed".

Of course the actors might consider it necessary not to begin or end exactly at that point but that is the passage I want to use. In any case I would let you know beforehand exactly where the chosen passage is to begin and end.

I shall be very grateful if you would allow us to do this and also if you would let us know your decision as early as possible.[2]

Yours truly
George Orwell
Talks Producer
Indian Section

1. George Bernard Shaw (1856–1950); a biographical note to the BBC pamphlet *Books and Authors* (1946) simply gives his date of birth and states that he 'is thus 90 years old this year.'

2. Shaw replied on 26 December. He did not wish any of the first act of *Arms and the Man* broadcast and suggested instead the passage when Raina and Bluntschli are alone together for the first time after his return, from 'You look ever so much nicer than when we last met' to 'I wish I had never met you,' prefaced by an outline of the story to that point in the play. Orwell, on 15 January 1942, accepted this arrangement; see *1824*. Shaw would have much preferred passages from his prose works, or Caesar's first soliloquy or the prologue to *Caesar and Cleopatra*, or the Devil's speech on death from Act III of *Man and Superman*; the dialogue of *Arms and the Man* had no particular literary pretensions, whereas the passages he suggested were deliberately rhetorical. Orwell was, of course, tied to the Calcutta University syllabus.

1758. Memorandum to Miss Playle, *The Listener*

21 December 1942   Original   EB/NP

NEW SERIES OF TALKS ON LITERATURE—CALLING ALL STUDENTS

On December 25th we are starting a new series of talks to India, covering some of the set books in the B.A. course in English literature at Calcutta University. This will be more or less similar to the series MASTERPIECES OF ENGLISH LITERATURE, some of which you used before, but we propose this time to publish the six talks in the form of a pamphlet in Calcutta so as to appear before the University examinations. There are six talks in all, as follows:

1. Shakespeare—with special reference to JULIUS CAESAR. E. M. Forster.
2. Milton, with special reference to the shorter poems. George Sampson
3. Hardy with special reference to FAR FROM THE MADDING CROWD. Blunden.
4. Hazlitt—with some remarks about English Essays in general. Mr. Nicol Smith.
5. Shaw—with special reference to ARMS & THE MAN. George Orwell.
6. The Book of Job. Walter J. Turner (Literary Editor of The Spectator).

The whole series is being arranged and presented by Edmund Blunden. I attach a copy of Forster's script on Julius Caesar. The talks are of 15 minutes' duration.

[Signed] N. H. Parratt
for Eric Blair

1759. Venu Chitale's Programme Preview

22 December 1942

Miss Chitale previewed forthcoming programmes each month. Her talk on 22 December 1942 contains three items of interest to this edition. There is a reminder to listen 'to George Orwell's News Commentary. Every Saturday at 11.15 G.M.T., 5.45 I[ndian] S[tandard] T[ime] you can hear George Orwell talking about the events of the week.' There is an interesting advance notice of what is claimed to be the first broadcast by the BBC of an Indian play in English for Indian listeners, *Mālatī and Mādhava*. But perhaps of most interest is Miss Chitale's description of Orwell's wife, Eileen Blair.

In describing a new Eastern Service series, 'In Your Kitchen' (which came under Orwell's aegis), she said it would be inaugurated by 'Eileen Blair, who will give an introductory talk on cooking recipes taken mainly from the BBC Home Service programme called "The Kitchen Front". I wish you could talk to Mrs. Blair yourselves. She and her colleagues at the Ministry of Food are responsible for all the recipes which go out on the radio to the millions of British housewives. Mrs. Blair has a reservoir of quiet humour, and again and again some of it seems to come out in between an amused smile and a penetrating remark. For instance, talking about food the other day, she said many battles have surely been lost because the Field-Marshal concerned had not had his proper allocation of vitamins and calories. I think it is this delightful humour that makes her love the work she is doing at the Ministry of Food. She finds it real fun besides it being very useful. Proper dieting keeps the nation fit and happy; helps to keep the morale high . . . after all there is nothing like a satisfying and enjoyable meal, more so in wartime. Mrs. Blair is a graduate of Oxford University and she read Psychology for her subject. When I asked her how she had drifted to food from psychology she said "Perhaps it is the psychological reactions to food and cooking that interest me more than food for its own sake." Of course that explained the Field-Marshal's vitamins and calories to me! Another interesting remark of Mrs. Blair's was that she found cooking most creative. Anyway let Mrs. Blair convince you of the psychological value and the creative character of . . . . FOOD!'

Corrections made to this script by hand look suspiciously like Orwell's, but it is difficult to be sure. He certainly revised an earlier Programme Preview extensively; see *1351*.

1760. Talk by Eileen Blair, for the Kitchen Front Broadcasts

Eastern Service, 23 December 1942

The typescript carries censors' stamps showing it has been passed for Policy and Security. There are no changes to the script and it is marked 'As broadcast.'

Every morning for 2½ years now there has been a broadcast from London called the Kitchen Front. It's part of the ordinary B.B.C. programme, but the idea behind it is that for 5 minutes the Ministry of Food shall try to help British women to do a very difficult job. And that is to give their families the food they need—and food they'll *like*—in spite of wartime restrictions. We haven't really any hardship to complain about. There is enough food for everyone, extra allowances for children and invalids and so on. But on the other hand two things have combined to convert catering from a habit into a research. Many women here, of course, have always cooked for their families—but now they have to cook without foodstuffs that they always relied on and to make up for their absence by using new foods, like dried eggs and dried milk, or foods that always existed but were not so important in peacetime. The other change is that many women are now cooking for the first time—they may know how to write a book or do a complicated surgical operation or teach philosophy, but they don't know how to make a vegetable stew and pre-war cookery books aren't much use to them. Obviously it's more than ever important that meals should be well cooked and well balanced, and the Kitchen Front tries to show how they can be both.

We have all kinds of speakers. Once a week the radio doctor explains the essential food values, the function of vitamins, proteins and calories in the diet, and particularly the importance of child-feeding. But the other talks are generally recipe talks—interpreting the results of scientific experiment in terms of actual dishes. Often the recipes come from the Ministry of Food's kitchens, where new dishes are tried out every day. Then once a week a foreign housewife tells us something about cooking in her country—at least not always a housewife exactly—one of our speakers was the High Commissioner for India who gave us a very good lesson on how to make Indian curries. Then once a week we broadcast recipes that have been sent in to us by ordinary housewives up and down the country—sometimes recipes for special dishes that their mothers and grand-mothers made, sometimes recipes that they themselves have invented on the very day they write to us. But wherever they come from they're *fighting* recipes—they're very economical in rationed food, they don't need any of the foods that are scarce, they're good sound nourishment, and they're attractive too. We are ambitious. We hope that one good result of this war may be that many more people will recognise that cooking is both an art and a science, worth all the intelligence and originality that anyone can put into it.

Well this programme has been going on, as I said, for 2½ years. That's a lot of recipes, and looking back it seems extraordinary that they haven't come to an end yet. But on the contrary, we haven't time to broadcast nearly all we'd like to. The shortage of foods we used to have in abundance has inspired all the good cooks in the country to get the same effect from something else or to find new ways of cooking the foods we have got. Especially vegetables. We can grow vegetables in England, vegetables of some kind all the year round, but many of us never appreciated them till now. For instance, before the war nearly everyone in England ate potatoes every day. And very nearly every day they ate *boiled* potatoes. Now we have over 100 ways of cooking potatoes, plain and savoury and sweet, and we've learnt how to preserve their very important food values too. Our foreign speakers help us a lot with vegetable recipes. People in Central Europe particularly have always lived mainly on vegetables (potatoes and cabbage, many of them) and now they're telling us how they ate them. The cabbage has come to England as an ambassador, and a very good internationalising influence it is, full of Vitamin C.

That's the story of the Kitchen Front broadcast. And now once a week you're going to hear one or two of our recipes. At least I hope you're going to hear them. Miss Panthaki is going to broadcast them anyway. Some of them will be new to you I expect, as they are to us. Some of them may seem pretty odd to you—a lot of them seemed very odd to us until we cooked them and found that they were good. And some of our traditional English and Scottish and Welsh dishes may be new to you too, but perhaps you may like them, even adapted as they have had to be for wartime. If you do, if you share our excitement in this adventuring after new experiences in eating, you might like to tell us something about your food. We have lentils, we have some rice and spices too, as well as fresh vegetables, and if we were to broadcast a recipe sent specially from India millions of English listeners would appreciate it and thousands of them would be cooking it the same day. That would be another internationalising influence.

1761. BBC Talks Booking Form, 22.12.42

Sir Aziz-ul-Huque: 'The High Commissioner Talks to you';[1] 13½-minute talk about Indians in this country; broadcast 29.12.42 and 26.1.43; fee £10.10s each talk. Signed: M Blackburn for I.P.O.

1. On 14 December, Bokhari sent Orwell a memorandum from India in which he said that the Eastern Service Director had agreed that Sir Aziz-ul-Huque's monthly talks should be given this title instead of 'Indians in Great Britain.' Orwell's office was asked to see that 'this information reaches the usual Publicity people in time.'

1762. BBC Talks Booking Form, 22.12.42

Mulk Raj Anand: 'Voice,' 6; 'half hour programme of poems etc., with discussions lasting about 5 min. Mr. Anand helped to put the programme together & will take part in discussion'; broadcast 29.12.42; fee £5.5s, 'Usual fee' (in Blackburn's handwriting). Signed: M Blackburn for I.P.O.; marked 'Cancelled' by M. Cunningham, Talks Booking Manager.

1763. BBC Talks Booking Form, 22.12.42

Lady Grigg: 'Women Generally Speaking'; broadcast 6, 13, 20, and 27.1.43; fee £8.8s each broadcast. Signed: M Blackburn for I.P.O.

1764. BBC Talks Booking Form, 22.12.42

Herbert Read: 'Voice,' 6; 'reading poems and taking part in discussions in this 30 minute programme'; broadcast 29.12.42; fee £4.4s, to cover reading of poems and part in discussions. Signed: M Blackburn for I.P.O.

1765. To Edmund Blunden

23 December 1942   07/ES/EB

Dear Mr. Blunden
We have fixed a recording for Mr. D. Nichol Smith[1] to do his talk on Hazlitt. The date of the recording is the 8th January at 10.45 to 11.15 a.m.
Would you please be here with Mr. Nichol Smith at 10.15 for a rehearsal. I hope this is quite convenient for you.

Yours sincerely
[Initialled] E. A. B
George Orwell
Talks Producer
Indian Section

1. David Nichol Smith (1875–1962), distinguished editor and scholar. His books include *Eighteenth Century° Essays on Shakespeare* (1903), *The Oxford Book of Eighteenth-century Verse* (1926), *Some Observations on Eighteenth-century Poetry* (1937), *The Poems of Samuel Johnson* (with E. L. McAdam) (1941), and *John Dryden* (1950).

1766. To W. J. Turner

23 December 1942   07/ES/EB/WMB

Dear Mr. Turner
Thank you very much for your script on the Book of JOB, which has arrived quite safely. This is very interesting and we are looking forward to your broadcast.

Yours sincerely
[Initialled] E. A. B
George Orwell
Talks Producer
Indian Section

1767. BBC Talks Booking Form, 23.12.42

Shridhar Telkar: 'Behind the Headlines'; broadcast 7, 14, 21, and 28.1.43; fee £9.9s each talk. Signed: M Blackburn for I.P.O.

1768. Review of *An Unknown Land* by Viscount Samuel

The Listener, 24 December 1942

Founded ultimately on Bacon's *New Atlantis*, this book is a 'favourable' Utopia, and it fails at just the same point as all other books of this type—that is, in being unable to describe a society which is anywhere near perfection and which any normal human being would want to live in.

The author, so the story goes, has always believed that the country known as the New Atlantis was a real island which some sea-captain had described to Bacon, and after a long voyage of exploration he succeeds in finding it and spends about a year there. It is only a smallish island situated in a remote part of the South Pacific, so that it has remained undiscovered, partly owing to the precautions of the inhabitants. They are aware of the outside world and periodically send out 'missioners' to put them in touch with the latest scientific discoveries, but they keep the existence of their own island secret, not having any wish to be invaded and conquered.

Internally, of course, the island has all the characteristics we have come to associate with 'favourable' Utopias—the hygiene, the labour-saving devices, the fantastic machines, the emphasis on Science, the all-round reasonableness tempered by a rather watery religiosity. The people work a nine-hour week and spend the rest of their time in scientific or artistic pursuits. There is no war, no crime, no disease, no poverty, no class-distinctions, etc., etc. Why is it that such 'ideal' conditions as these are always so profoundly unappetising to read about? One is driven to conclude that fully human life is not thinkable without a considerable intermixture of evil. It is obvious, to take only one instance, that humour and the sense of fun, ultimately dependent on the existence of evil, have no place in any Utopia. As Lunacharsky remarked long ago in the introduction to *The Little Golden Calf*,[1] in a perfect society there would be nothing to laugh at. The people in Lord Samuel's Utopia are occasionally described as laughing, but only at the habits of foreigners, not at anything in their own lives. A certain smugness and a tendency to self-praise are common failings in the inhabitants of Utopias, as a study of Mr. H. G. Wells' work would show.

It is noticeable that a 'perfect' society only becomes thinkable if the human mind and even the human physiology are somehow got rid of. The inhabitants of Lord Samuel's Utopia have artificially enlarged skulls which allow their brains to reach a prodigious development, but which make them, from our point of view, only doubtfully human. Swift, when he wanted to describe good instead of evil, had to turn from men to horses. It might be worth Lord Samuel's while to reflect that though the first three parts of *Gulliver's Travels* are disgusting and sometimes horrifying, they are hilariously funny and full of brilliant invention, and it is only in the final part, the Land of the Houyhnhnms, where Swift is describing as best he can the

---

1. See XII, 227 and *229*.

way in which reasonable beings would live, that a note of melancholy intrudes and the narrative even becomes boring.[2]

1769. To Arthur Wynn, Music Bookings Manager
24 December 1942   Original   EB/WMB

INTERLUDE IN 1115 TO 1130 GMT PERIOD

As from today, the 24th, we are doing a short interlude approximately 5 minutes, between the programmes BEHIND THE HEADLINES and BEHIND THE BATTLEFRONT, which is given at 1130 to 1200 GMT. This interlude is going to be filled by a recorded poem chosen by Mr. Blair and Dr. Menon is choosing appropriate music in relation to the poem.

We shall be glad, therefore, if you will issue a contract for Mr. Naravana Menon, 151 Sussex Gardens, London, W.2. to the end of January, commencing today, the 24th, and continuing for the 31st Dec. 7th January, 14th, 21st and 28th January 1943.

[Signed] M Blackburn
(For Eric Blair)

P.S. Mr. Blair suggests a fee of half a guinea each time.

1770. News Commentary in English for Malaya, 13
25 December 1942

This was written and read by George Orwell. No script has been traced.

1771. English News Commentary, 53
26 December 1942

There are unusual aspects to the script for this Newsletter. It has two different openings, the long, original, opening having been replaced by a much shorter text. The contents are much the same, and there is no ground for believing that the original opening was censored. The cut version is marked in Orwell's hand, 'As b' cast 13' 8"'; the running times marked on the script total $13\frac{1}{4}$ minutes. The script was apparently changed to fit the time available and done at the last moment, because it includes an update to the news: 'He was due to be executed this morning.' The original opening paragraph read:

I said in recent news commentaries that before long the British and United States governments were likely to issue some official statement defining the position of Admiral Darlan, the High Commissioner for French North and West Africa. Well, it so happens that his position has been defined in another way. He is dead, having been assassinated in Algiers the day before yesterday. The assassin was captured, but we don't yet know who he is or

---

2. Orwell was paid £2.2s for this review, which was unsigned.

what his motives were. No doubt the world will be enlightened on those points within the next few days. Meanwhile I should like to emphasise that Darlan's death makes no difference to the general situation. The stability of the regime in French Africa did not depend upon him, and there is no reason to think that the loyalty to the United Nations of the French troops in Africa will be in any way affected. For the moment General Giraud, who escaped recently from Germany and reached Africa via Vichy France, has taken over the command of the French forces in Africa. A successor to Darlan will no doubt be appointed shortly. During the past week or two a great deal of evidence had accumulated as to Darlan's unpopularity with the French North African population, who presumably didn't forget his record as a "collaborator" in the Vichy government, and didn't feel that his having changed sides a second time necessarily wiped out the first time. The cause of the United Nations will be a lot better off if as successor to Darlan we get someone who has been less conspicuously associated with the policy of surrender to the Nazis.

> The script looks as if it has been typed by Orwell, possibly on his own machine; the typewriter is certainly not one normally used for producing scripts of Newsletters. The replacement slip was typed on yet another machine, probably by someone unfamiliar with its idiosyncracies. It looks as if its carriage moved forward sluggishly in contrast to the typist's speed, for in some 120 words there are fifteen instances in which words run into the next, as well as other typing errors. The Christmas holiday may have meant that Orwell was not relying on the regular secretarial staff. The timings shown are those marked in the margin of the script. PasB has 'News Review written and broadcast by George Orwell.' The script was read for Policy and Security by S. Ramaam and in his hand is the indication 'For English & Bengali' on the first page of the amended text. The very slight verbal changes are also in Ramaam's hand but these may record Orwell's own amendments; they have no implications of censorship. This script seems to have been the basis for Bengali Newsletter, 24 (see 1772), but whether this was simply a saving of time at Christmas or a regular practice is not known.

I said in earlier commentaries that before long there would be some official pronouncement defining the position of Admiral Darlan, High commissioner° for French North and West Africa. Well, it so happens that his position has been defined in another way. He is dead. He was assassinated two days ago. The assassin was captured and tried by a French court martial. He was due to be executed this morning.[1] That is all we know at present, except that General Giraud[2] has taken over Darlan's position as commander of the French forces in north and west Africa° for the time being. The administration is proceeding as before [, and this incident will not in any way upset the United Nations' war effort].

Apart from the assassination of Admiral Darlan, the chief [1 min] development this week on the North African front has been the continued and rapid retreat of the Germans in Libya. At the time when I delivered my commentary last week the rearguard of General Rommel's army had just been cut off west of el Agheila and seemed likely to be completely destroyed.

Most of that rearguard ultimately got away, though not without losing fairly heavily in guns and other material, besides a few hundreds of prisoners. But the retreat has gone on, and our advance patrols are now in contact with the Germans somewhere near Sirte, about 150 miles west of el Agheila. It looks as though the Germans are about to abandon Sirte, and ultimately, in all probability, the whole of Libya, though no doubt they will fight a delaying action in defence of Tripoli. They are still doing their best to slow up the Eighth Army's advance by sowing anti-tank mines, and by ploughing up the airfields they have to abandon; when this is done it is some days before the airfields can be used by Allied planes. Also, within the last few days German airplanes have begun to reappear on the Libyan front, after about a week in which almost the only air activity had been that of the Allies. No doubt the German commander hopes to hold the Eighth Army till the bulk of the German forces have got away, probably into Tunisia or, possibly, back to Sicily by sea.

From the German point of view the complete abandonment of Libya has the disadvantage that it means giving up the last scrap of the Italian Empire and thus robbing the Italians of any motive they may still have for continuing the war. There is much evidence that morale in Italy is already low, the food situation is bad, and the British [3 min] air raids have caused much panic and disorganisation. There has even been serious talk of declaring Rome an open city to save it from being bombed. If this is done it will be a tremendous blow to Axis prestige and an open admission that Italian morale is shaky. The Germans, however, are not likely to be affected by any concern for Italian feelings. However much the Italian people may hate the war they are not in a position to make any anti-war move while the German army is quartered upon them. And for the Germans, to abandon Libya altogether and concentrate on holding on to Tunisia would have considerable advantages. If they could hold Tunisia permanently—which, however, isn't likely—they could completely bar the passage through the Mediterranean to Allied shipping. But even if they can only hold it for a while they can cut their losses and get out of Africa less disastrously than if they risked having a whole army destroyed in Libya. Also their supply problem in Bizerta and Tunis is very much simpler than it is in Tripoli. To supply Tripoli means a constant loss of ships and transport planes. Throughout the present operations the Axis have been losing on an average a ship a day—far more than they can afford with their limited amount of shipping. So my forecast for North Africa would be that the Germans are likely to defend Bizerta and Tunis as long as possible, but not to make an all-out effort to defend Tripoli.

Since last week the Russians have opened up fresh offensives,[3] this time on the middle Don, north west of Stalingrad *and also in the Caucasus.* They broke through the German defensive positions almost immediately, and in [5¼ min] just over a week they have made an advance of about 100 miles and claim 50000[4] prisoners, besides great captures of war material. The advance the Russians have made in a south-westerly direction makes it still harder for the German army before Stalingrad to get out of its uncomfortable position. How decisive this Russian victory will be we can't yet say. A feature of the winter fighting in Russia is the difficulty either side has of making any *prolonged* offensive, owing to the severe weather conditions and consequent break-down of communications. But the series of limited offensives which the Russians have now made at widely-separated points along the front have added greatly to the Germans' problems. The Russians are now in several places across the railway connecting Voronezh with Rostov, which makes lateral communication much harder for the Germans. If you look at the map of the Russian front, from Leningrad down to the Caucasus, you will notice that the line occupied by the German armies is roughly twice as long as it need be, owing to the huge salients in it. The Germans could shorten it by means of a general retreat, but considerations of prestige make that difficult for them. And the Germans have again failed to capture large cities in which to winter their troops. Last year thousands of Germans—we do not know how many thousands—were frozen to death because of the failure to capture Moscow and Leningrad. This year thousands more will die of cold because of the failure to capture Stalingrad and to get across the Caucasus Mountains. And the more activity the Red Army can keep up during the winter months, the harder for the Germans to rest their armies and get ready for the Anglo-American offensive [7½ min] next year.

Last week I suggested that the Japanese bombing of Chittagong might mean that the Allies intended some move in the area of the India-Burma frontier. This has been confirmed by the advance that British and Indian forces have made into Burma in the direction of Akyab. The fact that the Japanese have three times bombed Calcutta suggests that they take this move seriously. We ought not, however, to expect any *immediate* great results from the Allied advance. It is probably only a reconnaissance to test Japanese strength and also to make contact with the Burmese and discover their reactions to the Japanese occupation. Akyab is not of itself an objective worth fighting a serious battle for. There is only one really important objective in Burma, and that is Rangoon, the only port of entry through which war materials could once again be sent to the Burma Road. The Allies would have to capture Rangoon to make any campaign in Burma worth while. A more significant bit of news, which has attracted less attention, is the air raid on the island of Sumatra by British planes which must have come from an aircraft carrier. This is significant because it shows how the balance of naval power is shifting against[5] Japan. This is the first action the Allies have taken against Sumatra since March of this year, and till a few months ago no Allied aircraft carrier could possibly have got near Sumatra. Japanese naval superiority is waning even on the eastern side of the Bay of Bengal, thanks to the heavy losses they have had in the South Pacific and the much faster rate of Allied construction in ships and [9½ min] planes. The British raid on Sumatra is a demonstration of this, but it must have had some direct military purpose as well, and it may have been connected with the advance into Burma. It would be worth keeping an eye on the Andaman Islands, which lie south-west of Burma and command the approaches to Rangoon and Singapore.

This is the fourth Christmas of war, and in the minute or two remaining to me I should like to glance back, as I have sometimes done in earlier commentaries, and say something about the development of the war as a whole. Look back two years, to the Christmas of 1940. Britain was alone, fighting desperately with her back to the wall, and London and other British cities were being bombed to pieces. America was neutral, Soviet Russia also neutral and only very doubtfully friendly.[6] An Italian army had been destroyed in Cyrenaica and the air battle over Britain had been won, but the Germans had conquered the whole of western Europe and there was no kind of certainty that the New Order would not be a success. Now look back one year, to the Christmas of 1941. Then too the outlook was black enough. Hong Kong had just fallen, an unannounced attack had temporarily crippled the American fleet at Pearl Harbour, and the Japanese had started on their career of conquest which—so it appeared at the time—was certain to lead on to the invasion of India and of Australia. But there were compensations there had not been the year before. Russia and the United States were in the war, the attempt to knock out Russia at one blow had visibly failed, and the German army was still breaking its teeth [*11½ min*] on Moscow. Moreover Britain's strength, in arms and trained men, had grown enormously in the intervening year. And now look at the situation as it now stands. In Russia the Germans have suffered huge losses for no corresponding gain, and they have another winter in the snow ahead of them. The Japanese are where they stood seven months ago, they have lost scores of irreplaceable warships, and in the South Pacific the struggle has begun to turn against them. Most of Libya has been lost to the Axis, and the whole north-west corner of Africa, with its good ports and airfields and its important raw materials, has passed into Allied control. Both American and British arms production have got into full swing. As for the New Order, even the Germans themselves have almost stopped pretending that it is a success. There have been moments even during 1942—especially during the middle of the summer—when things looked dark enough, but we can see now with certainty that the tide has turned. Just at what moment it turned is disputable. It might have been the Battle of Britain in 1940, or the failure of the Germans before Moscow in 1941 or the Anglo-American invasion of North Africa in 1942—but it has turned, and one can tell even from the speeches of the Axis leaders themselves that they know very well it won't flow their way again. [*13¼ min*]

1. For Darlan, see *803, n. 1* and *1195, n. 9*.
2. General Henri Giraud (1879–1949) had served in World War I and in the Rif campaign in Morocco in the 1920s. He had belatedly taken over the French Ninth Army in May 1940, was captured, but escaped and was taken by British submarine from Gibraltar to North Africa. De Gaulle reluctantly allowed him to succeed Darlan as High Commissioner for French North Africa, and they served as co-presidents of the Committee of National Liberation from November 1943 until Giraud was forced out by de Gaulle.
3. fresh offensives] a fresh offensive
4. *50000*] 36,000
5. 'against' is doubly underlined in ink by Ramaam or Orwell.
6. The Soviet Union was, at least nominally, still an ally of Nazi Germany.

1772. Bengali Newsletter, 24

26 December 1942

PasB states 'written by Eric Blair, staff, translated and read by S. K. Das Gupta, followed by paragraph of news of interest to Bengali women written and read by Mrs. Renu Ghosh.' This is the only PasB entry for the Bengali Newsletter to mention Orwell. From PasB a timing of 12 minutes may be assumed. To fill the time HMV record N 15761 / OML 220-1 was played for 1½'. No script has been traced.

1773. Gujarati Newsletter, 44

28 December 1942

This was written by Orwell and recast and translated by R. R. Desai, who took over completely from No. 45. PasB says written and read by Desai. The timing is given as 11' 02". No script has been traced.

Because Orwell's involvement in the Gujarati Newsletter is from this time on restricted to checking, on Mondays, the English translation of what Desai had broadcast the previous day, no further details will be given of this series of Newsletters.

1774. For Z. A. Bokhari to P. Chatterjee

28 December 1942   07/ES/ZAB/ED

Dear Dr. Chatterjee,
[As] promised, here is a copy of the English version of the Bengali Newsletter, which was broadcast on Saturday last, from 3.30–3.45 p.m.

We shall be glad if you will write a trial Newsletter in Bengali, covering the news of the current week, and bring it along on Saturday next, the 2nd January, together with an English version. We will expect you some time during the morning on Saturday, if that is convenient to you.

Yours sincerely,
[Initialled] MB
for Z. A. Bokhari
Indian Programme Organiser

1775. BBC Talks Booking Form, 28.12.42

Edmund Blunden: 'Calling All Students,' 3, talk on Hardy with special reference to FAR FROM THE MADDING CROWD; broadcast 8.1.43; fee £9.9s. Signed: M Blackburn for I.P.O. Remarks: 'Edmund Blunden is giving the actual talk and not the introduction this time.'

1776. BBC Talks Booking Form, 28.12.42

S. K. Das Gupta: to translate & read the Bengali Newsletters written in English by E. Blair (Staff); broadcast 2, 9, 16, 23, and 30.1.43; fee £3.3s for the first[1] and £5.5s for the others. Signed: M Blackburn for Z. A. Bokhari.

1. This was to be a shorter and special broadcast: see Bengali Newsletter, 25, 2 January 1943, *1794.*

1777. BBC Talks Booking Form, 28.12.42

W. J. Turner: 'Calling All Students,' 6, THE BOOK OF JOB;[1] broadcast 29.1.43; fee £9.9s. Signed: M Blackburn for I.P.O.

1. The title evidently caused some surprise and is annotated in capitals, underlined twice, 'BIBLE.'

1778. 'Voice,' 6: A Magazine Programme
29 December 1942

The text of 'Voice,' 6, the last of the series, is reproduced from a typescript used in the broadcast. It has been amended by several hands, one of which is Orwell's. The script is almost certainly that used by Herbert Read, for his name, crossed through, appears at the top of the first page with the timing, 29¼ minutes, and 'As broadcast.'

The text is reproduced as modified for the broadcast, though there are a few places where the amendments are not clear and some guesswork has been necessary. The notes record changes and uncertainties. The surviving type-script, a top copy, has enough mistypings and overtypings to suggest that it is not the work of a professional typist. The small x's used to cross out words indicate that the typist was probably not Orwell. There is no list of participants, but, from the closing announcement, they were: Herbert Read, William Empson, George Orwell, Venu Chitale, and Christopher Pemberton; a BBC recording was used to transmit T. S. Eliot's contribution. Not all the speakers' names are given in this typescript; the original's SOMEONE has been left standing.

The typescript gives the commercial record numbers of the discs used in the broadcast; details of performers have been added in italic within square brackets.

'Voice,' 6 was transmitted from 11.15 to 11.45 GMT, and at 11.34 there was a one-minute news flash. The subject is not noted in PasB.

ANNOUNCER: This is London Calling. Here is the sixth number of VOICE, our monthly radio magazine.
> FADE UP 'ADESTE FIDELES'—HMV. DB. 984. for 1'
> [*John McCormack with Trinity Choir, mixed chorus, and orchestra*]

ORWELL: This is a special Christmas number, and we are departing from our usual practice and having music in it. But as usual we want to start off by making sure what we are talking about. Christmas is something integral to the West and we all take its importance for granted, but we are talking to an audience to whom the festival of Christmas may not be so familiar. What is the essential thing about Christmas? What does it really stand for?

CHITALE: Well, first of all, I suppose, for the anniversary of the birth of Christ.

EMPSON: Not first in order[1] of time. There was a pre-Christian festival at the same date, or about the same date. The ancient Saxon tribes that we are descended from used to celebrate something or other on Christmas day. The mistletoe hung[2] up in English houses at Christmas time was[3] a sacred plant when the aboriginal Britons were savages; its° an evergreen in winter. That's[4] a natural thing in a cold northern climate. You must have a break somewhere in the long winter, and an excuse for a little feasting: this comes just after the days have started to get longer.[5]

ORWELL: There seem to be three ideas mixed up in the Christmas festival. One is winter and snow, another is the Nativity of Christ, and the other is feasting and the giving of gifts. Of course some of it is a development of the last hundred years. I think the giving of Christmas presents is a modern custom, isn't it?

SOMEONE: No. Christmas presents are supposed to have originated when the three kings from the East brought their gifts of gold and frankincense and myrrh to Bethlehem. In India the custom is that the child is given presents 12 days after birth.[6]

ORWELL: Well, we'll try to cover those three aspects of Christmas. Let's start off with something about the snow and the characteristic winter plants, the holly and the ivy and the mistletoe.

EMPSON: You'll have great difficulty in finding much about snow in English literature. It's never praised,[7] at any rate until the last hundred years. That's natural. This is a cold country, and we don't write in praise of cold.

PEMBERTON: There's a poem by Robert Bridges, LONDON SNOW. I've got it here. That's in praise of snow.

ORWELL: All right, let's have that one. I tell you how we'll do it. First of all we'll have the carol "See amid the winter's snow", then we'll have the poem—LONDON SNOW by Robert Bridges—and then another carol, The Holly and the Ivy. I think we'll go straight through them with only pauses between.

RECORD: HMV. B. 8073 SEE AMID THE WINTER'S SNOW. I[1]

[*Royal Choral Society with organ accompaniment conducted by Dr. Malcolm Sargent*]

LONDON SNOW by Robert Bridges

PEMBERTON: When men were all asleep the snow came flying,
In large white flakes falling on the city brown,
Stealthily and perpetually settling and loosely lying,
   Hushing the latest traffic of the drowsy town;
Deadening, muffling, stifling its murmurs failing;

Lazily and incessantly floating down and down:
 Silently sifting and veiling road, roof and railing;
Hiding difference, making unevenness even,
Into angles and crevices softly drifting and sailing.
 All night it fell, and when full inches seven
It lay in the depth of its uncompacted lightness,
The clouds blew off from a high and frosty heaven;
 And all woke earlier for the unaccustomed brightness
Of the winter dawning, the strange unheavenly glare:
The eye marvelled—marvelled at the dazzling whiteness;
The ear hearkened to the stillness of the solemn air;
No sound of wheel rumbling nor of foot falling,
And the busy morning cries came thin and spare.
 Then boys I heard, as they went to school, calling,
They gathered up the crystal manna to freeze
Their tongues with tasting, their hands with snowballing;
 Or rioted in a drift, plunging up to the knees;
Or peering up from under the white-mossed wonder,
'O look at the trees!' they cried, 'O look at the trees!'
 With lessened load a few carts creak and blunder,
Following along the white deserted way,
A country company long dispersed asunder;
 When now already the sun, in pale display
Standing by Paul's high dome, spread forth below ·
His sparkling beams, and awoke the stir of the day.
 For now doors open, and war is waged with the snow;
And trains of sombre men, past tale of number,
Tread long brown paths, as toward their toil they go:
 But even for them awhile no cares encumber
Their minds diverted; the daily word is unspoken,
The daily thoughts of labour and sorrow slumber
At the sight of the beauty that greets them, for the charm they have broken.

RECORD: THE HOLLY & THE IVY HMV. BD. 768 45″ approx.

[*St Brandon's School Choir, Bristol, arranged, and orchestra conducted, by Leslie Woodgate*]

READ:[8] It's time we had something dealing with the birth of Christ itself, which is what the Christmas festival properly commemorates.[9]

ORWELL: Let's start with a carol specially dealing with that time.[10] For instance, The Seven Joys of Mary.

RECORD: THE SEVEN JOYS OF MARY VICTOR: 2018 1′ 50″ approx.

[*John Jacob Niles (tenor), with dulcimer accompaniment*]

ORWELL: I think we ought to read the story itself before reading any poems about it. What is the absolutely essential thing about the story of the birth of Christ, I wonder?

READ:[11] I think the essential thing—that is, the thing everyone remembers—is the idea of power and wisdom abasing themselves before innocence and poverty. Everyone who has ever heard of the birth of Christ remembers two picturesque details which don't, in fact, have anything to do with Christian doctrine. One is the child lying in the manger, and the other is the three Kings from the East coming with their gifts. The story is so perfectly right that it has become traditional, and it's acted every year in thousands of churches all over the world. But in fact not one of the versions in the Bible gives quite the full story.[12]

ORWELL: I think we'll have the version from the Gospel according to St. Matthew. That's the fullest one. Perhaps Venu Chitale will read it for us. Here it is then—from the second chapter of the Gospel of St. Matthew.

[CHITALE:] From THE GOSPEL ACCORDING TO ST. MATTHEW. Ch. II, 1–4, 7–15.

Now when Jesus was born in Bethlehem of Judaea in the days of Herod the king, behold, there came wise men from the east to Jerusalem, saying, Where is he that is born King of the Jews? for we have seen his star in the east, and are come to worship him. When Herod the king had heard these things, he was troubled, and all Jerusalem with him.

And when he had gathered all the chief priests and scribes of the people together, he demanded of them where Christ should be born.

Then Herod, when he had privily called the wise men, inquired of them diligently what time the star appeared.

And he sent them to Bethlehem, and said, Go and search diligently for the young child; and when ye have found him, bring me word again, that I may come and worship him also.

When they had heard the king, they departed; and, lo, the star, which they saw in the east, went before them, till it came and stood over where the young child was.

When they saw the star, they rejoiced with exceeding great joy.

And when they were come into the house, they saw the young child with Mary his mother, and fell down, and worshipped him: and when they had opened their treasures, they presented unto him gifts: gold, and frankincense, and myrrh.

And being warned of God in a dream that they should not return to Herod, they departed into their own country another way.

And when they were departed, behold, the angel of the Lord appeareth to Joseph in a dream, saying, Arise, and take the young child and his mother, and flee into Egypt, and be thou there until I bring thee word: for Herod will seek the young child to destroy him.

When he arose, he took the young child and his mother by night, and departed into Egypt:

And was there until the death of Herod: that it might be fulfilled which was spoken of the Lord by the prophet, saying, Out of Egypt have I called my son.[13]

ORWELL: And now what poems shall we have?

EMPSON: We ought to have Milton's Hymn on the Nativity. I'm sure Herbert Read would read that very nicely.

SOMEONE: And what about having T. S. Eliot's poem, THE JOURNEY OF THE MAGI? That would give a good contrast.

ORWELL: Yes, that's a good idea. We've got a recording of that which Eliot made himself. The Hymn on the Nativity is rather long, so perhaps we should have another carol in between the two poems. Let's have in

Excelsis Gloria.° First of all Milton,[14] then the carol, then THE
JOURNEY OF THE MAGI. Here they are then.

READ: It was the Winter wilde,
While the Heav'n-borne-childe,
   All meanly wrapt in the rude manger lies;
Nature in aw to him
Had doff't her gawdy trim,
   With her great Master so to sympathize:
It was no season then for her
To wanton with the Sun her lusty Paramour. . . .

No War, or Battails sound
Was heard the World around,
   The idle spear and shield were high up hung;
The hookèd Chariot stood
Unstain'd with hostile blood,
   The Trumpet spake not to the armèd throng,
And Kings sate still with awfull eye,
As if they surely knew their sovran Lord was by.

But peacefull was the night
Wherein the Prince of light
   His raign of peace upon the earth began:
The Windes with wonder whist,
Smoothly the waters kist,
   Whispering new joyes to the milde Ocean,
Who now hath quite forgot to rave,
While Birds of Calm sit brooding on the charmèd wave,

The Stars with deep amaze
Stand fixt in stedfast gaze,
   Bending one way their pretious influence,
And will not take their flight,
For all the morning light,
   Or Lucifer that often warn'd them thence;
But in their glimmering Orbs did glow,
Untill their Lord himself bespake, and bid them go. . . .

The Shepherds on the Lawn,
Or ere the point of dawn,
   Sate simply chatting in a rustick row;
Full little thought they than,
That the mighty Pan
   Was kindly com to live with them below;
Perhaps their loves, or els their sheep,
Was all that did their silly thoughts so busie keep. . . .

At last surrounds their sight
A Globe of circular light,
   That with long beams the shame-fac't night array'd,
The helmèd Cherubim
And sworded Seraphim,
   Are seen in glittering ranks with wings displaid,

Harping in loud and solemn quire,
With unexpressive notes to Heav'ns new-born Heir.

Such musick (as 'tis said)
Before was never made,
    But when of old the sons of morning sung,
While the Creator Great
His constellations set,
    And the well-ballanc't world on hinges hung,
And cast the dark foundations deep,
And bid the weltring waves their oozy channel keep. . . .

The Oracles are dumm,
No voice or hideous humm
    Runs through the arched roof in words deceiving.
Apollo from his shrine
Can no more divine,
    With hollow shreik the steep of Delphos leaving.
No nightly trance, or breathèd spell,
Inspires the pale-ey'd Priest from the prophetic cell. . . .

Peor, and Baalim,
Forsake their Temples dim,
    With that twise-batter'd god of Palestine,
And moonèd Ashtaroth,
Heav'ns Queen and Mother both,
    Now sits not girt with Tapers holy shine,
The Libyc Hammon shrinks his horn,
In vain the Tyrian Maids their wounded Thamuz mourn.

And sullen Moloch fled,
Hath left in shadows dred,
    His burning Idol all of blackest hue,
In vain with Cymbals ring,
They call the grisly king.
    In dismall dance about the furnace blue;
The brutish gods of Nile as fast,
Isis and Orus, and the Dog Anubis hast.

Nor is Osiris seen
In Memphian Grove, or Green,
    Trampling the unshowr'd Grasse with lowings loud:
Nor can he be at rest
Within his sacred chest,
    Naught but profoundest hell can be his shroud,
In vain with Timbrel'd Anthems dark
The sable-stolèd Sorcerers bear his worshipt Ark.

He feels from Juda's Land
The dredded Infants hand,
    The rayes of Bethlehem blind his dusky eyn;
Nor all the gods beside,
Longer dare abide,
    Not Typhon huge ending in snaky twine:
Our Babe to shew his Godhead true,
Can in his swadling bands countroul the damnèd crew,

So when the Sun in bed,
Curtain'd with cloudy red,
  Pillows his chin upon an Orient wave,
The flocking shadows pale,
Troop to th'infernall jail,
  Each fetter'd Ghost slips to his severall grave,
And the yellow-skirted Fayes,
Fly after the Night-steeds, leaving their Moon-lov'd maze.
But see the Virgin blest,
Hath laid her Babe to rest.
  Time is our tedious Song should here have ending,
Heav'ns youngest teemèd Star,
Hath fixt her polisht Car,
  Her sleeping Lord with Handmaid Lamp attending:
And all about the Courtly Stable,
Bright-harnest Angels sit in order serviceable.
RECORD: GLORIA IN EXCELSIS. COL: DX. 581. 1¼′ approx.
[*Version of King Henry VI sung by Nashdom Abbey Singers*]
JOURNEY OF THE MAGI by T. S. Eliot
(L.T.S.[15] RECORDING: 10PH 8167. 2′ 20″)

[ELIOT]: 'A cold coming we had of it,
        Just the worst time of the year
        For a journey, and such a long journey:
        The ways deep and the weather sharp,
        The very dead of the winter.'
        And the camels galled, sore-footed, refractory,
        Lying down in the melting snow.
        There were times we regretted
        The summer palaces on slopes, the terraces,
        And the silken girls bringing sherbet.
        Then the camel men cursing and grumbling
        And running away, and wanting their liquor and women,
        And the night-fires going out, and the lack of shelters,
        And the cities hostile and the towns unfriendly
        And the villages dirty and charging high prices:
        A hard time we had of it.
        At the end we preferred to travel all night,
        Sleeping in snatches,
        With the voices singing in our ears, saying
        That this was all folly.

        Then at dawn we came down to a temperate valley,
        Wet, below the snow line, smelling of vegetation;
        With a running stream and a water-mill beating the darkness,
        And three trees on the low sky,
        And an old white horse galloped away in the meadow.
        Then we came to a tavern with vine-leaves over the lintel,
        Six hands at an open door dicing for pieces of silver,
        And feet kicking the empty wine-skins.
        But there was no information, and so we continued
        And arrived at evening, not a moment too soon
        Finding the place; it was (you may say) satisfactory.

267

All this was a long time ago, I remember,
And I would do it again, but set down
This set down
This: were we led all that way for
Birth or Death? There was a Birth, certainly,
We had evidence and no doubt. I had seen birth and death,
But had thought they were different; this Birth was
Hard and bitter agony for us, like Death, our death.
We returned to our places, these Kingdoms,
But no longer at ease here, in the old dispensation,
With an alien people clutching their gods.
I should be glad of another death.

ORWELL: We've dealt with winter and the snow, and with the Nativity of Christ. We still haven't dealt with Christmas as it now is—the public holiday, the turkeys and plum puddings, Santa Claus and the reindeer, the Christmas parties and all the rest of it.

EMPSON: There's not so much about it in our literature, till the Victorian stress on it, and that seems to have come in from Northern Europe and America. Dickens is very good on it, especially the PICKWICK PAPERS, but they're too long to quote.[16]

READ: And perhaps they are hardly appropriate for a wartime Xmas. There's another poem of Robert Bridges which seems to me to give the feeling of the festival as it was celebrated this year, when after a long interval we heard the church bells again.[17]

ORWELL: Yes, that's a good idea. Perhaps Empson will read it for us. We'll have the poem, and then straight after it another carol to end up with. We'll have IN DULCE JUBILO, or as much of it as we've got time for.

[EMPSON:]   CHRISTMAS EVE 1913 by Robert Bridges.

A frosty Christmas Eve
    When the stars were shining
Fared I forth alone
    where westward falls the hill,
And from many a village
    in the water'd valley
Distant music reach'd me
    peals of bells aringing;
The constellated sounds
    ran sprinkling on earth's floor
As the dark vault above
    with stars was spangled o'er.

Then sped my thoughts to keep
    that first Christmas of all
When the shepherds watching
    by their folds ere the dawn
Heard music in the fields
    and marvelling could not tell
Whether it were angels
    or the bright stars singing.

Now blessed be the tow'rs
　　that crown England so fair
That stand up strong in prayer
　　unto God for our souls:
Blessed be their founders
　　(said I) an' our country folk
Who are ringing for Christ
　　in the belfries tonight
With arms lifted to clutch
　　the rattling ropes that race
Into the dark above
　　and the mad romping din.

But to me heard afar
　　it was starry music
Angels' song, comforting
　　as the comfort of Christ
When he spake tenderly
　　to his sorrowful flock:
The old words came to me
　　by the riches of time
Mellow'd and transfigured
　　as I stood on the hill
Heark'ning in the aspect
　　of th' eternal silence.

RECORD: IN DULCI JUBILO. HMV. C. 2070.

[*Royal Choral Society, unaccompanied, conducted by Dr. Malcolm Sargent*]

ANNOUNCER:　That is the end of the sixth number of VOICE, our monthly radio magazine. Those taking part were Herbert Read, William Empson, George Orwell, Venu Chitale and Christopher Pemberton. Owing to the rearrangement of our schedule, the next number of VOICE will not appear until March 19th 1943, after which it will appear every four weeks as before.[18]

The first reading is that of the amended text as printed; the second gives the reading of the original typescript and details of uncertainties.

1. order] point
2. The mistletoe hung] and the mistletoe which is still hung
   Originally the sentence started 'For that with. . . .' These words and a typed "and" were not crossed out.
3. was] also
4. savages; its° an evergreen in winter. That's] savages who painted their bodies blue with woad. It's
   In the margin: 'After lengthening days' (crossed through); 'its° an evergreen' is preceded by 'because,' which is also crossed through.
5. feasting: this comes . . . get longer] feasting.
   'following' is written, but crossed through, before 'longer.'
6. In India . . . after birth] *handwritten addition*
7. difficulty in finding much . . . never praised] great difficulty in finding anything about snow in English literature. It's hardly ever mentioned
8. READ] SOMEONE
9. birth of Christ . . . commemorates] Nativity of Christ, *but not crossed out*
   This reading is awkward. The handwritten alteration (by Read?) evidently first read 'festival

269

celebrates' but the last letter of 'festival' and the first six of 'celebrates' are crossed through; then (in Orwell's hand?) is written 'properly commemorates,' with an arrow to that last word but with 'commemorates' crossed through.

10. Let's start . . . that time] Let's have another carol to bring it in with
11. READ] SOMEONE
12. not one of . . . the full story] the version that is given in the Bible doesn't quite agree with the tradition
13. It looks as if it had been intended to cut the last two verses, but the marginal marking has been crossed out. The typescript runs the first two verses together.
14. Orwell omitted stanzas 2, 3, 7, 9, 10, 13–18, 20 and 21; stanza 23 (the tenth printed here) was crossed out. Elipses have been added to indicate cuts. Orwell did not underline for italicisation (as customary in seventeenth-century texts), perhaps fearing that would be a distraction in reading; his practice has been followed here. One or two typographical errors have been silently corrected and linear indention supplied.
15. London Transcription Service; therefore a BBC recording, not for commercial release.
16. There's not so much . . . too long to quote] There's curiously little about it in our literature, although it's so much a part of our lives. There's Dickens's CHRISTMAS CAROL, but that's been done to death. The Christmas chapters in the PICKWICK PAPERS are better, but they're too long to quote
17. READ: And perhaps . . . the church bells again] SOMEONE: There's another poem by Robert Bridges, CHRISTMAS EVE. I think that gives you the feeling of a modern Christmas.
   In wartime, the ringing of church bells was to be a sign that a German invasion was imminent. By Christmas 1942 the danger had receded sufficiently to permit the ringing of bells for Christmas. See *1658*.
18. In the event, the series was not continued.

1779. To E. C. Bowyer

29 December 1942   07/ES/EB

On 22 December, E. C. Bowyer wrote to Orwell agreeing to do the series of talks proposed by Orwell on 17 December; see *1748*. Orwell annotated Bowyer's letter:

Please let him have a card giving the date (or have we done so already?)

E. A. B

Winifred Bedwell obliged with this note:

Dear Mr. Bowyer
Thank you very much for your letter of the 22nd and I am very glad to hear that you are able to do the broadcasts for us.
   The date of the first broadcast is Friday, 22nd January 1943 at 12.45 p.m. British Summer Time.

Yours sincerely
[Initialled] W B
For George Orwell
Talks Producer
Indian Section

1780. To F. R. Daruvala

29 December 1942   Handwritten draft and typed versions
07/ES/EB/WMB

On 4 December, Cadet Daruvala had sent Orwell a Gujarati script he had written. He wrote again on 26 December giving his new address and asking if the script had been approved. Orwell wrote out this reply on the back of Daruvala's letter of the 24th, which Winifred Bedwell then typed.

Dear Mr. Daruvala
I am sorry to say I cannot commission any Gujerati° translations. I handed the specimen translation you did to our Gujerati° translator, who did not consider it up to standard. You will understand that I have to abide by his decision.

Thank you very much for the Christmas card you sent me. It was kind of you to think of me.

Yours sincerely
[Initialled] W B
For Eric Blair
Talks Producer
Indian Section

1781. To John Beavan

30 December 1942   07/ES/EB/WMB

Dear Beavan[1]
You will remember my ringing you up last week and suggesting the importance of giving prominence not only to the persecution of the Jews[2] but to any proposed relief scheme in order to forestal° the Axis claims that this is some sort of Jewish invasion of Palestine and other countries. I enclose an extract from the Japanese radio of three days ago aimed at India.[3] This is the sort of thing that will be said and it seems to me important to forestal° it, especially if the British Government really intends any relief measures.

Yours sincerely
[Initialled] G. O.
George Orwell
Talks Producer
Indian Section

1. John Cowburn Beavan (1910–1994; Life Peer, 1970, as Lord Ardwick of Barnes), a journalist, joined the London staff of the *Manchester Evening News* in 1933 and was its news editor in Manchester in 1936. He subsequently worked for the London *Evening Standard*, 1940; *The Observer*, 1942, and again the *Manchester Evening News*, from 1943; was editor of the *Daily Herald*, 1960–62, and political adviser to the *Daily Mirror* group 1962–76. As editor of the *Manchester Evening News* he commissioned Orwell to write for that newspaper from December 1943. He was a Trustee of the Orwell Archive from its setting up in 1960 until his death.

2. 'Jews' is underlined in ink, perhaps by Orwell when he initialled the carbon copy.
3. This broadcast argued that 'Britain should refuse to countenance the shipping of more Jews to Palestine.' It said the British government, having promised the Arabs a state of their own when wanting Arab help against the Turks in World War I, was now prepared to support the admission of 50,000 Jewish refugees into Palestine. Britain, the broadcast maintained, 'will be playing with fire if she makes the Arabs' lot any harder.' West: *Broadcasts* gives the text, 293.

1782. To Edmund Blunden

30 December 1942   07/ES/EB

Dear Blunden
I suppose it is O.K. for Friday and George Sampson will be here in good time to do his Milton talk. As to the reading afterwards, I thought the best thing to have would be a passage from Lycidas, taking about five minutes, and the intervening music will be chosen by Menon, as before. I don't know whether Professor Sampson wants to read Lycidas himself. If he specially wants to do so, well and good, but we often find it better to have a change of voice, and we have a young man here who would do the reading very nicely.

You will be glad to hear that the Shakespeare talk went off very well. I couldn't listen to all of it as I was on the air most part° of the time, but others listened and said it was very good. I believe the LISTENER is going to print this series of talks en bloc,[1] but we, unfortunately, don't get any rake-off[2] from them.

I have passed the business about your fees on to the right quarter and I think it will be all right. Will let you know on Friday.

Yours sincerely
[Initialled] Geo. O.
George Orwell
Talks Producer
Indian Section

1. en bloc] or part, *Orwell's handwritten amendment*
2. rake-off] record, *Orwell's handwritten amendment*. The nature of these two errors suggests that this letter was dictated by Orwell and not, as sometimes, typed from a version he had written out.

1783. To T. S. Eliot

30 December 1942   07/ES/EB/WMB

Dear Eliot
Herewith copy of the photograph of which I spoke to you.[1]

I wonder if you could come to my place for dinner on Tuesday, the 12th January. The address is 10A Mortimer Crescent, N.W.6. You can get there on the 53 bus, stopping at Alexandra Road or from Kilburn Park tube station.

It would be much better if you stayed the night and we can make you quite comfortable.

Perhaps you could let me know about this.

Yours sincerely
[Initialled] G. O.
George Orwell
Talks Producer
Indian Section

1. See Orwell's letter to Eliot, 21 November 1942 (*1673*). Eliot acknowledged this on 1 January 1943 and, because he thought the picture 'a very good one,' asked for another print. He found he had double-booked 12 January and asked if they could arrange a later date for dinner.

1784. To Desmond Hawkins

30 December 1942   O7/ES/EB

Dear Hawkins

I am sorry to say that as I suggested might be the case there's being trouble about the speeches on pages 7. and 8. of your script.[1] The ones objected to are (a) Shopkeeper, who describes himself as behaving like shopkeepers everywhere, (b) the Jolly Chap who does ditto, and (c) the Oppressed, who ask for death when it is thought better propaganda that they should ask for revenge.

I don't think one can alter those passages in the sense required, while keeping those characters. It might be possible to simply cut out that passage, but we don't want to cut the feature if we can help it because it is on the short side already. However, Douglas Cleverdon wishes to produce it and he, no doubt, will know how to fill up with music and so forth. I understand you are seeing him on Friday next, so we might leave the matter open until then.

Yours sincerely,
[Signed] Geo. Orwell
George Orwell
(Talks Producer)

1. Perhaps his 'Anniversary of the Month' programme.

1785. To Bahadur Singh

30 December 1942   07/ES/EB/WMB

Dear Bahadur Singh

Would you like to do a short broadcast (8 minutes) for us on Wednesday next, the 6th January.[1] We have a series called IN THE PUBLIC EYE, dealing with the leading personality of the week. I can't tell you yet whom we shall choose for next week as we don't definitely make the selection till the Monday. When suitable, we sometimes take the material from the PROFILES column in the OBSERVER.

If you can't do it next week you might like to do some subsequent week—but please let me know by return.

Yours sincerely
[Signed] Eric Blair
Eric Blair
Talks Producer
Indian Section

1. The date should be 13 January; see *1798*.

1786. To Stevie Smith

30 December 1942   07/ES/EB/WMB

Dear Stevie

I'm sorry it fell through about the special Christmas number.[1] In the end we made up a programme almost entirely of carols, which was easy to arrange, as of course all those are recorded. We have had to alter the schedule so that the next number is not until March 19th, and I think we are going to have an animal number, that is a number dealing with poetry and other literature about animals. I will let you know, however, with more certainty about this later on.

Yours
[Initialled] G. O.
George Orwell
Talks Producer
Indian Section

1. See *1696*.

1787. To Arthur Wynn, Music Bookings Manager

30 December 1942   Original   EB/WMB

INTERLUDE IN 1115 to 1145 GMT period, Fridays (Red Network)

As from the 25th December, we are doing a short interlude, 6 or 7 minutes between the reading of script on the chosen author and an extract from one of the works of the author, in our series CALLING ALL STUDENTS, which is broadcast every Friday at 1115 to 1145 GMT. This interlude is filled with music, selected by Mr. Narayana Menon, which will appeal to Indian listeners. There will be six talks in all, and the dates are given above.° Mr. Menon of course is choosing music which he feels will approximate to the idea of the work of the author that is given.

We shall be glad, therefore, if you will issue a contract for Mr. Narayana Menon, 151 Sussex Gardens, London, W.2., for these six dates, commencing from 25th December and continuing for the 1st, 8th, 15th, 22nd and 29th January. A fee of half-a-guinea each time is suggested.

(For Eric Blair)
[Signed] M Blackburn

1788. Memorandum to L. F. Rushbrook Williams (E.S.D.)

[31 December 1942?]   Original   EB/WMB

This memorandum is not dated and its position here is conjectural. West: *Broadcasts* places it between two letters dated 27 March 1942 (184), but gives no explanation for this. HMS *Repulse* was sunk off Malaya, some 150 miles north of Singapore (not *at* Singapore) on 10 December 1941, with the loss of 513 men. That suggests a broadcast a little after that date. However, this memorandum was typed by Winifred Bedwell, who did not become Orwell's secretary until almost a year after the loss of *Repulse,* and the address from which the memorandum was sent, 200 Oxford Street, was not used by Orwell until June 1942. Sir James Grigg's clumsy error in confusing *Renown* for *Repulse* suggests that the event—devastating at the time, for HMS *Prince of Wales* was also lost— was not fresh in his mind. On 30 December 1942, Grigg appeared on his wife's programme, 'Women Generally Speaking,' 109, and, described as 'Finance Member of the Government of India from 1934 to 1939, now Secretary of State for War,' and introduced by his wife, gave a live talk, 'The British Army in 1942.' It looks as if he strayed into discussing the Royal Navy as well.

Lady Grigg's Broadcasts (Women Generally Speaking)

I wonder if it would be possible for us to get Lady Grigg's broadcasts somewhat more under our own control, as we have to bear the responsibility for them.

This morning everything went wrong that could have gone wrong. The talk had not been properly timed and was far too long. When I pointed out that it was too long and had better be cut I was told this had been timed to 12½ minutes. I then said that I would signal if it were going to over-run and had to be cut. After about two pages I saw that it must over-run considerably and prepared a cut and went in with this to Lady Grigg. She offered it to Sir James who refused to take it and cut it himself in transit, with the result that Lady Grigg's closing announcement was cut out and there was a lot of rustling and whispering. In addition, Sir James referred to the sinking of H.M.S. "RENOWN" (instead of the REPULSE) at Singapore. This was in his own script and it had been copied from that into the censored script. He read from his own however.

I don't, in most cases, see Lady Grigg's scripts before transmission, as Tuesday is supposed to be my day off, and they are not usually in before then; I think it would be better if it were[1] made a rule that Lady Grigg's scripts were always in not later than Monday, and also that the Talks Producer could have some control over the way they're put on.

We had trouble only a week or two ago as can be seen from the attached memo. On another occasion, when Miss Ellen Wilkinson[2] was broadcasting she did not follow her script at all but almost composed a fresh talk on the spot. I know, of course, that eminent speakers have to be given more latitude but it is difficult for us to bear the responsibility when the speaker is practically not under our control.

[Signed] Eric Blair
(Eric Blair)

1. The text as typed has 'I' for 'it were,' but Orwell made this tactful amendment in ink.
2. For Ellen Cicely Wilkinson, Labour M.P. for Jarrow; see *422, n. 3* and *1471, n. 2.*

1789. To Bahadur Singh

31 December 1942

OUR LETTER 30th DECEMBER STOP SORRY WOULD LIKE YOU TO BROADCAST WEDNESDAY 11th[1] JANUARY AND NOT 6th. BLAIR

1. Singh replied on 1 January 1943, pointing out that Wednesday 11th should be Wednesday 13th. The letter is annotated 'Yes—my mistake WB' (Winifred Bedwell, Orwell's secretary).

1790. BBC Talks Booking Form, 31.12.42

E. C. Bowyer: Modern Aircraft; 'Mr Bowyer is doing six $13\frac{1}{2}$ mins. talks and writing his own scripts'; broadcast 22 and 29.1.43 and 5, 12, 19, and 26.2.43; fee £8.8s each talk. Signed: M Blackburn for I.P.O.

1943

1791. Review of *The Development of William Butler Yeats* by
V. K. Narayana Menon

Horizon, January 1943

This review was reprinted in Orwell's *Critical Essays* (1946) with the title 'W. B.
Yeats.' It is reproduced here from the second impression (May 1946) of that
book. Despite the letters received, and Orwell's answers, that followed the
review's publication, he made no verbal changes for the book. Although *Critical
Essays* has 'ready made' as one word, omits the comma after 'Van Dyck faces,'
and spells 'civilisation' with a 'z,' these changes are probably not Orwell's and
are not reproduced here, the forms used in *Horizon* being retained.

One thing that Marxist criticism has not succeeded in doing is to trace the
connection between 'tendency' and literary style. The subject-matter and
imagery of a book can be explained in sociological terms, but its texture
seemingly cannot. Yet some such connection there must be. One knows, for
instance, that a Socialist would not write like Chesterton or a Tory
imperialist like Bernard Shaw, though *how* one knows is not easy to say. In
the case of Yeats, there must be some kind of connection between his
wayward, even tortured style of writing and his rather sinister vision of life.
Mr. Menon is chiefly concerned with the esoteric philosophy underlying
Yeats's work, but the quotations which are scattered all through his
interesting book serve to remind one how artifical Yeats's manner of writing
was. As a rule, this artificiality is accepted as Irishism, or Yeats is even
credited with simplicity because he uses short words, but in fact one seldom
comes on six consecutive lines of his verse in which there is not an archaism or
an affected turn of speech. To take the nearest example:

> Grant me an old man's Frenzy,
> My self must I remake
> Till I am Timon and Lear
> Or that William Blake
> Who beat upon the wall
> Till Truth obeyed his call.[1]

The unnecessary 'that' imports a feeling of affectation, and the same tendency
is present in all but Yeats's best passages. One is seldom long away from a
suspicion of 'quaintness', something that links up not only with the 'nineties,
the Ivory Tower and the 'calf covers of pissed-on green', but also with
Rackham's drawings, Liberty art-fabrics and the *Peter Pan* never-never land,
of which, after all, *The Happy Townland* is merely a more appetising

example. This does not matter, because, on the whole, Yeats gets away with it, and if his straining after effect is often irritating it can also produce phrases ('the chill, footless years', 'the mackerel-crowded seas') which suddenly overwhelm one like a girl's face seen across a room. He is an exception to the rule that poets do not use poetical language:

> How many centuries spent
> The sedentary soul
> In toils of measurement
> Beyond eagle or mole,
> Beyond hearing or seeing,
> Or Archimedes' guess,
> To raise into being
> That loveliness?[2]

Here he does not flinch from a squashy vulgar word like 'loveliness', and after all it does not seriously spoil this wonderful passage. But the same tendencies, together with a sort of raggedness which is no doubt intentional, weaken his epigrams and polemical poems. For instance (I am quoting from memory), the epigram against the critics who damned *The Playboy of the Western World*:

> Once when midnight smote the air
> Eunuchs ran through Hell and met
> On every crowded street to stare,
> Upon great Juan riding by;
> Even like these to rail and sweat,
> Staring upon his sinewy thigh.[3]

The power which Yeats has within himself gives him the analogy ready made and produces the tremendous scorn of the last line, but even in this short poem there are six or seven unnecessary words. It would probably have been deadlier if it had been neater.

Mr. Menon's book is incidentally a short biography of Yeats, but he is above all interested in Yeats's philosophical 'system', which in his opinion supplies the subject-matter of more of Yeats's poems than is generally recognized. This system is set forth fragmentarily in various places, and at full length in *A Vision*, a privately printed book which I have never read but which Mr. Menon quotes from extensively. Yeats gave conflicting accounts of its origin, and Mr. Menon hints pretty broadly that the 'documents' on which it was ostensibly founded were imaginary. Yeats's philosophical system, says Mr. Menon, 'was at the back of his intellectual life almost from the beginning. His poetry is full of it. Without it his later poetry becomes almost completely unintelligible.' As soon as we begin to read about the so-called system we are in the middle of a hocus-pocus of Great Wheels, gyres, cycles of the moon, reincarnation, disembodied spirits, astrology, and what-not. Yeats hedges as to the literalness with which he believed in all this, but he certainly dabbled in spiritualism and astrology and in earlier life had made experiments in alchemy. Although almost buried under explanations, very difficult to understand, about the phases of the moon, the central idea of his philosophical system seems to be our old friend, the cyclical universe, in which everything happens over and over again. One has not, perhaps, the right to laugh at Yeats for his mystical beliefs—for I believe it could be shown that *some* degree of belief in magic is almost universal—but neither ought one to write such things off as mere unimportant eccentricities. It is Mr. Menon's perception of this that gives his book its deepest interest. 'In the first flush of admiration and enthusiasm,' he says, 'most people dismissed the fantastical philosophy as the price we have to pay for a great and curious intellect. One did not quite realize where he was heading. And those who did, like Pound and perhaps Eliot, approved the stand that he finally took. The first reaction to this did not come, as one might have expected, from the politically minded young English poets. They were puzzled because a less rigid or artificial system than that of *A Vision* might not have produced the great poetry of Yeats's last days.' It might not, and yet Yeats's philosophy has some very sinister implications, as Mr. Menon points out.

Translated into political terms, Yeats's tendency is Fascist. Throughout most of his life, and long before Fascism was ever heard of, he had had the outlook of those who reach Fascism by the aristocratic route. He is a great hater of democracy, of the modern world, science, machinery, the concept of progress—above all, of the idea of human equality. Much of the imagery of his work is feudal, and it is clear that he was not altogether free from ordinary snobbishness. Later these tendencies took clearer shape and led him to 'the exultant acceptance of authoritarianism as the only solution. Even violence and tyranny are not necessarily evil because the people, knowing not evil and good, would become perfectly acquiescent to tyranny. . . . Everything must come from the top. Nothing can come from the masses.' Not much interested in politics, and no doubt disgusted by his brief incursions into public life, Yeats nevertheless makes political pronouncements. He is too big a man to share the illusions of Liberalism, and as early as 1920 he foretells in a justly famous passage ('The Second Coming') the kind of world that we have actually moved into. But he appears to welcome the coming age, which is to be 'hierarchical, masculine, harsh, surgical', and he is influenced both by Ezra Pound and by various Italian Fascist writers. He describes the new civilization which he hopes and believes will arrive: 'an aristocratic civilisa-tion in its most completed form, every detail of life hierarchical, every great man's door crowded at dawn by petitioners, great wealth everywhere in a few men's hands, all dependent upon a few, up to the Emperor himself, who is a God dependent on a greater God, and everywhere, in Court, in the family, an inequality made law.' The innocence of this statement is as interesting as its snobbishness. To begin with, in a single phrase, 'great wealth in a few men's hands', Yeats lays bare the central reality of Fascism, which the whole of its propaganda is designed to cover up. The merely political Fascist claims always to be fighting for justice; Yeats, the poet, sees at a glance that Fascism means injustice, and acclaims it for that very reason. But at the same time he fails to see that the new authoritarian civilisation, if it arrives, will not be aristocratic, or what he means by aristocratic. It will not be ruled by noblemen with Van Dyck faces, but by anonymous millionaires, shiny-bottomed bureaucrats and murdering gangsters. Others who have made the same mistake have afterwards changed their views, and one ought not to assume that Yeats, if he had lived longer, would necessarily have followed his friend Pound, even in sympathy. But the tendency of the passage I have quoted above is obvious, and its complete throwing overboard of whatever good the past two thousand years have achieved is a disquieting symptom.

How do Yeats's political ideas link up with his leaning towards occultism? It is not clear at first glance why hatred of democracy and a tendency to believe in crystal-gazing should go together. Mr. Menon only discusses this rather shortly, but it is possible to make two guesses. To begin with, the theory that civilisation moves in recurring cycles is one way out for people who hate the concept of human equality. If it is true that 'all this', or something like it, 'has happened before', then science and the modern world are debunked at one stroke and progress becomes for ever impossible. It does not much matter if the lower orders are getting above themselves, for, after all, we shall soon be returning to an age of tyranny. Yeats is by no means alone in this outlook. If the universe is moving round on a wheel, the future must be foreseeable, perhaps even in some detail. It is merely a question of discovering the laws of its motion, as the early astronomers discovered the solar year. Believe that, and it becomes difficult not to believe in astrology or some similar system. A year before the war, examining a copy of *Gringoire*, the French Fascist weekly, much read by army officers, I found in it no less than thirty-eight advertisements of clairvoyants. Secondly, the very concept of occultism carries with it the idea that knowledge must be a secret thing, limited to a small circle of initiates. But the same idea is integral to Fascism. Those who dread the prospect of universal suffrage, popular education, freedom of thought, emancipation of women, will start off with a predilection towards secret cults. There is another link between Fascism and magic in the profound hostility of both to the Christian ethical code.

No doubt Yeats wavered in his beliefs and held at different times many different opinions, some enlightened, some not. Mr. Menon repeats for him Eliot's claim that he had the longest period of development of any poet who has ever lived. But there is one thing that seems constant, at least in all of his work that I can remember, and that is his hatred of modern Western civilisation and desire to return to the Bronze Age, or perhaps to the Middle Ages. Like all such thinkers, he tends to write in praise of ignorance. The Fool in his remarkable play, *The Hour-Glass*, is a Chestertonian figure, 'God's fool', the 'natural born innocent', who is always wiser than the wise man. The philosopher in the play dies on the knowledge that all his lifetime of thought has been wasted (I am quoting from memory again):

> The stream of the world has changed its course,
> And with the stream my thoughts have run
> Into some cloudy, thunderous spring
> That is its mountain-source:
> Ay, to a frenzy of the mind,

> That all that we have done's undone,
> Our speculation but as the wind.[4]

Beautiful words, but by implication profoundly obscurantist and reaction-ary; for if it is really true that a village idiot, as such, is wiser than a philosopher, then it would be better if the alphabet had never been invented. Of course, all praise of the past is partly sentimental, because we do not live in the past. The poor do not praise poverty. Before you can despise the machine, the machine must set you free from brute labour. But that is not to say that Yeats's yearning for a more primitive and more hierarchical age was not sincere. How much of all this is traceable to mere snobbishness, product of Yeats's own position as an impoverished offshoot of the aristocracy, is a different question. And the connection between his obscurantist opinions and his tendency towards 'quaintness' of language remains to be worked out; Mr. Menon hardly touches upon it.

This is a very short book and I would greatly like to see Mr. Menon go ahead and write another book on Yeats, starting where this one leaves off.[5] 'If the greatest poet of our times is exultantly ringing in an era of Fascism, it seems a somewhat disturbing symptom', he says on the last page, and leaves it at that. It *is* a disturbing symptom, because it is not an isolated one. By and large the best writers of our time have been reactionary in tendency, and though Fascism does not offer any real return to the past, those who yearn for the past will accept Fascism sooner than its probable alternatives. But there are other lines of approach, as we have seen during the past two or three years. The relationship between Fascism and the literary intelligentsia badly needs investigating, and Yeats might well be the starting-point. He is best studied by someone like Mr. Menon, who can approach a poet primarily as a poet, but who also knows that a writer's political and religious beliefs are not excrescences to be laughed away, but something that will leave their mark even on the smallest detail of his work.

Considerable comment and correspondence followed this review, not in *Horizon* but in *The Times Literary Supplement*. On 20 February 1943, the column 'Menander's Mirror,' under the sub-head 'Poetry and Prejudice,' discussed, first, Louis Aragon's *Le Crève Coeur* (which had prefaces by d'André Labarthe and Cyril Connolly), and then commented on Orwell's review of Yeats. The column was published anonymously, but the author has been identified as the novelist Charles Morgan (1894–1958) by Alan Hollinghurst, deputy editor of the *TLS*, in a private communication of 12 January 1990. The relevant portions of Morgan's column are:

. . . Mr. Orwell is too perceptive a critic not to admire Yeats's poetry and too honest—and, one had always believed, too liberal—a man to wish his criticism to be distorted by politics. When he writes calmly he writes well, but he can be strangely diverted. One feels that, in him, politics is not so much a vice as an aberration, an irresistible itch that he cannot leave alone. It is astonishing that it should now disturb him in speaking of Yeats, of all men. That, in some quarters, political conformity is demanded of poets has long been known, and not conformity of spirit alone but the wearing of a linguistic badge, the use of a particular jargon, a prescribed imagery of the machine-shop, even the avoidance of particular words; but to this rule Yeats was always an exception. Why? Had the aristocracy of his temperament passed unobserved? Was anyone so deluded as to suppose him to be a proletarian? Of course not. Why, then? For the good reason, one had always supposed, for the best and sanest of all reasons—that, whatever his political inclination, his poetry stood upon its unpolitical merits. However that may have been, he was in fact invited to the party and no one presumed to tell him what language he should use. This, without doubt, is, for Mr. Orwell himself, in his calmer moments, the right critical approach to Yeats, and there are many passages in his present essay which prove him to be, in this sense, wise and liberal. But now and then the political itch overcomes him. His first sentence—"One thing that Marxist criticism has not succeeded in doing is to trace the connexion between 'tendency' and literary style"—is a warning. But this, it may be said, is only a theoretical prelude by which no harm is done so long as the writer does not, in practice, allow it to distort his view of Yeats. Very well. Continue. "Yeats's philosophy," Mr. Orwell says, "has some very sinister implications." And again: "Translated into political terms, Yeats's tendency is Fascist . . . he had the outlook of those who reach Fascism by the aristocratic route:" Then, in allowing to poor Yeats one political virtue, Mr. Orwell is betrayed into the following cry of self-revelation: "He is too big a man to share the illusions of Liberalism." . . .

Criticism of Yeats's verse is tormented by the same itch, though here Mr. Orwell is to be seen in a struggle not to be irritated into injustice, not to be unkind, not to forget that, after all, this sinister Fascist was, during his life, a guest at the party. Although Yeats did not adopt the prescribed jargon, a certain licence is to be allowed him. For this once, another key is to be fitted into the exclusive lock. "He is an exception to the rule," we are told, "that poets do not use poetical language." The rule? Who made and who obeys it? But Mr Orwell applies it gently. He quotes Yeats:—

> How many centuries spent
> The sedentary soul
> In toils of measurement
> Beyond eagle or mole,
> Beyond hearing or seeing,
> Or Archimedes' guess
> To raise into being
> That loveliness?

With good reason, Mr. Orwell admires these verses, but, while he says so, the Jargon Rule must be asserted lest he be accused of not knowing a blackleg when he sees one. "Here," he points out, "he does not flinch from a squashy vulgar word like 'loveliness,'" but politely adds: "and after all it does not seriously spoil this wonderful passage." The ghost of Yeats will bow its acknowledgment of this generous permission to use the English tongue.

Mr. Orwell's approach to Yeats is of interest because it shows how easily criticism which begins in politics can arrive by almost imperceptible degrees at absurdity. To discuss a poet's use of words is one of the duties of criticism; dislike of the word "loveliness" may seem to us an error of taste in the critic but is not a crime. But it is evidence of false critical principle when it arises from the application of an arbitrary rule against the use of "poetical words"—a rule, that is to say, which, for the sake of establishing the exclusive abracadabra of a sect, seeks a wholesale impoverishment of the language. It is legitimate to suggest that Yeats uses "loveliness" too often, or that he might have used a better word in this instance, or that he has placed it wrongly or laid a false emphasis upon it—a critic, if he is prepared to defend his position, may say any of these things without making himself ridiculous. But to attack the word itself as "squashy and vulgar," to put it upon an expurgatorial index, is to reduce criticism to the level of fashion—the most obvious, though not the most evil, consequence of a political approach to art.

Political critics of poetry have a formula of self-justification; they say that politics implies an attitude towards life, a philosophy, and can no more be left out of account in judging poetry than the writer's religion; but this plea will not serve to justify the exclusion of much political criticism. In a fanatical Communist or Nazi, who says frankly that art is for him meaningless except as propaganda, this heresy-hunting is comprehensible, but in a critic who believes that art has a value independent of politics it is a negation of all his values. And it is to be fought against even by men to whom art is not a primary interest, for, as has been shown in France, politics that becomes an obsession and embitters relationships which are not in themselves political can disintegrate society. . . .

Orwell's reply was published on 6 March 1943:

Sir,—I am sorry to have annoyed your reviewer by pointing out that W. B. Yeats had Fascist tendencies, but I should be glad if you would allow me to answer him, because he has misrepresented what I said besides attacking me for several incompatible reasons.

In the first place he accuses me of a "political itch" and appears to feel that there was something vulgar, not to say sacrilegious, in even noticing that Yeats had political tendencies. In the article he refers to I was criticizing a book which dealt quite largely with Yeats's Fascist leanings, but in any case it will not do to claim, as your reviewer seems to do, that poetry exists in a sort of water-tight or rather thought-tight world of its own. A writer's political and religious beliefs will always colour his aesthetic achievements, and to trace the connexion is one necessary function of criticism. A little later than this your reviewer drops his thesis that politics are irrelevant to poetry and defends Yeats against the charge of being a Fascist. He repeats my statement that "Yeats's philosophy has some very sinister implications" as though it were a sort of wicked blasphemy, and entirely omits mention of the quotations with which I backed it up. But apart from these quotations, the facts are notorious. Did not Yeats write a "marching song" for O'Duffy's Blueshirts? Your reviewer then accuses me of applying something called the "Jargon Rule" and seems to suggest that I only admire writers who are politically "left." But I specifically said in my article, what I have been saying for years, that on the whole the best writers of our time have been reactionary in tendency: and I used Yeats himself as an instance.

Finally, your reviewer forgets all about my "political itch" and suddenly goes for me because after all I have aesthetic preferences. My particular offence is to dislike the word "loveliness," which leads to a whole paragraph in which I am charged with wishing to "impoverish the language" in order to "establish the exclusive abracadabra of a sect." May I suggest that the whole art of writing consists in preferring some words to others? It could be argued that no word is inherently ugly, but it is beyond question that certain words become vulgarized by association, and I object to a word like "loveliness" because in our own age it inevitably calls up a picture of pink sunsets, Dorothy Lamour, soft-centre chocolates, &c. If your reviewer is so attached to "loveliness" I wonder what he thinks of T. E. Brown's "lovesome"? I stand by my statement that on the whole poets do not use poetical language.

GEO. ORWELL.

Menander writes:—

Mr. Orwell generously gives me my case. What matters is not whether a marching-song was written "for O'Duffy's Blueshirts" or for the Tomsk Cycling Club, but whether it is a good song. . . . As for "loveliness." A critic may show why he considers a word to have been misused or misplaced, but to suggest that this word, and all "poetical" words, are now inadmissible is to exercise an insolent censorship. Mr. Orwell is entitled to believe that he knows better than Yeats but not to bowdlerize literature. He must not red-pencil the dictionary.

The following letters were published on 20 March 1943:

Sir,—I am afraid Mr. Orwell is a word-snob. He seems to think that a writer should be careful only to employ language that is considered good form among "the best people" of the literary world. "Do not use loveliness," he adjures us, "or people will take you for one of those dreadful creatures who like soft-centred chocolates." But a good writer is not afflicted by this lady-like squeamishness. Intent only on saying what he means as expressively as he can, he is prepared to use any word, ancient or modern, rare or popular, that will convey his meaning. He knows that a word used aptly and in its correct sense will always assume dignity, however much it may have been vulgarized by misuse. If this were not so, language would become progressively impoverished, as more people explored its capacities. As it is, I suppose that if poor Mr. Orwell wants to convey the meaning of loveliness, he has to search frantically about for some elegant periphrasis, like the French pedant who thought "chien" inadmissible in tragedy, and so was forced to say "de la fidélité respectable soutien." Words are the writer's servants, not his masters. "Lovesome" no doubt is unappetizing as used by T. E. Brown: but does Mr. Orwell object to Etherege's "wild, witty, lovesome, beautiful and young"?

Incidentally, the associations called up in Mr. Orwell's mind by the word "loveliness" cast a sinister light on the mental atmosphere in which he moves. No doubt there are persons to whom it "inevitably" suggests soft-centred chocolates, Miss Dorothy Lamour. But he may be surprised to learn that there are many others not so benightedly philistine. They might, I admit, call a sunset lovely. But Mr. Orwell is the first person I have come across so genteel as to think a sunset vulgar.

David Cecil[6]

Sir,—Why does Mr. Orwell say that in our age the word "loveliness" inevitably calls up a picture of pink sunsets, Dorothy Lamour, soft-centre chocolates, &c.? It may do to him, and also perhaps to that coterie of self-appointed and somewhat self-conscious arbitrators of literary worth of which some of us are becoming a little tired. But Mr. Sassoon certainly had none of Mr. Orwell's associations in mind when he wrote of "A Poplar and the Moon":—

> And I've no magic to express,
> The moment of that loveliness.

J. F. Head

Orwell responded in the next issue of *The Times Literary Supplement*, 27 March 1943, and Lord Alfred Douglas came to the defence of 'loveliness.'

Sir,—If being a word-snob means thinking that one ought to fight for decent English, then I am certainly a word-snob. But Lord David Cecil shows a more familiar kind of snobbery when he seeks to crush me by triumphantly pointing out that "lovesome" was used by Etherege. The reasoning, if any, appears to be that a word which is 300 years old must be all right. Age is no disinfectant, however, and to my ear the word "lovesome" sounds just as weak and silly in this context as it would in a modern one. Lord David Cecil also asserts that "a word used aptly and in its correct sense will always assume dignity," apparently claiming that there is no such thing as an inherently vulgar or ugly word. I could think of perhaps 500 examples, but since we started out with derivatives of "love," how about "love-nest"? I will pay him five shillings if he can produce a sentence—for a line of verse I will make it seven and sixpence—in which this word "assumes dignity." If he fails, I must be forgiven for thinking that there is a hole in his argument.

GEO. ORWELL.

Sir,—Having used the word "loveliness" in one of my sonnets, written in 1913,

> We clothed with bright and shining loveliness
> The soul of the belovèd; and anon
> We saw it gleam, red hate, behind her eyes,

I find myself interested in Mr. Orwell's attack on the word. It never occurred to me that any *soi-disant* appraiser of words would fail to recognize it as a beautiful word. Looking round for support I fall back on Shakespeare: In *Othello* (Act 2, Scene 1) Iago says "loveliness in favour." Although as far as I know Shakespeare only used the word once,[7] his authority is quite enough for me.

Alfred Douglas.

Correspondence continued in the issues of 10 and 17 April. Cecil responded to Orwell's challenge (see below) and Nora Monckton and Sydney Jeffery illustrated the use of 'love-nest' in 'Four Variations upon William Browne of Tavistock' by Sacheverell Sitwell and Hardy's 'The Discovery' respectively.

Sir,—I accept Mr. Orwell's challenge. I do not put forward my entries as examples of good writing; but I claim that in them "love-nest" is disinfected of its vulgar associations. Here is my prose sentence. "This lady's eyes were at once so tranquil, so radiant, that a poet once compared them, in his phantasie, to two love-nests or bowers of Cupid, whither the little god would betake himself to rest, when wearied with roving the world on his impish sport." My verse line is more modern; and can be imagined to be taken from a poem on The Nativity written in the Hopkins° manner.

"Oh but praise for the winter-white heaven-hallowed love-nest, dove-nest of Mary's son."

I cannot forbear from quoting, though quotations may not come under the conditions of the contest, two much more brilliant suggestions sent me by a friend.

AN EPITAPH

"Lo, here, a love-nest. Whereof is it made?
A pick, a shovel, and this cypress shade."

THE PHOENIX

The Phoenix of aromatic twigs erects a pyre, and having of her own ardours set it on fire, rises anew from its ashes; this pyre is called by the inhabitants of those parts her love-nest.

Yours truly,
David Cecil

On 22 April 1943, Cecil wrote Orwell a friendly letter. Evidently *The Times* had been asked to adjudicate Orwell's challenge and to decide whether the bet was payable. 'How like the Times to refuse to arbitrate! The fence is their home in everything,' wrote Cecil. He suggested, 'We had better call it quits. Anyway I don't know who could arbitrate on such a matter.' He concluded by saying he had noticed that Orwell was advertised as coming to speak at Oxford and asked him to look him up. On 23 April 1943, Orwell invited Cecil to give a talk to be broadcast to India by the BBC.

1. From 'An Acre of Grass.' Orwell capitalises 'frenzy' and makes 'Myself' two words in contrast to *The Variorum Edition of the Poems of W. B. Yeats*, edited by Peter Allt and Russell K. Alspach (New York 1957, 576). *W. B. Yeats. The Poems. A new edition*, edited by Richard J. Finneran (1983), has a full-point, not a comma, after 'frenzy.'
2. From the First Musician's opening speech of the play *The Only Jealousy of Emer*, Allt and Alspach, 788.
3. 'On those that hated *The Playboy of the Western World*, 1907.' The punctuation differs in Allt and Alspach, which has commas after 'Once' and 'air'; no comma after 'stare'; a colon after 'riding by'; and no comma after 'sweat.'
4. From the 1912 verse version of *The Hour Glass*. In *Responsibilities and Other Poems* (1916), there is no comma after 'cloudy'; 'mountain-source' is not hyphenated and is followed by a dash, not a colon; it is 'Aye, to some frenzy'; and, in the penultimate line, 'For all that.'
5. He did not write a longer book on Yeats; indeed, the British Library lists no other book by Narayana Menon.
6. Lord David Cecil (1902–1986; CH, 1949), scholar and author, was a Fellow of New College, Oxford, 1939–69; Goldsmiths' Professor of English Literature, Oxford, 1948–69. Among the books he had written by the time Orwell corresponded with him were *Sir Walter Scott* (1933), *Early Victorian Novelists* (1934), *Jane Austen* (1935), *The Young Melbourne* (1939), and *Hardy, The Novelist* (1943).
7. Shakespeare also has 'Unthrifty loveliness' at the start of Sonnet 4.

1792. News Commentary in English for Malaya, 14

1 January 1943

This was written and read by George Orwell. No script has been traced.

1793. News Review, 54

2 January 1943

No script has survived for this News Review but it is recorded in PasB as having been given by George Orwell. It was shorter than usual—6' 15". The time was filled with two recorded talks: 'Salute to Calcutta' by Sir Alec Aikman, Director of Andrew Mule & Co Ltd, 3' 9", and 'Salute to Calcutta' by Sir Alfred Watson, Editorial Director of Great Britain and the East, 3' 49". Total time: 13' 13".

1794. Bengali Newsletter, 25

2 January 1943

The English original was written by Orwell. No script has been traced. PasB implies a timing of 7' 47".

On 1 January a memorandum was sent to Miss E. W. D. Boughen, Talks Bookings, on behalf of the Indian Programme Organiser, explaining a change to be made in this broadcast:

Will you please amend Mr. S. K. Das Gupta's contract for tomorrow, 2nd January, 1943, for the Bengali Newsletter translation and reading. Instead of the usual 13-minute newsletter in Bengali, the 1430–1445 GMT period tomorrow will include a talk of approximately 6 minutes duration, given by Miss A. Sen Gupta, sympathising with the people in Calcutta and congratulating them on the brave way in which they have stood up to recent bombing. Mr Das Gupta's contribution will therefore be about half its usual length, i.e. approximately 6 minutes. This alteration applies only to tomorrow, 2nd January.

[Signed] M Blackburn
for Z. A. Bokhari

This arrangement had been planned as early as 28 December 1942, and the talks booking form for that date stipulates a fee of £3.3s instead of the regular £5.5s for this broadcast; see 1776. The news flash in the Newsletter in English when Orwell broadcast to India on 19 December may refer to the bombing of Calcutta, which took place for the first time on 20 December, although the time differential of 5½ hours is not quite sufficient to equate the dates.

1795. To R. R. Desai

2 January 1943   07/ES/EB

Dear Desai

I don't think I have any positive hints this week. Negatively we are still expected to keep off commenting on Admiral Darlan and his assassin. I should play up the Russian offensives,[1] provided this fits in to your general plan, but I would drop a hint to the effect that we cannot expect the Russian successes to continue equally spectacular.° My own line is that the Russians deliberately do limited offensives on separate parts of the Front to prevent the Germans from resting their troops during the winter.

There doesn't seem a lot of news from the Far East except that the Japanese shipping situation appears to be getting serious. There were two interesting articles in the News-Chronicle on Friday and Saturday, about conditions in Timor, which sounded reasonably authentic, and which you might find useful. This can, perhaps, be tied on to remarks about very similar German behaviour in Europe.

I merely make these suggestions tentatively and don't wish to force anything on to you.

Yours sincerely
[Initialled] E A B
Eric Blair
Talks Producer
Indian Section

1. Albert Gentry records in his diary for 29 December 1942 that news had reached the internees in Bangkok 'of a big Russian drive towards Rostov—said to be the biggest offensive of the war to date.'

1796. To Dwight Macdonald

3 January 1943   Typewritten

10a Mortimer Crescent   London   NW 6

Dear Macdonald,[1]

I send you for the first time a London Letter unsolicited, hoping you can use it. I did so because it is just possible—I am afraid only just possible—that I may get a job which would take me out of England for a while.[2] In case that happened I thought I would like to send you one last letter. It was a pity about my not being able to send you the additions to the last one, but the posts seem very variable nowadays. I haven't received the November–December PR, and nor has anybody else—not gone to the bottom of the Atlantic, I hope. I don't know what the position is about sending American periodicals here nowadays—I believe there is some quota business, but if it were possible for you to send more copies across you could certainly work up a circulation here. I have shown copies to various people who are very enthusiastic about it. There is no comparable review in England at present. You might let me know about this, and if it *is* possible to send more copies I think I could get together a list of subscribers.

An American publisher to whom you had kindly given my name wrote asking what books of mine had been published in the USA. I sent him some particulars, but I don't fancy it will come to anything because most of my books are now so completely out of print that I can't procure even one copy. They say 6 million books were destroyed in the big fire in 1940, and it completely wiped out at least 2 of mine.[3] Do you know if "New Directions" still exists? They were to print my essay on Henry Miller about a year and a half ago, and I believe did so, but I never had a copy. They sent me a cheque for it, but either the cheque was sunk on its way across or on its way back—I forget which, but the upshot was I never got paid. They are now trying to start something corresponding to New Directions in England. It is being run by Alex Comfort, the one who wrote to PR attacking me. I wrote them something for it. Did you know David Martin, a Canadian journalist, one-time Trotskyist? I rather think he said he knew you. He has just joined the RAF and is disliking it very much as everyone seems to at first.

Yours sincerely
Geo. Orwell

1. Dwight Macdonald (1906–1982), libertarian critic, pamphleteer, and scholar, was at this time an associate editor of *Partisan Review*. Later he founded *Politics*, of which he was editor, 1944–49, and to which Orwell contributed in November 1944 and September 1946; see Orwell's letter to Philip Rahv, 9 December 1943, *2390*.
2. The reason is not known. Much later, on 28 August 1943, Ivor Brown wrote to Orwell asking him if he would like to go to Algiers and Sicily for the *Observer* (*2255*, XV/208). It may be that Orwell was having discussions about going abroad as early as January 1943. The North African campaign was then going well and on 14 January 1943 Churchill and Roosevelt were to meet at Casablanca.
3. The type for *Homage to Catalonia* and *The Lion and the Unicorn* was destroyed in the air raids on Plymouth, 20 and 21 March 1940. Copies of *Inside the Whale* were also lost in an air raid.

1797. A Letter from England, 3 January 1943

Partisan Review, March–April 1943

Dear Editors,

It is just on two years since I wrote you my first letter. I wrote that one to the tune of AA guns, when we were in desperate straits and also on what appeared to be the edge of a rapid political advance. I begin this one at a time when the military situation is enormously better but the political outlook is blacker than it has ever been. My last letter but one, which I wrote in May of this year, you headed on your own initiative "The British Crisis." Well, that crisis is over and the forces of reaction have won hands down. Churchill is firm in the saddle again, Cripps has flung away his chances, no other leftwing leader or movement has appeared, and what is more important, it is hard to see how any revolutionary situation can recur till the Western end of the war is finished. We have had two opportunities, Dunkirk and Singapore, and we took neither. Before trying to predict the consequences of this, let me sketch out the main tendencies of this year as I see them.

Although the individual incidents don't fit in so neatly as they might, the rule has held good that the Government moves to the Right in moments of success and to the Left in moments of disaster. Collapse in the Far East— Cripps taken into the Government, Cripps' mission to India (this was probably so framed as to make sure that it should not be accepted, but was at least a big concession to popular feeling in this country). American victories in the Pacific, German failure to reach Alexandria—Indian Congress leaders arrested. British victory in Egypt, American invasion of North Africa—tie-up with Darlan and fresh bum-kissing for Franco. But over the whole year— indeed I have mentioned it in earlier letters—there has been visible a steady growth of blimpishness and a more conscious elbowing-out of the "reds" who were useful when morale needed pepping up but can now be dispensed with. The sudden sacking of Cripps merely symbolises a process which is occurring all over the place. Apart from the general rightward swing there have been two other developments which seem to me significant. One is the Second Front agitation, which reached its peak about July and thereafter took on a more definitely political colour than before. The North African campaign has temporarily silenced the clamour for a second front, but in the preceding months the controversy had not really been a military one but was a struggle between pro-Russians and anti-Russians. The other development is the growth of anti-American feeling, together with increased American control over British policy. The popular attitude towards America has I believe changed in the last few months, and I will return to this in a moment. Meanwhile the growing suspicion that we may all have underrated the strength of Capitalism and that the Right may, after all, be able to win the war off its own bat without resorting to any radical change, is very depressing to anyone who thinks. Cynicism about "after the war" is widespread, and the "we're all in it together" feeling of 1940 had faded away. The great political topic of the last few weeks has been the Beveridge report on Social Security. People seem to feel that this very moderate measure of reform is almost too good to be true. Except for the tiny interested minority, everyone is pro-Beveridge—including leftwing papers which a few years ago would have denounced such a scheme as semi-fascist—and at the same time no one believes that Beveridge's plan will actually be adopted. The usual opinion is that "they" (the Government) will make a pretence of accepting the Beveridge Report and then simply let it drop. The sense of impotence seems to be growing and is reflected in the lower and lower voting figures at by-elections. The last public demonstrations of any magnitude were those demanding a Second Front in the late summer. No demonstrations against the Darlan deal, though disapproval of it was almost general; nor over the India business, though, again, popular feeling is pro-Congress. The extreme Left still tends to be defeatist, except as regards the Russian front, and at each stage of the African campaign its press has clung almost desperately to a pessimistic interpretation of events. I think it is worth noting that the military experts favoured by the Left are all of them defeatist, and haven't suffered in reputation when their gloomy prophecies are falsified, any more than the cheery optimists favoured by the Right. However, this comes partly from jealousy and "opposition mentality": few people now really believe in a German victory. As to the real moral of the last three years—that the Right has more guts and ability than the Left—no one will face up to it.

Now a word about Anglo-American relations. In an earlier letter I tried to indicate very briefly the various currents of pro- and anti-American feeling in this country. Since then there has been an obvious growth of animosity against America, and this now extends to people who were previously pro-American, such as the literary intelligentsia. It is important to realise that for about fifteen years Britain has differed from most countries in having no nationalist intelligentsia worth speaking of. The average English intellectual is anti-British, and though chiefly worshipping the USSR has also tended to look on America as being not only more efficient and up-to-date than Britain, but more genuinely democratic. During the period 1935–9 the Left intelligentsia were taken in to a surprising extent by the "anti-fascist" antics in which so many American newspapers indulged. There was also a tendency to crouch culturally towards America and urge the superiority of the American language and even the American accent. This attitude is changing, however, as it begins to be grasped that the U. S. A. is potentially imperialist and politically a long way behind Britain. A favourite saying nowadays is that whereas Chamberlain appeased Germany, Churchill appeases America. It is, indeed, obvious enough that the British ruling class is being propped up by American arms, and may thereby get a new lease on life it would not otherwise have had. People now blame the U. S. A. for every reactionary move, more even than is justified. For instance, even quite well-informed people believed the Darlan job to have been "put over" by the Americans without our knowledge, though in fact the British Government must have been privy to it.

There is also widespread anti-American feeling among the working class, thanks to the presence of the American soldiers, and, I believe, very bitter anti-British feeling among the soldiers themselves. I have to speak here on second-hand evidence, because it is almost impossible to make contact with an American soldier. They are to be seen everywhere in the streets, but they don't go to the ordinary pubs, and even in the hotels and cocktail bars which they do frequent they keep by themselves and hardly answer if spoken to. American civilians who are in contact with them say that apart from the normal grumbling about the food, the climate, etc., they complain of being inhospitably treated and of having to pay for their amusements, and are disgusted by the dinginess, the old-fashionedness and the general poverty of life in England. Certainly it cannot be pleasant to be suddenly transferred from the comforts of American civilization to some smoky and rainy Midland town, battered by three years of war and short of every kind of consumption goods. I doubt, however, whether the average American would find England tolerable even in peacetime. The cultural differences are very deep, perhaps irreconcilable, and the Americans obviously have the profoundest contempt for England, rather like the contempt which the ordinary lowbrow Englishman has for the Latin races. All who are in contact with the American troops report them as saying that this is "their" war, they have done all the fighting in it, the British are no good at anything except running away, etc. The lack of contact between the Americans and the locals is startling. It is now more than eight months since the first American troops arrived, and I have not yet seen a British soldier and an American soldier together. Officers very occasionally, soldiers never. The early good impression which the American troops made on the women seems to have worn off. One never sees them except with tarts or near-tarts, and the same thing is reported from most parts of the country. Relations are said to be better in Scotland, however, where the people are certainly more hospitable than in England. Also, people seem to prefer the Negroes to the white Americans.

If you ask people why they dislike Americans, you get first of all the answer that they are "always boasting" and then come upon a more solid grievance in the matter of the soldiers' pay and food. An American private soldier gets 10 shillings a day and all found, which—with wages and income tax as they now are—means that the whole American army is financially in the middle class, and fairly high up in it. As to the food, I do not imagine that people would resent the troops being better fed than civilians, since the British army is also better fed, so far as the ingredients of food go, but the Americans are given foodstuffs otherwise reserved for children, and also imported luxuries which obviously waste shipping space. They are even importing beer, since they will not drink English beer. People point out with some bitterness that sailors have to be drowned in bringing this stuff across. You can imagine also the petty jealousies centering round the fact that American officers monopolise all the taxis, drink up all the whisky and have inflated the rents of furnished rooms to unheard-of levels. The usual comment is "I wouldn't mind if they were fighting, not just talking." This is said out of spite, but it is a fact that the attitude will change deeply if and when the American army is engaged in Europe. At present the parallel with our own relations with France during the phony war is all too obvious.

Whether this state of affairs could be altered by better propaganda methods is disputable. I note that people newly returned from the U. S. A., or with knowledge of conditions there, especially Canadians, are concerned about Anglo-American relations and very anxious that the British war-effort should be more loudly boosted in the U. S. A. Britain's propaganda problems, however, are more complex than most people realise. To take one example, it is politically necessary to flatter the Dominions, which involves playing down the British. As a result the Germans are able to say plausibly that Britain's fighting is done for her by colonial troops, but this is held to be a lesser evil than offending the Australians, who are only very loosely attached to the Empire and culturally hostile to Britain. This dilemma presents itself over and over again, in endless variations. As to America, some propagandists actually hold that it is better for the Americans to be anti-British, as this gives them a good opinion of themselves and "keeps their morale up." Others are dismayed because we are represented in America by people like Lord Halifax[1]—who, it is feared, may be taken for a typical Englishman. The usual line is "Why can't we send over a few workingmen from Wigan or Bradford to show them we're ordinary decent people like themselves?" This seems to me sentimentality. It is true, of course, that Lord Halifax is just about as representative of Britain as a Red Indian chieftain is of the United States, but the theory that the common peoples of all nations love each other at sight is not backed up by experience. The common people nearly everywhere are xenophobe, because they cannot accustom themselves to foreign food and foreign habits. Holding leftwing opinions makes no difference to this, a fact which impressed itself on me in the Spanish civil war. The popular goodwill towards the USSR in this country partly depends on the fact that few Englishmen have ever seen a Russian. And one has only to look round the English-speaking world, with its labyrinth of cultural hatreds, to see that speaking the same language is no guarantee of friendship.

Whatever happens, Britain will not go the way that France went, and the growing animosity between British and Americans may not have any real importance till the war is over. But it might have a direct influence on events if—as is now widely expected—Germany is defeated some time in 1943 or 1944 and it then takes about two more years to settle Japan. In that case the war against Japan might quite easily be represented as "an American war," a more plausible variant of "a Jewish war." The masses in Britain have it fixed in their minds that Hitler is *the* enemy, and it is quite common to hear soldiers say "I'm packing up as soon as Germany is finished." That doesn't mean that they genuinely intend or would be able to do this, and I think in practice majority opinion would be for staying in the war, unless by that time Russia had changed sides again. But the question "What are we fighting for?" is bound to come up in a sharper form when Germany is knocked out, and there are pro-Japanese elements in this country which might be clever enough to make use of popular war-weariness. From the point of view of the man in the street the war in the Far East is a war for the rubber companies and the Americans, and in that context American unpopularity might be important. The British ruling class has never stated its real war aims, which happen to be unmentionable, and so long as things went badly Britain was driven part of the way towards a revolutionary strategy. There was always the possibility, therefore, of democratising the war without losing it in the process. Now, however, the tide begins to turn and immediately the dreary world which the American millionaires and their British hangers-on intend to impose upon us begins to take shape. The British people, in the mass, don't want such a world, and might say so fairly vigorously when the Nazis are out of the way. What they want, so far as they formulate their thoughts at all, is some kind of United States of Europe dominated by a close alliance between Britain and the USSR. Sentimentally, the majority of people in this country would far rather be in a tie-up with Russia than with America, and it is possible to imagine situations in which the popular cause would become the anti-American cause. There were signs of this alignment in the reactions to the Darlan business. Whether any leader or party capable of giving a voice to these tendencies will arise even when Hitler is gone and Europe is in turmoil, I do not know. None is visible at this moment, and the reactionaries are tightening their grip everywhere. But one can at least foresee at what point a radical change will again become possible.

There is not much more news. Another Fascist party has started up, the British National Party. It is the usual stuff—anti-Bolshevik, anti-Big Business, etc. These people have got hold of some money from somewhere but do not appear to have a serious following. The Common Wealth people have quarreled and split, but the main group is probably making headway. There have been further signs of the growth of a left-wing faction in the Church of England, which has had tendencies in this direction for some years past. These centre not, as one might expect in the "modernists" but in the Anglo-Catholics, dogmatically the extreme "right wing" of the Church. The Church Times, which is more or less the official paper of the C. of E. (enormous circulation in country vicarages), has for some years past been a mildly leftwing paper and politically quite intelligent. Parts of the Roman Catholic press have gone more markedly pro-Fascist since the Darlan affair. There is evidently a split in the Catholic intelligentsia over the whole question of Fascism, and they have been attacking one another in public in a way they usually avoid doing. There is still anti-semitism, but no sign that it is growing. Our food is much as usual. The Christmas puddings, my clue to the shipping situation, were about the same colour as last year. It is getting hard to live with prices and taxes as they now are, and what between long working-hours and then fire-watching, the Home Guard, A.R.P. or what-not, one seems to have less and less spare time, especially as all journeys now are slow and uncomfortable. Good luck for 1943.

1. Edward Frederick Lindley Wood, First Earl of Halifax (see *763, n. 9*), served as British Ambassador to the United States from 1940 to 1946. The *DNB* describes his character as one 'of baffling opaqueness.'

1798. To Bahadur Singh

4 January 1943   07/ES/EB/WMB

Dear Bahadur Singh

Thank you for your letter of the 1st January and I am glad you will be able to do the broadcast for us. The correct date is, of course, Wednesday, the *13th January*. The 11th, mentioned in our telegram, was a mistake. I have explained the details of the broadcast in my letter of the 30th December. Last week, for example, it was Mr. Wendel Willkie.° Perhaps you will have some ideas of your own for next week, but, in any case, the person must be a topical personality.

I will telephone you next Monday about the matter.

Yours sincerely
[Initialled] E. A. B
Eric Blair
Talks Producer
Indian Section

1799. Memorandum to L. F. Rushbrook Williams

4 January 1943   Handwritten

E.S.D.

The attached is a specimen Bengali newsletter composed by P. Chatterji, who is anxious for the job of announcer-translator. Could we get it sent to the School of Oriental Studies & get an opinion on the Bengali? Attached also is an English translation of the newsletter made by Mr Chatterji himself.

Meanwhile I am informed that Miss Sen Gupta, who did a Bengali message to the people of Calcutta for us on Saturday last, speaks very good Bengali & has a good microphone manner. Our present announcer-translator, Mr Das Gupta, is I am almost certain unsatisfactory.[1]

Eric Blair   4.1.43

1. The note is annotated 'Professor Firth — Could you have this vetted? LFW.' For Firth, see *846, n. 13.*

1800. BBC Talks Booking Form, 5.1.43

Bahadur Singh: 'In the Public Eye,' 4; '8 minute talk on the outstanding personality of the week'; broadcast 13.1.43; fee £3 3s 0d + 13s 2d. Signed: M Blackburn for I.P.O. Remarks: 'This broadcast is normally an adaptation of a newspaper article not involving very much work & I suggest that £3.3.0. would be a suitable average fee for the 8 minutes.'

1801. BBC Talks Booking Form, 5.1.43

Marjorie Leaf: 'Women Generally Speaking'; two 13-minute talks arranged and presented as usual by Lady Grigg. 'Miss Leaf will be talking about the activities of the Victoria League — how we look after the troops from the Empire; broadcast 13 and 20.1.43; fee £7.7s. Signed: M Blackburn for I.P.O.

1802. To E. C. Bowyer

6 January 1943   Handwritten draft and typed versions
07/ES/EB/WMB

Dear Mr. Bowyer

Very many thanks for the script,[1] which is just the kind of thing we wanted. I am going to alter a phrase or two in order to simplify the language very slightly, but the general tone and the number of types mentioned is just right. The alterations are very small ones and I'll let you see them when made.

You will be on the air for the first talk at 12.45 on the 22nd January, so perhaps you could arrive soon after 12 noon.

Yours sincerely
[Initialled] E. A. B
George Orwell
Talks Producer
Indian Section

1. Bowyer had sent a first draft for his talk on bombers, to be given on 22 January. At the foot, Orwell wrote 'P.T.O.' and on the verso a handwritten version of this reply. Miss Bedwell typed this in two- instead of one-paragraph form.

1803. To Desmond Hawkins

6 January 1943   07/ES/EB/WMB

Dear Hawkins

Our next ANNIVERSARIES OF THE MONTH Feature programme is scheduled for Tuesday, February 2nd, the usual time, 1145 to 1200 GMT. Do you again feel like writing the script for this programme? I shall be glad if you will do it.

I am enclosing a list of the Anniversaries for February. Will you be kind enough to return this to us, without fail, as soon as possible.

Yours sincerely,
[Initialled] E. A. B
George Orwell
Talks Producer
Indian Section

1804. Extract from Minutes of Eastern Service Meeting

6 January 1943

'Calling All Students.' E.S.D. drew attention to this excellent series' under Edmund Blunden's editorship. Mr. Brook reported publication arrangements in train.[1]

1. The series was organised by Orwell. In a letter to Ian Angus of 5 September 1983, Laurence Brander confirmed that he and Orwell chose the BBC scripts for the two pamphlets published by Oxford University Press in Bombay from the series 'Calling All Students.' Brander edited the texts and arranged with R. E. Hawkins, General Manager of the OUP in Bombay, for the pamphlets to be printed and distributed. BBC Pamphlet No 2, *Books and Authors*, comprised: E. M. Forster: Shakespeare's *Julius Caesar*, George Sampson: Milton's Shorter Poems, Edmund Blunden: Thomas Hardy, D. Nichol Smith: William Hazlitt, George Orwell: Bernard Shaw's *Arms and the Man*, W. J. Turner: *The Book of Job*. These were all proposed by Orwell to Blunden in December 1942; see *1712* and *3101*.
   BBC Pamphlet No 3, *Landmarks in American Literature*, comprised: Herbert Read: Nathaniel Hawthorne, T. S. Eliot: Edgar Allan Poe, Geoffrey Grigson: Herman Melville, V. S. Pritchett: Mark Twain, George Orwell: Jack London, Rayner Heppenstall: The Contemporary American Short Story. There were two exceptions in this list to the titles proposed by Orwell to Read on 4 December 1942; see *1718*. O'Henry and Hemingway were dropped, and Heppenstall's talk substituted.
   No 2 was published on 29 October 1946 in an edition of 2,500 copies, of which 2,103 were pulped in February 1949. No 3 was published in an edition of 1,500 copies on 21 October 1946 (according to the file copy in Bombay) or also on the 29th. It was 'Declared out of print on 12.12.49,' but OUP Bombay could not say whether that meant all copies were sold or copies had been pulped.

1805. Introduction to 'Calling All Students,' 3

8 January 1943

Edmund Blunden introduced speakers in this series, but when he himself spoke, Orwell made the introduction. The text reproduced here is from the typescript used for this broadcast; manuscript amendments have been incorporated, and the original text is given in the notes. The name 'Miss Playle' (of *The Listener*) is written on the typescript and also on Blunden's script. Presumably both typescripts were sent to her following Orwell's memorandum to her of 21 December 1942 (see *1758*), in which he described the series and the intention to publish the talks in India.

Today we are having a departure from the usual arrangement of these talks. The introducer of all the others has been Mr. Edmund Blunden who has been chiefly responsible for arranging the whole series. Today, however, Mr. Blunden is delivering the talk himself. So I am here to introduce him to you, as he has introduced so many others.

As a matter of fact, it ought not to be necessary to introduce Edmund Blunden to any audience interested in English literature for his name has been familiar to the reading public for not far short of thirty years. Although he is primarily a poet and would perhaps wish to be thought of as a poet, Edmund Blunden is best known for a prose work "Undertones of War". The war of

1914 to 1918 produced a great spate of literature in England but it only produced some half dozen books which seem worth reading after a lapse of years. Well[1] among these "Undertones of War" has an assured place. As its title implies, it is a restrained unemphatic book. It describes[2] the reactions of a sensitive and intelligent human being when brought into contact with the horrors of modern mechanised war but it doesn't deal[3] in any kind of sensationalism. Like Edmund Blunden's poems it expresses a quiet acceptance of the world as it is and a love of the surface of the earth—even nature worship if you prefer that name for it. It has never failed him even in the extremest hardship and danger. I believe nobody else who wrote about the war of 1914 to 1918 remained so aware of the procession of the seasons and the birds[4] and wild flowers which somehow managed to survive even on the edges of the battle-field. Even if you had never read Edmund Blunden's poetry you could hardly glance into "Undertones of War" without realising that here was a man whose love of the countryside was his ruling passion. Today, Edmund Blunden is speaking to you about Thomas Hardy's novel, "Far From the Madding Crowd".[5] Few people could be more suitable, for perhaps Hardy's greatest quality is his power of invoking a picture of the English countryside which Edmund Blunden loves so well. Now here is Edmund Blunden to talk to you about Thomas Hardy.

1. Well among] Among. *There is no comma.*
2. book. It describes] book describing. *The amendment has what appears to be a comma after* book, *but* It *clearly has a capital 'I,' so it may have been intended to score out the original punctuation mark here, or it may be a badly marked period.*
3. it doesn't deal] not dealing
4. the birds] birds
5. "Far From the Madding Crowd"] "The Return of the Native" *in the typescript. When this was scored through, the quotation marks were also crossed out; they have been added editorially.*

1806. News Commentary in English for Malaya, 15

8 January 1943

This was written and read by Orwell. No script has been traced.

1807. Review of Pamphlet Literature

The New Statesman and Nation, 9 January 1943

One cannot adequately review fifteen pamphlets in a thousand words, and if I have picked out that number it is because between them they make a representative selection of eight out of the nine main trends in current pamphleteering. (The missing trend is pacifism: I don't happen to have a recent pacifist pamphlet by me.) I list them under their separate headings, with short comments, before trying to explain certain rather curious features in the revival of pamphleteering during recent years.

1. Anti-left and crypto-fascist. *A Soldier's New World*. 2d. (Sub-titled "An anti-crank pamphlet written in camp," this wallops the highbrow and proves that the common man does not want Socialism. Key phrase: "The Clever Ones have never learned to delight in simple things.") *Gollancz in the German Wonderland*. 1s. (Vansittartite). *World Order or World Ruin*. 6d. (Anti-planning. G. D. H. Cole demolished).

2. Conservative. *Bomber Command Continues*. 7d. (good specimen of an official pamphlet).

3. Social Democrat. *The Case of Austria*. 6d. (published by the Free Austrian Movement).

4. Communist. *Clear out Hitler's Agents*. 2d. (sub-titled "An exposure of Trotskyist disruption being organised in Britain." Exceptionally mendacious.)

5. Trotskyist and Anarchist. *The Kronstadt Revolt*. 2d. (Anarchist pamphlet, largely an attack on Trotsky).

6. Non-party radical. *What's Wrong with the Army?* 6d. (a Hurricane Book. Well-informed and well-written anti-blimp document). *I, James Blunt*. 6d. (good flesh-creeper, founded on the justified assumption that the mass of the English people haven't yet heard of Fascism). *Battle of Giants*. Unpriced, probably 6d (interesting specimen of popular non-Communist Russophile literature).

7. Religious. *A Letter to a Country Clergyman*. 2d. (Fabian pamphlet, left-wing Anglican). *Fighters Ever*. 6d (Buchman vindicated).

8. Lunatic. *Britain's Triumphant Destiny, or Righteousness no longer on the Defensive*. 6d. (British Israel, profusely illustrated). *When Russia Invades Palestine*. 1s. (The author, A. J. Ferris, B.A., has written a long series of pamphlets on kindred subjects, some of them enjoying enormous sales. His *When Russia Bombs Germany*, published in 1940, sold over 60,000). *Hitler's Story and Programme to Conquer England*, by Civis Britannicus Sum. 1s. (Specimen passage: "It is a grand thing to 'play the game,' and to know that one is doing it. Then, when the day comes that stumps are drawn or the whistle blows for the last time:

> "The *Great Scorer* will come to write against your name,
>   Not if you have 'won or lost; but *How you Played the Game*.'")

These few that I have named are only a drop in the ocean of pamphlet literature, and for the sake of giving a good cross-section I have included several that the average reader is likely to have heard of. What conclusions can one draw from this small sample? The interesting fact, not easily explicable, is that pamphleteering has revived upon an enormous scale since about 1935, and has done so without producing anything of real value. My own collection, made during the past six years, would run into several hundreds, but probably does not represent anywhere near 10 per cent. of the total output. Some of these pamphlets have had huge sales, especially the religio-patriotic ones, such as those of Mr. Ferris, B.A., and the scurrilous ones, such as *Hitler's Last Will and Testament*, which is said to have sold several millions. Directly political pamphlets sometimes sell in big numbers, but the circulation of any pamphlet which is "party line" (any party) is likely to be spurious. Looking through my collection, I find that it is practically all trash, interesting only to bibliophiles. Though I have classified current pamphlets under nine headings they could be finally reduced to two main schools, roughly describable as Party Line and Astrology. There is totalitarian rubbish and paranoiac rubbish, but in each case it *is* rubbish. Even the well-informed Fabian pamphlets are hopelessly dull, considered as reading matter. The liveliest pamphlets are almost always non-party, a good example being *Bless 'em All*, which should be regarded as a pamphlet, though it costs one and sixpence.

The reason why the badness of contemporary pamphlets is somewhat suprising is that the pamphlet ought to be *the* literary form of an age like our own. We live in a time when political passions run high, channels of free expression are dwindling, and organised lying exists on a scale never before known. For plugging the holes in history the pamphlet is the ideal form. Yet lively pamphlets are very few, and the only explanation I can offer—a rather lame one—is that the publishing trade and the literary papers have never gone to the trouble of making the reading public pamphlet-conscious. One difficulty of collecting pamphlets is that they are not issued in any regular manner, cannot always be procured even in the libraries of museums, and are seldom advertised and still more seldom reviewed. A good writer with something he passionately wanted to say—and the essence of pamphleteering is to have something you want to say *now*, to as many people as possible— would hesitate to cast it in pamphlet form, because he would hardly know how to set about getting it published, and would be doubtful whether the people he wanted to reach would ever read it. Probably he would water his idea down into a newspaper article or pad it out into a book. As a result by far the greater number of pamphlets are either written by lonely lunatics who publish at their own expense, or belong to the subworld of the crank religions, or are issued by political parties. The normal way of publishing a pamphlet is through a political party, and the party will see to it that any "deviation"—and hence any literary value—is kept out. There have been a few good pamphlets in fairly recent years. D. H. Lawrence's *Pornography and Obscenity* was one, Potocki de Montalk's *Snobbery with Violence* was another, and some of Wyndham Lewis's essays in *The Enemy* really come under this heading. At present the most hopeful symptom is the appearance of the non-party Left Wing pamphlet, such as the Hurricane Books. If productions of this type were as sure of being noticed in the press as are novels or books of verse, something would have been done towards bringing the pamphlet back to the attention of its proper public, and the level of the whole genre might rise. When one considers how flexible a form the pamphlet is, and how badly some of the events of our time need documenting, this is a thing to be desired.[1]

1. At least two of Orwell's readers wrote to him. E. J. Wyburne suggested that he should have included educational pamphlets, and sent him one called *Britain's Schools*, published by the Communist Party; he proposed it be reviewed. Ruth Fry wrote a charming letter as 'a pretty ardent pamphleteer,' whom Orwell would probably categorise as 'a crank who passionately

wants to say something.' She sent Orwell some of her pamphlets for his collection to give him 'the pleasure of laughing at them.' See Appendix 10, *3733*, for an account of Orwell's pamphlet collection (which includes Miss Fry's pamphlets) and his Classified List.

1808. Weekly News Review, 55

9 January 1943

This text is reproduced from the typescript used for the broadcast, a carbon copy. Some slight manuscript amendments in Orwell's hand are here recorded in the notes; a longer typewritten insertion, which seems to have been made after the Newsletter was completed, is in *n. 3*. It is single- instead of double-spaced and has been typed directly on the carbon copy. Commas have been added liberally, perhaps to aid delivery; these are silently incorporated. Words shown in italic are handwritten inserts. The timings recorded on the script are in italic in square brackets. The 'As broadcast' timing was given as 12′ 10″ but there are two other final timings, 12′ 50″ and 13′ plus some unreadable seconds. These may indicate that the script was censored—Rushbrook Williams acted as censor—or there may have been errors in recording timings during rehearsal or an attempt to speed up the reading. To complicate matters, the transmission time given by PasB (which would include preliminary and closing announcements) is 14′ 17″. Despite their apparent precision, too much reliance cannot be placed on the timings. According to PasB, the script was read by Orwell. The typescript spells 'Solomon' as 'Soloman.'

This week there is little fresh news except from the Russian front, and I propose to devote most of my commentary to that. But I would like first to summarise shortly the news from the other fronts, so as to get the Russian front into its proper perspective.

In North Africa, there has hardly been any fresh developments. In Tunisia the struggle seasaws to and fro, neither side gaining or losing much ground and both sides are evidently building up their forces for the big battle yet to come. The Germans in Tunisia have evidently been re-inforced in tanks as well as men, in spite of their losses at sea, which continue to be serious. Malta has been re-inforced now that the naval position in the Mediterranean has shifted in favour of the Allies and air activity based on Malta is increasing.

Free French forces moving northward across the desert from Lake Tchad in equatorial Africa, have[1] driven in the Axis outposts in the Libyan desert and captured an important oasis about 400 miles south of Tripoli. This manoeuvre has meant a march of about 1,000 miles largely over desert. An attack coming from this direction is an added threat to the Axis positions, both in Tripolitania and in Tunisia, but it is very difficult to move large numbers of men or vehicles across the desert, not only because of the lack of water but because of the time taken in building up petrol dumps. That is about all the news from North Africa. [*1′ 55″; 1′ 45″*]

In Eastern New Guinea, Japanese resistance at Buna has been finally overcome. The only Japanese forces now left in this part of the island are at Sanananda, about 50 miles to the west, where they were landed a few weeks ago. The Allies are now re-grouping for the final attack on Sanananda. The Japanese loss of Eastern New Guinea and of Guadacanal° in the Solomon islands,° will have upset their plans in the South Pacific, but it does not look as though they had yet given up all hope of attacking Australia. Air reconnaisance shows that they have assembled another big fleet of warships and transports in Rabaul, in New Britain, and some observers report that this is the biggest fleet which they have yet assembled. We don't[2] yet know what operation they are intending but it has been suggested that they might make another effort at invading Australia somewhere on the northwest coast. They would probably have another try at retrieving the situation in New Guinea and the Solomons before doing so. This threat is taken seriously in Australia where conscription, both for the armed forces and for war industries is being extended.

British and American air-raids along the coast of Burma have been increasing in volume and they have ranged all the way from the Arakan coast to Pagoda Point and as far inland as Mandalay. We have not at present very much evidence of how things are going for the Japanese in their occupied territories but what evidence there is all shows that local resistance is increasing everywhere. The latest bit of news is the announcement by the Japanese wireless that they have just executed a number of Burmese for sabotage and destruction and also two [2'; 4' 10"] Indians on the charge of sabotaging railways. The Japanese have also issued orders that the people of Burma are forbidden to listen-in to foreign broadcasting stations—a sure sign that Allied broadcasts are attracting attention.[3] We are probably safe in guessing that the Burmese are already beginning to find out the real nature of the Japanese new order.

I don't think that during this week there have been any other events on the Asiatic fronts on which I can significantly comment.

Now as to the Russian Front. The Russians have followed up the capture of Veliki Luki° near the Latvian border, by capturing Mozdok and Nalchik on the Caucasus front, hundreds of miles to the south. The loss of Nalchik puts the seal on the failure of the German Caucasus campaign. If you look at a map of Russia on which the present approximate position of the armies is marked, you will see that the German army in the Caucasus is doing nothing except to maintain a huge salient which has no direct value. When the Germans advanced southward in the summer they expected, and a good deal of the rest of the world expected, too, that they would cross the Caucasus mountains and get to the Baku oilfields before the winter. At the least it was expected, that they would remain in possession of the key towns, commanding the passes[4] over the Caucasus mountains and would be able to renew their offensive early in the spring. Now they're being driven back and they° evidently retreating rapidly. They can hardly make another stand before they get to the Kuma river and may have to go much further *back* than that, for, at the same time as the German army in the south has lost its footing, the Russian armies west of Stalingrad are still advancing along the Don. They are now[5] [6'] thought to be only about 75 miles from Roztov. If they should reach Roztov, which is not impossible, the whole German army in the

Caucasus area will either have to retreat hurriedly or run the risk of being completely cut off. Undoubtedly the right thing to do would be to retreat now but German strategy is not governed altogether by military considerations. The Germans have had huge and useless losses because Hitler did not care to abandon Stalingrad after boasting that he would take it, and the same story may be repeated in the south.

Meanwhile, the German public is apparently being prepared for bad news. If one studies the German wireless and newspapers, one notices two propaganda tricks constantly employed. One is that place names are mentioned as seldom as possible, the commentators merely stating that fighting is in progress in such and such an area, and by not mentioning names avoiding stating whether the German armies are advancing or retreating.[6] The other device is to dwell on the immense difficulties of the Russian campaign and especially the severity of the Russian winter. It is also admitted, however, by some German commentators, that the Russian troops are fighting well and are not short of tanks and weapons generally. There are even some quite detailed accounts of the special methods[7] the Russians use, to overcome the difficulty of moving over deep snow. All this suggests that the Germans are contemplating a big retreat and are trying in advance to make this acceptable to the public. The articles in the German press and on the wireless [1' 50"; 7' 50"; 8' 40"] emphasising the strength and numbers of the Red Army do not fit in very well with the official statement of more than a year ago that the Red Army had been destroyed once and for all but the people in totalitarian countries are expected to have short memories. At present it looks as though the Nazi leaders can see no good news ahead, at any rate on the Russian front, and are excusing this as best they can by implying that the task before them is superhuman.

President Roosevelt's speech on January 6th, when he addressed the United States Congress, has already had a lot of publicity but I should like to re-emphasize two points in it because a speech of this kind is in it-self° an event and can be *just* as important as anything that happens on the battle field.

In the first place the President added some more figures of American war production to the ones I was able to give you last week. For instance, he revealed that during 1942, the United States has produced 48,000 military aeroplanes, which is more than the production of Germany, Italy and Japan, put together. By December the United States was producing aeroplanes at the rate of over 60,000 a year. Again, in 1942 the United States produced 56,000 fighting vehicles, such as tanks or self[8] propelling artillery. Again during the past year the United States armed forces have grown from a strength of 2 million men to over 7 million men. *Now* it is no use reading out long lists of figures which after a little while only become confusing, but the up-shot is [9' 45"; 10' 40"] that during the past year the whole of America's war production has enormously increased, sometimes by an increase of several hundreds per cent over 1941 and still is increasing rapidly. American food production has increased as well.

The other outstanding point in the President's speech was the complete *and* uncompromising break he made with isolationism. He said quite clearly and at considerable length that Americans realised more clearly than ever before that the whole world is now potentially one unit and that no nation can stand aloof, either from the job of preventing aggression or from the job of supplying the wants of the common people everywhere. "We cannot", he said, "make America an island in either a military or economic sense. Victory in this war is the first and greatest goal before us. Victory in the peace is the next. That means striving towards the enlargement of the security of men here and throughout the world, and finally striving for freedom from fear." "The United Nations," he added, "are the mightiest military coalition in history. Bound together in solemn agreement that they themselves will not commit acts of aggression or conquest, the United Nations can and must remain united for the maintenance of peace by preventing any attempt to re-arm in Germany, in Japan and in Italy. There are cynics and sceptics who say it cannot be done. The American people and all freedom loving peoples of this earth are now demanding that it must be done and the will of these peoples shall prevail." This is a great step forward from the isolationism and the purely nationalistic conception of security and prosperity with which the United States, as well as some other nations, ended the last war. [12' 10"; 13'; 12' 50"]

1. have] has
2. don't] do not. *This slight change shows Orwell adapting the formal written form for speech.*
3. The Japanese have also . . . are attracting attention.] *typed insert squeezed into top margin*
4. passes] bases
5. They are now] *written in by Orwell. The three words were originally typed between the two preceding lines.*
6. advancing or retreating] retreating or advancing. *In typescript over 'retreating' is a figure 2 and over 'advancing' a figure 1, indicating the order should be reversed.*
7. methods] method. *The 's' is a manuscript addition.*
8. self] heavy

1809. Bengali Newsletter, 26

9 January 1943

The English original was written by Orwell. No script has been traced. PasB gives timing as 11' 4".

1810. To K. K. Ardaschir

9 January 1943   07/ES/EB

Dear Ardaschir
Thanks for your letter of January 7th. I am sorry the suggestions were not acknowledged.
    I would like a talk on the second of the two subjects you suggested, that is to say, From Victoria Station, Bombay, to Victoria Station, London. I have a

blank period into which I could fit this talk, on Friday, March 12th—usual length 13½ minutes, and the time of broadcast—12.45 p.m. British Summer Time. I would like it if I could have the script in a week before the date.

I am sorry but I am sure I gave you back the wicker basket. I distinctly remember tying the string round again and bringing it down to the office.

You may be interested to hear the black hen is now beginning to lay, as well, and lays a very nice light brown egg.

Yours sincerely
[Initialled] E. A. B
Eric Blair
Talks Producer
Indian Section

1811. To R. R. Desai

9 January 1943   07/ES/EB

Dear Desai

As to this week's hints there is not much that we want to avoid mentioning this week except that one should not overplay the probability of the Russians re-taking Rostov.[1] I don't suppose you will do so anyway.

As to positive hints; it does not much matter whether you do this now or in later weeks, but I would like it if some time you could say something about the way in which the Germans and the Japanese swindle the inhabitants of occupied territory by means of spurious currency. This is a thing it is important to rub in and I usually mention it about once in two months.

I also include, in case it should be useful to you, some quotations from Japanese propaganda showing the change of tone during the past year. Please let me have this back.[2]

Yours
[Initialled] E. A. B
Eric Blair
Talks Producer
Indian Section

1. Churchill wrote to Stalin on 14 February 1943 congratulating him on the liberation of Rostov (*The Second World War*, IV, 667; U.S.: *The Hinge of Fate*, 744).
2. Not traced.

1812. To K. K. Ardaschir

11 January 1943   07/ES/EB/WMB

Dear Ardaschir

I am sending back the enclosed script as you requested as after some consideration I find that I simply have not got room for it. You had my note about the other talk we want you to do I think.

Yours sincerely
[Initialled] E. A. B
Eric Blair
Talks Producer
Indian Section

1813. To Sidney Horniblow

11 January 1943   07/ES/EB/WMB

Dear Mr. Horniblow
I must apologise for not replying earlier to your letter[1] but I waited over until I had got my new schedule into shape, so that I could see whether we could make room for you.

I would like to continue the IN BLACK AND WHITE item, as a fortnightly broadcast, starting from Friday, the 12th March, at 12.45 p.m. British Summer Time. This is a quarter-of-an-hour programme, as before. Could you send me a line to let me know whether you are able to carry on as from that date.

Yours sincerely
[Signed] Eric Blair
Eric Blair
Talks Producer
Indian Section

1. Horniblow wrote to Orwell on 16 December 1942 submitting ideas for programmes for India in response to a request from Orwell. He made four suggestions: 1. In Black and White, which summarised leading articles from British newspapers and which Horniblow was keen to continue; this, in effect, was a variation on the series The Leaders which had made way for Orwell's news commentaries in English for India; 2. Man in the News, a weekly personality sketch; 3. Home Front Fighters, typical members of the public explaining how they were helping to bring victory to 'the United Nations'; 4. Victory News, a weekly review of items showing how the United Nations were getting stronger and advancing towards victory. Horniblow's letter is annotated 'Answered' by Orwell—presumably this letter of 11 January 1943.

1814. To Marjorie Leaf

11 January 1943   07/ES/EB

Dear Marjorie
Very many thanks for your letter of the 8th January, and for your script (Number one) on the Victoria League. This should be an interesting talk. With this letter, I am sending round to you a flimsy copy of your script. (A top copy will be waiting for you at 200 Oxford Street on Wednesday next, 13th January, the day of the broadcast). If you are here about 12.0 noon, the

script can be rehearsed and timed and if we find it necessary, cuts can be made. The actual time of the broadcast is from 12.45 to 1.0 p.m. BST.

The broadcast can be heard on the shortwave, on the following metre bands: 16, 19, 25 and 31. It is not usually easily heard in this country, but on a good shortwave set, it can sometimes be picked up. The programme immediately before your broadcast is a 15-minute programme of music. This may make it simpler to tune-in before your talk starts.

Yours sincerely,
[Initialled] MB
for Eric Blair
(Talks Producer)

1815. Laurence Brander's Report on Indian Programmes

11 January 1943

The BBC and individual members of its staff showed anxiety over how its broadcasts to India were received, even if, as earlier reports indicate, Laurence Brander's analyses tended to be re-interpreted in London. Direct requests for information were not uncommon. Thus, on 24 November 1942, Mary Blackburn asked that a cable be sent to Ahmed Ali[1] inviting criticism and comments on the Gujarati Newsletter and its presenter (R. R. Desai). This was initiated by Desai and said that 'by "criticisms" he doesn't mean "praise", but comments, both adverse and favourable.'

On 11 January, Brander, in his capacity as the BBC's Intelligence Officer for India, submitted a full report on the programmes transmitted to India. Some of these emanated from the section for which Orwell worked; some from the Hindustani section under Sir Malcolm Darling at Evesham. The report illustrates the difficult task the BBC faced and how limited were the numbers of those who could hear the broadcasts. The report is relevant to Orwell and the work he did as well as to the Eastern Service as a whole, and for understanding the nature of the audiences served. It is given here as an appendix; see 2374.

It is not known whether Orwell read this report but it is extremely likely that he knew of its contents from conversations with Brander; see 1546.

1. Ahmed Ali is decribed in Brander's report as 'a wellknown° Urdu writer of the Delhi School.' See also 1103, n. 3.

1816. Memorandum to E. W. D. Boughen

13 January 1943   EB/WMB

BEHIND THE HEADLINES — talk by Shridhar Telkar

Today we have issued a Booking Slip for Sir Mohammed Zafrullah Khan who is giving an 8 minute talk on Thursday, 21st January 1943 at 1115–1130 GMT on the PACIFIC RELATIONS COUNCIL. This talk will be recorded on Saturday, the 16th January, at 3.45 to 4.15 BST. in St.2, Oxford Street.

We wished to fit this talk in while Sir Mohammed is in this country, and we are therefore putting him in, in the place of Shridhar Telkar's talk, BEHIND THE HEADLINES, which he was to have given on the 21st January, at 1115–1130 GMT. Please note, therefore, that Shridhar Telkar's talk is cancelled for that date.[1]

[Signed] Eric Blair
(Eric Blair)

1. A letter cancelling the arrangement was sent by Miss Boughen on 15 January 1943.

1817. BBC Talks Booking Form, 13.1.43

Bahadur Singh: 'In the Public Eye,' 5; broadcast 20.1.43; fee £3.3s + travel voucher. Signed: M Blackburn for I.P.O.

1818. BBC Talks Booking Form, 13.1.43

Professor E. D. Edwards:[1] 'Women Generally Speaking,' Chinese decorations and deeds of heroism; broadcast 27.1.43; fee £8.8s. Signed: M Blackburn for I.P.O.[2]

1. Evangeline Dora Edwards (1888–1957) was born in New Zealand and was Professor of Chinese Literature, University of London. She wrote a number of books on Chinese literature, including *Chinese Prose Literature of the T'ang Period*, and on the Chinese language; she also wrote a book on Confucius and edited an anthology, *Bamboo, Lotus and Palm*.
2. Professor Edwards submitted her script on 21 January. Orwell was away, sick, and Mary Blackburn replied on behalf of Bokhari, who was also away. She said it was a little on the long side but 'I seem to remember that you read fairly quickly . . . a cut may not be necessary.' A time was suggested for her to arrive for rehearsal before transmission.

1819. To E. C. Bowyer

14 January 1943   07/ES/EB/WMB

Dear Mr. Bowyer

After, I am afraid, some delay, I am sending a copy of your script. You will see that I have made some very minor alterations with the idea of using even more non-technical language. If I have deformed your meaning by any of these, please alter it back again. It is merely that we are talking to a public which does not speak English as its native language and cannot be assumed to know very much about aircraft.[1]

Your talk will go for censorship in the usual way and I don't suppose anything in it will be altered.

You will be on the air on Friday next, the 22nd, at 12.45 p.m. (British Summer Time). I wonder if you could be good enough to get here about 12.

> Yours sincerely,
> [Initialled] G. O.
> George Orwell
> Talks Producer
> Indian Section

1. Bowyer replied on 18 January and suggested striking out a reference to Japanese medium bombers that might imply a degree of praise that would be welcomed in Japanese propaganda. Orwell annotated the letter for his secretary: 'Send p.c. telling him of changes made by the Air Ministry. E.A.B.' Miss Bedwell scribbled through that and wrote 'done' above it. The reference to the Air Ministry shows the script had been submitted for censorship.

1820. To Sidney Horniblow

14 January 1943   07/ES/EB/WMB

Dear Mr. Horniblow

I think I asked you whether you could re-open the series IN BLACK AND WHITE as from March 12th. I am sorry I shall have to wash that out and make it start as from March 26th. I have only just discovered that we have a talk already booked for the first date. Otherwise, I would like you to continue with the talks fortnightly as arranged.

> Yours sincerely
> [Initialled] WMB
> Eric Blair
> Talks Producer
> Indian Section

1821. To Herbert Read

14 January 1943   07/ES/EB/WMB

Dear Read

There seems to be a muddle somewhere. I find, by my schedule, that we have not got 7 talks on American literature but 6, so it is a question of either not proceeding with the Whitman talk or else dropping mine. I don't think we can drop out the talk on Steinbeck, as we must have something from contemporary literature. Will you let me know which you think it would be better to drop, Whitman or Jack London.

> Yours sincerely
> [Initialled] G. O.
> George Orwell
> Talks Producer
> Indian Section

1822. News Commentary in English for Malaya, 16

15 January 1943

This was written and read by Orwell. No script has been traced.

1823. To K. K. Ardaschir

15 January 1943   07/ES/EB/WMB

Dear Ardaschir

Thanks for your letter of January 13th. I cannot use the suggested talk about America's overseas possession, nor any others at this moment, except for the one you are doing on March 12th. I simply have not got any space to dispose of.

I am passing on the two ideas you sent me to the Hindustani section in case they should have any room. I think it possible that the Balkan one might be usable but as to the other idea I don't think one could get [far?] at this time with any discussion of the Russian regime along those lines. I am sorry I cannot be more helpful.

As to the other business about the Near Eastern Section; if any query comes my way I will do what I can.

Yours sincerely
[Initialled] E. A. B
Eric Blair
Talks Producer
Indian Section

1824. To George Bernard Shaw

15 January 1943   07/ES/EB/WMB

Dear Mr. Shaw

Many thanks for your letter dated 26th December. We have decided to broadcast the passage named by you from Act 3, ARMS AND THE MAN, beginning—"You look ever so much nicer than when we last met" and ending, "and I wish I had never met you".

The Contracts Department will get in touch with you over the question of the fee.

The passage acted will of course be prefaced by an explanation of the preceding events in the play, but, in any case the plot of the play will have been outlined in the first part of the programme, which is a talk on your work with special reference to ARMS AND THE MAN.

Yours truly
[Initialled] G. O.
George Orwell
Talks Producer
Indian Section

1825. Weekly News Review, 56

16 January 1943

The typescript used for this broadcast, reproduced here, has, at the top of its first page, 'Announcer/Trans: S. K. Das Gupta.' This script apparently served as the basis for Das Gupta's Bengali Newsletter for this same day. PasB suggests a timing of 13 minutes, probably including the announcement. Bengali Newsletter, 27, was approximately 9 minutes, so there was evidently considerable adaptation. Orwell read the News Review for India.

During this week there have been only two events of major importance and I should like to devote most of my commentary, as I do from time to time, to giving a general survey of the war as it now stands. But first let me just mention those two events which I spoke of as important—one of them military, the other political.

The important military news is that the Russian offensives on four separate parts of the Front are all continuing and making headway. I said last week that the Germans retreating in the Caucasus might make another stand on the Kuma river about Georgievsk and already Georgievsk is in Russian hands and the Russians are well over the Kuma river and are still advancing. The advance along the Don towards Stalingrad is also continuing, though less rapidly. It is important not to expect Rostov itself to fall at all rapidly or easily. The Germans are now falling back on Rostov from all directions and are certain to defend it obstinately. If they should lose it their whole Caucasus campaign will have gone for nothing and in all probability a large body of men further south would be cut off with only a rather slender chance of escaping by sea.

The other important event of this week is the final signature of the treaty between China, Great Britain and the United States. By this treaty extra territorial rights in China are formally relinquished. One hundred years ago treaties were made with the[1] Chinese by which the nationals of various countries enjoyed privileges in China's territory which were not compatible with China's existence as a sovereign state. They were exempt from China's law and payment of taxes and their warships had the right to navigate in Chinese rivers. All this has now been signed away once and for all by the British and American Governments. The Japanese, [not to be outdone on the propaganda front,] are making a pretence of some similar arrangement but as they are in actual possession of about a quarter of China, with the status of conquerors, their claims cannot be taken very seriously. Simultaneously with this, the Japanese have ordered the so-called Government of Nangking to declare war on the United Nations. This is not of very great importance, as the Nangking Government has no real existence, being merely a marionette show put on by Japan and in any case the few Chinese who have sided with the Japanese were for all intents and purposes at war with the United Nations already. The Anglo-Chinese treaty has caused great satisfaction in this country, perhaps almost as great as it has caused in China. It is one of those events like the settlement with Abyssinia which shows that the claim of the

United Nations to be fighting for liberty and against aggression[2] and tyranny is not simply a show of words. Incidentally, it is rather interesting to couple with this the results of a survey of public opinion taken recently in Britain on the question of feeding Europe after the war. A representative cross-section of the British public were asked "if it is necessary in order to prevent starvation in Europe would you be ready to continue with food rationing in Britain when the war is over". Eighty percent answered "Yes" and only seven percent answered with a definite "No". Things like this tell one more about the real reasons for which the ordinary man is fighting than declarations of war aims expressed in high sounding and general terms.

I said I was going to attempt a general survey of the war situation at the beginning of 1943. The first point which would be conceded, even by our enemies, is that the situation is enormously better for the Allies than it was at the beginning of 1942. Even Dr. Goebbels, in his weekly article in the newspaper DAS REICH warns the German public that their position is more difficult and dangerous now than it was at the beginning of the war. If one looks at the past year, in spite of the many and brilliant successes of the Axis, there are three main facts which stand out. These facts are, first the failure of the Japanese to keep up the initial impetus of their attack against the United Nations, the second is the failure of the German campaign in Russia to gain any of its major objectives. The third, is the quite obviously growing strength of Britain and the United States, by means of which the danger to Egypt and the Suez Canal has been removed and a whole corner of Africa, larger than Europe in area, has passed into the control of the Allies. The most immediately important of these three events is the German failure in Russia with all its damaging effects, present and to come, in losses of men, materials and prestige, and it is important when one assesses this to remember that the successes the Russians have had, though chiefly due to their own courage and energy, also owe a great deal to the less obvious efforts of Great Britain and the United States. We hear less about the convoys to Murmansk than we hear about the Russian battle fields, but it is important to remember that the British supply of war materials to Russia has never flagged, even in the face of the greatest difficulties and even when the need for arms on other fronts was most acute. For example, Britain has already delivered for Russian use, 3,000 aeroplanes, 4,000 tanks and many thousands of tons of war materials of all descriptions, including medical supplies.[3] The United States has similarly contributed and has also sent Russia a good deal of food but the chief help which Britain and America have brought to their Ally has been indirect. By the threat to invade Western Europe, which it is known will be carried out sooner or later, they have forced the Germans to keep at least 35 divisions in Western Europe, and consequently, to deplete their strength on the Russian Front to that extent. The British army in Libya keeps another 10 or more Axis divisions busy and this diversion becomes more serious owing to the German effort to hold on to Tunisia. During this year the Germans will probably find it necessary to hold and fortify the whole of Southern Europe on the same scale as Western Europe, with a corresponding drainage on their man power. The peculiar features of the New Order have ensured that the German man power problem is now serious. If the Germans had kept the various promises to the European peoples with which they started the war, they might possibly have had, by this time, a large reliable European army fighting on their side, and a huge fluid labour force. The whole of European industry might have been working at top speed for their benefit. As it is, they have no Ally in Europe whom they can really rely upon, for even Italy is almost as much a liability as an asset, and though they have been able to force the European peoples to work, they have not been able to make them work with the speed and willingness which total war demands.

A year ago, when the Japanese offensive was at its height, it was possible to outline the grand strategy on which the Axis powers based their plans. It was evident that Germany and Japan had a rendezvous somewhere in the neighbourhood of the Persian Gulf. The Japanese were to dominate the Indian Ocean and probably India itself, and the Germans were to cross the Caucasus mountains from the north and break through to[4] Suez from the west. The United Nations would then be separated from one another— Soviet Russia would be isolated and its armies would probably have to retreat behind the Ural mountains while China would be completely cut off and could be destroyed at leisure. After this, Britain could be attacked with the full weight of the German war machine and if Britain was conquered America could be dealt with at some time in the future. That was the Axis grand strategy. It was possible to discern it both from what the Axis military commanders were doing and from what their propagandists were saying. It should hardly be necessary to point out that this has failed completely, and however hard the struggle ahead may be, it is never likely to come so near success again. The Japanese are involved in a difficult struggle in the South Pacific in which they are losing ships and planes far faster than they can replace them, and the defences of India have been so strengthened that no attempted invasion is now likely. Japanese naval supremacy which once threatened to cover the whole Eastern part of the Indian Ocean has now receded to the Western Pacific. The Germans have failed to reach the Caucasus mountains and have lost enormously in a vain effort to reach the Caspian Sea. British strength is just about reaching its peak and American strength will do so some time during next year.

That is the picture as it appears at the beginning of 1943, and we ought to keep that picture in mind when we consider the less visible aspects of war. Probably the best card which the Germans have left is the U-Boat warfare which still, without any question, causes the Allies heavy losses in shipping and reduces their offensive capacity. For about a year past, the Government has adopted the practice of not publishing shipping losses regularly and this practice is probably justified since it keeps the enemy guessing about the truth of the shipping situation. The Germans were caught napping by the Anglo-American move into North Africa and this was partly because they had under-rated our true shipping capacity. I don't care to offer an opinion on something which is an official secret, but I may add that we have a clue to the shipping situation in the fact that the food rations have not altered in Britain during the past year. The German propagandists are making the most they can of the U-Boat warfare, because at the present they have not much else with which to comfort the German home public. In general, we can say this much of the situation as it now stands: the end is not in sight and we cannot safely prophecy that any of the Axis powers will be out of the war before 1943 is ended, but we can safely prophecy that 1943 will be the year in which the United Nations will hold the initiative and will be strong enough to pass over from mere self defence to an aggressive strategy.

1. made with the Chinese] imposed on the unwilling Chinese; *Orwell's handwritten amendment*
2. aggression] agression; *a spelling used by Orwell from childhood to the writing of* Nineteen Eighty-Four. *The typescript has several spelling errors, which have been silently corrected, and it is likely that Orwell was the typist.*
3. West: *Commentaries* notes that 'Orwell's source for these figures has not been found. In a speech in the House of Lords on 3 February Lord Portal gave the figures to 31 December 1942 as 2,480 planes under the Anglo-Russian Agreement (3,000 including those outside it) and 2,974 tanks' (204).
4. to] the *in typescript*

1826. Bengali Newsletter, 27

16 January 1943

The English original for this Newsletter was based on the News Review broadcast to India on the same day; see *1825*. PasB gives a timing of approximately 9 minutes, four minutes shorter than that of the English Weekly News Review. No script has been traced.

1827. To Herbert Read

18 January 1943   07/ES/EB/WMB

Dear Read
I think it is a very good idea to have Rayner Heppenstall for the last talk as he has an excellent voice. If he cannot get away from his unit we can quite easily record the talk at Leeds or somewhere. I think, however, that—
  a) His subject should be the one you have indicated, i.e. The American Short Story, dealing with a number of contemporary writers, and not merely concentrating on one rather obscure one like Saroyan, and
  b) He would need a lot of prodding to make him deliver his stuff on time.
  Could you get in touch with him and tell him that we are putting his name down in the Publicity and that I am really keen for him to do this talk. I did not know he was free to do talks or I would have approached him before this.
  I will send out contracts for all the others.

Yours
[Initialled] G. O.
George Orwell
Talks Producer
Indian Section

P.S. [on verso] Could you please let us have Rayner Heppenstall's[1] address.

1. Rayner Heppenstall (see *238, n. 2*) met Orwell in 1935 and shared a flat with him for a time. For his account of Orwell, see his *Four Absentees* (1960), extracts of which are in *Orwell Remembered* (106–15). A biographical note to the BBC pamphlet *Landmarks in American Literature* (1946) states that he 'is on the staff of the B.B.C. [as of 1945] as a Producer in the Features Department. He has published two novels, *The Blaze of Noon* and *Saturnine*. He has also several books of verse to his credit which include *Blind Men's Flowers are Green* and *Sebastian*.'

1828. To Marjorie Leaf

19 January 1943   07/ES/EB

Dear Miss Leaf,[1]
Thank you very much for your letter and for the script of your talk for Wednesday next, 20th January. I am enclosing a flimsy copy of the script, but a top copy will be waiting for you at 200 Oxford Street on Wednesday next. It will be nice if you can manage to be here about 12 noon, so that you may rehearse it and time it accurately. The actual time of the broadcast is as before from 12.45 to 1.0 p.m. BST.

I was glad to hear that you reached your meeting in time, last Wednesday. I shall just love to have lunch with you tomorrow. Thank you very much.

Yours sincerely,
[Initialled] MB

1. 'Marjorie' was typed in the salutation but then crossed out on the carbon copy and 'Miss Leaf' written in, in what looks like Mary Blackburn's hand. Orwell was away sick on 20 January, so he may have dictated this letter and Blackburn read it through, changed the salutation to something more formal, and initialled it for him. 'I shall just love to have lunch with you' is unusually effusive for Orwell or Miss Blackburn.

1829. To B. H. Alexander, Copyright Department

19 January 1943   Original   EB/WMB

On 18 January, Miss B. H. Alexander wrote a memorandum to Orwell confirming that George Bernard Shaw had agreed to allow passages from *Arms and the Man* to be broadcast at a fee of £1.1s per minute; Orwell was asked to put the timing of the passage quoted on the PasB. This gives a timing of 5' 54". A fee of £7.7s maximum was allowed and £6.6s was paid.

Miss Alexander then continued: 'I do not think it is very desirable that both you and I should write to Shaw about such matters. For one thing it makes the Corporation look rather silly, and for another, we (copyright) are the only department who are really qualified to say whether it is necessary to obtain permission or not. We happen to know that Shaw interprets the expression "reasonable quotation" very liberally and does not think that permission need be obtained for extracts which others might consider fairly substantial. Moreover whenever a fee has to be negotiated the question should, of course, be dealt with by this department. Would you therefore leave me to make application in cases of this sort in future?'

Miss Alexander's memorandum and the ensuing exchange are indicative of the tensions existing between a long-established organisation and those newly recruited. Orwell replied on 19 January:

With reference to your memo. I did not write to Mr. Shaw about his fee nor have I ever meddled with the question of fees for speakers, but it is absolutely necessary that in many cases I should be the first to approach the speaker to ask whether his work may be used or whether he is willing to broadcast. Even in this case Shaw refused to allow the first passage suggested to be broadcast and asked for the substitution of another. Had he been approached by the Copyright Department in the way you suggested he would probably have refused to allow any passage whatever from ARMS AND THE MAN to be broadcast.

I am only too willing to leave to the Copyright Department the whole business of negotiation over fees, etc., but I cannot possibly give up my right to make independent approaches to speakers who in many cases are deeply suspicious of the B.B.C. but will broadcast or lend their work as a favour to me personally.

On 21 January (when Orwell was off sick), Miss Alexander responded:

Thank you for your memo of the 19th January. I am afraid, however, that I do not quite understand it. You speak of the necessity for your being able to approach *speakers* direct, which, of course, no one disputes. A producer must always be the first to contact speakers, and also authors who are going to write scripts specially for broadcasting, so as to ascertain whether they are willing to do the work. It is only when they have agreed to his proposal that Programme Contracts or Copyright Department come into the picture in order to arrange terms. The case is, however, quite different where it is a question of our broadcasting published material or any other material not specially written for broadcasting: then it is the function of this department to ask for permission and arrange terms.

To put the point in a nutshell, there is all the difference between an approach to a speaker or writer who is to be asked to do work specially for the Corporation, and an approach to an author for permission to use published material which involves no work on his part, but merely the granting of a licence to perform.

Shaw is certainly not 'deeply suspicious' of the B.B.C.—in fact we are on very good terms with him. If you had told us the special arguments you wished to be put before him in connection with the proposed 'Arms and the Man' broadcast I do not think you would have found he would have turned down our application simply because it came from Copyright Department and not from you. (We would of course have mentioned your name as the producer.)

If the producer is a close friend of the author of published material which we wish to use and if the author has not had any previous dealings with the

Corporation and does not know much about broadcasting then I think there may be a case for the producer making a preliminary contact with him. In that case of course, this department should be told in order that when we write him the official letter we can refer to the approach that has already been made.

1830. Orwell's Sick Leave

Orwell's personal file shows that he was sick from Wednesday, 20 January, to Thursday, 11 February 1943. His sick notes show that he was suffering from bronchitis. (For a summary of his sick leaves, see *867*.)

Correspondence written on his behalf relevant to the programmes he was organising is given here in order to complete the record.

Instead of a Newsletter for India on 23 January, a talk, 'Turkey Today,' was broadcast; see *1839* and *1840*. The Newsletters for 30 January and 6 and 13 February were written and read by Anthony Weymouth. Orwell's next contribution in this series was on 20 February 1943.

The News Commentaries in English for Malaya were: No. 17: 22 January, written by Orwell, read by D. Prentice (an announcer in the Overseas Presentation Unit); 18: 29 January, written and read by G. E. Rowan Davies (a Transcription Assistant when Orwell joined the Eastern Service but listed as School Broadcasting Manager, 21.8.43); 19: 5 February, written and read by G. E. Rowan Davies; 20: 12 February 1943, written and read by Sir Richard Winstedt.[1]

Orwell wrote and read No. 21 on 19 February 1943.

1. For Sir Richard Winstedt, authority on Malay language and history, see *1669, n. 1*.

1831. Venu Chitale to Desmond Hawkins

20 January 1943   07/ES/EB/WMB

Dear Mr. Hawkins

Mr. Blair tells me that you have already chosen your subjects for the ANNIVERSARIES OF THE MONTH Feature programme, for Tuesday, February 2nd—1145 to 1200 GMT.

I am looking forward to receiving your script on the Saturday before the broadcast.

Yours sincerely,
[Initialled] V. C.
Venu Chitale
Indian Section

1832. Mary Blackburn to L. F. Rushbrook Williams, E.S.D.

c. 20 January 1943

Bengali Newsletters.

May we, on the att'd report,[1] go ahead and use Dr P. Chatterjee, to write in Bengali and broadcast the Bengali Newsletter for a few weeks in February? It would be a good idea to have a change from Das Gupta whose present Contract expires after the last Sat. in Jan. Mr. Blair thinks it might be a good idea, occasionally, to use Miss A. Sen Gupta to give a 3 to 4 min. Bengali item specially of interest to Bengali women. She was very good when she gave the message to the bombed areas and the Indian Staff say her voice is excellent and her Bengali good.

Rushbrook Williams annotated Miss Blackburn's memorandum, 'Yes certainly.' On 22 February, he wrote to Chatterjee's employer, the General Manager of the Mercantile Overseas Trust Ltd in Old Broad St., London, explaining Chatterjee's appointment and its importance to the war. There were, he said, few competent Bengali speakers available to the BBC to address 'this very important community in India.' He asked if Chatterjee could be free every Saturday morning to write the Bengali Newsletter and prepare an English version. The General Manager replied on 24 February that the firm was very pleased to agree to the request.

On 25 January, Miss Blackburn, and on 22 February, Orwell invited Chatterjee to write the Newsletters in Bengali for 6 and 13 February, and 6, 13, 20, and 27 March. This would leave 23 and 30 January and 20 and 27 February for Orwell, but he was ill for the first two of these dates. It would appear from Chatterjee's letter of 22 March to Orwell, which refers to the seven Newsletters he had by then written, that he wrote the first two scheduled for Orwell. That would bring the total of Bengali Newsletters written by Orwell to 29. Orwell continued to be associated with the production of this Newsletter, however, for he checked the English translations. Chatterjee continued writing the Newsletters until he was commissioned in August 1943. Special four-minute features of interest to women listeners were given by Miss Anima Sen Gupta on 6 February (on Ellen Wilkinson, M.P.) and 6 and 20 March; those on 5, 12, 19, and 26 December 1942 were given by Mrs. Renu Ghosh. For Chatterjee, see also *858, n. 2.*

1. A report on Chatterjee's capabilities, prepared by Miss G. M. Summers, found that the Bengali was good, with a wide choice of vocabulary but yet not falling into the trap of being stiff and over-literary; the style was simple and easy and suitable for broadcasting. The English translation (which Orwell was to check) was accurate if not always grammatical.

1833. Unsigned Review of *The Pub and the People* by Mass-Observation

The Listener, 21 January 1943

It is a pity that this large and careful survey could not have had a short appendix indicating what effect the war has had on our drinking habits. It seems to have been compiled just before the war, and even in that short period of time beer has doubled in price and been heavily diluted.

Writing at a time when 'mild' was still fivepence a pint (between 1936 and 1941 rearmament only raised it by a penny), the Mass-Observers found that in 'Worktown' the regular pub-goer was putting away, on average, between fifteen and twenty pints a week. This sounds a good deal, but it is unquestionable that in the past seventy years the annual consumption of beer per head has decreased by nearly two-thirds, and it is the Mass-Observers' conclusion that 'the pub as a cultural institution is at present declining'. This happens not merely because of persecution by Nonconformist Town Councils, nor even primarily because of the increased price of drink, but because the whole trend of the age is away from creative communal amusements and towards solitary mechanical ones. The pub, with its elaborate social ritual, its animated conversations and—at any rate in the North of England—its songs and week-end comedians, is gradually replaced by the passive, drug-like pleasures of the cinema and the radio. This is only a cause for rejoicing if one believes, as a few Temperance fanatics still do, that people go to pubs to get drunk. The Mass-Observers, however, have no difficulty in showing that there was extraordinarily little drunkenness in the period they were studying: for every five thousand hours that the average pub stays open, only one of its clients is drunk and disorderly.

Working on the more old-fashioned provincial pubs where the various bars are still separate rooms and not, as in London, merely one long counter separated by partitions, the authors of this book have unearthed much curious information. In a short review it is impossible to dilate on the complex social code that differentiates the saloon bar from the public bar, or on the delicate ritual that centres round treating, or the cultural implications of the trend towards bottled beer, or the rivalry between church and pub and the consequent guilt-feelings associated with drinking; but the average reader is likely to find Chapters V, VI and VII the most interesting. At least one of the Observers seems to have taken the extreme step of being initiated into the Buffaloes, about which there are some surprising revelations. A questionnaire issued through the local press, asking people why they drink beer, elicited from more than half the answer that they drank it for their health—probably an echo of the brewers' advertisements which talk of beer as though it were a kind of medicine. There were some who answered more frankly, however: 'A middle-aged man of about 40 of labouring type says, "What the bloody hell dost tha tak it for?" I said for my health; he said "Th'art a —— liar". I paid for him a gill'.[1]

And one woman answered the questionnaire thus:

My reason is, because I always liked to see my grandmother having a drink of beer at night. She did seem to enjoy it, and she could pick up a dry crust of bread and cheese, and it seemed like a feast. She said if you have a drink of beer you will live to be one hundred, she died at ninety-two. I shall never refuse a drink of beer. There is no bad ale, so Grandma said.

This little piece of prose, which impresses itself upon the memory like a poem, would in itself be a sufficient justification of beer, if indeed it needed justifying.

Orwell was paid a fee of £2.2s. for this review.

1. A gill is a quarter of a pint except in areas indicated by the accent, where it is half a pint..

1834. BBC Talks Booking Form, 21.1.43

T. S. Eliot: 'Landmarks in American Literature,' 2; 'Mr. Eliot is writing a script on "Edgar Allen° Poe" and is reading it'; 13½ minutes approx.; broadcast 12.2.43; fee £15.15s. Signed: M Blackburn for I.P.O.

1835. BBC Talks Booking Form, 21.1.43

V. S. Pritchett:[1] 'Landmarks in American Literature,' 4; 'Mr. Pritchett is writing a script on "Mark Twain" and is reading it'; 13½ minutes approx.; broadcast 26.2.43; fee £12.12s + 11s for the fare. Signed: M Blackburn for I.P.O.

1. Victor Sawdon Pritchett (1900–1997; Kt., 1975), author and critic, particularly noted as a writer of short stories. The biographical note to the BBC pamphlet, *Landmarks in American Literature*, gave his year of birth as 1901, and noted 'His best-known works are *Nothing Like Heather* (a novel, 1935), *You Make your° own Life* (short stories, 1938), *In my Good Books* (critical essays, 1942).' By this time he had also written *Marching Spain* (a travel book, 1928), *The Spanish Virgin and Other Stories* (1930), *Dead Men Leading* (1937), and a number of other books.

1836. BBC Talks Booking Form, 21.1.43

Herbert Read: 'Landmarks in American Literature,' 1; 'H. Read is writing the script and reading the first talk in this series, on "Nathaniel Hawthorne", he is also compèring the five other talks in this series'; broadcast 5.2 (N. Hawthorne), 12, 19 and 26.2.43 and 5 and 12.3.43; fee 'usual' and split into two rates, £12.12s and £5.5s; Talks Booking Manager agreed to '12gns each talk.' Signed: M Blackburn for I.P.O.

1837. News Commentary in English for Malaya, 17

22 January 1943

This was written by Orwell before he was taken ill and read by D. Prentice (Staff). No script has been traced.

1838. 'Calling All Students,' 5: George Bernard Shaw,
Arms and the Man

Broadcast 22 January 1943

The text for Orwell's talk on *Arms and the Man* exists as the typescript used by Orwell for recording the talk (just before he was taken ill) and in the form printed in 1946 by Oxford University Press in Bombay, BBC Pamphlet No 2, *Books and Authors*. The published form is reproduced here; the few differences from the typescript are given in the notes. Rushbrook Williams passed the script for Policy and Security, and it is marked, in Orwell's hand, 'As recorded   14' 20" E.A.B'. PasB records:

Talk on George Bernard Shaw, with special reference to *Arms and the Man*, by George Orwell, rec: DOX 9909, 14' 20"
Introduction by Edmund Blunden, rec: DOX 9909 3½'
'The Soldier's Tale' by Stravinsky, COL LX 197 Pt 1, 2½'; COL LX 199 2½'
(Chosen by Narayana Menon)
Extract from *Arms and the Man*, Act III, acted by Belle Crystal and Laidman Browne, rec. 20.1.43, DOX 10034, 5' 54".

Arms and the Man was performed for the first time in 1894, when Bernard Shaw was 38 years old and was at the height of his powers as a dramatist. It is probably the wittiest play he ever wrote, the most faultless technically, and, in spite of being a very light comedy, the most telling. But before discussing the play in general terms I must say something, as short as possible, about its theme and plot.

Briefly, *Arms and the Man* is a debunking of military glory and the romance of the warrior. The action takes place in the little Balkan state of Bulgaria—it doesn't, of course, matter whether the local colour is correct or not: the events might just as well have happened in England or Germany or America—at a time when a war between Bulgaria and Serbia has just ended in a Bulgarian victory. The heroine, Raina she is called, a romantic young girl, has just heard at the beginning of the first act that her lover, Sergius Saranoff, has won the crucial battle of the war by charging at the head of his regiment of cavalry through the enemy's machine-guns. Naturally she is wild with pride. She is standing at her window, gazing out on the mountains and dreaming of her lover, when the defeated Serbian army begins to stream through the town with the Bulgarians pursuing them. One hunted man climbs up the waterpipe and takes refuge in her bedroom. He is hardly there when Raina finds herself violating what she believes to be the code of true patriotism by helping him to hide, and even telling lies to protect him when the pursuers come to look for him. But the short conversation she has with him punctures her illusions much more completely than that. The hunted man turns out to be a Swiss professional soldier, Captain Bluntschli by name, and the most hopelessly prosaic person it is possible to imagine. He can hardly open his mouth without outraging the notions of military glory on which Raina has been brought up. He assures her that all soldiers are frightened of death, that a man who has been under fire for three days loses his nerve until he is ready to cry like a child, and that in battle food is far more important than

323

ammunition. 'You can always tell an old soldier by the insides of his holsters and cartridge boxes', he says. 'The young ones carry pistols and cartridges: the old ones, grub.' But then an even worse disillusionment occurs. It turns out that Captain Bluntschli was in command of the Serbian machine-gun battery which was destroyed when Sergius, Raina's lover, made his heroic cavalry charge. And he is able to explain why it was that the charge succeeded—the machine-gunners had been sent the wrong ammunition and were unable to fire. If the guns had gone off not a man would have survived; so Sergius has in fact won the battle by mistake. In the later acts some more illusions are exploded. Sergius, a magnificent romantic figure with flashing eyes and sweeping moustaches, a character out of Byron's early poems, turns out to be an almost complete fraud. He tells Raina that he regards her as a saint and himself as her knight errant, but he begins making love to the maidservant the moment Raina's back is turned. Raina herself is exposed as a habitual liar and as laying claim to lofty emotions which she does not feel, and all the other characters are in their various ways impostors. The play ends by Raina marrying the prosaic Swiss soldier, the first man who has ever seen through her romantic pretentions to the real woman underneath.

Shaw is what is called a 'writer with a purpose', every one of his plays is designed to point some moral or other, and undoubtedly one reason why *Arms and the Man* has worn better than some of the other plays he wrote at about the same time, is that its moral, or 'message', still needs pointing. Shaw is saying, in effect, that war, though sometimes necessary, is not glorious, not romantic. Killing and being killed isn't the heroic, picturesque business that the propagandists make it out to be, and, moreover, wars will usually be won by those who plan for them scientifically and not romantically. Nearly fifty years after the play was written this is still worth saying, because the romantic view of war dies very hard and tends to revive after every disillusionment. It so happens that I have seen *Arms and the Man* acted twice. The first time was in 1918, and the theatre was full of soldiers fresh from the front in France. They saw the point of it, because their experiences had taught them the same thing. There is a passage early in the play where Bluntschli is telling Raina what a cavalry charge is really like. 'It is', he says, 'like slinging a handful of peas against a window pane: first one comes; then two or three close behind him; and then all the rest in a lump.' Raina, thinking of Sergius, her lover, charging at the head of his regiment, clasps her hands ecstatically and says, 'Yes, first comes One! The bravest of the brave!' 'Ah,' says Bluntschli, 'but you should see the poor devil pulling at his horse!' At this line the audience of simple soldiers burst into a laugh which almost lifted the roof off. The next time I saw the play acted was in 1935, at an experimental theatre before a much more high-brow audience. This time Bluntschli's line didn't get a laugh. War was far away and very few people in the audience knew what it was like to have to face bullets.

If you examine Shaw's other plays of the same period, you find that some of them, equally brilliant in execution—for every one of Shaw's early plays is a masterpiece of technique, with never a false note or a wasted word—don't have the same freshness today, because in them he is attacking illusions which no one any longer believes in. The play which caused a terrific scandal when it first appeared and did, perhaps, more than anything else to make Shaw famous is *Mrs Warren's Profession*. This play deals with prostitution, and its theme is that the causes of prostitution are largely economic. This idea was a novelty in the eighteen-nineties, but now, when everyone has read Marx, it seems a commonplace, hardly worth uttering. So also with *Widowers' Houses*, an attack on slum landlordism. Slums still exist and people still make a profit out of them, but at least no one thinks this normal and proper any longer. Or so again with a somewhat later play, *John Bull's Other Island*. The satire in this play depends largely on Ireland being under English rule, a state of affairs which has long ceased to exist. *Pygmalion*, one of the wittiest of Shaw's plays, revolves round class-distinctions which at this date are nothing like so strongly marked as they used to be, and even *Major Barbara* and *Androcles and the Lion* depended for their first impact on orthodox religious belief being very much more general than it is today.[1] I don't, however, want to give the impression that Shaw is one of those writers, like the French dramatist Brieux or the English novelist Charles Reade, who squander their talents on 'showing up' some local and temporary abuse which will probably have disappeared of its own accord within a few years. Shaw deals in generalities, not in details. He is criticizing society as a whole, and not merely its aberrations. Yet there is a reason why his early attack has lost something of its sting, and it raises certain questions about the whole position of satirists and political writers generally.

Briefly, Shaw is a debunking writer, what people used to call a 'shocker'. Now it is obvious that you can only play this part successfully when there is something to be debunked. For the background, the springboard as it were, of his witticisms, Shaw needed the solidity, the power and the self-righteousness of the late-Victorian society in which he first lived and worked. Shaw was born in 1856 and first came to England at the age of about twenty, and quite apart from his natural talent he was especially fitted to satirize English society because he was an Irishman and able to look at it from the outside as a native Englishman could hardly do. The two great vices of England, now as then,[2] are hypocrisy and stupidity. But late-Victorian society differed from that of today in that it was far more self-confident, more Philistine, more frankly acquisitive. What we should call 'enlightened' people were relatively far fewer. Class privilege was more assured, there were no left-wing political parties worth bothering about, popular education and cheap newspapers had not yet had their full effect, art and literature had lost contact with Europe in the early part of the century and not yet regained it. The world of late-Victorian England was easy meat for a satirical writer. Indeed, Shaw was not the first of his kind. In the prefaces to some of his plays he has discussed his own literary ancestry, and though he admittedly owes much to Ibsen, the great Norwegian dramatist, he seems to feel that he owes even more to Samuel Butler, the English novelist, who a few decades earlier had criticized English society from somewhat the same angle as Shaw himself. Butler, it is worth noticing, utterly failed to reach the big public and only received recognition after his death: Shaw, born twenty years later, remained obscure till he was nearly forty but lived to be the best-known literary man of his age. The difference is partly one of time. Butler's great novel, *The Way of All Flesh*, was at once hailed as a masterpiece when it was published round about 1905, but it would probably have fallen flat if he had published it in the eighties, when he actually wrote it. Shaw happened upon the scene when the colossus of Victorian society was still there, as imposing and self-satisfied as ever, but was actually due to fall to pieces within a few years. He was attacking something still strong enough to be worth attacking, and yet not so strong as to make the attack hopeless. People found it amusing to be shocked, but they were still capable of being shocked. These conditions existed to perfection in the years 1890–1910, the years when Shaw's best work was done, but they exist no longer. No one, nowadays, could make his reputation as a 'shocker'. What is there any longer to be shocked at? What conventions survive to be outraged? The self-satisfied, prudish, money-ruled world that Shaw made fun of has been washed away by the spread of scepticism and enlightenment: and for that scepticism and enlightenment Shaw himself, as much as any one writer of our time, is responsible.

In this short space I have necessarily dealt with only one aspect of Shaw's work, his debunking of current society and the consequent inevitable 'dating' of certain of his plays. But it would be an absurdity to regard Shaw as a pamphleteer and nothing more. The sense of purpose with which he always writes would get him nowhere if he were not also an artist. In illustration of this I point once again to *Arms and the Man*. Whoever examines this play in detail will notice that it is not only a witty satire on one of the abiding illusions of humanity, but a miracle of stage technique. There are only eight characters in it—two of them are small parts—and by the time any one of those eight has spoken half a dozen sentences you have the feeling that you would recognize him at a glance if you met him in the street. Nowhere is there a false emphasis or a clumsily contrived incident; the play gives the impression of having grown as naturally as a plant. There are not even any verbal fireworks; brilliant as the dialogue is, every word of it helps the action along. In this play, and in two or three others written about the same time, Shaw's genius reached its high-water mark.[3] If I were asked to tabulate Shaw's plays in order of merit, I should bracket together at the top *Arms and the Man* and *The Devil's Disciple*, his play about the American War of Independence. In both of those there is a strong central theme that may grow familiar but never grows stale, and in both there is the most perfect mastery of character, dialogue and situation. A little way below those two I should put *Captain Brassbound's Conversion*, *Caesar and Cleopatra*, *Androcles and the Lion* and *The Man of Destiny*, all of them brilliantly witty comedies. The volume of Shaw's work that will survive on its own merits is much greater than that, and it includes not only plays but dramatic criticism and at least one of his early novels, *Cashel Byron's Profession*. But whoever has read or seen those six plays that I have named has skimmed the cream off Shaw. Those are the works of his prime, done when he knew himself for what he really was, a dramatist, and before he had mistaken himself for a philosopher and begun to produce unwieldy plays like *Man and Superman* and *Back to Methuselah*, already unactable and unreadable.

1. 'The play which caused a terrific scandal . . . than it is today' is within square brackets in the typescript but is not crossed out. This probably indicates a provisional cut. The full script could have been read in 14′ 20″; cutting these lines would have reduced this time by about 75 seconds.
2. ', now as then' is crossed out in the typescript but retained in the 1946 printed text.
3. high-water mark] high water-mark *in typescript*

1839. To E. W. D. Boughen, Talks Booking

22 January 1943   Original   EB/WMB

Owing to illness, Orwell could not broadcast a Newsletter to India on 23 January and, at short notice, a talk, 'Turkey Today,' was substituted. Mary Blackburn made the arrangements.

BRIG. GEN. SIR WYNDHAM DEEDES, C.M.G.[1]

The above is doing a talk in English for us, entitled TURKEY TODAY, at very short notice, to take the place of George Orwell, who is away ill. This will be broadcast tomorrow, the 23rd January, at 1115 to 1130 GMT, in the Eastern Service (Red Network).

Would you please issue a contract for Sir Wyndham Deedes, and send it to this office immediately (today) so that we may hand it to Sir Wyndham Deedes tomorrow.

[Signed] M Blackburn
(For Eric Blair)

1. Sir Wyndham Deedes, CMG (1883–1956) had been a distinguished soldier in the Boer War and World War I. He had learned Turkish and was charged with organising the Turkish gendarmerie in an area of North Africa four times the size of France. He also served in Palestine and supported the Zionist movement. In 1923 he retired from the army and devoted himself to social work in the East End of London. He helped found the Turkish Centre in London, translated Turkish novels, and regularly broadcast in Turkish to Turkey. He was Labour member for North-East Bethnal Green on the London County Council, 1941–46, and was chief air-raid warden for Bethnal Green.

1840. BBC Talks Booking Form, 22.1.43

Brig. Gen. Sir Wyndham Deedes, C.M.G.: 'Turkey Today'; a 13-minute talk in English, requested at very short notice, written and read by him; broadcast 23.1.43; fee £12.12s. Signed: M Blackburn for I.P.O.

On 25 January, Miss Blackburn wrote to Mrs. Talbot Rice, Near East Section, Ministry of Information, a Turkish specialist (see *1125, n. 1*) to express thanks for help in putting the Indian Section in touch with General Deedes at short notice. The talk was later translated into Hindustani and transmitted in the vernacular programme to India on 7 February; General Deedes provided an additional introductory paragraph 'on the Prime Minister's recent visit to Turkey.' Churchill had met the President of Turkey, Ismet Inönü, and his ministers at Adana on 30 January 1943; see *The Second World War*, IV, 626–37; U.S.: *The Hinge of Fate*, 704–12.

1841. To A. L. C. Bullock, European Service Talks Director

25 January 1943   Handwritten draft and carbon copy
07/ES/EB/WMB

Dear Mr. Bullock
Thank you for your letter of the 22nd January. I will do the suggested talk[1] with pleasure, if I can be reasonably frank. But[2] I am not going to say anything I regard as untruthful.

> Yours sincerely
> [Initialled] G. O.
> George Orwell
> Talks Producer
> Indian Section

1. Orwell was to give a talk of 600 to 800 words 'on the social changes in the town since the war' as one of seventeen talks given during 'British Week' in a series called Britain Today. It was scheduled for 4 February 1943, and he evidently expected to be better by then. Because he was still ill, however, Stephen Spender spoke on 'The Town and War,' on 2 (not 4) February 1943.
2. 'But' appears only in the draft, but a space has been left for a word of that length in the carbon copy of the typed version.

1842. To Public Relations, Section 4, Air Ministry

25 January 1943   07/ES/EB/ED

Dear Sir,
I enclose the second script in our series "Modern Aircraft", by E. C. Bowyer. We propose to broadcast this talk on "Fighters" on Friday next, 29th January, at 1145–1200 GMT, in our Eastern Service, and shall be glad to receive your approval as soon as possible.

> Yours faithfully,
> [Initialled] E. A. B[1]
> (Eric Blair)
> Talks Producer

1. Although Orwell was ill with bronchitis, the carbon copy of this letter has been initalled by him. An annotation gives the telephone number Abbey 3411.

1843. BBC Talks Booking Form, 25.1.43

Princess Indira of Kapurthala: 'The Debate Continues'; broadcast 25.1.43; fee £12.12s. Signed: M Blackburn for I.P.O.

1844. BBC Talks Booking Form, 25.1.43

Dr. P. Chatterjee: to write Newsletter in Bengali and supply an English version; the one on 6 February approx. 10 minutes, the one on the 13th approx. 13½ minutes; broadcast 6 and 13.2.43; fees £9.9s and £10.10s. Signed: M Blackburn for I.P.O.

1845. On Orwell's behalf to Noel Sircar

26 January 1943   07/ES/EB

Dear Mr. Sircar

Will you be able to do our talk in the series IN THE PUBLIC EYE, on Wednesday, February 10th. You know the procedure, as you have done two for us already. If the personality in the Profiles column in THE OBSERVER on the Sunday previous is an interesting one, you can take that, or perhaps you have some other ideas of your own. Will you please confirm that you are able to do this.

Yours sincerely
[Initialled] MB
For Eric Blair
Talks Producer
Indian Section

1846. BBC Talks Booking Form, 26.1.43

K. K. Ardaschir: 'Victoria Station Bombay to Victoria Station London'; 13½-minute talk; broadcast 12.3.43; fee £9.9s. Signed: M Blackburn for I.P.O.

1847. BBC Talks Booking Form, 26.1.43

Lady Grigg: 'Women Generally Speaking'; broadcast 3, 10, 17 and 24.2.43; fee £8.8s each broadcast. Signed: M Blackburn for I.P.O.

1848. BBC Talks Booking Form, 26.1.43

Shridhar Telkar: 'Behind the Headlines'; broadcast 3, 10, 17, and 24.2.43;[1] fee
£9.9s each talk. Signed: M Blackburn for I.P.O.

1. On 6 February, Orwell's secretary, Winifred Bedwell, wrote to Ronald Boswell, Talks
Booking Manager, to correct dates for these talks to 4, 11, 18, and 25 February.

1849. Memorandum on Orwell's behalf to E. W. D. Boughen

27 January 1943   Original   EB/WMB

RECORDING BY SIR AZIZ-UL-HUQUE,
High Commissioner for India

Owing to a technical hitch, the recording of the High Commissioner's talk
did not take place yesterday, during transmission time, as previously
arranged. (It was arranged that his talk should be recorded when he came
to broadcast live on Tuesday, January 26th at 1145–1200 GMT). The talk
was, however, recorded as follows:—

On Wednesday, January 26th, at 3.45 to 4.15 BST. in St. 2, Oxford St.
"THE HIGH COMMISSIONER SPEAKS TO YOU" (Eastern Service—Red
Network) DOX. 10325. Recording time 10' 55". The recording was quite
satisfactory.

The High Commissioner had to record this talk specially, which meant
an extra ¾ hour of his time, after he had given a live talk in the Hindustani
Service previously. Therefore, we feel, he should be paid an extra fee for
this.[1]

[Signed] Winifred Bedwell
(For Eric Blair)

1. The memorandum is annotated, '4 gns.'

1850. BBC Talks Booking Form, 27.1.43

Catherine Lacey: 'Women Generally Speaking'; Producer 'Mr Eric Blair';
broadcast 10.2.43; fee £8.8s + repeat fees. Signed: SFA, Programme Contracts
Department.

1851. To E. M. Forster

c. 28 January 1943

SENDING REGISTERED POST FURTHER COPY HENRY PONSONBY[1]   ORWELL
ILL PLEASE PROCEED AS YOU THINK BEST SECRETARY[2]

1. West: *Commentaries* prints Forster's letter to Orwell of 26 January 1943 regretting that Orwell is ill and asking for two books: 'Lord Ponsonby's life of his father,' identified by West as *Henry Ponsonby: His Life from his Letters* by Arthur Ponsonby, a copy of which he had mislaid, and 'the book about Max Plowman' (240). Sir Henry Ponsonby (1825–1895), was private secretary to Queen Victoria. The second book was probably *The Right to Live*, a collection of Plowman's essays, edited by his wife, Dorothy. For the Plowmans' long friendship with Orwell, see *95, 418*, and *817*.
2. Presumably Winifred Bedwell. Venu Chitale also took over some of Orwell's work whilst he was ill. On 27 January she asked Desmond Hawkins to bring in his Anniversaries script on the next day because Orwell was sick. She seems then to have taken over as producer of these programmes. On 16 February she wrote to Hawkins saying she thought 'the idea of John Donne for our March feature is a marvellous one' but proposed to decide on Barnum (for April or May) 'till we have finished with March.'

1852. BBC Talks Booking Form, 28.1.43

Naomi Royde-Smith:[1] 'Women Generally Speaking'; three 13½-minute talks in English, 'Illustrated Talks on Poetry Produced in Wars'; broadcast 17.2.43, 17.3.43, and 21.4.43; fee £15.15s for each talk + 13s 6d fare. Signed: M Blackburn for I.P.O.

1. Naomi Royde-Smith (1875–1964), novelist and literary editor of the *Westminster Gazette*, 1912–22, wrote more than forty novels, of which *The Tortoiseshell Cat* (1925) is particularly well regarded, a number of plays, one on Mrs. Siddons (1931), of whom she also wrote a biography (1933). In 1941 she published *Outside Information: Being a Diary of Rumours collated by N. Royde Smith* (no hyphen).

1853. To E. M. Forster[1]

c. 29 January 1943

UNABLE TO OBTAIN BOOK ON MAX PLOWMAN OUT OF STOCK STOP DO YOU WISH TO SUGGEST ANOTHER   ORWELL BROADCASTS

1. Presumably sent on Orwell's behalf by Winifred Bedwell; see *1851, n. 2*.

1854. On Orwell's behalf to S. K. Das Gupta

29 January 1943   07/ES/EB

Dear Mr. Das Gupta

I should like to take this opportunity of thanking you personally, and also on behalf of the Indian Section for your kind co-operation and untiring keenness and interest in translating and broadcasting the Bengali Newsletters to India. We are most grateful for all your help.

In order to bring variety into our Bengali News Commentaries, we have been asked to introduce some more voices and we feel that we must take notice of these requests which we have received. We are therefore arranging temporarily for someone else to read the Bengali Newsletters for a short time. We ought to emphasise that there is nothing permanent as yet in this arrangement. We shall be grateful for your continued help and interest, if and when the opportunity occurs.

Yours sincerely,
[Initialled] MB
for Eric Blair
(Talks Producer)

1855. On Orwell's behalf to Arthur Wynn, Music Bookings Manager

29 January 1943   Original   EB/WMB

As from Friday, February 5th, we are giving an interlude of music (about 7 minutes) in our new series, LANDMARKS IN AMERICAN LITERATURE. This series of six talks will be broadcast at 1115 to 1145 GMT on Fridays, beginning 5th February and continuing the 12th, 19th, 26th and 5th and 12th March. Mr. Narayana Menon is choosing appropriate music for this seven minute interlude to fit in with these talks.

We shall be glad, therefore, if you will issue a contract for Mr. Narayana Menon, 151 Sussex Gardens, London, W.2. for these six periods. Mr. Menon has to carefully choose music, which will interest Indian listeners, and appropriate to this American Literature series. The interlude will fill 7 minutes of the programme and the music will need thoughtful choosing, which will take some time—therefore, we feel that the fee should be a higher one than for his previous work. [We] suggest £2–2–0.

[Signed] M Blackburn
(For Eric Blair)

1856. On Orwell's behalf to Public Relations, Section 4, Air Ministry

30 January 1943   07/ES/EB

Dear Sir

I enclose the third script in our series 'Modern Aircraft' by E. C. Bowyer.

We propose to broadcast this talk on "Dive Bombers and Torpedo 'Planes" on Friday next, the 5th February at 1145–1200 GMT (12.45 to 1.0 p.m. BST), in our Eastern Service. We shall be most grateful to receive your approval as soon as possible.

Yours faithfully,
[Initialled] MB
for — (Eric Blair)
Talks Producer

1857. BBC Talks Booking Form, 30.1.43

Princess Indira of Kapurthala: 'The Debate Continues'; broadcast 1.2.43; fee £12.12s. Signed: M Blackburn for I.P.O.[1] Remarks: 'Miss Ellen Wilkinson was to have done 4–min. talk within this period but its° cancelled.'

1. This talks booking form was initiated by 'I.P.O's Office (in Mr. Blair's absence).'

1858. Morocco Is Poor but Happy

World Digest, February 1943

This was a shortened version of 'Background of French Morocco,' which appeared in *Tribune*, 20 November 1942; see *1668*.

1859. On Orwell's behalf to Herbert Read

1 February 1943   07/AS/GB/HEM

Dear Herbert Read

In George Orwell's absence I[1] am looking after the programme on Friday, and your Hawthorne script has therefore been passed on to me. Will it be convenient to you to come here (200 Oxford Street) at about 11 o'clock, so that we can rehearse for timing and so on.

Yours sincerely

1. This letter is initialled, but the initials are illegible. It was probably written by Gerald Bullett, Talks Producer. Rendall's memorandum of 20 August 1941 indicates that Bullett was to lend Orwell assistance when he started at the BBC, and the letter to Martin Armstrong, 9 September 1942 (see *1465*), shows he still did so, at least from time to time. For Gerald Bullett, see *846, n. 7*.

1860. Memorandum to B. H. Alexander

1 February 1943   Original   EB/WMB

Mr. Sidney Horniblow

We have asked Mr. Sidney Horniblow, of 56 Curzon Street, W.1. to do a 13 minute programme for us entitled IN BLACK AND WHITE, on the lines of the one he previously wrote for us. This programme is to run fortnightly in the Eastern Service (Red Network) on the following dates:— March 26th, 9th, 23rd April, 7th, 21st May and 4th June. This series is for broadcast between 1145 and 1200 GMT. Will you kindly arrange payment for these scripts.[1]

This series are Featurised Talks and they are based, to a certain extent, on the leading articles from the Press of Great Britain, because the idea is to let

Indian listeners have up-to-date information about what our press is saying.

[Signed] Winifred Bedwell
(Eric Blair)

1. Miss Alexander wrote to Horniblow on 2 February. She argued that because the original series had been paid for at a rate of £10.10s under the misapprehension that the programmes consisted of original material, it was hoped he would agree to a reduced fee of not more than £8.8s for each broadcast. The letter has two annotations: 'Agreed 10 on phone' and 'Cancelled!' See letter from Rushbrook Williams to Horniblow, 5 February 1943, *1872*.

1861. BBC Talks Booking Form, 1.2.43

Dr. N. Gangulee:[1] 'In Your Kitchen: Diet'; 'Dr. Gangulee is going to write and broadcast a 5-min. talk on diet. These talks will entail a good deal of research work'; broadcast 3 and 17.2.43 and 3 and 17.3.43; fee £4.4s each talk. Signed: M Blackburn for I.P.O.[2]

1. Dr. Gangulee had been Professor of Agriculture and Rural Economics at the University of Calcutta. He was active in the 'Free India' movement in England. An advertisement in *Tribune*, 7 April 1944, bills him as chairman of a meeting to be held on 16 April 1944 to 'Wipe out the memory' of Amritsar (where nearly 400 people were killed by troops under the command of General Dyer in 1919) 'with a Free India Now! Public Meeting.' As well as unnamed Indians, speakers included Sir Richard Acland (see *609, n. 2*) and Fenner Brockway (see *363, n. 4*), Gangulee is described in Orwell's memorandum of 3 February 1943 as the son-in-law of poet and Nobel Prizewinner (1913) Rabindranath Tagore (1861–1941).
2. This, and the next four forms, are stated to be from 'Eric Blair Indian Section,' but they were evidently prepared in his absence.

1862. BBC Talks Booking Form, 2.2.43

Mrs. K. C. Roy: 'In Your Kitchen'; 'Mrs. Roy will choose and broadcast a recipe appropriate to Dr. Gangulee's broadcast of the previous week in this series. Duration abt. 5 mins. Mrs. Roy will broadcast alternately with Dr. Gangulee'; broadcast 10 and 24.2.43 and 10 and 24.3.43; fee £4.4s each talk. Signed: M Blackburn for I.P.O.

1863. Memorandum to R. A. Rendall, Assistant Controller, Overseas Service

3 February 1943   EB/WMB

Subject: New Speakers—"IN YOUR KITCHEN". Eastern Service (Red Netwk)
To: A.C.(O.S.) Copies to D.E.P. E.S.D. E.P.P. I.P.O. Room 321, Mr. Goatman, Overseas Pub. Emp. Prog.

Compilation, Mr. Brenard, Langham Hotel, E.T.M. Mrs. Short, N.A.S.D. P.S.D. A.S.D. Mr. Brander.

After Wednesday, January 27th, Miss Shireen Panthaki ceases to broadcast the cooking recipe in the series IN YOUR KITCHEN. Commencing Wednesday, the 3rd February, and continuing *fortnightly*, Dr. Gangulee, who is the son-in-law of Rabindranath Tagore, will broadcast a talk on food and diet, in the series IN YOUR KITCHEN.

Commencing Wednesday, February 10th, and continuing *fortnightly*, Mrs. Roy, will broadcast a recipe, based on the previous week's talk by Dr. Gangulee. Dr. Gangulee's and Mrs. Roy's talks will be given every week, alternately. I don't know how long these talks will last but I will inform you when I receive the information.

These talks will be broadcast in the Eastern Service, (Red Network) every Wednesday, commencing February 3rd, at 1124 to 1130 GMT.

[Signed] Winifred Bedwell
(For Eric Blair)

Several copies of this memorandum survive, including that sent to R. A. Rendall. He annotated his copy for Rushbrook Williams's benefit, starting at the foot of the side containing Orwell's memorandum and continuing on the verso until he had no more room to voice his complaints. His reply carries a bold rubber-stamp: 'PRIVATE & CONFIDENTIAL.' West: *Broadcasts* reproduces the first part but omits points iii and iv, there are a number of transcription errors, and the reply is wrongly dated 1942.

This is the third of these notes that I have received recently. I don't like the look of them because it suggests that Blair is setting up an independant° business as an Eastern Talks Director. I have a high regard for his general abilities and I know that he would not deliberately attempt to do this in a self-advertising or separatist way: and I know that you have been badly affected by illness in your dept. But I must point out (i) that I have asked more than once to be consulted in advance of new series (ii) that coordination & general notification is Collins job and that he equally should be informed in advance, (iii) that the "regionalising" of talks producers was arranged on the assumption that S.D.s[1] would accept the considerable responsibility involved in talks direction and (iv) that Blair is not a policing scrutineer, nor has he shown himself particularly sensitive to considerations of broadcasting technique. I have no room to mention manpower arguments for earlier coordination and several other points! Let's discuss   R.A.R.   3.2.43.

On 5 February 1943, Rushbrook Williams replied to Rendall, marking his memorandum 'Private & Confidential':

Notification from Mr. Blair's Office

I am afraid this was a pure secretarial error. The normal course of procedure, as soon as a suggestion for a talks series has been approved by the Indian Programme Meeting, and details have been arranged, is to notify E.T.M.[2] I will see that this is done for the future.

The protracted absence of Mr. Blair on sick leave has greatly complicated the execution of my intention radically to overhaul both the arrangements for, and the contents of, the period devoted to English-knowing Indians in the Eastern Service.

This was annotated by Rendell:

E.T.M. To see. And please discuss with me the improvement of advance notification of talks plans etc.

R.A.   6.2.43

1. Service Directors; for example, the Eastern Service Director and the North African Service Director, to whom Orwell had sent copies of his memorandum.
2. Empire Talks Manager, Norman Collins.

1864. Extracts from Minutes of Eastern Service Meeting

3 February 1943

a)   <u>Chatham House Surveys of Foreign Press</u>. Mr. E. A. Blair to bear in mind using information from Surveys of Foreign Press.

b)   RECEPTION
     D.E.P. to secure technical guidance on slow reading being affected by intrusion of atmospherics: for report next week. Loss of fluency due to slow pace to be watched.
     <u>Ionosphere storm warnings</u>. E.S.D. reported Service Directors to be notified of ionosphere disturbances likely to make listening difficult: when warnings received announcers to be cautioned to read slowly and clearly.

c)   INTELLIGENCE
     Mr. Blair[1] outlined the constitution and functions of the Calcutta Committee. Report considered. Mr. Blair undertook (a) to ascertain from the Committee the provenance of the various reports and whether comments on the Hindustani Service were derived from Hindustani speaking areas, and (b) to ask that the original report be sent to the Government of India. Committee to consider points for further questionnaire.

1. The absence of the initials 'E. A.' and the subject—the Calcutta Committee—indicate that this is not Orwell, but a Mr. Blair of the Ministry of Information. For possible identifications of this Blair, see 882, n. 1.

1865. BBC Talks Booking Form, 3.2.43

Bahadur Singh: 'In the Public Eye,' 8; broadcast 10.2.43; fee £6.6s.[1] Signed: M Blackburn for I.P.O.

1. The fee was to be the usual £3.3s because the work to be done—adaptation of a newspaper article—was not great. However, on 9 February Miss Bedwell wrote to Miss Boughen explaining that Singh had had to prepare an original script (on President Inönü, the Turkish Premier), and a higher fee was appropriate. Miss Boughen wrote to Singh the following day offering £6.6s.

1866. Venu Chitale to Dr. Gangulee

4 February 1943

Venu Chitale wrote to Dr. Gangulee to thank him for suggestions for the series 'In the Public Eye.' She also referred to arrangements for co-ordinating his contributions to the series 'In Your Kitchen' with those by Mrs. Roy, and she gave him this progress report on Orwell's illness: 'Mr. Blair is much better now but I am afraid he will not be back in the office for at least a week, but I shall certainly pass on your suggestions to him.'

1867. Venu Chitale to B. H. Alexander, Copyright Department

4 February 1943   Original   VC/WMB

INDIAN PLAY NO. 2: MROCCHAKATIKA (The Little Clay Cart)

Narayana Menon has adapted the Indian play THE LITTLE CLAY CART from a translation by Arthur William Ryder,[1] the Sanscrit scholar. It is a 15 minute feature and the original play in Sanscrit is traditionally attributed to an ancient king named SHUDRAKA of India.

The rehearsal takes place on Monday, the 8th, and the transmission on Tuesday, February 9th, at 1145–1200 GMT, in the Eastern Service (Red Network).

[Signed] Venu Chitalé[2]
(Venu Chitale)

P.S. Will you please arrange payment to Dr. Menon accordingly. For your information I am enclosing a copy of the play.

1. Arthur William Ryder (1877–1938) translated a number of Sanskrit texts. *The Little Clay Cart* was published by Harvard University Press in 1905. University of Chicago Press published his versions of *The Pancatantra* (1925), *Gold's Gloom: Tales from the Pancatantra* (1925), and *The Bhagavad-gita* (1929).
2. Venu Chitale here signed her name with an accent: é.

1868. On Orwell's behalf to E. M. Forster

4 February 1943   07/ES/EB

Dear Mr. Forster

I am sorry to have to worry you but our library is making enquiries about the books we lent you. I think they are THE SCREWTAPE LETTERS, THE PROBLEM OF PAIN and MAN, THE MASTER—also Lord Ponsonby's life of his father.[1] Would you kindly return them so that I may hand them over.

Your broadcast was a very good one indeed and I enjoyed listening to it.

Your next broadcast SOME BOOKS will be on Wednesday, March 3rd, but I will send our usual card of reminder beforehand.

Yours sincerely
[Initialled] WB
(For Eric Blair)
Talks Producer
Indian Section

1. On 5 April 1943, Miss F. Milnes, BBC Librarian, wrote to Orwell 'through Mrs. Hunt,' to say that she was sorry 'you have lost the Times Book Club copy of "Arthur Ponsonby."' Because this was a new book, the Times Book Club demanded a refund of 12s 6d, and Orwell was asked to let her have this amount as soon as possible. Orwell annotated that memorandum 'Keep pending till Forster replies.'

1869. Venu Chitale to Eileen Blair

4 February 1943   07/ES/VC/JBL

Dear Mrs. Blair,

Here I am again to trouble you. Sometime ago you promised me some recipes of biscuits and cakes etc. I shall be very glad if you can let me have some of them. I should be very grateful for any recipes of salads, soups and pies and also special recipes of biscuits and sweets for children, I believe some were given on the Home Service sometime ago.

Venu Chitale
Assistant (Programmes)

1870. BBC Talks Booking Form, 4.2.43

Sir Aziz-ul-Huque: 'The High Commissioner Talks to You'; broadcast 23.2.43; fee £10.10s. Signed: M Blackburn for I.P.O.

1871. BBC Talks Booking Form, 4.2.43

E. M. Forster: 'Some Books'; usual monthly series: 13½-minute talk; broadcast 3.3.43 and 7.4.43; fee £21 each talk. Signed: M Blackburn for I.P.O.[1]

1. Separate requisitions were re-issued for these two talks on 19 February 1943.

1872. L. F. Rushbrook Williams to Sidney Horniblow

5 February 1943   07/ES/LFRW/WMB

Dear Mr. Horniblow

In the absence of Mr. Blair on sick leave, I am writing immediately to let you know about an unexpected, but unavoidable change which we have to prepare for in our English programmes to India in the Eastern Service. I'm very sorry to have to tell you that this change will unfortunately affect IN BLACK AND WHITE—the programme which we had asked you to supply us with, of topical items from the British Press of the week, and which we originally planned to put out fortnightly, starting on March 26th. The change in the advance planning of our programmes has been caused by a variety of reasons and programmes have had to be somewhat drastically re-arranged since we wrote to you on the 11th January.

I understand that you felt that these programmes would entail a great deal of work and would take up a considerable amount of your valuable time, and you will, therefore, not be altogether disappointed at the idea of having them postponed for the time being.

We do appreciate your kind offer of help and co-operation and the detailed suggestions which you made in your letter of the 16th December.

Yours sincerely
L. F. Rushbrook Williams
Eastern Service Director

1873. BBC Talks Booking Form, 5.2.43

Miss Indira Roy:[1] Indian Play, 2, 'The Little Clay Cart';[2] broadcast 9.2.43; fee £4.4s. Signed: M Blackburn for I.P.O. Remarks: 'They are rehearsing this play from 3.15 to 4 o'clock on Monday afternoon and from 7.15 to 9.15 on Monday evening'; Empire Programme Executive Remarks: 'This fee is suggested by the Producer as being reasonable for the amount of work involved.'

1. Indira Roy was, presumably, Mrs. K. C. Roy's daughter. The booking forms for both have the same home address in St Albans.
2. Orwell was ahead of his time. In January 1986 this 8th-century play, translated from Sanskrit and attributed to King Śūdraka, was presented on a large scale by the Tara Arts Group at the Arts Theatre, London. The play has ten acts, so only a very short excerpt was broadcast. In the

full version, the play combines a love story and political intrigue. Presumably the BBC's version did not include the descriptions of the prostitute's palace and the technique of burglary which are a feature of the original.

1874. BBC Talks Booking Form, 5.2.43

Miss Lilla Erulkar: [similar to form above, *1873*].

1875. On Orwell's behalf to Public Relations, Section 4, Air Ministry

6 February 1943   07/ES/EB

Dear Sir,
I enclose the fourth talk by Mr. E. C. Bowyer in our series "Modern Aircraft". We propose to broadcast it in our Eastern Service on Friday, 12th February, 1943, 1145–1200 GMT, and shall be glad to receive your approval of the script as soon as possible.[1]

Yours faithfully,
[Initialled] E. D.[2]
for Eric Blair
(Talks Producer)

1. The reply to this letter, from S/Ldr J. B. B. Atherton, to Orwell, 9 February 1943, gives some indication of the formalities he and other talks producers faced. He was advised that because the talk was on naval aircraft, the script should first be submitted to the Admiralty, the U.S.A.A.F., and the Ministry of Information censors; if they cleared the talk, then, when the Air Ministry had been informed, it would give its approval.
2. Probably Miss E. Dunstan, listed on 21 August 1943 as secretary to the Director, Overseas Presentation.

1876. To Press Division, Admiralty

8 February 1943   Original and carbon copy version
07/ES/EB/ED

Dear Sir,
In our Eastern Service, we are broadcasting a series of talks directed especially to India on "Modern Aircraft". We enclose herewith the script of the fourth talk, which we propose to broadcast on Friday next, 12th February, 1145–1200 GMT. We submitted a copy of this script to P.R.4, Air Ministry, and they have instructed us to get in touch with you as the

subject of this talk is 'Naval Aircraft'. We shall be glad, therefore, to receive your approval of the talk as soon as possible.

> Yours faithfully,
> [Top copy signed] M Blackburn
> (for Eric Blair)
> Talks Producer

1877. On Orwell's behalf to Harry W. Todd

> 8 February 1943   07/ES/EB/WMB

Dear Mr. Todd

Thank you for your letter of the 30th January, on the question of the British Council documentaries which have been sent out by you for distribution in India.

I regret that this letter has not been answered sooner but I have been expecting to see Mr. Blair, who has been away ill, back in the Office. I understand, however, that he will be returning on Thursday next,[1] when I will place your letter before him and he will doubtless be writing to you again.

> Yours very truly
> [Initialled] M B
> [Handwritten] Secretary For Eric Blair
> Talks Producer
> Indian Section

1. 11 February 1943, but see letter to Todd, 10 February 1943, *1879* The letter was addressed to Todd at the Film Department of the British Council.

1878. BBC Talks Booking Form, 8.2.43

Oliver Bell:[1] 'Women Generally Speaking'; Films of the Month; broadcast 24.2.43; fee £9.9s. Signed: M Blackburn for I.P.O.

1. Oliver Bell (1898–1952) served on the staff of the League of Nations Union, 1923–34, and was Press Officer for the Conservative Central Office, 1934–36, and Director of the British Film Institute, 1936–49.

1879. To Harry W. Todd

> 10 February 1943   07/ES/EB

Dear Mr. Todd

Many thanks for your letter of the 30th January. I am sorry about the delay in answering but as you perhaps know I have been ill and have been away.[1] We had to discontinue the film talks because there was so much uncertainty as to what films were being produced in India that we were no longer able to give any useful information about forthcoming films. If the position improves again, as I fancy it will, so that it will be possible to know in advance exactly what films are coming, then I shall be very glad to take up your suggestion about giving special publicity to shorts and documentaries produced by the British Council, but, at the moment, I do not care to broadcast on these alone while we are unable to say anything about ordinary commercial films.

Yours truly
Eric Blair
Talks Producer
Indian Section

1. Despite Miss Blackburn's expectation that Orwell would return on 11 February, it would seem he came back on the 10th.

1880. To K. K. Ardaschir

13 February 1943   Handwritten draft and typed versions
07/ES/EB/WMB

Dear Ardaschir

I am returning the script we are *not* using.[1] I liked the VICTORIA STATION one very much.

As I think you have heard, I have been ill three weeks but am now about again. I hope your wife is getting better.

How are the hens doing.? Ours didn't do so badly. Those two you sold me laid about 25 eggs between them during January. Now only one is laying but we get about two a week from her.

Yours sincerely
[Initialled] E. A. B
Eric Blair
Talks Producer
Indian Section

1. On 14 December 1942, Tamara Talbot Rice, of the Ministry of Information, Middle East Section, wrote to Bokhari (absent in India) to say that a talk proposed by Mr. Ardaschir called 'The Storm nears Turkey,' though an excellent idea, needed so much alteration that it would be wiser to rewrite it. Among the points she raised was that the decorousness of Turks was such that disparaging remarks by a Turk (Ardaschir) about Britain's enemies would be inappropriate. Either such disparagement should be expressed by an Englishman or, if a Turk was to speak, pro-British sentiments should be voiced. Various passages were described in such terms as 'totally unsuitable' and a particular point, that 'the President does not like references to his short stature,' was raised. It may well be that this is the script that Orwell was, belatedly, returning.

1881. To Director, Press Division, Admiralty

13 February 1943   07/ES/EB/WMB

Dear Sir

We are submitting a copy of the script SEAPLANES AND FLYING-BOATS, by
E. C. Bowyer, and shall be glad to receive your approval of this talk as soon
as possible.

This talk will be broadcast in our Eastern Service on Friday next, the 19th
February at 1145–1200 GMT (12.45 to 1.0 p.m. BST).

As this talk is on Seaplanes and Flying-Boats, and we were instructed by
the P.R.4., Air Ministry, when we submitted the previous week's talk to
them on NAVAL AIRCRAFT, to get in touch with you, we are therefore also
submitting to you a copy of this week's talk on SEAPLANES.

Yours faithfully
(For Eric Blair)[1]
Talks Producer

1. Although marked 'For Eric Blair,' Orwell had completed his sick leave on 10 February.

1882. To Public Relations, Section 4, Air Ministry

13 February 1943   07/ES/EB

Dear Sir

I enclose the fifth script in our series MODERN AIRCRAFT by E. C. Bowyer.

We propose to broadcast this talk on SEAPLANES AND FLYING-BOATS on
Friday next, the 19th February at 1145–1200 GMT (12.45 to 1.0 p.m. BST) in
our Eastern Service. We shall be most grateful to receive your approval as
soon as possible.

As this script is on Seaplanes and Flying-Boats we are also submitting a
copy of this script to the Admiralty.

Yours faithfully
(For Eric Blair)
Talks Producer

1883. To Norman Collins, Empire Talks Manager

13 February 1943   Original   EB/WMB

APPROACHING DISTINGUISHED OR WELL-KNOWN PEOPLE IN REGARD
TO BROADCAST TALKS.

We are going to approach the following M.P's, to do five minute talks on

subjects of current interest, to be included in THE DEBATE CONTINUES period
on Mondays at 1115 to 1130 GMT.

Dr. Edith Summerskill[1]
Cyril Lakin[2]
Will Lawson[3]

[Signed] Eric Blair
13.2.43
(Eric Blair)

1. Dr. Edith Summerskill (1901–1980; Baroness Summerskill of Ken Wood, 1961), Labour
   M.P., 1938–55, held office in the post-war Labour governments, 1945–51.
2. Cyril Lakin (1893–1948), journalist, barrister, broadcaster, was assistant editor, *Daily
   Telegraph*, 1928–33; literary editor, *Sunday Times* and *Daily Telegraph*, 1933–37; assistant
   editor and literary editor, *Sunday Times*, 1933–45, and National Unionist M.P. for Llandaff &
   Barry, 1942–45.
3. There was no M.P. of this name. It is probably an error for William Lawther (1889–1976; Kt.,
   1949, always known as 'Will'), who had been a Labour M.P., 1928–31, and was at this time an
   important miners' leader and member of the Trades Union Congress General Council, 1935–
   54. Around 1939, he began a shift to the right of the labour movement, opposing Aneurin
   Bevan, and helped bring about the defeat of many Communist and left-wing initiatives.
   Another possibility, but less probable, was John James Lawson (1881–1965; Baron Lawson,
   1950). He served in the Royal Artillery, 1914–18 and was M.P. for Chester-le-Street, 1919–
   49. From 1939 to 1944 he was Deputy Commissioner for Civil Defence, North Region; from
   1945 to 1946 Secretary of State for War in the first Labour government.

1884. Note to L. F. Rushbrook Williams, E.S.D.

13 February 1943   Handwritten

On 18 January 1943, G. V. Desani wrote a personal and an official letter to
Rushbrook Williams, following a meeting with him on 1 January, outlining his
background, qualifications, and suitability as a broadcaster and giving suggestions for talks. On the 20th, Williams's secretary, Miss P. J. Orr, wrote to
Desani to say that Williams was on sick leave. The carbon of that letter is
annotated by Williams: '*Mr Blair* Could you look?' It is also annotated by
Orwell:

E.S.D.
I have been thro' Mr Desani's suggestions. I think in the present full-up state
of our schedule we can't possibly commission any talks.

Eric Blair   13.2.43

Meantime, B. Sahni, Programme Assistant, had written to Desani on 2
February to say he would be glad to receive 'the script of "Ausan,"' and that A.
L. Bakaya, of the Indian Section staff, was translating Desani's talk 'My Lecture
Tours' into Hindustani. He gave a time of day, but not a date, for the
transmission of this talk; it was probably 11 February, for a timing rehearsal was
arranged for earlier that day.

On 16 February, Rushbrook Williams wrote to Desani explaining that the
schedule was very full and, though he had 'plainly a great flair for lecturing,' he

could not be fitted in. Furthermore, 'Before very long, the Service of which I am in charge will be remodelled: and there will be very little English talk going out in it.' In Orwell's pamphlet collection is a copy of Desani's *India Invites* (1941); see *3732*

1885. BBC Talks Booking Form, 13.2.43

Bahadur Singh: 'In the Public Eye,' 10, '"Madame Chiang Kai-Shek" — an original script — not taken from a newspaper'; broadcast 24.2.43; fee £6.6s. Signed: M Blackburn for I.P.O.

1886. To V. S. Pritchett

15 February 1943   07/ES/EB

Dear Pritchett

Thank you for your letter of the 14th, together with your script on MARK TWAIN.

I have fixed a recording for you, from 4.30 to 5.15 pm. on Wednesday afternoon, the 17th. We can only get the Studio for ¾ of an hour so any rehearsal you need should be done beforehand. Do you think you could manage to get here at 4 o'clock.

I don't know what passage you have picked out to read from MARK TWAIN and whether you are doing this yourself—if so, we can record that at the same time as your talk, but please let me know. It should be a passage taking not more than about 5 minutes.

Yours
George Orwell
Talks Producer
Indian Section

1887. R. A. Rendall, Assistant Controller (Overseas Services) to S. J. de Lotbinière (D.E.P.) and L. F. Rushbrook Williams (E.S.D.)

15 February 1943

The following memorandum refers to a script by Ellen Wilkinson, M.P., Joint Parliamentary Secretary to the Ministry of Home Security (see *422, n. 3*), proposed for the series 'Why We Shall Win.' It gives a vivid picture of problems Orwell and his colleagues faced in addition to the usual difficulties of organisation in wartime, shortages, censorship, and so forth. Miss Wilkinson had broadcast under Orwell's auspices on 14 October 1942 (see *1471*) on 'The House of Commons' in the series 'Women Generally Speaking.' Half her fee for this script was paid to the Ministry of Home Security.

I agree that there does not seem to be any very good reason for turning this script down, but unfortunately we are not in a strong position ourselves to argue the matter with the Ministry as we didn't handle it in the agreed way. It does not seem to be clearly understood in the Eastern Department that the procedure now in force is that the Ministry should be approached before the proposed speaker. Any informal approaches on our part to the speakers in advance of Ministry permission are likely to result in an embarrassing situation, such as is only too clearly shown by the case of Noel Baker[1] and Princess Indira as well as in this case. Actually, at the time when Miss Wilkinson was first approached, primary approaches on our part were in order. But that does not explain the fact that the Eastern Department were in negotiation with Miss Wilkinson over a period of six months and that Miss Wilkinson had accepted, and yet neither D.E.P. nor the Ministry had been told anything about it.

If E.S.D. is very anxious to take it up again with the Ministry on the strength of the value of this script and if he is sure that the India Office will back him in this, then I think we can say to the Ministry that we are sorry to place them in this position vis-à-vis Miss Wilkinson (a position which should not arise according to the new procedure), but that in this instance it is due to the fact that the script has been submitted suddenly and unexpectedly as a result of an informal arrangement made a long time previously. But I think we should be ill-advised to press the matter very hard in view of the more serious complications that have arisen lately over Noel Baker, in which case we really have no excuse at all for an embarrassment which is being heavily underlined by a P.Q.[2]

I hope that E.S.D. will make the new position very clear to every member of his Department and even to Programme Contract staff (such as Princess Indira and Lady Grigg) for whose activities we cannot really deny responsibility. It is particularly important that they should not operate on the lines implied in the last paragraph of E.S.D.'s minute of February 11th.

Rushbrook Williams annotated this memorandum and returned it to Rendall on 17 February: 'I agree that in view of subsequent developments, there is nothing to be gained by pressing the Ministry. Both these incidents, in combination, form the *reductio ad absurdum* of Ministry red-tape. But Eastern Department now realises that *inter arma ratio abest*[3] and that Ministry permission must be obtained even before it is known whether a Parliamentary Undersecretary (even) is willing to speak or not.'

1. Philip Noel-Baker (1889–1982; Baron Noel-Baker, 1977), a Quaker who actively campaigned for peace and disarmament, commanded Friends' Ambulance Units, 1914–18 (decorated for valour), was Labour M.P., from 1929 and held offices in Labour governments, 1945–51. He received the Nobel Peace Prize in 1959, and the French Legion d'Honneur in 1976.
2. Probably a Parliamentary Question.
3. Perhaps 'between conflicting interests, reason has no place.'

1888. To H. D. Graves-Law[1]

16 February 1943   07/ES/EB/ED

Dear Sir,

Mr. Rushbrook Williams, the Eastern Service Director, has asked me to send you the enclosed script[2] for approval, before we go ahead with the broadcast on the 12th March, 1943. I shall be glad to hear from you in due course that it will be in order for us to broadcast the talk.

Yours faithfully,
[Initialled] E. D.
for (Eric Blair)
Talks Producer

1. Graves-Law's initials and hyphenated form of his name come from a later letter. He was a Companion of the Order of the Indian Empire, and at this time in the Middle East Section of the Ministry of Information.
2. The script was by K. K. Ardaschir, possibly 'Victoria Station Bombay to Victoria Station London,' broadcast 12 March 1943. Orwell returned another script to Ardaschir, unused, on 8 March 1943.

1889. L. F. Rushbrook Williams to Chinna Durai

19 February 1943

Chinna Durai gave some talks in the early part of Orwell's service with the BBC and submitted a number of suggestions for further programmes towards the end of 1942. Balraj Sahni on 14 December and A. L. Bakaya on 6 January wrote to him, the former expressing some interest in the possibility of his writing Hindustani feature scripts, the latter saying he was unable to find a place for the talk 'All Eyes on Britain' in the Hindustani service and he understood that the English Talks Section also had found no place for it. Orwell had considered a script but found no place for it; see *1884*. Durai became dissatisfied with the delay in getting a script placed, and this was aggravated by Orwell's absence when he was ill. Considerable correspondence ensued and, in case Durai took legal action, the advice of the BBC's legal department was sought by the Eastern Service Department. On 19 February, Rushbrook Williams wrote to Durai:

I have now been able to ask Mr. Blair about your script. He informs me that he told you over the telephone that he liked the script. So he did; but that did not mean that he was able to find space for it. He could not do this for two reasons. First, his schedule was planned far ahead and could not be upset; secondly, the theme of your talk had, broadly speaking, been inspiring other broadcasts for some time.

Your script was then passed to the Hindustani Section, to know whether they could use it in that language. They considered it very carefully; but on the upshot decided that they also were unable to make use of it, as Mr. Bakaya informed you in his letter of 6th January when he returned the script to you.

I regret that you should have been disappointed; but our time on the air is so limited that we are only able to use a very small fraction of scripts dealing with themes which we have discussed with authors.

I cannot agree that the Corporation is under any legal liability but, as there was some unavoidable delay in returning the script, I am prepared to recommend an ex gratia payment of ten guineas which I hope will be satisfactory to you.

In due course, Durai accepted this settlement.

1890. News Commentary in English for Malaya, 21

19 February 1943

This was written and read by George Orwell. No script has been traced.

1891. To Arthur Wynn, Music Bookings Manager

19 February 1943   Original   EB/WMB

We are asking Dr. Narayana Menon of 151 Sussex Gardens, London, W.2. to plan and choose a 15 minute programme of gramophone records, which will take place fortnightly in the Red Network, Eastern Service, starting in Week 12, 25th March, and continuing fortnightly thereafter on the following dates—8th April, 22nd April and 6th May, at 1130–1145 GMT, Eastern Service (Red Network). We are asking him to choose this music because of his wide knowledge of Western music and also because he knows what will appeal to Indian listeners and what they will not like in the way of Western music. There will be a minimum of announcement only, which he will help us to compile, and which will be read by the announcer on duty on the day of the broadcasts.

Will you kindly arrange a contract and payment for Dr. Menon for this work.[1]

[Signed] Eric Blair

1. The memorandum is annotated '3 gns ea.'

1892. BBC Talks Booking Form, 19.2.43

E. M. Forster: 'Some Books'; usual monthly series; 13½-minute talk; broadcast 3.3.43; fee £21. Signed: M Blackburn for I.P.O.

1893. BBC Talks Booking Form, 19.2.43

E. M. Forster: 'Some Books'; used monthly series; 13½-minute talk; broadcast 31.3.43; fee £21. Signed: M Blackburn for I.P.O. This and the form above (*1892*) are re-requisitions for those issued 4 February 1943, for broadcasts on 3.3.43 and 7.4.43. Someone had failed to notice that there were five Wednesdays in March 1943.

1894. BBC Talks Booking Form, 19.2.43

Commander Stephen King-Hall: within 'The Debate Continues'; 'approx. 4 mins. talk — "What we shall do when the Nazis Surrender Unconditionally" '; broadcast 22.2.43; fee £4.4s. Signed: M Blackburn for I.P.O. Remarks: 'The rest of the period will be as usual Princess Indira.'

1895. Weekly News Review, 57

20 February 1943

The text is reproduced from the typescript used for the broadcast. It has been amended slightly, but several corrections are of mistypings. Rushbrook Williams acted as censor. The script, the first he had written since returning from his illness, was read by Orwell, and at the top of the first page he wrote 'As b'cast 13′ E.A.B'. Timings for each page of the typescript are in italic within square brackets.

Since the Japanese evacuated Guadalcanal there has been no very big event in the Far Eastern end of the War and this week I would like to talk chiefly about the Russian and North African Fronts and also to say something about Madame Chiang-Kai-Shek's° visit to Washington and about the Debates on the Beveridge Social Insurance scheme in this country.

I don't need to tell you what are the big events of the week. Anyone who is listening to this broadcast will have heard of the capture by the Red Army of Rostov and Kharkov. This is a very great victory, probably the most important single event in the whole course of the Russo–German War. The capture of Kharkov, which the Russians failed to achieve last winter, is even more important than the re-capture of Rostov. Kharkov is not only a great industrial city but a great railway junction at which all the communications of the Ukraine cross. The Germans have not only lost heavily in territory, men and materials, but they're going to lose more, for one Army is all but cut off on the shores of the Sea of Azov and another somewhere in the rear of Rostov is threatened by the same fate. The Russians are not only driving westward from Rostov but another column has struck southward from the neighbour-hood of Krasnoarmeisk and is moving more or less in the direction of Mariupol on the northern shore of the Sea of Azov. [*1¾′*]

The Germans in that area will have to get out quickly if they're not going to suffer the same destruction as has already happened to the German Sixth Army at Stalingrad and threatens the Army which is isolated in the Caucasus. Last year, when the Russians re-took Rostov, they did not get further westward than Taganrog, about 50 miles to[1] the west, and the Germans were able to hold on to the Crimean Peninsula. This year, the Russian offensive is much more far-reaching in its effects and it is generally believed that the Germans will have to go back to the line of the Dnieper, thus leaving themselves in a position considerably worse than they were before their 1942 campaign started. Some observers *including Dr Benes, President of Czechoslovakia,*[2] even think that they will retreat as far as the river Dneister, which means standing[3] on the borders of Poland and Roumania and abandoning the whole of the Russian territory which they have over-run. This may be an over-optimistic forecast but at any rate enough has happened already to make it undisguisedly clear to the German man in the street that the 1942 campaign, with all its enormous losses, has been fought for exactly nothing.

You can imagine, even if you haven't read, the sort of dope that is being handed out to the German masses to explain away the mistakes of their leaders. Hitler himself has been silent and apparently in retirement for some weeks past but his underlings, particularly Goebbels, have been very active. What Goebbels says to the German people is not of great importance to us but it is important to examine the propaganda line which is being handed out to the world at large because this propaganda is intended to deceive and weaken us [4'] and it is as well to be armed against it in advance.

Briefly, the main line now being followed is the Bolshevik bogey. It is being put out crudely by the German propagandists and somewhat more subtly by those of Italy and other satellite States. According to Goebbels's broadcasts, Europe is now faced with the fearful danger of a Communist invasion, which will not stop at its Eastern borders but sweep as far as the English channel and beyond, engulfing Britain as well as the other European countries. The Germans, it now appears, only took up arms in order to defend Europe from this Bolshevik peril, and by allying themselves with the Bolsheviks, Britain and the United States have betrayed European civilisation. All the talk which the Germans were uttering about the need for living space, or Lebensraum as it is called, and the divine right of Germany to rule the world, appears to have been forgotten for the time being. Germany's war is purely defensive, so Dr. Goebbels says. It can be seen, quite clearly, of course, that the real drift of these speeches[4] is to appeal to those sections in Britain and America who are frightened of seeing Soviet Russia become too powerful and might be willing to consider a compromise peace. This is augmented by the Italian publicists, who are openly talking about a compromise, and the duty of Britain to collaborate with the Axis powers against the Bolshevik danger.

All this is foredoomed to failure because the anti-Russian sentiment on which the Axis propagandists seem to be playing is almost non-existent in the Anglo-Saxon countries. So far as Britain is concerned, Soviet Russia was never more popular than at this moment. [6¼'] But we ought not to underrate the danger of Fascist propaganda which has scored such great triumphs in the past. Even if the anti–Bolshevik line of thought does not achieve much in Britain, it may find listeners among the wealthier classes all over Europe and in addition the hints which have been dropped by the Italian propagandists may be followed up later by very attractive-sounding peace offers. Towards India, of course, German propaganda will take a different line. The talk about defending Western civilisation is only for European consumption. To India the propaganda line will be that Soviet Russia is the Ally of Great Britain and therefore shares the responsibility for any grievances which the *Indian Nationalists*[5] have, or believe they have. We can best deal with these propaganda campaigns, if we start with the knowledge that they are in essence, simply strategic manoeuvres and take no more account of the truth than a military commander does when he disposes his army so as to deceive the enemy.

In Tunisia, the Germans have had a considerable local success during this week. It probably won't effect the final outcome but unquestionably the Axis Forces in Tunisia have turned out to be stronger in armoured vehicles and in the air than had been anticipated. During this week the Germans have attacked westward in Southern Tunisia, driven back the American troops opposing them, and captured several advance airfields. The main object of this manoeuvre is probably to drive a wedge between the British First Army in Tunisia and the British Eighth Army which is advancing from Tripoli. The British [8½'] Eighth Army has now reached the outposts of the Mareth Line, the fortified area which guards the approaches to Gabes. We can't expect their progress to be rapid for communications hardly exist in this area and the Eighth Army is now a long way from its base. Probably the nearest sea-port it can make full use of is Benghazi. Also the North African rainy season is still on, which makes the movement of heavy vehicles difficult. However, it is unlikely that the Germans will be able to hang on in Tunisia indefinitely, and some observers on the spot believe that they do not intend to do so. Quite possibly, they're only fighting a delaying action in the hope of getting as many as possible of their forces away by sea. General Catroux the Fighting French Commander has given his opinion that the Germans will be out of Tunisia in two months.

The Beveridge scheme of social security[6] is still under debate. The Government has already proposed the adoption of the greater part of it but a Labour Amendment in the House of Commons demanding the adoption of the scheme in its entirety received as many as 117 votes. I have spoken of the Beveridge scheme in earlier News Commentaries and don't want to detail its provisions again. I merely mention the Debate now taking place in order to emphasize two things. One is, that whatever else goes through, Family Allowances are certain to be adopted though it is not yet certain on what scale. The other is that the principle of Social Insurance has come to stay and even the most reactionary thinkers in Great Britain would now hardly dare to oppose this. The Beveridge scheme may ultimately be adopted in the [10¾'] somewhat mutilated form but it is something of an achievement even to be debating such a thing in the middle of a desperate war in which we are still fighting for survival.

Madame Chiang-Kai-Shek,° the wife of the Generalissimo, who has been staying in Washington as the guest of President and Mrs. Roosevelt, has addressed both of the American Houses of Congress. She was cheered when she warned the United Nations against the danger of allowing Japan to remain as a potential threat after the war is won. And also, when she pleaded for a peace settlement, which would not be either vindictive or nationalistic in concept. China, she said, was ready to co-operate in laying the foundations of a sane world society. She also, speaking out of her own experience, warned the Americans against under-rating the strength of the Japanese, whose power will grow if they're left too long in possession of the territories they've over-run. Parts of Madame Chiang-Kai-Shek's° speech were re-broadcast in this country and aroused great interest. It is recognised in this country that the Chinese who have now been fighting in the common struggle for five-and-a-half years have suffered far more than any of the other of the United Nations, and can hardly be blamed if they now complain that their Western Allies have done very little to help them. Madame Chiang-Kai-Shek's° visit to the United States will have done a great deal to promote good relations between China and the rest of the United Nations. [*12¾'*]

1. The typescript has 'from the west'. Taganrog lies to the east of Rostov. It fell to the Germans in October 1941; thousands of civilians were victims of mass shootings by the Germans. It was retaken by the Red Army on 30 August 1943. Very sadly, by July 1995, its citizens could no longer afford the gas bill to keep the 'eternal' flame alight that honoured its dead. Albert Gentry, imprisoned in Bangkok, recorded in his diary for 11 February 1943 that he had heard on the radio that Rostov had been retaken; on 20 February he heard that Taganrog had also been retaken by the Russians.
2. '*including . . . Czechoslovakia*' was added in Orwell's handwriting. There is a question mark in the margin beside it. This may have been added to draw attention to the original placement of the insert, which had been marked to follow 'think.'
3. 'standing' is a handwritten correction of the typescript's 'landing.'
4. A question mark has been written in the margin by this line.
5. *Indian Nationalists*] Internationalists *in typescript; an aural error which may indicate that the script was dictated to a typist*
6. William Beveridge, 1879–1963; Kt., 1919; Baron, 1946), economist and social reformer; Director of the London School of Economics, 1919–37; Master of University College, Oxford, 1937–45; Liberal M.P., 1944–46, was the author of the *Report on Social Insurance and Allied Services*, popularly known as the *Beveridge Report*, 1942, which laid the foundations of the welfare state in Britain.

1896. Bengali Newsletter, 32

20 February 1943

The English original was probably written by Orwell; see Blackburn's 20 January memorandum to Rushbrook Williams, *1832*. No script has been traced. Assumed timing from PasB: 9' 3".

1897. To Public Relations, Section 4, Air Ministry

20 February 1943   07/ES/EB/MB

Dear Sir

We enclose the sixth and last script in the series MODERN AIRCRAFT, by Edward C. Bowyer.

We propose to broadcast this talk on Friday next, 26th February at 1145–1200 GMT (12.45 to 1.0 p.m. BST) in our Eastern Service. We shall be most grateful to receive your approval as soon as possible.

Yours faithfully
[Initialled] MB
(for Eric Blair)
Talks Producer

1. Although Orwell was back at work and this letter bears his reference, the typist's reference and the style indicate that it was Mary Blackburn's work; it was by this time a regular routine. On 1 March, Bowyer wrote to Orwell to tell him that a friend's daughter in Southern India had heard at least one of Bowyer's talks very clearly.

1898. To P. Chatterjee

22 February 1943   07/ES/EB/MB

Dear Dr. Chatterjee

I understand that you are willing to continue to help us by broadcasting the Bengali Newsletter weekly, at any rate for the present: we are therefore asking our Contracts Department to get into touch with you regarding the broadcast dates in March—which are the 6th, 13th, 20th and 27th.

We are still anxious to arrange for a woman to broadcast in Bengali fortnightly and we are therefore asking Miss Anima Sen Gupta to do a four to four-and-a-half minute Bengali talk within the Newsletter period on the 6th and 20th March. I understand that you have no objection to this arrangement.

We are writing to the Managing Director of your firm about the question of your having every Saturday free, as suggested by you.

Yours sincerely,
[Signed] Eric Blair
Eric Blair
Talks Producer

1899. To E. M. Forster

22 February 1943   07/ES/EB

Dear Mr. Forster

Mr. Blair has asked me to send you the enclosed book—"Mr. Bowling buys a Newspaper"[1]—about which I understand he has already spoken to you.

I hope it reaches you safely, and in time.

Yours sincerely,
[Initialled] MB
for Eric Blair
Talks Producer

1. By Donald Landels Henderson, published in 1943, who also wrote under the name Stephanie Landels. Had the name Bowling attracted Orwell's attention? The principal character of *Coming Up for Air* is George Bowling.

1900. To Herbert Read

23 February 1943   07/ES/EB/WMB

Dear Mr. Read

Mr. Blair has asked me to send you the enclosed book LIFE ON THE MISSISSIPPI by Mark Twain. He has marked two passages in blue pencil, either of which you could read, one, the beginning of Chapter 4, on pages 20 to 21, and the other, beginning at the bottom of page 43 to the end of Chapter 9 on page 45.

Would you please let us know which of these two passages you are choosing to read.

Yours sincerely
[Initialled] WB
for Eric Blair
Talks Producer

1901. To Norman Collins, Empire Talks Manager

24 February 1943   Original   EB/WMB

APPROACHING EMINENT SPEAKERS

In connection with our new literary series (GREAT DRAMATISTS) to start in Week 11, on the completion of LANDMARKS IN AMERICAN LITERATURE, we propose approaching Bernard Shaw for a talk on IBSEN. This would be the fourth talk in the series and would therefore be broadcast on Thursday of Week 17. It would be a ten minute talk and would go out on Thursday, April, 29th. In the same series we also propose approaching T. S. Eliot and James Stephens.[1] I do not know whether these two will come under the heading of "eminent speakers".

[Signed] Eric Blair
(Eric Blair)

Collins sent a copy of this memorandum to R. A. Rendall, Assistant Controller, Overseas Service, on 1 March 1943, with this note: 'Cd you pse advise me on this question of approaching G.B.S. Other Services wd. like to carry the talk (in isolation) if it *can* be got. But I thought that you shd. be consulted first.' He replied to Orwell the same day:

I will raise the matter of G.B.S. and let you know at the earliest possible moment.

As regards the other points:

a) Go ahead with Eliot whom you use much more than we do.
b) James Stephens has done quite a lot for us lately and it occurs to me that unless you have any special brief for him, one of his performances in the African or Pacific Services might be repeated for you. Unfortunately the man who knows most about J. S. is Gerald Bullett, who is away at the moment, but if, as I say, you have no special directive for Stephens, you might suggest that he repeats something that he has done. (If he agrees, would you please advise Boswell who should be able to arrange some small reduction in fee). If, on the other hand, he does something entirely new, you might please let me know about it in advance, as we might possibly use it.

Orwell wrote a reply on the same day on the verso of this memorandum:

Mr Collins:
I want to use Stephens in our "Great Dramatists" series to do a talk on W. B. Yeats. Even if he has previously done something on Yeats I don't fancy it would fit into this series, the programmes in which are all constructed on one plan.
If it would help I can explain exactly what I want Shaw to do (it is not a talk likely to give him much scope for making a nuisance of himself).

[Signed] Eric Blair 1.3.43

Collins replied on 2 March, approving the engagement of Stephens. He asked to see the script in advance so that he could decide whether to record it for use in other services. He also took up Orwell's offer of further details of what was proposed for Shaw.

On 3 March, Collins sent another memorandum to Orwell, telling him that he had spoken to Rendall, and it was thought that Orwell should not approach Shaw directly, especially because the Home Service was 'anxious to get something out of Shaw.' George Barnes, the Director of Talks, thought it possible that if Orwell could get Shaw on Ibsen, then the Home Service might carry that talk also: 'I gather the Home Service are anxious for G.B.S. rather than G.B.S. on any particular subject.' For Orwell's reply, see *1927*.

1. James Stephens (1882–1950), Irish poet and novelist, published his first book of poetry, *Insurrections* in 1909, and two years later helped found the *Irish Review* and published his first novel, *The Charwoman's Daughter*. James Joyce considered him to be the only person capable of completing *Finnegans Wake* should it be left unfinished. He was a member of Sinn Féin and contributed to its journal. The sentence has been marked, probably by Collins, and annotated

'SD's Monday' (the meeting of area service directors). Orwell is, of course, being ironic at Collins's expense.

1902. To Bonamy Dobrée

24 February 1943   07/ES/EB/WMB

Dear Mr. Dobrée[1]

I wonder if you would care to do a 10 minutes talk in a forthcoming series which we are calling GREAT DRAMATISTS. I will explain the purpose and lay-out of these programmes, each of which will take half-an-hour in all.

The programme consists of a 10 minutes talk on the chosen author, a scene from one of his plays, acted by the B.B.C. Repertory Company, and taking 8 or 10 minutes, and about 8 minutes of music. The lay-out will be as follows:—

　1. Opening Announcement
　2. About a minute taken from the scene to be acted.
　3. Talk
　4. Music
　5. Scene from chosen dramatist

You can see, therefore, that the speaker's opening words should refer to the fragment of the scene which has just been heard. He should start off—"Those lines you have just heard were written by John Dryden"—(or whoever it may be).

The one we want you to undertake is JOHN DRYDEN, and the play from which we propose chosing a scene is THE INDIAN EMPRESS. The date of your talk would be Thursday, April 1st, at 12.30 to 1 p.m. (British Summer Time). If this date is not convenient to you we can easily record the talk beforehand. Would you be kind enough to let me know, as early as possible whether you can undertake this.

Yours sincerely
[Initialled] G. O.
George Orwell
Talks Producer
Indian Section

P.S. The plays we shall choose are not absolutely fixed yet and I am open to suggestions.

1. Bonamy Dobrée (1891–1974), Professor of English Literature, University of Leeds, 1936–55, served in the army before and throughout World Wars I and II. He was a prolific author of critical books, especially on seventeenth- and eighteenth-century topics. He also wrote on modern authors, including Ibsen, Kipling, Forster, and T. S. Eliot. His books on Restoration comedy (1924) and tragedy (1929) were much used by undergraduates. His British Council pamphlet on Dryden was first published in 1956. See also *856, n. 3.*

1903. To James Stephens

24 February 1943   07/ES/EB/WMB

This letter asking Stephens to discuss *The Hour Glass*[1] by W. B. Yeats on 27 May 1943 in the GREAT DRAMATISTS series was the same essentially as Orwell's letter to Bonamy Dobrée; see *1902*.

1. *The Hour Glass: A Morality* (1903). Verse and prose versions of the play were published in 1922.

1904. To T. S. Eliot

24 February 1943   07/ES/EB/WMB

Dear Eliot

I wonder if you would like to do us a ten minutes talk on Christopher Marlowe on Thursday, the 13th March. If that date is not itself convenient to you we can always record beforehand. I should explain the purpose of this series of talks and the way we intend doing them.

This is a series called GREAT DRAMATISTS and each talk will consist of a ten minutes talk, a scene from the chosen dramatist taking 8 to 10 minutes and about 8 minutes of music. We propose, at the opening of each programme, to trail about a minute of the scene which is to be acted in full at the end of the programme and the talk will come immmediately after this. The speaker's opening words should therefore refer to the fragment of a scene which has just been heard. In this case we're going to have a scene from DR. FAUSTUS, though I haven't yet decided which. You could perhaps start off therefore—"Those lines you have just heard come from a scene in Marlowe's Dr. Faustus which you will be hearing acted in a few minutes time," or words to that effect. I should be glad if you would let me know as early as possible whether you can undertake this. I hope you will as this ought to be an interesting series and we want to start it with a good talk.

Yours sincerely
[Signed] Geo. Orwell
George Orwell
Talks Producer
Indian Section

1905. To Arthur Wynn, Music Bookings Manager

24 February 1943   EB/WMB

As the point has been queried, we are asking Dr. Menon to choose the 15 minute musical programmes in weeks 12, 14, etc., because he has shown himself competent in selecting programmes of this type, and he has the advantage of being a student both of European and Indian music. He is therefore probably a good judge of the types of European music likely to appeal to Indian listeners.

To arrange his contract on a weekly basis would no doubt be a better arrangement and we will do so.

This is being sent through E.S.D. for his approval.

[Signed] Eric Blair
(Eric Blair)

1906. To Sir Aziz-ul-Huque

25 February 1943   07/ES/EB/WMB

Dear Sir Aziz-ul-Huque

We are going shortly to revive a series of talks which had a good reception in India, entitled BOOKS THAT CHANGED THE WORLD. On the previous occasion we discussed six great European books which might be considered as having a direct affect upon human history. We want to follow this up with six talks on comparable Asiatic books and we would be very much honoured if you could do the first talk for us on the KORAN. This would be a talk of the same length as you do for us every month and the date would be March 26th (Friday)—transmission time 12.45 to 1 pm. (British Summer Time).

If you are willing to undertake this we can let you have further particulars.[1]

Yours truly
[Signed] Eric Blair
Eric Blair
Talks Producer
Indian Section

1. A reply was sent on behalf of the High Commissioner for India on 1 March regretting that he would be unable to give this talk; he would be out of England by 26 March.

1907. BBC Talks Booking Form, 25.2.43

Lady Grigg: 'Women Generally Speaking'; broadcast 3, 10, 17, 24, and 31.3.43; fee £8.8s each broadcast. Signed: M Blackburn for I.P.O.

1908. BBC Talks Booking Form, 25.2.43

Desmond Hawkins: 'Anniversary of the Month'; 'Mr. Hawkins will take part in this Feature Programme on March 2nd at 1145–1200 GMT. Rehearsal at 10 am. transmission 1245 to 1 pm.'; fee £5.5s + 19s fare (95p). Signed: M Blackburn for I.P.O. Remarks: 'This is a 13 min. Feature Broadcast, for which Desmond Hawkins has written the script, and for which copyright payment has been requested through Miss Alexander.'

1909. News Commentary in English for Malaya, 22
26 February 1943

This was written and read by George Orwell. No script has been traced.

1910. BBC Talks Booking Form, 26.2.43

Shridhar Telkar: 'Behind the Headlines'; broadcast 4, 18, and 25.3.43; fee £9.9s each talk. Signed: M Blackburn for I.P.O. Remarks: 'Mr. Telkar will not give his broadcast on the 11th March, as a talk on the INDIAN RED CROSS will be given in that time.'[1]

1. An interesting sidelight on programme organisation is provided by a letter from Balraj Sahni, Programme Assistant, to Telkar dated 2 March 1943. He invites Telkar to a tea party to be given by 'Professor Rushbrook Williams' at 200 Oxford Street on 23 March in order that 'authors who help us by writing scripts for our Hindustani feature programmes' might meet. He is invited to hear one such programme before the tea party.

1911. Weekly News Review, 58
27 February 1943

Written and read by Orwell, the text is reproduced from a typescript used for the broadcast. The script was not initialled by him, nor has he added his usual 'As b'cast' indication. However, the usual typed line at the beginning of these scripts, 'NOT CHECKED WITH BROADCAST,' has had the first word crossed out. Some pages have timings, given here in italic within square brackets. Room was made in the quarter-hour available for announcing details of the Essay Competition for March. The censor was F. Singleton. There are one or two slight typing errors, silently corrected here except for the addition of '[al]' to 'internation.' 'Medenine' was typed incorrectly but amended by hand, probably by Orwell.

During this week the only major military developments have been in Tunisia and on the southern part of the Russian Front, near the shores of the Sea of Azov. There have also been heavy bombing of Japanese concentrations of shipping in the Solomons and New Britain, and a British sea-borne raid on the coast of Burma, but so far as the eastern end of the war is concerned one can't say that the military situation has changed. I should like to spend my time this week in discussing the Russian and North African Fronts and then to say something about the speech which Hitler composed but failed to deliver three days ago.

In Southern Tunisia there has been a dramatic change during the past three days and the situation which looked threatening a week ago has probably, though not absolutely certainly, been restored. The Germans have attacked westward through the Kasserine Pass, almost the only Pass through the Atlas mountains in this area. They not only captured three airfields but they came within a very few miles of capturing the town of Thala, which is an important spot from the point of view of communications. However, the Allied commander on the spot seems to have thrown in all his aircraft in a heavy attack and the Germans were driven back through the Pass with considerable losses of men and material. Evidently both the Germans and the Allies have lost heavily in tanks. It is too early to say with absolute certainty that the situation is restored because the airfields they have captured give the Germans a local air superiority in central Tunisia and also because we don't yet know what reserves of tanks they possess. We do know that they're now using a new mark of heavy tank, weighing 55 tons and carrying an 88 mm. gun which has not made its appearance before.[1] However, the Minister for War, has just stated in Parliament that the armour of this tank has been successfully pierced by our 6 pounder guns,[2] and also that the new British tank, the latest model of the Churchill tank, is now in action in Tunisia in large numbers.

Both the Allies and the Germans in North Africa are fighting against time. It is important for the Allies to clear the North African coast as rapidly as possible and it is also important for the German commander, if he can manage it, to drive the British First Army back into Algeria before the Eighth Army arrives in his rear. The Eighth Army has now occupied Medenine, one of the chief outposts of the Mareth Line, and also Djerba, which is so placed that it might make a very valuable airfield or a jumping off place for seaborne attacks against the coast.

During this week there has been a considerable revival of the rumour that the Germans are going to invade Spain. They are, so it is said, rushing troops in very large numbers to the Spanish border at the eastern end of the Pyrenees. We have no way of confirming this and we ought to remember that a German invasion of Spain has been one of the recurrent rumours of this war and in some cases has been put about by the Germans themselves. At the same time a German invasion of Spain is by no means impossible and we ought always to keep it in mind because it is one method by which the Germans might hope to retrieve the situation in North Africa and so stall off an Allied invasion of Europe. If the Germans could cross Spain rapidly and then get across the Straits of Gibraltar into Spanish Morocco they would then present a tremendous threat to the whole Allied position in Africa and the Allies would have to scrap the idea of any offensive operations until they had driven the Germans out again. The Germans could, of course, only bring this off if they could capture Gibraltar on the way. Gibraltar is not a mere Naval base like Singapore. It is an immensely powerful fortress, which has been strengthened through three years of war, and it is probably the strength of Gibraltar rather than any consideration for internation[al] law which has prevented the Germans from invading Spain much earlier than this.

The political situation in North Africa appears to have improved somewhat and a military mission representing General de Gaulle and the Fighting French is expected to arrive shortly and confer with General Giraud, the High Commissioner of French North Africa. Probably it will be headed by General Catroux. We may hope, therefore, that an agreement between the two main groups of Frenchmen outside France will be arrived at before long.

Since last week the Russian advance has continued but it has slowed down somewhat, partly owing to the weather, partly to the stiffening of German resistance. The whole of this winter has been abnormally mild and great areas in the Ukraine, which would usually be frozen hard at this time of the year, are now a sea of mud, which makes it difficult for armoured vehicles to move. But the Germans have also been resisting more successfully and during the past two days the tone of their [6'] communiqués has been somewhat less pessimistic. I mentioned last week that on the southern Front, north-west of Rostov, the Russians were moving southward in the direction of Mariupol and the whole German Forces in that area were menaced with encirclement. It is here that the Germans have counter-attacked. They claim to have re-captured two towns east of Stalino. This is not confirmed [yet] but it does appear that the Germans have managed to slow down the Russian advance and that the German troops, who are still in the neighbourhood of Rostov, may get away. Further north, on the central Front, Orel, which is one of the key points of the whole German line, is [still] in very great danger and its communications are cut in every direction except towards the west. In general the news from the Russian Front is less resounding than it was last week but the tide is still flowing strongly against the Germans.

The Anniversary celebrations of the foundation of the Nazi Party took place three days ago. Hitler has always spoken on these occasions and this time he did emerge from his retirement to the extent of sending a written speech which was read out by somebody else. The pretext given was that Hitler is too busy directing the war on the eastern Front to be able to spare time to come to the microphone. It will be noticed that since things began to go wrong in Russia, Hitler has not shown himself publicly, nor made a speech in his own voice. In this speech he made absolutely no reference to the disaster of Stalingrad or to his own promise that Stalingrad should be captured nor any admission whatever of being responsible for the way things have turned out. This, although Hitler publicly assumed supreme command of the German armies some months ago. It is worth remembering that when Singapore fell, the British public first learned the fact from Mr. Churchill himself, who came straight to the microphone to deliver the news. This makes something of a contrast with Hitler, who grabs any credit that may be available when things are going well, but disappears into retirement and leaves the explanations to other people when things go badly. However, that is not of great importance. What is of more interest is to notice the content of Hitler's speech and its probable bearing on German policy. The speech was addressed ostensibly, at any rate, to the members of the Nazi Party, rather than to the German people as a whole, and it consisted almost entirely of ravings against the Jews, the Bolsheviks and the traitors and saboteurs, who are alleged to be still numerous *in Germany* itself. Hitler made two quite plain undisguised threats. One was, that he intended to kill off every Jew in Europe—he said this quite plainly—and the other was that in the moment of danger Germany could not afford to be over-scrupulous in her treatment of what he called "aliens". This remark was somewhat less clear than the threats against the Jews, but translated into plainer terms it [10'] means more forced labour and lower rations for the subject European populations. Hitler also uttered threats against traitors, saboteurs and idlers. This agrees with the general tone of German public announcements recently and with the huge extension in the ages of people in Germany now liable for military service or compulsory labour. All this points to the serious shortage of German man power which was bound to arise sooner or later and which is now almost certainly beginning to become acute. On the other hand the shouting against the Jews and Bolsheviks was more probably directed at Western Europe and seems to bear out what I said last week that the Germans are going to play the Bolshevik bogey for all it is worth in hopes of stimulating the fear of communism in Britain and America and thus paving the way for a compromise peace. I pointed out last week how vain this German manoeuvre is and the celebrations in London of the 25th anniversary of the Red Army have underlined this. Soviet Russia is more popular in Britain than any foreign country except possibly China. All in all, Hitler's most recent speech and the inferences which can be legitimately drawn from it should be encouraging to all the enemies of Fascism. [11' 35"]

1. This was the Tiger-1, or PzKw-VI (Panzerkraftwagen). In addition to its 88-mm KwK gun, it carried two 7.9 mm machine guns. It had a maximum speed of 23½ mph; the Mk VII Churchill's was 20 mph.
2. Despite Sir James Grigg's comfortable assurance to Parliament, as Louis L. Snyder records, 'astonished Allied gunners saw their heavy shells bounce harmlessly off the *Tiger's* especially designed armored plate' (*Historical Guide to World War II,* 687).

1912. Bengali Newsletter, 33

27 February 1943

For attribution of the English text to Orwell, see Mary Blackburn's memorandum of c. 20 January, *1833.* No script has been traced.

This appears to be the last English version that Orwell prepared from which a Bengali Newsletter was translated. Dr. P. Chatterjee took over from 6 March (see *1898*) until he was commissioned in the army at the end of August 1943. Orwell checked the English translation made by Chatterjee each Monday morning. His involvement is not further recorded here.

1913. To the Editor of *Picture Post*

27 February 1943

On 6 February 1943, *Picture Post* published a short illustrated article on the Society of Individualists (22–23); this sketched the shift from a laisser-faire attitude in English society which left everything to 'Chance or "Free Competition,"' to changes wrought by Lord Shaftesbury that limited 'what men should do in their lust for profits: for example, it wasn't quite right to employ children under a certain age, to make women work excessive hours, to leave unguarded machines which maimed workers. . . .' Now, it stated, this growth in social conscience or, as the Individualists would say, this 'national decay,' had reached such a pitch that Sir William Beveridge envisaged 'a state of society in which every member will be given security.' Now was the time, Individualists thought, to organise and protest against the proposed Welfare State in particular. The illustrations showed leading members of the society: W. W. Paine, Director of Lloyd's Bank, author of *The Menace of Socialism*, and an 'active propagandist against the nationalisation of industry'; Dr. C. K. Allen, one of the two Honorary Treasurers and Warden of Rhodes House and Fellow of University College, Oxford; Donovan Touche, Honorary Secretary, senior partner of the firm of chartered accountants bearing his name and 'against the League of Nations and any form of federal union or world society'; Sir Frederick Hamilton, the other Honorary Treasurer, a director of several finance and mining companies and, at seventy-six, president of the National Liberal Conference; Viscount Leverhulme, Chairman; Colin Brooks, editor of *Truth* and author of *Can 1931 Come Again?*, which advocated a lower standard of living; and Sir Ernest Benn, President, 'arch-enemy of all "planning,"' a regular contributor to *Truth*. Orwell's letter was titled (probably by *Picture Post*) 'The Truth about "Truth"' and was written from Mortimer Crescent, London, NW6. The ellipsis indicates a cut made by *Picture Post*.

Further to your article on the "Individualists", and your reference to *Truth*, I note an extraordinary paragraph in that paper of January 22, to the effect that between the Spanish War and the present war, the French paper *Gringoire* "seemed to most of us to be one of the few influences working against the mental, moral and financial corruption of both France in particular and Europe in general . . . it had an old-fashioned prejudice in favour of religion and patriotism, which it expressed pungently and with wit."

This paragraph is extraordinary, because *Gringoire* was frankly pro-Fascist and was partly owned by Chiappe,[1] former Prefect of Police in Paris, and one of the first to go over to the Germans. It took a disgusting attitude during the Spanish Civil War. Its political section, devoted to buttering up Mussolini and baiting Blum and Jouhaux and other politicians of the Left, used to publish cartoons which were pornographic as well as libellous. To give but one example: it published a cartoon, consisting of an imaginary picture of Leon Blum in bed with his own sister. Perhaps this is what the Editors of *Truth* meant by "an old-fashioned prejudice in favour of religion. . . ."

1. For *Gringoire*, see *1668, n. 1*. Jean Chiappe was described by Eugen Weber as a reincarnation of Fouché, Napoleon's unprincipled minister of police (*The Hollow Years*, p. 203).

1914. To Desmond Hawkins

27 February 1943   07/ES/EB/WMB

Dear Hawkins

Thanks for the script of the "Feature"[1] which is now being roneod.

Miss Blackburn tells me you would like to take a part yourself. I think this would be O.K. but I don't think you ought to take the part of Donne himself because I don't think your voice is suited to this.[2] Would you like to take one of the other parts?

The rehearsal is at 10.30 a.m. Tuesday morning, in Studio 6, Oxford Street. Don't be late will you.

Yours sincerely
[Initialled] G. O.
George Orwell
Talks Producer
Indian Section

1. 'Anniversary of the Month'; see *1908*.
2. this: perhaps 'his' was meant.

1915. Speaker's Form[1]

Name: ROY, Mrs. K.C
Empire: "In your kitchen": 10.2.43.

QUALIFICATIONS: Some knowledge of cookery, Good English. Poor b'caster.

SUBJECTS: Cookery

[Signed] Eric Blair   27.2.43

1. The form is typewritten; Orwell's comments are written in by him.

INDEX

Volume XIV

This is an index of names of people, places, and institutions, and of titles of books, periodicals, broadcasts, and articles; it is not (with a very few exceptions) a topical index. It indexes all titles of books and articles in the text, headnotes and afternotes; incidental references to people and places are unindexed. In order to avoid cluttering the index (and wasting the reader's time), names and places that appear very frequently are only listed when a specific point is being made and Orwell's tentative suggestions for talks and his speculations as to the way the war might develop, are only lightly indexed. Numbered footnotes are indexed more selectively; for example, books listed by an author who is the subject of a footnote are not themselves indexed unless significant to Orwell. Unless there is a significant comment or information, the BBC is not itself indexed. At the BBC Orwell was usually referred to as Blair; such references are indexed under Orwell. Titles of broadcasts are entered under their author's name and, if they form a coherent group (such as "How it Works") under the title of the series; miscellaneous broadcasts given in such series as "We Speak to India" and "Through Eastern Eyes" are indexed individually. All broadcasts are denoted as such by '(B)' and are listed chronologically. Talks Booking Forms (TBFs) and Programmes as Broadcast (PasBs) are not themselves indexed (though the programmes and people to which they refer are). Orwell's news commentaries are given various descriptions (Newsletter, News Review, News Commentary, etc.: see XIII 82–92), but they are all indexed under News Review; the description used is given at the page referred to. Information about broadcasts is dependent upon what can be recovered from the Archive and, inevitably, there are some loose ends.

Orwell's book titles are printed in CAPITALS; his poems, essays, articles, broadcasts, etc., are printed in upper and lower case roman within single quotation marks. Book titles by authors other than Orwell are in italic; if Orwell reviewed the book (in this volume), this is noted by 'Rev:' followed by the pagination and a semi-colon; other references follow. Both books and authors are individually listed unless a reference is insignificant. If Orwell does not give an author's name, when known this is added in parentheses after the title. Articles and broadcasts by authors other than Orwell are placed within double quotation marks. Page references are in roman except for those to numbered footnotes, which are in italic. The order of roman and italic is related to the order of references on the page. Editorial notes are printed in roman upper and lower without quotation marks. If an editorial note follows a title it is abbreviated to 'ed. note:' and the pagination follows. First and last page numbers are given of articles and these are placed before general references and followed by a semi-colon; specific pages are given for each book reviewed in a group. The initial page number is given for letters. Punctuation is placed outside quotation marks to help separate information.

Letters by Orwell, and those written on his behalf (for example, when he was ill) are given under the addressee's name and the first letter is preceded by 'L:', which stands for letters, memoranda, letter-cards, and postcards; telegrams are distinguished by 'T:' to draw attention to their urgency. If secretaries sign letters on Orwell's behalf, they are not indexed. However, the convention, 'L:' is *not* used in association with the organisation of broadcasts unless the letter contains other information. Against each

Index

Index

Index

Index

Index

Index